PRESERVING ON PAPER

Seventeenth-Century Englishwomen's Receipt Books

Edited by Kristine Kowalchuk

Apricot wine and stewed calf's head, melancholy medicine and "ointment of roses."
Preserving on Paper is a critical edition of three seventeenth-century receipt books – handwritten manuals that included a combination of culinary recipes, medical remedies, and household tips that documented the work of women at home. Kristine Kowalchuk argues that receipt books served as a form of folk writing, where knowledge was shared and passed between generations. These texts played an important role in the history of women's writing and literacy and contributed greatly to issues of authorship, authority, and book history. Kowalchuk's revelatory interdisciplinary study offers unique insights into early modern women's writings and the original sharing economy.

(Studies in Book and Print Culture)

KRISTINE KOWALCHUK is an instructor of critical reading and writing at the Northern Alberta Institute of Technology.

PRESERVING ON PAPER

SEVENTEENTH-CENTURY ENGLISHWOMEN'S RECEIPT BOOKS

Edited by Kristine Kowalchuk

UNIVERSITY OF TORONTO PRESS
Toronto Buffalo London

ISBN 978-1-4875-0006-1 (cloth)   ISBN 978-1-4875-2003-8 (paper)

Studies in Book and Print Culture

Library and Archives Canada Cataloguing in Publication

Preserving on paper : seventeenth-century Englishwomen's
receipt books / edited by Kristine Kowalchuk.

(Studies in book and print culture)
Includes bibliographical references and index.
ISBN 978-1-4875-0006-1 (cloth). – ISBN 978-1-4875-2003-8 (softcover)

1. Cooking, English – Early works to 1800. 2. Formulas, recipes,
etc. – Early works to 1800. 3. Home economics – Early works to 1800.
4. English literature – Women authors. 5. English literature – Early
modern, 1500–1700. 6. Women and literature – Great Britain –
History – 17th century. I. Kowalchuk, Kristine, 1974–, editor
II. Series: Studies in book and print culture

TX705.P74 2017   641.5   C2017-900529-4

This book has been published with the help of a grant from the Federation
for the Humanities and Social Sciences, through the Awards to Scholarly
Publications Program, using funds provided by the Social Sciences and
Humanities Research Council of Canada.

University of Toronto Press acknowledges the financial assistance to its
publishing program of the Canada Council for the Arts and the Ontario
Arts Council, an agency of the Government of Ontario.

Canada Council   Conseil des Arts
for the Arts   du Canada

ONTARIO ARTS COUNCIL
CONSEIL DES ARTS DE L'ONTARIO
an Ontario government agency
un organisme du gouvernement de l'Ontario

Funded by the   Financé par le
Government   gouvernement
of Canada   du Canada

For my parents

… the life of the average Elizabethan woman must be scattered about somewhere, could one collect it and make a book of it.

– Virginia Woolf

… leafing through a cookbook is like peering through a kitchen window. The cookbook … evokes a universe inhabited by women both in harmony and in tension with their families, their communities, and the larger social world.

– Janet Theophano

What importance, after all, can recipes have to the reading, writing mind?

– Susan Leonardi

… there is a connection between the search for authenticity in the written and printed word and the search for it in culinary matters.

– Patience Gray

Contents

Illustrations

Acknowledgments

Many people contributed to this project, and I am deeply grateful to all of them. Firstly, I would like to thank Siobhan McMenemy at the University of Toronto Press; I could not have asked for a more capable and gracious editor. I am also thankful to Patricia Demers for her enthusiasm, model efficiency, and open-minded thinking, and for setting everything into play for this project to be possible. The work greatly benefited from the assistance of John Considine, who proofread the transcriptions letter for letter, helped trace the meaning of sticky terms (including *hoxy croxy*, on which we published an article in *Notes & Queries*), lent insight on recipe instructions, offered biographical clues on the Granville family, and provided valuable advice throughout the writing process. Beverly Lemire offered continuous encouragement and helped round out my knowledge of seventeenth-century material culture; I have gained so much from her generosity and her fascinating, broad perspective of the period. Stephen Reimer introduced me to the delights of medieval literature and offered important feedback and suggestions for my Note on the Text. Robert Merrett's insightful public lecture on cookbooks, which I attended before embarking upon my doctorate, helped me realize such study was possible. Mary Marshall and Kim Brown in the University of Alberta's English department office were always helpful. The librarians at the Folger Shakespeare Library offered many good leads and suggestions (and a warm sweater). Victoria Burke provided feedback that was extremely valuable for this published edition. Ann de León lent her time and expertise in checking my translations of the Spanish recipes in the Granville text. Juliet McMaster perfectly demonstrated how to handle a historical text with respect, and I borrowed greatly from her example as I worked out my own methodology. Alex McGuckin shared his time and expertise in bookbinding and antiquarian texts to help me better understand the physical details of the manuscripts. Through a Rural Museum network discussion, Jenny Humphris, Sandi Shallcross, and David Walker of the South West Heritage Trust helped me discover a possible meaning of "a sriprius bagg" and learn more about the history of sedge-weaving in England; Roy Vickery of the Plant-Lore archive and historian Stuart Peachey also lent insight. My anonymous peer reviewers offered deeply thoughtful feedback, questions, and encouragement, and the final work is much better for their insight; thank you both. Judy Williams performed excellent copyediting, for which I am most grateful. Mark Thompson, Barbara Porter, Luciano Nicassio, Marilyn McCormack, and the designers at University of Toronto Press were all helpful and professional and a pleasure to work with. Ellen Schoeck supported me in many ways, including getting me started on organic gardening, which benefited this project on many levels. Bert Almon and Olga Costopoulos offered invaluable encouragement and guidance early in my literary career. Dawn Morgan's enthusiasm for seventeenth-century literature and culture sparked my own curiosity and interest in the period. Joe Varughese and David Schmaus at NAIT offered moral support and lightened my teaching duties during a critical point in this project. Many of my friends and students took an interest in my work, and their reinforcement always seemed to come when I needed it most; particular thanks to my longtime food-loving friends Rachel Needoba, Julie Belanger, Patricia Dean, Cindy Broda, and Robert Pendergast. I am also grateful to the many scholars before me whose work this edition builds upon and pushes back against; their ideas enabled my own thinking. Finally, my mom, a proud housewife, inspired this project through family stories and family recipes, which I have come to recognize as the greatest gifts. My sister ensured that I kept a sense of humour throughout the process. They both supported me in countless ways and were also willing participants when I made dishes from these receipt books. My dad, who passed away in 2010, always believed in me and taught me to follow my own path.

Preserving on Paper

Historical Introduction

Early modern women's writing in England has, over the past few decades, received increased attention from literary, cultural, and women's studies scholars. A recurring theme across these fields of research is the need for a widened consideration of what actually constitutes women's writing in order to reach an accurate understanding of the subject. For, while Virginia Woolf legitimately claimed that she could find few early modern women's books on the library shelves, women did indeed write; they just did not often publish their works in print form, and their works were not always literary. Consideration of women's writing has thus extended to manuscripts and to a broader spectrum of genres. Open any recent anthology of early modern writing and women are finally more fully represented; open any anthology of early modern *women's* writing, and besides poetry, drama, and fiction, the contents might include letters, diaries, religious writing, translations, and excerpts from miscellanies and commonplace books. Helen Ostovich and Elizabeth Sauer, in their 2004 *Reading Early Modern Women: An Anthology of Texts in Manuscript and Print, 1550–1700*, explicitly list ten purposes for their collection, including "to identify and present a substantial selection of materials from original editions of women's writings, which have traditionally been underrepresented in early modern literary studies," and "to display the wide array of private and public genres in which women wrote" (5).

However, one genre is still overlooked by Ostovich and Sauer's anthology, and continues to be largely unconsidered or misunderstood by most scholarship on early modern women's writing, even though seventeenth-century Englishwomen developed and dominated the form, and even though it was "an intricate part of women's manuscript participation in the culture of early modern writing" (Wall, "Women" 106), and that is the receipt book: highly collaborative, handwritten domestic manuals that included a combination of culinary recipes, medical remedies, and household tips – works that reflect, in Joan Thirsk's words, "the unseen doings of women at home in their kitchens" (*Food* 181). The persistent dismissal of this genre in literary scholarship until only very recently undoubtedly stems from the prejudice that domestic writing is less important than purely literary writing, revealing both continued disrespect for traditional women's work and knowledge, and a narrow conception of authorship. And unfortunately, the recent scholarship on the genre that has begun risks perpetuating the same prejudice, as it tends to either denounce the genre as evidence of women's repression or, conversely, to regard it as evidence of women's emerging modern subjectivity. In very few instances are receipt books considered within their historical and cultural context, which is key to understanding them; instead, they are subjected to modern values. The result of this imposition of the present on the past is not only a serious misinterpretation of the genre, the culture of the period, and the history of women's writing, but also a missed opportunity to recognize the wider possibilities of the written word. Receipt books are interesting and important precisely because they do *not* fit our current, conventional understanding of authority, authorship, and even the way a book works; they require a wholly different frame – and they are exciting because they illuminate the limitations of the one we have been using.

This work focuses on receipt books as an important yet largely overlooked and misunderstood genre. Its most simple aim is to broaden access to seventeenth-century Englishwomen's receipt books, few of which have been published. Most critical analyses of receipt books are not accompanied by reproduction of receipt books themselves, while those receipt books that have been published are not generally approached through deep critical analysis of the genre. (Published receipt books to date include Ann Wallis Blencowe's edition of *The Receipt Book of Mrs. Ann Blencowe*; Raymond A. Anselment's edition of *The Remembrances of Elizabeth Freke, 1671–1714*; Hilary Spurling's edition of *Elinor Fettiplace's Receipt Book*; David E. Schoonover's edition of *Ladie Borlase's Receiptes Booke*; and the Folger Shakespeare Library's transcription of *Mrs. Sarah Longe, Her Receipt Book* for its 2011 exhibit *Beyond Home Remedy: Women, Medicine, and Science*.) This simple aim then relates to others more ambitious: to acknowledge the receipt book as an important historical form of women's writing; to explore the role of receipt books in furthering women's literacy skills; to recognize the unique contribution of receipt books to critical issues of authorship, authority, and book history; and to expand understanding of the

history of food and medicine through new consideration of the genre.
To meet these aims, both simple and ambitious, this work provides a
semi-diplomatic edition of three previously unpublished manuscripts
held at the Folger Shakespeare Library: MS V.a.430, otherwise known as
Receipt Book attributed to Mary Granville and Anne Granville D'Ewes
(c. 1640–1750); MS V.a.20, otherwise known as *Receipt Book* attributed to
Constance Hall (c. 1672); and MS V.a.450, otherwise known as *Cookery
and Medical Receipt Book* attributed to Lettice Pudsey (c. 1675). I have
chosen these works in particular for a few reasons: digital scans of these
texts are available on *Perdita Manuscripts: Women Writers, 1500–1700*,
as well as partially on the Folger Shakespeare Library's *Digital Image
Collection* (*Luna*); all three have benefited from previous scholarly discussion; and while receipt books are a fluid genre with few constant
characteristics, each of these texts is "typical" of the genre in containing
a mixture of recipes, remedies, and household tips written in multiple
hands and compiled over time. I chose to include three works as this
allows the reader to begin to discern patterns in the genre, as well as
to witness the surprising diversity within it. Presentation of these texts
alongside a historical introduction to the genre, a brief textual introduction to each work, notes explaining textual particularities, and a glossary of seventeenth-century culinary, medical, and household terms
aims to situate receipt books within their historical and cultural context.

The editorial and analytical approach of this work stands upon Susan
Leonardi's aphorism that "A recipe is … an embedded discourse" (340).
To understand a discourse means to understand a culture and a world
view, so while my own background means that my perspective is primarily a literary one, I have aimed for a more complete understanding of receipt books through valuing interdisciplinarity and borrowing
from various strategies of interpretation. I draw on Peter Beale's argument that manuscripts should be considered "first and foremost as
physical artifacts which have their own peculiar nature and mode
of being" (v); D.F. McKenzie's sociological approach to texts, paying
attention to the relationship of the meaning of the text and the book
as a material object; Margaret Ezell's suggestion that receipt books be
considered from a perspective that is both new historicist and French
feminist, recognizing the difference of the past from the present, and
of women's experience in the past from that in the present (*Writing*
8); Anne Laurence's point that we must move away from evolutionary ways of regarding history ("a view of the past which gives greatest weight to people exercising power and doing things, and to forces
of dynamism and change in society") towards historical recognition of

ordinary life, through greater archival work and study of the material world (4); Derek Pearsall's note that manuscript study calls for a degree of "adventurousness" similar to the boldness and openness of an archaeologist's hypothesis (176) (which helps me balance my sharing of Joan Thirsk's experience: "Over and over again, my searches among the archives have made me revise and refine my viewpoint, sometimes driving me to despair at my arrogance in ever claiming to generalize" [*Food* ix]); Frances Dolan's emphasis on the need to understand manuscripts as inherently nonlinear:

> We need to abandon the notion of an evidentiary point of origin ... thinking instead about charting ripple effects, splatters, aftershocks, feedback loops, and contact networks rather than tracing a line to the beginning or digging down to the bottom. Each fragment of evidence is valuable as a piece of a larger puzzle; but its value does not depend on its proximity to the event, the facts, or the truth of what it represents. Each fragment, whether it is a deposition, a diary entry, or a ballad, has invariably been shaped by the process of its own production, by generic conventions, and by an awareness of audience or market. Everything needs to be read warily; everything requires interpretation; each morsel makes most sense when it is read against others, but a different sense depending on what others [say] (Dolan 164);

and Elizabeth Spiller's point that "[i]t may be that the only way to read a cookbook is to bring it into the kitchen" ("Printed" 526). Taken together, these strategies of interpretation comprise an approach that recognizes receipt books as a special genre: as manuscripts rather than print, *and* as texts written by women rather than men, *and* as domestic rather than literary or professional works, *and* as texts that arose out of a particular world view that was nonlinear, collective, and originated in oral folk culture. Ignoring any one of these elements means missing the mark because each element is critical to how receipt books originated, how they functioned, and what they mean. Likewise, keeping all of these elements in mind is extremely rewarding, as together they allow us a glimpse into early modern Englishwomen's work, wisdom, and writing – the average woman's life that Virginia Woolf sought, and knew must lie recorded somewhere – and as such, enables a redrawing of the boundaries of literary studies in general. This new consideration of receipt books thus impacts the fields of Renaissance and early modern literature, history, cultural studies, book history, women's studies, culinary studies, and the history of medicine.

Folk Culture, Food, and the Renaissance

In aiming to situate seventeenth-century Englishwomen's receipt books within the historical and cultural context out of which they arose, it is important to establish a broad understanding of the context in the first place. A particularly useful work for beginning such study is Mikhail Bakhtin's *Rabelais and His World* because it convincingly looks forward to the seventeenth century from its medieval roots (as based on François Rabelais's *Gargantua and Pantagruel* [c. 1532]) rather than backward from a modern perspective. In this text, Bakhtin illuminates the folk culture that "existed in all countries of medieval Europe and shaped Renaissance culture" and which was "a world in which all medieval people participated more or less" (6); indeed, the folk culture Bakhtin describes is evident throughout Shakespeare's plays and other medieval and Renaissance texts. Folk culture was agrarian, gendered but collective, oral, acutely aware of the physicality of nature, and structured around the rhythmic cycle of the seasons. It also sought escape from the officialdom of the church, allegorical/artificial culture, monologism, and focus on deprivation and death through their opposites: carnivalesque topsyturvydom, collective feasting, and celebration of the regenerative ability of the body – that is, of life literally out of death. The triumph of rebirth is central to folk culture, and indeed, as Bakhtin emphasizes, rebirth is the literal meaning of *renaissance*: this term does "not mean a revival of the ancient arts and sciences. It [is] an immensely important and significant word, rooted in the very depths of the ritualistic, ideological, and visual imagery of mankind ... [t]he striving toward renewal and a new birth" (57). The period we call the Renaissance, he later notes, was the time in which the "carnival attitude" peaked in "human consciousness, philosophy, and literature" (273). The Renaissance was thus the height of folk culture and its cyclical world view, meaning that "early modern" is what came *after* the Renaissance, rather than being an equivalent name. From here on, this edition will thus refer to the culture and world view on which it focuses as "the Renaissance."

The philosophy of rebirth as a form of harmony (death is always followed by, and thus is balanced by, life) permeated folk culture's conceptions of health, nature, time, and social organization. Galenic medicine was based upon balance of the four humours of the body (black bile, yellow bile, phlegm, and blood), and imbalances were corrected by the "virtues" of ingested plants, animals, and minerals; thus, the balance of the parts was required for the good of the whole. Such harmony mattered not only within the body, but also in the body's place within nature and the cosmos, as is evident in the consideration of the stars and phases of the moon in the collection, preparation, and use of plants for medicinal purposes. As Piero Camporesi notes,

> [A] perfect ... herbalist ... had to bear in mind the constellations and the "sites and aspects" of the stars ... Pietro Castelli [Italian physician and botanist, 1574–1662] wrote, "All the things that the apothecary does in order to preserve [herbs] at length, he must do during the waning of the moon so that they don't spoil quickly, as in the gathering of roots, herbs, flowers and seeds." And he warned that liquid syrups and preparations simmer and expand when the moon waxes. (Camporesi 143–4)

The microcosm/macrocosm relationship between the individual and nature is exemplified in Shakespeare's *King Lear*, in Lear's raging on the heath during a stormy night: Lear achieves understanding and, ultimately, peace only after he and nature are aligned. In terms of time, the agrarian calendar balanced the scarcity of winter and Lent with seasonal feasting and the excess of carnival (the latter's "festive release" paralleling Galenism's bloodletting/evacuation of excess humours). Likewise, the cyclical conception of time based on the collective celebration of nature's seasons gave temporal balance from year to year. A social parallel to this balance existed in collective society, in which the "health" of the community depended upon harmony between individuals; similarly, the health of the entire kingdom depended upon the accord between the "body" of the people and the monarch as their "head." In each of these cases, balance of the individual parts created collective harmony and enabled the continuity of life. It is important to recognize that this philosophy of rebirth constituted an entire world view that was very different from the modern world view; as Michael Schoenfeldt points out,

> It is easy for us, benefiting daily from our own very different medical and psychological regimens, to underestimate both the seductive coherence of Galenic humoral theory and its experiential suppleness. This theory possesses a remarkable capacity to relate the body to its environment, and to explain the literal influences that flow into it from a universe composed of analogous elements. (3)

Conceptions of food in folk culture were also, of course, intricately bound up with a philosophy of rebirth and harmony. People collectively sourced and consumed food: common lands and rivers provided areas for public gathering of wild foods, pasturing of animals, collection of firewood, and fishing under the feudal system until at least the Tenures

Abolition Act of 1660 (although in reality foraging continued for much longer) and the hedgerows that increasingly enclosed those lands in the sixteenth and seventeenth centuries also provided common food. Likewise, group harvests, markets, and feasts brought people together in a collective procurement and celebration of food; as Pieter Bruegel the Elder's peasant paintings and the woodcuts in Holinshed's *Chronicles* suggest, these events were social spaces in which everyone participated. Such sharing again maintained social harmony; waste, selfishness, and grossly unequal access were seen as unhealthy "surfeits" or excesses (again showing a clear parallel to Galenism) and gluttony and greed represented two of the seven deadly sins. Unequal access to food led to violence; as Roy Porter notes, "the promise of food moved peasants to revolt more than the abstractions of justice" ("Preface" in Camporesi 11). John Hales in *The Discourse of the Commonweal of this Realm England* (1549) also specifically wrote against gluttony and suggested that it "stirred up dissension in the nation" (Thirsk *Food* 19), and Rabelais clearly denounces gluttony and the selfishness of the individual eating alone in *Gargantua and Pantagruel*.

A deep value of harmony and strong social bonds was especially critical in preventing social unrest in the late medieval and Renaissance period, due to frequent food shortages and disease: "[f]rom the time of the Black Death in 1348–9 to the Great Plague of London in 1665 England was seldom, if ever, completely free from plague" (Sloan 153), and agrarian disasters repeatedly befell Europe between 1500 and 1650, part of a cool period sometimes called the Little Ice Age (although there is little scholarly consensus on this period's precise dates) that was perhaps caused by reforestation after "the shrinking back of the margin of cultivation … after the Black Death" (Mennell 25). Poor weather and failed harvests are reflected in literature of the period, such as the "winds, fogs, floods, rotted crops, sickly flocks, forests and ice of Shakespeare's *A Midsummer Night's Dream*," and "the wretched weather of *Macbeth*" (Franklin 28), as well as in the equating of unusual weather events with witchcraft (Sharpe 657). Famines occurred repeatedly across Europe in this period, sometimes regionally, sometimes across the continent; in England one-sixth of harvests failed between 1500 and 1660 (Mennell 25). War often exacerbated food shortages, "by destroying crops and animals, and yet demanding food supplies to be available at a moment's notice in random places dictated by the constantly changing location of the main battlefields" (Thirsk "Agricultural Policy" 301). The result of these shortages was that "one of the most characteristic features of [Renaissance and] early modern Europe was 'the obsession with starving to death'" (Mennell and Mandrou in Mennell 27) – meaning that not only receipt books, but all literature of the period, should be read in such context. It is important to keep folk culture's philosophy of rebirth and harmony in mind to understand medieval and Renaissance people's psychological response to famine. While ecocritic Simon Estok sees the effect to be the seed of modern "ecophobia," a deep fear of nature and a desire to control it, this interpretation misses the very essence of folk culture. When King Lear cries out in the storm, it is not because he wants to control nature, but because he realizes that he has upset a fundamental natural balance and set himself apart from the body of his kingdom – "the folk" who, as Bakhtin emphasizes, recognized that they were part of a natural and agrarian cycle and did not aim to overcome it, but rather collectively celebrated its endless regenerative ability. The scene ends with Lear grateful for a hovel, where he takes shelter with the Fool. So instead of denial or fear, one might see this psychological underpinning as a full and constant awareness of death, yet acceptance of its necessity as part of a regenerative cycle, and an ultimate carnivalesque laughing at it.

Folk culture's focus on rebirth and harmony as a response to vulnerability explains the recurring theme of food-centred utopias in late medieval and Renaissance literature. This theme runs through Rabelais's *Gargantua and Pantagruel*, and appears in the lack of want in Thomas More's *Utopia*, in Don Quixote's meditation on harmony while sharing a simple meal of acorns with Sancho and shepherds, and in Gonzalo's vision in *The Tempest* of a utopia in which nature simply offers up everything without need for work. (It also appears in art, as in Pieter Bruegel the Elder's *The Land of Cockaigne*.) While it does seem true that the concept of utopia generally shifted through the sixteenth and seventeenth centuries from one of carnivalesque excess to one of humanist moderation and manners – "[t]he medieval Land of Cockaigne and its impossible, laughable super-abundance gave way to the [early modern] utopia and its rationalized, egalitarian sufficiency" (Appelbaum 14) – both forms exist in *Gargantua and Pantagruel*. Furthermore, perhaps they are not as opposite as they seem if one recalls that both prioritized balance. In any case, until modernity, utopia was considered as achieving equilibrium with nature, not overcoming it. And dreams of food were a natural response to the prevalence of hunger throughout the medieval and Renaissance period:

The conditions of producing and consuming food in premodern Europe – conditions where surpluses could not be taken for granted, where the distribution of goods was obscenely unequal, where the rhythm of life was also a rhythm of uneven consumption, and where the hopes of whole classes could thus be fixed upon the foodways of the world[1] – meant that utopia itself, in almost any of its forms, was necessarily and first of all a utopia of food ... We need to take seriously the experience of hunger that would motivate a daydream world like the Land of Cockaigne. (Appelbaum 122–6)

The profoundly interesting thing about folk wisdom, including its ideals, is that the symbols are not arbitrary. This point is often forgotten in literature and other cultural studies, where one cannot think of bread and wine, for example, without linking them to the Christian meanings they have assumed. However, food in particular ties to meaning that reaches deeper than metaphor because of our dependence on it for survival, which is an instinct that comes before all others; this explains humans' very assignment of religious meaning to food in the first place.[2] As Bakhtin points out, "Bread stolen from the people does not cease to be bread, wine is always wine, even when the Pope drinks it. Bread and wine have their own truth, their own irresistible tendency toward superabundance. They have the indestructible connotation of victory and merriment" (292). They mean, literally, life over death. Medieval and Renaissance people, because of their close connection to the land and cyclical conception of time, perceived this deeper literal meaning. Such an understanding is completely distinct from an ecophobic desire to control nature; indeed, ecophobia is part of the shift to modernity, based on a linear conception of time that is fearful because it ends with death.

Utopias of food perhaps inevitably led to thoughts of the Garden of Eden, and to spiritual questions of how God meant for humans to eat, and this questioning likely connected to the period's increased interest in vegetarianism – a diet, furthermore, whose Galenic parallel is clear in its value of harmony with nature. Thomas Tryon was the move-

---

1 Receipt books in fact suggest a large dependency on local ingredients and dietary equality. (Otherwise, this assessment is valid.)
2 In fact, while Bakhtin sees folk culture as opposed to the church, it might instead be possible to see it first as a response to physical matters. That is, folk culture's focus on rebirth and harmony might have arisen in opposition to death itself – as a biologically and anthropologically fuelled response to winter and hunger, which *then* came to be associated with the church through its introduction and increased enforcement of fasting rituals to deal with scarcity, such as fishdays and Lent.

ment's greatest promoter, writing numerous manuals on the vegetarian diet, but other prominent vegetarians of the period included John Evelyn, Sir Thomas Browne, Sir William Temple, René Descartes, and Francis Bacon (Stuart 7). An interest in vegetarianism permeates literary works of the period as well. Bakhtin notes that Panurge's list in *Gargantua and Pantagruel* of all the ways seeds are protected in nature – through "husks, cases, scurfs and swads, hulls, cods, stones, films, cartels, shells, ears, rinds, barks, skins, ridges and prickles" – contrasted with the unprotected nakedness of human genitalia (Rabelais 3.VIII) suggests that humans are meant to live peacefully in nature (Bakhtin 314). In *Don Quixote*, Sancho also alludes to the ethics of vegetarianism in denouncing the cruelty of hunting, calling it "a diversion which, in my opinion, hardly deserves the name, as it consists in murdering a poor beast that never committed any crime" (808). In Shakespeare's *Twelfth Night* when the Clown asks Malvolio, "What is the opinion of Pythagoras concerning wildfowl?" and Malvolio replies, "That the soul of our grandma might haply inhabit a bird" (4.2.48–52), he is referring to Pythagorus's interest in Brahminism, which involves a vegetarian diet and a belief in reincarnation. In his fascinating article "The Chameleon's Dish: Shakespeare and the Omnivore's Dilemma," Todd A. Borlik notes references to vegetarianism in a number of Shakespeare's plays, and especially focuses on a questioning of Judeo-Christian meat-eating in *Hamlet*. It is hard to say to what extent these literary sources concerned with animal consumption and welfare reflected general thinking, as recipes from the period use matter-of-fact language in calling for the killing of animals, a seeming contradiction also noticed by ecofeminist scholars such as Michelle DiMeo, Rebecca Laroche, and David Goldstein. However, Bakhtin's reminder of the meaning of *renaissance* might again lead towards reconciliation: folk culture's acceptance of death as necessary for rebirth might mean it was possible to frankly kill an animal while also appreciating the gift of the animal as food (this is certainly the case for indigenous cultures around the world). DiMeo and Laroche do gesture towards this interpretation too, noting that the housewife, even in killing animals, had "a more intimate sense" of nature than most modern people do (100), and Borlik similarly notes that "[e]arly moderns ... were much closer to the meat industry than moderns, and rather than de-sensitizing them to the violence the shambles were a constant reminder of the bloodshed required to put beef upon their plate" (13). Goldstein likewise observes that women's attitude towards animals and nature seemed neither romantic nor dominating, but rather a practical matter of survival, and that premodern people held a different understanding of "correspondence" between the human and natural worlds than we do in modern Western culture ("Woolley's Mouse" 111). This view seems reasonable, and is indeed reflected in the archive, in an example DiMeo and Laroche mention only in a footnote: Anne Nevile, in a 1679 letter to Margaret Boscawen, notes, "I haue sent you here above written the purge my Mother gave many … take your moles alive three or fower and given them a knock only to kill them from being too cruell to burn them alive …" (103). It will be interesting to see research unfold in the relatively new field of premodern and early modern ecocriticism – particularly if this research involves deeper consideration of the archives, art, and other material sources[3] – on historical and alternative understanding of the relationship between humans and nature.

Folk culture's valuing of social harmony meant that its response to the food insecurity of the late medieval and Renaissance period was not only utopian dreams but also real-life sharing and charity, and these acts had great impact on English diet and agriculture. In 1599 Richard Gardiner published a treatise on how he fed poor people on seven hundred cabbages and carrots prior to that year's harvest. This success prompted increased esteem for certain vegetables for their ability to feed many people and to last: "[h]enceforward, brassicas, and roots like turnips, carrots, parsnips and succor would be viewed in a fresh light, as the life-saving foods that could insure against starvation" (Thirsk, *Food* 34); these vegetables indeed all begin to appear in receipt books. At the same time, new vegetables, or superior varieties of known ones, were introduced from Italy, Spain, Holland, and the New World, and gardening techniques improved through introduction by immigrants from the Low Countries (Thick, "Root Crops" 279). These various influences enabled and encouraged further agricultural innovation in the period, with the aim of feeding more people. Eventually a great expansion of market gardens occurred around London: they grew from 10,000 acres in 1688 to 110,000 acres by the 1720s (Thirsk, *Food* 159). Fruit also increased in popularity, as is particularly evident in John Evelyn's and John Beale's promotion of the planting of apple trees in common grounds and hedgerows, and the resulting increase in the

---

3 An architectural "correspondence" between humans and animals seems evident in the heads carved into the beams above the sick room in the 1443 Hospices de Beaune in France; these heads suggest an amusing physiognomic equality between people and animals in a place where a modern visitor might instead expect to see angels.

consumption of cider as a home-grown libation. In tandem with this agricultural and dietary shift was the publication of numerous books on improved methods in agriculture, horticulture, and husbandry, as well as frugal living, such as Hugh Plat's *Sundrie New and Artificiall Remedies Against Famine. Written ... Uppon the Occasion of this Present Dearth* (1596), Gervase Markham's *Hunger's Preuention* (1621), and Thomas Tryon's various works, including *The Way to Save Wealth* (1695), which includes numerous recipes based on bread and water, and whose full title promises recipes for bread made from roots, herbs, and leaves of trees, to help one "live in cases of great scarcity or famine." A number of influential herbals were also published in this period, including John Gerard's well-known *Herball* (1597) (to which the glossary at the end of this edition frequently refers), John Parkinson's *Paradisi in Sole Paradisus Terrestris* (1629) and *Theatrum Botanicum* (1640), and William Turner's *A New Herball* (published in three parts from 1551 to 1568). Samuel Hartlib developed a network of correspondents (including Evelyn and Beale) to share new ideas on agriculture and husbandry, and the Royal Society was founded in 1660, largely as an institution dedicated to improved farming (Thirsk, "Agricultural Innovations" 564). While the clear emphasis on plant-growing in this period of innovation was "economical" in the seventeenth-century understanding of the term (simply, plant production is more efficient than animal production, and a plant-based national diet meant more people had access to food), it was also cultural: plant-growing's clear connections with Galenic medicine, utopian ideals, and vegetarianism make clear that it also tied back to physical, social, and spiritual harmony, as well as harmony with nature.

Folk culture's focus on harmony and the collective sourcing and sharing of food also underscores that, contrary to common belief, lower-class and upper-class diets were not mutually exclusive, at least into the beginning of the early modern period. "One is struck," writes Jean-François Revel, "by the fact that there was not as much difference between the diet of the people and that of the ruling classes in the Middle Ages [through the early seventeenth century] as there was to be later on, at the end of the seventeenth and eighteenth century" (95–6). He later adds, "Popular cuisine is less poor in quantity and quality than historians ordinarily lead us to believe" (145). At the same time, upper-class diets were less elaborate than we have commonly come to believe: even Sir Kenelm Digby (chancellor to Queen Henrietta Maria) includes numerous simple recipes for pottage in his cookbook, and household accounts reveal that royalty purchased simple foods from peasant neighbours (Sim 43). As Thirsk notes, "Rich, middling and poor did not live in separate worlds. Many, indeed most, ingredients in food at the castle and in the manor house were grown, reared, or trapped by ordinary folk living as neighbours in the same place" (*Food* 19). The well-to-do also often shared leftovers with servants and the poor, and sometimes the household members and servants even ate together (Robertson 57). Similarity of diet across social classes is also evident in literary works: in *Don Quixote*, the wedding feast is, except for spices, really not that different from Sancho's daily diet of bread, cheese, onion, wine, and the occasional wild foods and meat: there is a bullock stuffed with suckling pigs and spices, and pots containing "a whole shamble of meat," wine, loaves of the whitest bread, a great quantity of cheese, and honey (Cervantes 694). Revel also turns to Cervantes to emphasize that meat did not define the upper-class diet: "A mere three or four centuries ago beef in Europe was barely edible: at the beginning of *Don Quixote*, Cervantes offers as proof of the extreme material straits of his hero, who is about to become a knight, the fact that he 'ate beef more often than mutton'" (4).[4] Dietary difference was largely in *degree*; poorer people simply ate coarser bread, more wild fruits and vegetables, and tougher cuts of meat; indeed, such foods were regarded as better, according to Thomas Moffett[5] in his *Health's Improvement* (1595), for their constitution as labourers. As Thirsk concludes, a popular saying held true in premodern England: "We all eat the same food, 'the difference is only in the dressing'" (*Food* 210).

Greater consideration of archival sources and material artefacts over the past few decades has revealed how one must take care in linking apparent clues about diet and class in historical cookbooks. On the surface, methods of cooking might suggest class difference: the fact that "[m]eats to be roasted needed plenty of fat in them" (Robertson 91) suggests that roasting recipes would have indicated a rich household, and boiling or stewing recipes a poor one. However, people of more humble means might have collected recipes for enjoying roasted meat on special occasions. Likewise, meagre households who suffered after the imposition of the hearth tax might still have benefited

---

4   Thus, contrary to Robert Appelbaum's interpretation, Sir Andrew's beef-eating in *Twelfth Night* is completely in line with the fact he is "a thin, craven and silly man" (1). Both Revel and Thirsk note that mutton was of much better quality than beef at the time.

5   This writer's last name also appeared variously as Muffet and Moufet.

from the service of village bakers, who "baked items prepared by their customers and on Sundays lit their oven in order to bake joints of meat for those without the means of cooking them themselves" (Robertson 96). Imported items could also be misleading; currants, for example, were not only popular among the wealthy in Renaissance England, but also enjoyed by the poor during feast days (Wilson, *Food* 333). Likewise, the amount of citrus imported in the period suggests that its consumption could not have been limited to the upper class: it is estimated that in 1694–5, nine million oranges and lemons were imported into London (Thirsk, *Food* 136). Thus, even when recipes seem to reveal social and economic information about an individual or household, such information might be misleading.

It was not until the late seventeenth century, when the weather improved, better agricultural techniques were developed, food was increasingly commodified through importation of items such as cane sugar, and food needs were more fully met, that an upper-class diet lifted away from the diet of "the people"; as Stephen Mennell suggests, "the civilizing of appetite" occurred only once a satisfaction of quantity was achieved (32–3). This was also the period in which professional cooking fully diverged from the household recipe (and in which, at the professional level, cooking and medicine diverged). Thus, rather than a single folk culture based on a philosophy of rebirth, harmony, and collectivity, there were now two food worlds: the professional world of chefs and printed cookbooks, and the traditional world in which folk culture still reigned:

> The one was inhabited by food writers who ... pontificated about food and were happy to pronounce authoritatively, though none of them knew as much about food throughout England as they liked to think. The other world of the kitchen was inhabited by women and some men cooking food according to their social, local and family traditions, while adapting them in each generation to suit changing tastes and circumstances. (Thirsk, *Food* x)

Until recently, the professional cookbook was the main historical food record that was known and studied, and it painted an inaccurate picture of eating in the past because it focused on food that was not the norm. As Revel noted in 1982, "The meals which history has recorded are clearly memorable repasts, princely wedding banquets, the menus served on festive occasions. This is a drawback when one is attempting to trace the history of societies and of their everyday life" (24).

The Seventeenth-Century English Housewife: Her Work, Knowledge, and Authority

Since Revel's lamentation, scholarship has indeed uncovered many domestic texts that reflect "everyday life." One such genre is the receipt book. In order to understand how, and when, and why, the seventeenth-century English housewife began to write down her quotidian recipes, remedies, and household tips, we might first consider the housewife herself. A number of period texts give a good sense of the knowledge, skill, and comportment that the seventeenth-century housewife was meant to embody and the work she was expected to undertake. One important work is Gervase Markham's *The English Huswife*, a household manual reprinted numerous times from 1615 until 1683. Markham describes in detail a wide range of housewifery responsibilities: cooking, baking, preserving, collecting herbs, growing vegetables, dairy-making, animal husbandry, beekeeping, dyeing and weaving wool, sewing, making beer, choosing and keeping wines, distilling, creating curatives, healing the sick, and keeping household accounts. Besides fitting in all her daily work, she also had to prepare for times of scarcity: "[a] good housewife always had to have the winter at the back of her mind" (Sim 11). Methods for food preservation that Una Robertson lists in *The Illustrated History of the Housewife, 1650–1950* include open-air drying, smoking, salting, pickling, candying, and the making of jams and jellies, cheeses, butter, confits, ale, sometimes beer (which used hops, and kept better than ale), mead, metheglin, cider, perry, fruit wines, and medicinal waters. While such a list of household responsibilities is in itself impressive, Robertson describes the work and expertise each of these tasks actually involved – "The fireplace," for example, "had its own language" (92). And in every task, Markham emphasizes, the housewife must be economical and self-sufficient: "let [her food] proceede more from the prouision of her owne yard, then the furniture of the Markets" (4). These expectations of the housewife's extensive domestic work, careful planning, economy, and self-sufficiency are not unique to Markham but are also reflected in other household manuals of the period, including Thomas Tusser's *Fiue Hundreth Points of Good Husbandry* (1573), John Partridge's *Treasurie of Commodious Conceites* (1573), Thomas Dawson's *The Good Huswife's Jewell* (1585), Hugh Plat's *Delightes for Ladies* (1600), and Patrick Ruthven's *The Ladies Cabinet Enlarged and Opened* (1654). Such domestic demands and values are also evident in literature of the period. In Shakespeare's *The Merry Wives of Windsor*, Mistress Quickly is introduced in the play in association with domestic work when she promises to make an evening posset, and by the end of the scene, she exemplifies Markham's housewife as she lists the work she does for Dr Caius: "I keep his house, and I wash, wring, brew, bake, scour, dress meat and drink, make the beds and do all myself" (1.4.89–91). Similarly, in Cervantes's *Don Quixote*, the ideal Andalusian damsel, a "beautiful apparition" with a sweet voice and good sense (286), describes her own virtue as a daughter through her housewifery work:

> I was mistress of [my parents'] affection as well as their wealth. By my advice, they received and dismissed their servants: the tale and account of what was both sowed and reaped, passed thro' my hands. I managed the oil-mills, the vineyards, the herds and flocks, the beehives, and every thing that such a rich farmer as my father, may be supposed to possess: in short, I was steward and mistress, and acted with such care and œconomy, that I should not find it easy to exaggerate the pleasure and satisfaction which my parents enjoyed. Those parts of the day that remained, after I had given all due attention to the herdsmen, overseers, and other day-labourers, I employed in exercises equally decent and necessary for young women, such as lace-making, needle-work, and spinning; and, if at any time, I interrupted these employments, in order to re-create the mind, I entertained myself with some religious book, or diversified my amusement with the harp; being convinced by experience, that music lulls the disordered thoughts, and elevates the dejected spirits. Such was the life I led in my father's house ... (287)

While it is possible that the literature parodies the housewifery manuals, receipt books themselves, as is evident in the transcriptions that follow this introduction, also reflect the same domestic demands. So, too, does other evidence from the period: the diaries and account books of Lady Anne Clifford and Lady Margaret Hoby make clear their engagement with domestic duties (Wall, *Staging* 21), while the architecture of early modern kitchens and the tools used within them reflect the extensive work described in Markham's text, as well as his values of economy and self-sufficiency; as Pamela Sambrook and Peter Brears outline in *The Country House Kitchen 1650–1900*, the ideal kitchen included the scullery (for cleaning fish, dishes, etc.), pantry, various larders for fish, game, and other types of food, salting room, smoking house, dairy, pastry house, bakehouse, brewhouse, wine cellar, coal cellar, wood house, still room, china closet, and so on, each with its particular fittings and equipment and all conveniently located to minimize walking distance. Even if the country house did not represent the social norm, it was interconnected with the society that surrounded it, and it represented "the social target" (Sambrook, "Introduction" 3). In fact, as receipt books and country-house kitchens reveal, the myriad responsibilities of the housewife were not limited to lower-class women, but extended across social classes. While servants undoubtedly made things easier for the upper-class housewife, she still managed the household and was directly involved in administering cures in her community. Indeed, as popular recipes and remedies attributed to upper-class women such as the Countess of Kent and Queen Henrietta Maria attest, there was a particular expectation for socially prominent women to share helpful domestic knowledge. This heightened role of the upper-class housewife could even symbolically take on national significance: Sir Kenelm Digby's evocation of noblewomen's recipes in his own household manual served as "reminders of the ways that the domestic spaces of the English kitchen and stillroom were concerned with acts of *nouriture* [*sic*] and sustenance that were understood to extend outside the home and hearth to the political realm of the English state" (Spiller, "Printed" 528). Thus, it appears that women across social classes were deeply engaged in housewifery activities. And regardless of her social standing, Markham emphasizes, the housewife's value was directly tied to the quality of her work; in stating that every second day she must change the nettles wrapped around a ripening cheese, he notes, "for the more euen and fewer wrinkles that your Cheese hath, the more daintie is your Hous-wife accounted" (189).

While smoothly surfaced cheese might seem a frivolous concern, women's work was of course seriously related to survival: not only was the housewife ultimately responsible for feeding her family, including preparing for winter and periods of scarcity, she was also the family's and community's main medical authority. Markham writes,

> To begin then with one of the most principal vertues which doth belong to our English Hous-wife; you shal vnderstand, that sith the preseruation and care of the family touching their health and soundnesse of body consisteth most in the diligence: it is meet that she haue a physicall kind of knowledge, how to administer many wholesome receits or medicines for the good of their healths, as wel to preuent the first occasion of sicknesse, as to take away the effects and euill of the same, when it hath made seasure on the body. (4)

This expectation is not surprising, as food and medicine were interrelated fields in the seventeenth century, and domestic medicine was the sphere of care to which people had most access. Recipes and remedies followed "medicogastronomic" precepts (Revel 118) based on Galenic theory, which dominated European medical understanding until at least the emergence of Paracelsian philosophy in the 1550s (and much later at the household level). As noted above, Galenic theory held that health depended upon equilibrium among the four humours of the body, and curatives based on the "virtues" or intrinsic properties of individual plants, animals, and minerals acted on the humours to correct imbalances. For example, an ingredient with a heating and drying property, such as galangal, was good for balancing cold, wet humours. Plants in particular, likely because of their variety and availability, were widely used to create remedies. The housewife's knowledge of plants and their properties was thus extensive, and receipt books contain numerous herbal remedies calling for long lists of plants, many of which are little known today; "To make plague Water" in the receipt book attributed to Mary Granville and Anne Granville D'Ewes, for example, calls for agrimony, wormwood, sage, celandine, balme, mugwort, dragon, wood sorrell, scabius, wood betony, brown mayweed, avens, angelica, tormentil, pimpernel, carduus benedictus, elecampane, burnet, marigold, feverfew, hartshorn, and rosemary (41). As the behaviour of the virtues of plants was, furthermore, understood to be influenced by the stars and moon, the housewife's knowledge also incorporated this understanding in the preparing and administering of remedies; a remedy for "Palsie Water" in the Granville receipt book, for example, notes the water should be taken "Especially against the new, full, & Change of the Moon" ([193]). As receipt books make clear, women were keepers of intertwined food and medical knowledge: "[t]he person most commonly approached for medical advice was ... the woman of the house. Women were brought up to know how to make medicines and how to use them" (Sim 82). And especially since this was a period of frequent food shortage and plagues, the housewife's knowledge of food and medicine was critical and her authority was widely assumed.

As of the seventeenth century, however, the issue of authority became more complex. While at the household level food and medicine remained united as women's work and dominated by folk knowledge (as Thirsk emphasizes, "At no time before the late nineteenth century should we separate food from medicine, for throughout all ranks of society they were regarded as one and the same" [*Food* 6]), a new professional level also emerged, and, at least superficially, it split food and medicine into separate fields, both of which were dominated by men. This period saw a profusion of male-authored manuscript and print

texts dealing with food and medicine at both the household and professional level, and these texts were mixed in their acceptance of women's
authority. Generally, men's domestic texts recognized the housewife's
authority, while the professional texts instead claimed authority for
themselves. It might be most accurate, however, to see the relationship between gender and authority in the myriad texts dealing with
food and medicine in this period as a kind of spectrum, with women's
receipt books at one end, men's household manuals and agricultural/
husbandry manuals and herbals in the middle, and professional cookbooks and medical books at the other, with various grades of blending
in between. There was clearly a correlation between forms here as well;
while it is an oversimplification to state that manuscript culture was
the province of women and print of men (Ezell, *Social* 40), especially
since there were diverse manuscript cultures[6] representing degrees of
overlap with printed texts, it nevertheless seems inaccurate to say that
"manuscript recipe collections … by no means [reflect] gender-specific
terrain of medical information and encounters" (Leong and Pennell
138). The archive suggests that *more* women than men were involved in
the compilation of manuscript receipt books, just as it is true that *more*
men than women were involved in the creation of printed agricultural,
husbandry, and household texts, as well as professional cookbooks and
medical books.

A question naturally arises in considering the emergence of so many
texts dealing with food and medicine as of the turn of the seventeenth
century: why did English people begin writing down this knowledge –
which had been passed on orally since time immemorial? Furthermore,
was the answer the same for women as for men, and the same for
manuscripts as for printed books? The rise of literacy and writing in
this period is at best only a partial answer, as it still misses explaining incentive, and furthermore disregards the fact that writing in particular created a major cultural disruption and was sometimes equated
with class division and conflict. In Shakespeare's *King Henry VI, Part II*,
for example, the ability to write one's name rather than use a common
mark is a sign of villainy and treason (4.2.80–103), as it served as an

---

6 Besides receipt books, manuscript forms included men's husbandry/medical/
   veterinary manuscripts, literary manuscripts, scribally reproduced manuscripts,
   commonplace books, miscellanies, diaries, account books, almanacs, parish
   registers, and others; each originated and functioned in its own way. Harold Love,
   Margaret Ezell, Victoria Burke, and Adam Smyth provide good introduction to
   these forms.

act of distinction of the individual rather than self-identification within collective society. As Shakespeare acknowledges in this play (however anachronistically), the spread of the written word upset traditional social balance and harmony. Nor was there a general rush to write or print: as Michelle DiMeo, Sara Pennell, Patricia Fumerton, and other scholars have emphasized, there was by no means a smooth, linear, and complete transition from oral to written to printed media. Crossover between forms was, in fact, characteristic of the period: "The climate in which handwritten documents were produced in Renaissance England was not unlike a symbiotic and osmotic sphere, with information flowing from speech to manuscript to print and back again in a continuous, cross-fertilizing circle" (Wolfe, "Manuscripts" 115).

As men's domestic and professional texts generally appeared before women's receipt books, it makes sense to first explore the origins of the men's texts. Many scholars, including Wendy Wall and Elizabeth Spiller, have regarded men's household manuals such as Markham's *The English Huswife* in particular as the literary forbears of receipt books, suggesting that male authors pressured women into assuming a new domestic role or else incited women to assert their individual authority as a response to repression. These scholars have assumed men's household manuals to be meant for female readers, but neither the books' intended audience nor their actual readership is in fact certain. For one thing, while men's household manuals peaked in publication between 1570 and 1650, diverse evidence makes clear that the cooking and curing work outlined in these household manuals was nothing new for women. The medieval ballad "A Woman's Work Is Never Done," for example, shows that Markham's list reflected more or less the same work women had done for generations or longer – and as women's receipt books later indicate, it is the same work that continued for generations more (Dowd 2). These household manuals recognized women's work and knowledge and deferred to women's authority: Gervase Markham, Sir Kenelm Digby, John Gerard, Richard Surflet, and John Pechey all freely cite women as sources, and perhaps even use such references to support their own credibility. Gerard in his *Herball* (1597) makes frequent reference to women's use of particular herbs; Surflet notes in *The Countrie Farme* (1600; a translation of Charles Estienne's *Maison Rustique*), "You must not doubt but that I my self have learned many remedies from the experiments and observations of ... women" (207); while Pechey nods to women's knowledge in stating in *The Compleat Herbal of Physical Plants* (1694) that he has only included "such plants as grow in England and are not commonly known; for I thought it needless to trouble the reader with the description of those that every woman knows or keeps in her garden" (in The Preface, EEBO image 3). Nor could the male-written works have represented relegation of women to the kitchen, "intended to keep women submissive and focused on domestic affairs" (Ostovich and Sauer 6), for, as Wall herself notes, "How could women be 'relegated' to the household at a time in which it had not yet even superficially withdrawn from economic life or from some yet unborn public sphere?" (*Staging* 9). Men's household manuals were also, it should be noted, similarly detailed in laying out men's work, and Markham refers to husbandry and housewifery as complementary at the beginning of *The English Huswife*, while Tusser refers to husbandry and housewifery as "married" in his *Fiue Hundreth Pointes of Good Husbandry*. Men's household manuals therefore seem more descriptive than *pre*scriptive of women's work. This matters, because it signals deeper origins for women's receipt books than women's attempt to live up to some newly formulated, male-created domestic ideal. Thus it is problematic to see receipt books as working to "cultivate and inform overarching conceptions of domesticity in the period" (Wall, "Literacy" 386); instead, one might argue that women already held firmly established domestic roles in the household, as part of a world in which men also already held their own firmly established domestic roles in husbandry and farming, and that women accepted their roles because they were valued authorities in them. So, if women already knew about cooking and curing and their authority was already assumed in these areas, why would men like Markham have bothered to write and publish household manuals at all?

That household manuals were primarily intended for male readers is in fact suggested by a number of details in the books themselves. The full title of Partridge's *Treasurie of Commodious Conceites* (1573) notes that it is the result of "sundry experiments, lately practised by men of great knowledge" and is dedicated to "Master Richard Wistow, Gentleman." Similarly, Dawson's *The Good Huswife's Jewell* (1585) is dedicated to "husbandmen," while the very title focusing on husbandry of Tusser's book also suggests that its primary aim was men's work, not women's, even if the two spheres were connected as two sides of the same coin. Another clue exists in Markham's book: his long list of women's tasks does not include reading or writing. While Cervantes' damsel was literate, both Markham's and Cervantes' texts preceded women's receipt books, which did not peak until 1650–1700 – and which are the first evidence of women's wider literacy and writing ability. Joan Thirsk did groundbreaking work in tracing the Latin, academic influence on English domestic texts written by men (see "Agricultural Innovations and Their Diffusion" and "Making a Fresh Start"), and Elizabeth Spiller has shown how books of "secrets" (to which one can add books of "cabinets," "closets opened," "jewels," and "delights," all terms carrying sexual innuendo) also had academic origins, deriving from medieval and Arabic books of secrets. These books thus all descend, at least in part, from a formal, foreign, scholarly tradition – a world to which men belonged but from which women were largely excluded. And, to repeat the obvious point, the domestic knowledge in the books was far from "secret" to women. In fact, Spiller notes that the very promise of a secret distinguished these printed books from receipt books: "Recipes in manuscript collections were not understood to be 'secret'; paradoxically, it was only being printed that made them so" ("Printed" 524). Receipt books do occasionally refer to "secrets," but the recipes and remedies in which they appear are also often foreign rather than domestic in origin; see the remedy from Holland for consumption (61) in the Hall receipt book in this edition.

The attention male authors paid to the housewife's work might thus reflect men's *own* anxiety and nostalgia in a period of hunger, plague, and dearth when women's knowledge was critical, and amidst great social change and a departure from tradition that initially only impacted men. The breaking away of men's world from the folk community, to which everyone, men and women, had belonged, towards individuality may have "freed men from ancient constraints" (Laurence 274), but men most certainly would have felt the loss this shift represented as well. It makes sense, therefore, that a writer like Markham would regard the housewife as the "guardian" of English culture (Wall, *Staging* 218). Even if, as Wall suggests, printed publications "forged" greater national commonality than actually existed (*Staging* 42), these texts tied to a deeper *cultural* tradition, one bound up with women's work and knowledge of cooking, curing, and preservation for times of scarcity – profoundly ingrained cultural knowledge, that is, of comfort and survival. Spiller also notes the conservative nature of men's household manuals, and while she, too, focuses on a national level, and interprets this as nostalgia for the Stuart political past rather than the deeper, broader, cultural past, she emphasizes that these books "invoke gender and domesticity in ways that look back, rather than forward" ("Printed" 519). That these texts might have been "anxious" and perhaps even reflect a longing for maternal nurturing in a turbulent time does not preclude their authors' recognition of domesticity as a possible commodity; Markham and others may very well have seen the opportunity to capitalize on tradition that was no longer as stable as it once was, and sell their supposed "unique access" to it. This idea supports Laurence's note that increasing individualism "liberated men from the restraints of the community and gave them the whole market place in which to operate; it deprived women of the support of the community while not substantially increasing their opportunities for personal choice and action" (274). While one may debate whether or not women experienced a Renaissance at all (a question itself problematized by Bakhtin's persuasive definition of the term), it seems clear that the cultural and social changes of the seventeenth century happened first for men.

Meanwhile, the professional fields of cooking and medicine that arose out of the cultural break, and their corresponding cookbooks and medical texts, drew, to an even greater extent than men's domestic texts, from an academic tradition. As these fields actively worked to dissociate themselves from women's authority and folk culture, they purposely made use of print for wider, and less relationships-based, dissemination. Medical books were also often written in Latin (at least until Nicholas Culpeper's 1649 vernacular translation of the *Pharmacopoeia Londinensis*), thereby aiming to exclude women, who generally did not gain formal schooling in Latin, as readers. However, the force with which the professionals challenged and derided women's authority (about which Rebecca Laroche and Elaine Leong have written extensively) suggests that the latter was indeed powerful and pervasive. And ultimately, the professionals' attempt to distance themselves from household medicine was largely superficial. While professional medicine was based upon classical and Arabic sources, it is evident from the similarities between the professional texts and receipt books that professional medicine was deeply influenced by traditional remedies too. (And the existence of "An excellent approoued plaister for *the* spleene" in the Granville receipt book, which was apparently "giuen ouer by the Phisitians" [46], is evidence that receipt books managed to borrow from the published medical texts as well.) The professionals might denounce women's health remedies as superstitious – a claim that modern readers might agree with when encountering, for example, the Countess of Kent's remedy for an ache in the sciatica, which calls for a boiled and strained middle-aged badger (101) – but all men's texts included similar remedies.[7]

---

7   And indeed, as John Considine has shown, the preface makes clear that the Countess of Kent's book was actually compiled by the (undoubtedly male) publisher, W.I. Gent.

Men's domestic texts in particular included remedies one might regard as "superstitious": Thomas Dawson's remedy "For sinowes that be broken in two" calls for the practitioner to "Take wormes while they be knitte, and looke that they depart not, and stampe them, and lay it to the sore, and it will knit the sinowes that be broken in two" (50); John Gerard prescribes tying peony roots around children's necks to cure them of the falling sickness (984); and Thomas Tryon's "To cure an Ague" in *The Way to Save Wealth* (1695) calls for the practitioner to write "Abracadabra" in a triangle on a piece of parchment and hang it around the patient's neck (50). Thus, Wendy Wall is correct in noting that in *Macbeth*, "when the witches call for body parts in their grotesque brew, they don't invert medical remedies as much as exaggerate their sinister nature. After all, some of the ingredients in the cauldron ... aren't that different from the body parts that surface in household guides" (*Staging* 199). However, these remedies are not so different from those listed in professional medical books, either. The *Pharmacopoeia Londinensis* (1618) includes remedies calling for

> roots, bark, leaves, flowers, fruits and seeds of numerous plants, mostly indigenous wild flowers. Animals in the catalogue include earthworms, grasshoppers, vipers and woodlice; parts of animals include sparrow's brain's, crab's eyes,[8] frog's liver, man's skull and the greatly prized unicorn's horn. Another category, "Belonging to the sea," includes pearls, sea sand and spermaceti. Finally, "metals and stones" include bezoar (a concretion from the stomach of a ruminant), brimstone (sulphur), diamond, gold, lead, ruby and topaz ... Methods of preparation are given in considerable detail and a general introduction indicates how treatment should be modified in terms of the four temperaments and the importance of astrology in selecting the appropriate remedy. (Sloan 61)

The *Pharmacopoeia Londinensis* clearly drew on shared knowledge with household medicine, and as new medical books were printed, they also incorporated and built upon household remedies. For a long while, the medical profession did succeed in denying its roots: modern medicine has largely forgotten its pre-modern connection to, and great influence by, women's traditional knowledge and authority. However, household remedies are regaining attention today in the

---

8   See Glossary; this is actually a seed.

field of preventative medicine and in research on antibiotic resistance (see Harrison et al.).

Professional cookbooks were also almost exclusively written by men and were clearly intended for other male professional cooks: Robert May, for example, dedicated his 1660 work, *The Accomplish't Cook*, "To the Master Cooks, and to such young Practitioners of the Art of Cookery, to whom this Book may be useful ... To all honest well intending Men of our Profession." Even apparent exceptions must be read cautiously: while Joseph Cooper seemingly directs *The Art of Cookery* (1654) towards a female readership, his language follows that of the books of secrets, referring to women blushing at seeing recipes "prostituted," for example, and his inclusion of only culinary recipes (rather than the traditional intermingling of recipes, remedies, and household tips) reflects a split from women's work and authority; the same is true for Sir Kenelm Digby, who, while attributing many recipes in his cookbook to women, also omitted remedies and household tips. The professional cookbooks emphasized novelty and elaborate dishes, as well as the "perfection" of the recipes and the special knowledge and skill of the author/professional cook himself – thereby greatly departing from the concept of commonly shared folk knowledge. Generally, these cookbooks did not share the quotidian practicality and economy of folk recipes either: May includes a recipe for a model stag that released wine when an arrow was plucked from its side, and others for pies baked with live birds and frogs that flew and hopped away to delight and surprise the diners. "Everything," writes Gerald MacLean, "that May instructs [his cook] to make ... is designed to be wasted" (16). Professional cookbooks, even more so than men's domestic texts, are of a different origin from women's receipt books; as Elizabeth Spiller points out, they did not

> develop out of ... Galenic traditions so much as in opposition to them. Indeed, the historic emergence of the modern cookbook depended on key factors: print culture, a philosophical commitment to detailed measurement (recipes, rather than "receipts") and the emergence of food as a category that could be thought of as fundamentally distinct from health (cookbooks, rather than dietaries). ("Recipes" 55)

None of these qualities characterizes seventeenth-century English-women's receipt books. Receipt books have different roots. It is clear that women did not begin writing receipt books in response to pressure created by male-written domestic texts, or as a way of asserting their individual authority in household matters. Crossover did occur; just as men's domestic and professional texts incorporated women's knowledge, receipt books then incorporated men's knowledge as well – the Granville receipt book includes "Mr. Bamber's Medicine for an Horse has the Grypes" ([239]), as well as recipes attributed to a navy guard, a monk, and a Portuguese man, while numerous other receipt books contain recipes and remedies with phrasing and placement of line breaks nearly identical to those in various printed books. However, this incorporation of men's knowledge seems to have happened only when it related to women's own traditional knowledge and knowledge structures, and it is interesting to note what is *not* shared between men's texts and women's receipt books. As Wall notes, Tusser's *Fiue Hundreth Pointes of Good Husbandry* explains to the reader how to use the printed book itself; however, the conventions he outlines, such as preface, tables, and particular order of reading ("Literacy" 388–9), are almost entirely absent from receipt books, suggesting that many women even decades later were unfamiliar with this text – or, more likely, since many printed books utilized these conventions, that women simply did not find them appropriate for their own writing. This absence underscores the point that women also had their own, long-established means of ordering and circulating their knowledge long before men's writing appeared, and as receipt books show, these other means persisted. It was indeed out of the folk tradition of social networks women had long used for the acquiring and sharing of knowledge that receipt books emerged.

Seventeenth-Century Englishwomen's Literacy and Writing

Women's work in seventeenth-century England as described by Markham and others leads one to believe that women would have had little time to write. As Una Robertson notes:

> Cooking, cleaning, fetching water and fuel, making candles, washing and ironing, producing food from the garden, looking after poultry, pigs or bees, going to market to sell products of her own making or to buy in what was required, supervising servants, caring for children and other dependants [plus spinning wool or flax, sewing and hemming garments, distilling waters, and making creams, as listed in previous paragraphs] – in such a busy life so filled with the practicalities of running a household there can have been few moments left over for anything that could remotely be called leisure, let alone pleasure. (150)

Yet seventeenth-century women *did* write. And, according to the material evidence surviving today, one of their most common genres was the receipt book. The emergence of this writing within the context of such domestic demands suggests that the writing served a useful, practical purpose – and this hints at why women suddenly began writing down recipes that had circulated orally since time immemorial. Such a purpose could very well have been the recording and sharing of knowledge in a time of great cultural change, which threatened the loss of oral transmission. The central reason, really, for writing anything down is to preserve what would otherwise be lost. (This is particularly obvious today, unfortunately, in the creation of dictionaries of endangered oral languages.) The influx of foreign foods and ideas, the splitting of knowledge into distinct fields, the fragmenting of collective culture and rising prominence of the (male) individual, "the shift from a largely rural to a concentrated urban population" (Hunter 134), the lifting away of the upper class from the folk culture of the people, etc. – in short, the markers of change in the early modern period that initially only impacted men – ultimately impacted women as well, so that, fifty years after men wrote housewifery books praising women as the keepers of tradition, women then wrote for the same reason: as a response to cultural instability and risk of loss. Paradoxically, as the keepers of tradition in a changing culture, women were forced to adapt in order to actually *preserve* that tradition, by writing down the knowledge they had shared orally. Seventeenth-century women's manuscripts in general underscore women's role as record-keepers; Jill S. Millman, in her introduction to the *Perdita Manuscripts* database, notes: "the top genres of receipt books, religious and meditative writings, diaries and account books could all represent record-keeping activities" ("Genres" par. 1). Receipt books – especially as one of the least interior forms in this list – represent not women's new, emerging early modern subjectivity, but rather an act of holding on to the past to prevent its loss. Like jellies and pickles, they served as another form of women's work in preserving.

Consideration of receipt books greatly alters our understanding of Renaissance and early modern Englishwomen's literacy rates, writing abilities, and education, enabling us to look past traditional, inaccurate research methods. David Cressy's "illiteracy" figures are often quoted on the topic, but these are vague, and his research methods focus on men's worlds of formal schooling, book publication, book ownership, and the marking of wills. He concludes: "More than … nine-tenths of the women were so illiterate at the time of the civil war that they could not even write their own names" (2); he later states, "Most women did not need to be able to write" (128). Margaret Spufford suggests that more women could read than write, but she also ignores receipt books (and other manuscript writing) and bases her conclusions on publication history. Jennifer Anderson and Elizabeth Sauer have criticized this quantitative approach, referring to Cressy and Spufford as "counters of books and readers" (9) and noting the "loss of historical particularity in numerical data" (10). What Cressy's and Spufford's research does not consider is that many women might have become literate in other ways; their findings certainly do not account for how women were ever able to read and write receipt books. (And even male physicians assumed that women *could* read by the 1630s: when James Rueff notes that he wrote *The Expert Midwife* [1631] in English "for the benefit of midwives, most of whom are unlearned," he obviously means that women simply did not know university Latin; he assumes they could read in English [Sloan 121]). Caroline Bowden's research on early modern women's literacy, which takes a more qualitative approach and is based on comparisons with patterns of women's education in non-industrial nations today, seems more useful in understanding women's particular experiences in becoming literate. Bowden notes that, while few women in her study attended school, many were invested in learning, "creating their own opportunities and making their own educational spaces in their households" (91), and that many developed a "functional literacy" (86). She emphasizes that women learned at home from other, more experienced women, and points out that the opportunity for such learning depended upon the existence of mentors to fill the space of trained teachers, a place of learning with materials relevant to the life of the learner, the practising of skills in order to not lose them, and motivation (87) – all elements certainly present in the context of the seventeenth-century housewife's kitchen.

Bowden also specifically sees women's receipt books as evidence of practice of reading and writing in the seventeenth century:

> Still-rooms ... and kitchens were also transformed into educational spaces. Here women practiced and developed skills learned earlier and trained others to prepare the herbs and distillates for medicines used in the household and the local area. Numerous recipe collections testify to the existence of female networks of knowledge exchange. (92)

In "Literacy and the Domestic Arts," Wendy Wall also notes that many women might have engaged in "artisanal literacy" – that is, writing that was a domestic art akin to carving food, shaping edible tarts into letters or decorative knots, sewing, and embroidery, so that "[s]cribally produced recipes were 'writing matter' that emerged out of the inscriptional activities of housework" ("Literacy" 396) – an example of which is evident in the Pudsey receipt book in this edition, where a recipe for gooseberry cakes calls for the cook to cut "ether letters or what you please" on them ([10v]); cooking and writing were also interconnected through the use of paper from old manuscripts to line baking pans, in recipes for ink, and in common sourcing in the farmyard for food and quills for pens. Edith Snook likewise contends, "Domesticity was central to how women construed reading, for the household provided its space, rationale and schedule" (43). Janet Theophano emphasizes how this information was then passed on to daughters, and that many girls over time have developed literacy skills at home: "While working in the kitchen with children underfoot, mothers may have used recipes to teach their children – primarily daughters – how to read and write" (156):

> ... these documents show how kitchens and cookbooks were places where women could and did practice reading and writing and where they also taught others to do so. Manuscript recipe books and printed cookbooks provided women the opportunity to read, write, and reflect ... while working in the kitchen. (188)

Theophano uses Mrs Maddison's 1679 receipt book as an example of this kitchen writing. In this manuscript, Mrs Maddison's daughter Mary practises writing the letter "M" (Theophano 157), and Mrs Maddison herself uses the manuscript to practise reading and writing: she includes a recipe for Lady Kent's powder, copied nearly verbatim from the Countess of Kent's *A Choice Manual*, so that "even the funnel-shaped title of the receipt is written so as to resemble the printed version" (Theophano 181); at another point, after a few attempts at spelling an ingredient, she writes, "I cannot write it right" (in Theophano 161).

The sharing of knowledge among women traced in receipt books is dynamic, occurring not only from mother to daughter, but also between neighbours, from housekeeper to servant, or even the other way around (Pennell 243). Thus, literacy was not necessarily limited to upper-class women, but rather might have begun among a few elite or middle-class women and then spread in the mixed-class space of the kitchen. Even if recipes were sometimes read aloud in the kitchen (Margaret Hoby notes that "she listened to books read aloud as part of [her] 'Huswiffrie'" [Wall, "Women" 106]), they nevertheless represented an entry point for the written word into women's domestic space, rather than requiring a separate, formal educational environment. And access to the materials needed for writing was not limited to the upper class: as the multiple recipes for ink in the Granville receipt book show, ink could be made at home using reasonably common ingredients. Likewise, as noted above, a quill pen was as accessible as the nearest goose. Even access to paper, which has traditionally been regarded as a marker of means, might have been more widespread than originally thought: Mark Bland notes that any generalization regarding paper is risky because "There is reason to believe that at least c.95 per cent, possibly as much as 98 per cent, of the paper that was used in the sixteenth and seventeenth centuries has perished" (Bland 214). Similarly, Heather Wolfe at the Folger Shakespeare Library has undertaken research that suggests that paper, while still special and carefully reused, was not the rare and expensive commodity it was once believed to be ("Rethinking" par. 1). If paper was used to line cake pans, which we know from recipes was the case, then even servants would have had access to it. And that servants were at least somewhat literate is evident in that the printed household manual *The Compleat Servant Maid* (1677) (sometimes attributed – wrongly, Elaine Hobby argues – to Hannah Woolley [174]) includes instruction on how to make a quill pen, as well as instruction on how to write in secretary, italic, and mixed hand. Receipt books thus not only fulfilled a purpose of recording and sharing recipes and remedies in a time of change, they also served as literacy tools. As the manuscripts were written, read, used, and edited in the kitchen, this room became a space not only of cooking and curing but also of reading and writing. And the sheer number of surviving seventeenth-century receipt books (over two hundred between the Folger, Wellcome, Bodleian, and British Library collections, plus perhaps many still in private hands), despite the fact that these works were not simply read in a study but rather used in a kitchen, suggests that these manuscripts were common.[9]

Just as simply counting students or signatures does not reveal how many women were actually literate in the seventeenth century, publication numbers do not indicate how many women actually wrote in the

---

9 It is interesting to note that few receipt books have stains on them. This might suggest that only the *little-used* manuscripts have survived (although the comments on recipes indicate that this is not the case), or it might simply reflect careful treatment. However, the small size of some of the books, such as Sarah Longe's *Receipt Book* (1610), might point to the fact that the books were carried around rather than placed on a countertop; historian Beverly Lemire has suggested that the ubiquitous pockets tied under women's petticoats might have proven useful in just this way (personal communication, 4 September 2012).

period. Once manuscripts are considered, it is clear that the number of women writing in Renaissance and early modern England is much greater than previously believed when only counting first editions of printed works (Lunger Knoppers 10). As Margaret Ezell notes, the question is now "Who was writing and who was reading as opposed to who was printing and who was purchasing" (*Social* 2). As receipt books prove, women wrote, but relatively few of them published in print. Most literary scholars now recognize that print was not always the preferred form in the period, and that it did not simply replace the manuscript form, just as manuscripts did not simply replace oral culture:

> We should no longer see the conventions and properties of manuscript circulation as peripheral to a simple set of procedures established by a dominant world of print publication. Instead, it is necessary to look at manuscript culture as a persisting set of procedures with its own history and customs as well as balancing manuscripts and print as unfinished, in-process cultures with strong cross-fertilization. (Justice and Tinker 8)

The very inclusion of directions on how to make and hold a quill pen in *print* books, as noted above, reveals the concurrency and "cross-fertilization" of manscript and print cultures; manuscript texts did not only exist as "raw material for the presses" (Ezell, *Social* 16).

There are many hypotheses as to why women did not always seem to desire publication. The "stigma of print" (see J.W. Saunders's essay by this title) is a commonly offered explanation, suggesting that women accepted that it was immodest and unbecoming to expose themselves so publicly. But this idea assumes that manuscripts were private works – and much evidence, including the multiple hands in receipt books, proves they were not – as well as assumes a degree of submission on women's part that is not supported by women's authority and confidence in the writing itself. Perhaps a more convincing possibility is that print publication simply did not align with the purpose of the text, and so women would have felt no urge to publish this way. As Paul Eggert notes, this may be hard for anyone raised in mainstream modern Western culture to understand, because we have been conditioned *not* to understand:

> The economics of cultural production have for a very long time, perhaps always, tended to narrow our attention as viewers of works of art (or readers of works of literature) to the object that would sell most readily: the finished product. The idea has become so thoroughly naturalized that it has helped in turn to naturalize exaggerated doctrines about individual

inspiration and execution, doctrines born probably in the Renaissance but of course later greatly stimulated by the climate of Romanticism. (Eggert 59–60)

Receipt books, of course, were anything but finished products. Recipes and remedies were continuously added into the manuscript or annotated right in the kitchen, and this was done in a collaborative way: women applied their collective authority in the domestic sphere to a collective authority in receipt books. Print reproduces a text through largely uniform, multiple copies, and while that is often print's advantage over the manuscript form, it does not seem quite appropriate for a receipt book that in whole and in part depended upon variation, adaptability, and relationships. The fact that receipt books persisted as manuscripts, even after the publication of Hannah Woolley's *The Ladies Directory* in 1661[10] – and even, one might say, until today, in the recipe notebooks still kept and passed down in families, often along matriarchal lines – underscores the suitability of the handwritten form to the genre. Woolley's publication of her household manuals does not signify a triumph in some evolution of women's writing, and receipt books continued in their own right. Thus, while many scholars suggest that women wrote receipt books (and then published cookbooks) as subscription to new domestic pressures created by men or, conversely, to assert their authority in a patriarchal, repressive society, in reality it seems that the situation was quite different from either scenario. Yes, the world of premodern Englishwomen focused on the kitchen, but receipt books reflect neither submission nor an attempt to break free from domesticity – these works "should not be taken primarily as a marker of some kind of proto-feminist shift" (Spiller "Printed" 519). Instead, they represent continuity of a world in which women's authority was already assumed.

Receipt Books

Amidst the cultural instability of the seventeenth century, the kitchen remained the last bastion of folk culture. The main themes of carnival as described by Bakhtin – life and death and rebirth of the physical body – are, in effect, the themes of the kitchen, and the hearth in

---

10   While some scholars have regarded the Countess of Kent's *A Choice Manual* (1653) as the first printed cookbook by a woman, as noted above, John Considine points out the book's preface makes clear that it was compiled by the publisher, W.I. Gent.

particular was the place of both transformation and storytelling. Wendy Wall hints at the carnivalesque nature of the kitchen when she notes that women's receipt books include both butchery/carving and healing because women's world dealt with "all manners of the body" ("Women" 100), and that "housewifery involved a world of interchangeable, absorbable, and consumable body parts, extracted from live and dead beings," including frequent use of blood, urine, and dung for curing (*Staging* 199). The kitchen was an unofficial sphere, a noisy, mixed-class, spoken-word space of women's collective authority and sharing of traditional knowledge. This space paralleled the dialogism and topsyturvydom of carnival, which one might see as "organized in its own way, according to its own rules" (Bakhtin 255), rather than a crisis of domestic "*loci* out of control" (Wall, "Reading the Home" 182–3). The linking of the housewife and oral culture is reflected in Bartholomew Dowe's *A Dairie Booke for Good Huswives* (1588), as he includes songs his mother sang as she milked cows and made butter and cheese, and in Shakespeare's *The Merry Wives of Windsor*, of which Wall asks, "Is it a coincidence ... that it is in Shakespeare's most domestic play that a notorious housewife interrupts [in English] a Latin language lesson?" (Wall, *Staging* 93). Even as a new instability of this domestic sphere likely stimulated the writing down of recipes and remedies, receipt books served as an *extension* of its oral, collective, traditional nature rather than a break away from it.

Receipt books' function in preserving traditional folk knowledge is evident in both the content and structure of the recipes, remedies, and household tips they contain. These elements directly parallel women's work in cooking, curing, and cleaning, and their random placement reflects the conceptual inseparability of food and medicine in the period, at least in the household. This randomness also reflects day-to-day practical use as tasks happened at overlapping times, rather than the abstract standardization more characteristic of written language, and thus reveals a kind of "artisanal writing," to adapt Wendy Wall's useful term; these were books that were *used*, not "just" read. Such practical use is also evident when a sequence of recipes focuses on a single ingredient; the three recipes in a row calling for elderflowers in the Pudsey manuscript, for example, certainly suggest that they were written during elderflower season. Even receipt books commencing in one neat hand, suggesting that they began as presentation copies, contain traces of use and eventually fall into randomness, so that their "utility" seems "the key reason for passing them on, as much as their carriage of any symbolic value" (Leong and Pennell 142). Such randomness

can be disorienting for a modern reader, and the effect can also sometimes be startling: in Sarah Longe's receipt book, "For a stinking, or
poison of Snakes, or adders" is immediately followed by "To make fritters" (24) and "For a Vomitt" is followed by "Another way to make
snow" (36), while in Lady Grace Castleton's receipt book, a remedy
"too expell a dead chield" is followed by "To make Sirrip of Turnips"
(image 16 in the *Perdita* scan). The individual recipes and remedies,
meanwhile, reflect the extensive work that Markham and others
describe: in Granville's receipt book, "To make Diett cakes" calls for
the cook to beat the eggs and sugar with a stick for three hours (53),
while in Ann Blencowe's receipt book, "To Whiten Cloth" takes an
entire week, beginning with "Laye *the* cloth in this green water [made
from sheep's dung] on Saturday morning ..." (37). Often, a recipe's
instructions include dealing with the animals called for in the recipe:
in Granville's receipt book, "To make a thicke creame" begins, "Bring
2· or 3· Cowes according to the quantity / you will make, as neare the
place you set your creame / in as may bee, and milke them with all the
speed / that you can ..." (45); similarly, in Mary Baumfylde's receipt
book, "Howe to Coller a Pigg" calls for the cook to "Take a good fatt
pigg scald him and / cutt off the head & slit it down the back / & bone
it & throw him into fair water and / soe let him lie one night to soke
out the / bloud" (49r), and Pudsey's receipt book includes instructions
"To feed chickings geeses or duckes," which are themselves destined
as food ([8v]). Also occasionally included are veterinary remedies, such
as "Mr. Bamber's Medicine for an Horse has the Grypes" in Granville's
receipt book ([239]). Such everyday recipes and remedies imply that
these are practical texts reflecting the housewife's existing work and
intimate relationship with plants and animals, rather than aspirational
texts imagining an alternative reality. For the same reason it is also hard
to see them as *aides-mémoires* for special-occasion dishes, as various
scholars have asserted (e.g., Brears, "Ideal" 13).

The traditional/everyday nature of the knowledge contained in
receipt books is also revealed through the ingredients and tools called for
in the recipes. Most recipes list local, widely available ingredients such
as pippins (apples long cultivated in England), quinces, plums, apricots,
gooseberries, and walnuts, plus a plethora of wild herbs, many of which
are now unfamiliar. The inclusion of outdated ingredients particularly
underscores the long tradition represented in some recipes; for example, saffron appears frequently, as both a flavouring and a colouring,
even though Richard Hakluyt revealed as early as 1582 that saffron "is
gone out of great use" in England (98). While receipt books also call for

imported foods such as eastern spices, almonds, sugar, citrus, and currants, these were at least somewhat "established" ingredients, as they had been imported for centuries (and in some cases were now being grown on a small scale in England) and also appeared in medieval texts. Occasionally, recipes do call for novel ingredients such as chocolate, and they reflect an increasing interest in vegetables such as carrots, potatoes, and artichokes, thereby reflecting subtle changes in foods, diet, and techniques; however, there is no revolutionary change, and "new" recipes are always followed by traditional ones – as in the Granville receipt book, where "To ming /To pickle Artichoaks" (127) is followed a few pages later by "To Cure a Flux infaliably," a remedy based on oak bark (164). Seventeenth-century receipt books overwhelmingly look back, not forward: while these books are indeed a "transitional form" (Spiller, "Printed" 526), they only rarely reflect innovation, and instead serve as a "handy compendium of a long period of accumulated knowledge and skill" (Ezell, "Cooking the Books" 167). Tools and measurements likewise make use of readily available materials: Granville's receipt book describes using little bags of "pebblestones" to sink spices in a kettle (13), a feather to ice macaroons (50), and a stick with a flattened end to beat eggs and sugar (53), and Constance Hall's receipt book suggests drying tansy by swinging it in a coarse cloth ([22v]) and giving as much "as a walnut" of cough medicine to an adult and "a nutmeg" to a child (61), while Grace Randolph's receipt book calls for "as many herbs as will fill an egg" (image 17 in the *Perdita* scan).

Remedies are equally everyday/traditional, generally reflecting a Galenic understanding of health, with rare inclusion of new Paracelsian remedies as well. Granville's receipt book includes a recipe "To make an Admirable good Water against Melancholly" (12) and Pudsey's includes "To purge Malincoly without grife" ([3r]), while other remedies refer to healing according to the phases of the moon: the "Palsie Water" in Granville's receipt book was to be given "Especially against the new, full, & Change of the Moon" (193), and "Lady Katharine Windham's Receipt / Powder for Convulsion fitts" calls for the medicine to be administered "three / Days before a new Moon, & 3 days after, & the / Same before and after the full Moon" ([239]). Even the inclusion of multiple versions of a single remedy likely reflects Galenic principles in the need for cures suitable for a range of humoral and constitutional differences, so that receipt books serve as a kind of "textual medicine chest" of the period (Leong and Pennell 145). As with the culinary recipes, "new" remedies, such as "To make Paracelsus plaister" (59) in Granville's receipt book, are followed by more traditional remedies, so it is difficult to chart a development or "evolution" in either cooking or medicine in receipt books. More useful is to perform a detailed analysis of the layers of cultural knowledge embedded in each individual recipe, which is precisely what Elizabeth Spiller does with three seventeenth-century recipes in her article "Printed Recipe Books in Medical, Political, and Scientific Contexts" and what my own edition aims to offer in a more expanded form through its historical introduction and glossary alongside transcriptions of the manuscripts themselves.

Receipt books also reveal confident authority that implies long experience and repeated practice, as well as intimate knowledge of the land; these are not anxious books that tread new territory. Many recipes specify the time of year in which they should be made or their ingredients gathered: butter, for example, should be made in May, walnuts picked at the end of June before the shells become tough, hawthorn berries picked after a frost, and elderflowers collected, according to Pudsey's receipt book, "when / *they* are falling & will shake off" ([54r]). Similarly, a number of recipes distinguish between "pump water," "rain water," "river water," "fair water," and snow. However, the self-assuredness to experiment is also suggested in recipes that offer options: a contributor of "To make a Fricacee" in Granville's receipt book notes, "I Thinke that leamon wilbe better then Vinegre" (25); similarly, a contributor of "To Boyle a carpe" ([60v]) in Pudsey's receipt book notes, "if you have shelott it is much better / to putt in then onion" but that the reader should "season the / broth with salt to your likeing," and later, this same contributor follows a recipe "how to mack Shrewsberry cakes" with "as I mack it," outlining her own version of the recipe ([65r]). The contributors' confidence seems unwavering: while the Granville receipt book's remedy "Doctor Burges his direction a*gainst* the plague" notes, "in all the time of the / plague; vnder God trust to this for this neuer did faile / either man woman or child" (41), and the remedy for "The head pills" assures the reader that the patient will "[require] no confinement" (212), the contributor of Mrs Risley's "pills for the stone" in the Pudsey receipt book simply notes that "it may be thay will work: if not / thay will doe noe harme" ([15v]). And if a recipe went wrong, the cook's confident authority is also evident in her denunciation of the recipe: below a crossed-out recipe for pickles in the Pudsey book is the comment, "This Receipt is good for nothing" ([56r]). And yet others convey unspoken knowledge by what is left *out* of the recipe: "To make Bread A la Roine" in Granville's receipt book, for example, calls for "good" flour of "good" wheat, ground in a "good" mill, and notes, "the oven must not bee heated too much nor too / little but according to the Judgement of the Baker" (10). Such unspoken knowledge is proof that culture is embedded in recipes. The same is true, of course, for recipes of any given time and place.

Besides the traditional nature of the recipes, remedies, and tips, various structural and rhetorical elements of receipt books signal the oral, collective kitchen culture out of which they arose. The practice of handwriting noted above, and the spelling, which is often phonetic and is particularly inconsistent, even for the period, imply the informal schooling of the writers (between the Granville, Hall, and Pudsey receipt books, *cinnamon* is spelled seventeen different ways). They also intimate a sense of informality and even fun through their often messy writing, marginal doodles, and writing at various angles, including a series of upside-down recipes in Susanna Packe's receipt book. Most striking, however, is receipt books' collaborative character. Multiple hands, inscriptions, attributions, annotations, and other marginalia, as well as loose recipes tucked between the pages (obtained, presumably, during a visit paid to a relative or a friend or a neighbour), all show that these books were compiled by many women, and a few men, often over generations (the final entries in most archive receipt books date from around the 1740s). These texts thus not only preserved traditional knowledge, they also preserved, through a social activity that "lies somewhere between the processes of reading and writing" (Burke, "Manuscript" 55), the particular social culture upon which the sharing of that knowledge depended. The receipt book attributed to Mary Granville and Anne Granville D'Ewes, for example, seems to have been begun by someone other than Mary Granville; it was later acquired by Mary, who in turn passed it on to her daughter Anne, as is made clear by the inside-cover inscription: "Mrs. Ann[11] Granvilles Book / which I hope shee will make / a better use of then her mother / Mary Granville." This manuscript contains many recipes, remedies, and tips not in Mary Granville's handwriting – in fact, the manuscript contains no fewer than twenty-three different hands (a number that does not necessarily directly correspond to the number of its contributors, as the hand of a child practising her writing skills might reappear later as that of an adult). Many recipes and remedies are attributed to specific sources, and while it makes sense that compilers would have sought sources they deemed trustworthy (see Leong and Pennell 139), in some cases the contributor mentions the attribution quite casually – a remedy in Granville's receipt

---

11   The name appears as both "Ann" and "Anne" in the text.

book was "giuen me for Excellent by a Portuges" (92), while in another case Colonel Belasyse simply "had *the* receat *with* hime" (95). In most cases, the sources range from presumed neighbours, such as Goodwife Lawrence and Mr Bamber in Granville's receipt book, to upper-class women or well-known physicians who might have been beyond the writer's own immediate social circle, such as Doctor Chambers (whose medicinal water remedy appears in many other texts in the period).

And yet *these* people were not likely the creators of the recipes and remedies either. The particular elusiveness of authorship of receipt books, even over other manuscript forms, is evident when one considers the folk origins of the individual recipes, remedies, and tips that make up these texts. Unlike diaries, poems, or sermons, recipes and remedies never have an original author; even "new" recipes build upon pre-existing ones.[12] Thus, while all manuscript culture is collective – as Victoria Burke emphasizes, manuscripts are "fundamentally social forms" ("Manuscript" 55) – the aggregate nature of receipt books distinguishes them as particularly so, to the point that one might question the relevance of the term "authorship" to them at all.[13] In all cases, the "author" has been determined by a library, for simplicity's sake; without an author name, cataloguing these manuscripts would be even *more* confusing than it already is.[14] It does thus indeed seem true, as David Goldstein points out, that "The multiplicity of authorial practices in the manuscript recipe genre exceeds our present vocabulary of authorship and originality ... To attempt to describe the circulation of authorship in such a text is to approach the limits of our understanding of what 'author' can mean" (*Eating and Ethics* 259); neither "author," "scribe," "compiler," nor "commentator" accurately describes the contributors

---

12 The folk origin of recipes and remedies means that not only does a literary focus on individual authorship miss the point, so too does a historical search for "original" recipes; as Gilly Lehmann points out, "[the] very idea of originality belongs to a heroic narrative of culinary development, in which a defining moment can be isolated ... This is indeed a futile search" (96).

13 Traditional folk songs (including lullabies, nursery rhymes, and ballads) might be the only other genre to parallel receipt books' social origins, although they were not collaboratively compiled in a material way in the same way receipt books were.

14 Yet referring to a receipt book by its manuscript number feels deficient; "MS V.a.430" seems too impersonal for such a richly human text. Hence, this edition perpetuates the misleading – and, admittedly, considering my interpretation of these texts, somewhat contradictory – identification of individual receipt books through reference to a woman's name.

to receipt books (159).[15] "Reader," "private," "public," "narrative," and even "literature" are similarly problematic; in many ways, the language we use does not seem sufficient to accurately describe receipt books. These are truly open-ended texts; collectively created and shared orally from one generation to the next since time immemorial, the text is inseparable from a particular culture – rather than reflecting the life of an individual woman.

While some feminist critics are uncomfortable with the concept of the dissolution of the author, claiming that "to kill off the author is to ensure [her] continued silence" (Pacheco xv), this attitude does more of a disservice to women by subjecting them generally to modern values rather than considering them within their own historical and cultural context and remaining open to alternative possibilities of identity and authority. Shifting focus away from an "author" is not to say that receipt books, or the experiences of the women who contributed to them, are insignificant or homogeneous; indeed, that is far from the case – each work is a unique artefact, because it arose out of a cluster of particular lives (as is evident, for example, in the inclusion of Castilian recipes in Granville's receipt book from her family's time in Spain). Instead, it recognizes that women's experience and identity throughout history and across cultures are not uniform, and that alternatives exist to our own. Receipt books serve as evidence that seventeenth-century Englishwomen belonged to a culture that was much more collective, cyclical, and orally oriented than is the modern, mainstream, Western world. Thus, while consideration of individual contributors can and should be used as another source of clues to shed light on the origins and function of receipt books as a genre, the "author's" biography, or any similar emphasis on the individual, should not be the focus in receipt book study. Overemphasis on any single individual misses the point of how receipt books originated and functioned. One should also be cautious in drawing conclusions about the contributors' circumstances; as noted above, seemingly clear clues can be misleading. The commonality of food sources and shared values of economy and self-sufficiency across classes mean that receipt books reveal little about social standing; this explains why the receipt book attributed to a relatively wealthy woman such as Mary Granville includes recipes that make use of all parts of the animal, such as "To stew a Calues Head," thrifty recipes such as "To make Short Paist Without Butter," and recipes for preserved

---

15   This edition uses the term "contributors."

wild foods, such as "To make Gooseberry wine." Similarly, while many receipt books include recipes for confections and distillations, which called for expensive ingredients and were sometimes so labour-intensive that they could have been undertaken only in households with a certain number of servants (Thirsk, *Food* 107), it is not always clear whether these recipes were actually made, and although a recipe might include an attribution to the Countess of Kent, the fact that recipes travelled far beyond immediate social circles means that the writer did not necessarily know this noblewoman. (Simple dishes were more likely directly received: Lady Dorset's book [1649], for example, "cites recipes that she got from Goodwife Wells for rennet, Goodwife Rivers for liver cake, and Goodwife Cleaves for hog's cheek. These were plainly homely dishes made by homely neighbours, not recipes passed on by grand ladies" [Thirsk, *Food* 209].) As Michelle DiMeo notes at the end of her own attempt to trace individual women's networks through attributions in their receipt books, "the detailed case studies in this chapter highlight the potential problems with using such textual evidence to document an individual compiler's network" (42).

The deeply traditional and social nature of receipt books suggests that the structural and rhetorical qualities that a number of scholars have interpreted as evidence of emerging modern subjectivity represent something else entirely. The imperative form receipt books use, for example, might not represent the assertion of an individual woman's instructions, but rather a disembodied authority of tradition, implying the way something simply *is done*. Likewise, comments on the success of a recipe, or amendments needed, might not signify individual authority, but rather a general understanding of "the best way," a term that indeed often appears in receipt books (see, for example, Granville 17); similarly, the note *probatum est* at the end of recipes does not mean "I have proven this," as some scholars suggest, but rather the passive "it is proved," and it might even have been copied from the previous source as part of the recipe itself. In all of these cases, we might envision the cook/contributor as participating in a kitchen-like conversation with other women (including women in other kitchens, and other times) to create the recipe, in terms of both the dish and the text, together. Even seemingly straightforward indications of individual authorship or ownership should be read carefully in the context of receipt books' social origin and function. The note "my own," for example, does not seem to carry greater weight or importance than any other attribution, and thus might simply be read as an indication of the source. Keeping in mind that all recipes build on others, this statement likely means that the contributor has created her own version of a particular dish, not that she has come up with something strikingly new – and indeed, such a note in Mary Hookes's manuscript indicating that a recipe "To make Meade" is her own (image 12 in the *Perdita* scan) supports this point, as countless versions exist for mead recipes. Endless variety was (and is) a fundamental characteristic of recipes: in their exploration of the recipe for "oil of swallows," DiMeo and Laroche found twenty-three instances of the recipe in seventeenth-century print books and manuscripts, and no two were exactly the same (90). David Goldstein's argument is thus convincing that "use" of a recipe in the period meant not "following" it through an act of one-way transmission, but rather "practicing" it through active interaction with the recipe ("Woolley's Mouse" 115); such interaction is clearly a social act. Even a woman's writing of her name, such as "Lettice Pudsey, her Booke / of recipts, These following / are written with my owne hand" ([7v]), might not represent a definite claim of ownership, but rather a kind of record-keeping, a documenting of to whom the receipt book currently (and only temporarily) belongs. Such interpretation is supported by the fact that Pudsey's note appears partway through the manuscript; the book must have belonged to someone else before her, and Pudsey would have known this. Similarly, the variation in Ann(e)'s spelling of her name on the inside front cover of the Granville manuscript is already a clue that receipt books reflect a conception of the self that is very different from our own. All personal information in receipt books, such as signatures and important family dates, seems to have been simply listed without much attachment or internalization. The purpose of receipt books was clearly one of preserving and record-keeping.

A record-keeping purpose is also evident in writing forms of the seventeenth century that one would assume to be more personal. In his research on autobiography, Adam Smyth notes that Lady Anne Clifford's diary is more like a kind of daily accounting, to the point that at times it is structured as two columns, and he demonstrates how a "narrative/non-narrative dichotomy" is of limited relevance when comparing her chronicles and her financial accounts (see 85–90). Sharon Cadman Seelig observes the same quality in Lady Margaret Hoby's diary, noting that "the diary is detailed precisely where we might expect it to be minimal, and minimal precisely where we might expect it to be detailed" (218); she then acknowledges, "But if these entries seem insufficient to us, Margaret Hoby probably did not think she was omitting anything essential: the general lack of detail exemplifies the differences between her expectations and ours" (219). This is not to say that premodern people were devoid of self-reflection, but that, as Smyth suggests, their identity was often created by "looking out into the world, rather than within" (11). (Even the sketches and decorative flourishes in some receipt books, such as the book attributed to Constance Hall, while creative, in the same way needlework and pastry-making might be creative, are not necessarily expressions of inwardness.) Smyth also traces an oral public history and use of communal voice similar to what I see in receipt books in other forms of writing from the period as well – namely the printed almanac, annotated with handwritten notes; the financial account; the commonplace book; and the parish register. He notes that these forms, while not personal, still offer a kind of life record (13–14). Receipt books further highlight the distinction between our modern conception of life writing and that of the past; their folk-culture origins, oral conventions, and practical use all reflect their creation and functioning as social, not individual, texts. Receipt books preserve a collective, not individual, identity and authority.

Looking Back, Looking Forward: Scholarship on Receipt Books and a New Consideration of Cookbooks

Reading receipt books within their historical and cultural context illuminates seventeenth-century Englishwomen's experience and the way these texts, as social documents, worked to preserve that experience. While many scholars of receipt books have performed invaluable research that recognizes and supports the genre's social function, it is striking how, almost without exception, these same scholars still then automatically read these works as examples of individual authorship and women's emerging modern subjectivity. At the end of his insightful article "Using Language to Investigate Ellen Chantrill's Recipe Book," for example, Malcolm Thick notes, "A crucial task remains, to link my document with a specific Ellen Chantrill" (357). Why is this task crucial? Why is it necessary to attach the works to a specific individual? Why can we not fully accept receipt books as social texts, rather than texts belonging to and expressing the individual? Scholarship on receipt books perfectly proves Michel Foucault's point that so pervasive is modern Western culture's dependence upon the idea of the individual, subjective author as a means of achieving a certain unity in discourse that "literary anonymity is not tolerable" (285).

Considering receipt books backward from our own perspective rather than forward from their origin in folk culture inevitably leads to contradictions in their interpretation – and, I would argue, to continued misunderstanding of the genre. As is evident in the title of "'Many Hands Hands': Writing the Self in Early Modern Women's Recipe Books," for example, Catherine Field, while noting that the receipt book is "a communal and social project" (55), also considers the works as an "expression of the early modern self ... a site and strategy of female self-writing" (50), and she asks, "Nevertheless, the larger questions of authorship remain ... How to determine the author's sense of 'self' when the authorship/ownership of the book was multiple and multiplying?" (56). One problem in focusing on individual authorship when considering receipt books is apparent in the article's first sentence, which states, "Recent historians and critics have argued that during the Renaissance, the concept of 'self' was a distinctively negative one" (49). If this is true, then why would women aim for self-expression? While Field sees receipt books as a means by which women broke away from the negative conception of the individual, the issue here might be one of assumed values. She is right to suggest that the "self" was not desired in the Renaissance; however, this, for contemporaries, did not seem to be a problem. Lack of selfhood did not represent repression, as we might assume in the twenty-first-century Western world, but was necessary for preservation of the collective good and social harmony, which, as emphasized above, were important values rooted in folk culture.

Furthermore, reading receipt books as personal texts reflecting the individual leads to a host of other problems. A focus on negative conceptions of the "self," for example (a focus influenced by Gail Kern Paster's *The Body Embarrassed*), leads Field to view women of the period as submissive and self-effacing, so that "thinking and writing about the self ... often involved wrestling with the unruly, passionate self" (49). However, these qualities are not reflected in receipt books, which are practical, confident, and authoritative. Similarly, negative readings of the self lead to a perception of the premodern body as "vulnerable" (49), "leaky" (59), and in need of self-discipline (49), and to an interpretation of remedies focusing on the female body as expressions of shame, when the very opposite seems true. The sheer number of receipt book remedies and tips relating to child delivery, miscarriages, sore nipples, hemorrhaging, and anemia is seeming evidence of openly acknowledged women's health issues, as well as widely shared knowledge on how to deal with them. Furthermore, the random interspersion of these remedies between culinary recipes – such as the aforementioned occurrence of a remedy "Too expell a dead chield" on the page facing "To make a Sirrip of Turnips" in Lady Castleton's receipt book – suggests practicality and frankness about women's bodies. Such an attitude also seems supported by the literature of the period, which reflects a matter-of-fact view or even a joyful celebration of the body's shortcomings. The main theme of Rabelais's *Gargantua and Pantagruel* is the timeless, universal, regenerative ability of the body, so that its grotesque nature is exalted as life-giving – including in the birth of Gargantua out of Gargamelle's ear shortly after she ate too much tripe. Don Quixote and Sancho Panza, meanwhile, are associated with bodily excess at different ends of the spectrum, as Don Quixote never eats, while Sancho Panza (whose last name means *paunch*) continuously thinks of food, so that Don Quixote tells Sancho, in a kind of Rabelasian way, "I was born to live dying, and thou to die eating" (982); furthermore, the reader is led to laugh at and love both characters because, together, they create harmony: Don Quixote and Sancho prepare a lunch "which they ate together like good friends, laying aside all vain distinction of master and man" (141). In Shakespeare's *Merry Wives of Windsor*, Falstaff, who is continuously associated with eating, drinking, and carnal pleasure, is the object of good-humoured jokes inflicted upon him by the women he woos rather than serious scorn; similarly, Mistress Quickly notes she and Mistress Anne talked for an hour about Fenton's wart (1.4.140). Mistress Quickly also refers to her own youth as the "holiday time" of her beauty, indicating light-heartedness and acceptance of the aging of her body (2.1.2). As outlined earlier in this introduction, food was associated with utopia and harmony, rather than carrying negative connotations, and the food insecurity throughout the medieval and Renaissance periods that accentuated this meaning suggests that "self-control over appetite was scarcely a pressing problem for the vast majority of Europeans" (Mennell 27) – except perhaps during carnival, and this was a joyful time.[16] And indeed, far from being vulnerable, leaky, ashamed, and in need of discipline, women's bodies seem to be regarded in receipt books with openness and as ideally in equilibrium both internally and externally with the world around them. This is why

---

16 One might say that one of the markers between the Renaissance and early modernity was a shift away from carnivalesque joy toward disgust at the human body; this is a change Shakespeare recognized, as is evident in the very different treatments of the body in *The Merry Wives of Windsor* and *Hamlet*. The former – the traditional world to which receipt books belonged – represented joy, and the latter a new angst.

Field eventually notes, towards the end of her article, that receipt books in fact reflect wholeness and unity. Receipt books belong to a culture that precedes women's anxious sense of self and feeling of oppression; these attitudes are modern ones.

Regarding receipt books as personal texts reflecting the individual also leads to problematic interpretations of women's role in the history of science and medicine. While Field and others regard women's recipe writing as an example of subjectivity that emulated the emerging scientific method (Field 56), it might be more plausible – considering that women had been cooking and curing for millennia already, and were already, as Field emphasizes, authorities in these areas – that science was in fact influenced by women's long-established work in the kitchen. Likewise, the social construction of receipt books seems to run against the scientific method's emphasis on the individual observer. Regarding this history backwards – suggesting science primarily influenced women in the kitchen, rather than the other way around – fails to adequately recognize women's history and contribution to medicine. For example, while Elizabeth Tebeaux notes that printed recipes were "written in a style that still reflected oral-based language patterns" (37), she suggests that this is proof of women as simply *readers*, rather than writers: "The extensive number of books containing food and medicinal recipes suggests that women could read material that was probably familiar to them from oral transmission" (37); she makes no mention of women's receipt books. Similarly, she notes that Eucharius Roesslin's midwifery book, *The Birth of Mankinde*, also known as the *Womans Booke*, shifted from Latin to the vernacular because, "as a technical writer, he realized the importance of writing to his readers' knowledge level" (41). This patriarchal interpretation not only ignores women's long-established authority in midwifery, it also ignores how women – who were largely excluded from schools – became literate in the first place. Finally, focusing on a linear evolution of medicine also leads to misinterpretation of receipt books themselves. In noting that they counted twenty-three recipes for oil of swallows in seventeenth-century texts, and that none were exactly the same, Michelle DiMeo and Rebecca Laroche – who rightly note the need to overcome our own assumptions in reading receipt books (89) – then state that the differences between just two of these versions "demonstrate how the recipe evolved over more than a century" (91) and reveal the new scientific practices with which "elite women were experimenting" (92). Yet one of the qualities they note in the later recipe – inclusion of more herbal ingredients – runs against the time-saving development in recipes that David Goldstein notes in his essay in the very same volume (see "Woolley's Mouse"). Just because a recipe occurs in a more recently dated manuscript, or later in a manuscript that spans years or generations, does not mean the recipe itself is not old. And while the incorporation of new ingredients and methods (such as distillation) is certainly evident in receipt books, the important issue is not any evolutionary development of a particular recipe, but rather the adaptability of the housewife in her culinary and medical knowledge, and the endless variation that is intrinsic to the recipe form.[17]

The reflex to read cookbooks according to modern assumptions of subjectivity and individual authorship is pervasive. While Anne Bower, in "Cooking Up Stories: Narrative Elements in Community Cookbooks," recognizes the collective authorship and relationships focus of community cookbooks, she says that in this way they are "lacking" (31) as they never fully reveal any individual woman's story. Then, even though she has described the books as "a genre governed by distinct codes and conventions" (29), she reads the recipes as narratives – listing setting, characters, plot, and themes such as "the breaking of women's silence" (46–7) as literary elements she sees in the form – in an effort, she notes, "to bring new appreciation to these undervalued texts" (49). Thus, despite Bowers's recognition of the importance of *community* cookbooks, her approach perpetuates a patriarchal reading and privileging of the individual author. In *Aguecheek's Beef*, Robert Appelbaum aims to legitimize the early modern (printed) cookbook in a similar way, describing "what the cookbook looks like when it is viewed as literature" (109). Qualities he emphasizes include "persuasive and scientific language," "an engagement with artfulness," and "textual practice that increasingly became a part of the intellectual life of the era and as a sign of that increasingly engaged with the architectonics of the menu and the rhetorical negotiations of prefatory matter" (109); while Appelbaum is right in suggesting that cookbooks

---

17 One might also question current scholarship's understanding of the role of the self in early modern medicine in a deeper way than there is room for in this edition. Schoenfeldt's suggestion in *Bodies and Selves in Early Modern England* that humanist self-moderation empowered the individual subject seems problematic. How does self-moderation differ from Galenic balancing of one's own humours with herbs? Or, for that matter, an individual in a hunter-gatherer society self-administering a curative? Or an animal licking a wound? Each case describes a basic, biological self-awareness and response.

deserve greater appreciation, it is only through a purely literary lens that he sees this as possible. It seems most literary scholars are inclined to read cookbooks as we read purely literary texts because that is what we know how to do, and because purely literary texts are what we have been taught to value. However, emphasizing the opportunity for individual self-expression that receipt books offered women forces anachronistic modern values onto these manuscripts, and this leads to a not insignificant misunderstanding of the texts. When we look for only what we already know, we are blinded from seeing what is actually there. This narrow view is also perpetuated in popular misunderstanding of the recipe form and its history: as a recent *New York Times* food article notes, "[t]he recipe is being stretched and shattered" by digital recipe-sharing sites. "There was a time when a cake recipe was learned at a grandmother's elbow, codified on a worn recipe card or in a book with stained pages. It was a straightforward march: ingredients, instructions and maybe a tip or two scribbled in the margin" (Severson, par. 2 and 5). The first written English recipes, as is clear in the transcribed manuscripts that follow in this edition, did not follow this two-part form, and their use and sharing – partly as evidenced by those tips scribbled in the margins – shows that they were anything *but* a straightforward march. In the current obsession with cooking, food trends, and celebrity chefs, the fascinating folk history of recipes and the alternative story of women's work, knowledge, and writing they represent are overlooked.

Margaret Ezell has come the closest to reading seventeenth-century Englishwomen's receipt books in a way that fully recognizes the particular historical and cultural context of their creation and the specialness of their form. In *Social Authorship and the Advent of Print* (1999), she rightly identifies scholarship's gaps in understanding women's domestic manuscripts, noting that modern, normalized concepts of "writer" and "reader" simply do not work for the genre (40), and she challenges Harold Love's focus on scribal publication of manuscripts (which, she notes, largely follow print conventions) and his assumption of women's "pride" in creating purely literary texts rather than domestic ones (23). Then in her article "Domestic Papers: Manuscript Culture and Early Modern Women's Life Writing," she acknowledges a number of peculiarities unique to the genre. It is productive when considering any manuscript, she notes, to shift emphasis away from literary concerns such as the writer's emotions or the events described, and instead "investigate the situation of the creation of the text, then the formatting or physical presentation of its narrative, and finally how this information might affect its being read" (33–4). "Messy volumes" such as recipe manuscripts, she says, were "used by women for a much more complicated form of life record than their classification suggests … [These manuscripts] may indeed … stretch the assumed conventions of life writing" (41–2). She then notes how these volumes manipulate space, so that the entries act "like pieces in a kaleidoscope, the nature of the pattern changing as the container is inverted and reversed … This messy volume, in its very appropriation and distortion of the conventions of the printed page, offers us a complex example of 'domestic writing'" (43). Even Ezell, however, seems to slightly miss the full insight her observations actually convey; at the beginning of her article she still calls these manuscripts "single-author narratives of personal experiences" (33) despite the fact that she later refers to the works' multiple authors and notes that they are open-ended rather than linear. Then at the end she remarks that "the author *or authors*" (italics are mine) frequently laid "aggressive claim" to authorship (45) – when surely the multiple authors of a given work could not lay aggressive claim to authorship in the way a single author might. Thus, while it is true that our view of the past will always to some extent be influenced by the present, we must at least carefully *aim* to view the past as widely as possible, making use of numerous, diverse sources, to avoid imposing the present on historical texts – what Ezell has called elsewhere "the totalizing effect of the bland imposition of the present" over the past (*Writing* 12).

Recipes are, indeed, an embedded discourse. This means that collections of them – as in seventeenth-century Englishwomen's receipt books – are best considered as fully as possible within their historical and cultural context, through an approach that is as multidisciplinary as possible, as well as one that honestly acknowledges the texts' place in the kitchen. Receipt books should be the last writings we might consider as the products of modern subjectivity and individual authorship, and admitting this does not deny a woman's experience; instead, it recognizes the works as rich, multilayered, open-ended texts that serve as a material trace of the lives of many women in a cultural context very different from our own – their physical work, their expert knowledge of plants, animals, health, and medicine, their collective sharing of this knowledge, their concerns with recording the past, their particular engagement with the written word and acquisition of literacy, their family and social circles, their way of seeing themselves, and their way of ordering the world. The reason why Virginia Woolf and others searched in vain for a record of women's lives and writing is that they looked in the wrong places; it is true that Judith Shakespeare did not become a playwright because her world did not cultivate, or even largely conceive of, such a possibility. But she likely did become, as Woolf suggests, a "wise woman selling herbs" (49) – and was most certainly a housewife, using the herbs herself and sharing written recipes with other women. Without receipt books, the record of seventeenth-century Englishwomen's lives might have been largely lost.

So, too, might we have missed the opportunity to witness writing capable of redrawing the boundaries of literature itself. Had Foucault considered the receipt book genre, he might have seen that a perfect equivalent of the "postauthor utopia" he imagined taking place in the future, and which other scholars and food writers (such as that of the *New York Times* article above) have seen as a quality of digital culture, already existed in the past; we simply failed to recognize it, partly because of a prejudice against the value of domestic writing that led to long dismissal of the recipe and pervasive misunderstanding of its historical form. For the same questions he suggested we would ask, instead of old questions of authority and ownership, are precisely the questions receipt books pose:

> what are the modes of existence of this discourse? Where has it been used, how can it circulate, and who can appropriate it for himself? What are the places in it where there is room for possible subjects? Who can assume these various subject functions? And behind all these questions, we would hear hardly anything but the stirring of an indifference: What difference does it make who is speaking? (Foucault 291)

Not simply collections of formulae that modern cooks/readers might follow today, receipt books were carriers of an entire world view that was very different from our own; they preserve different meaning. Rather than forcing our own assumptions on receipt books in order to validate them, we gain much more insight by recognizing that the genre reflected, as Foucault would call it, an alternative mode of existence, with its own mode of circulation, valorization, attribution, and appropriation (290). This is precisely what makes receipt books an intriguing, special form and why they "repay close reading" (Leong and Pennell 149). One might argue they are the ultimate feminist texts.

Reading Receipt Books in the Kitchen

Considering that much of their meaning derives from their practical use, receipt books should indeed, as Elizabeth Spiller suggests, be read in the kitchen. Working through a recipe enables a deeper understanding of these texts, partly through simple clarification of the recipe, and partly through more acute awareness of the physical work required and the skills possessed by the seventeenth-century housewife. I know this first-hand as I have made recipes from each of the receipt books in this edition: "To make Bread A la Roine" (Granville 10); "Frittars of Eggs and herbes" (Hall [2v]); "A receit how to dress trout" (Pudsey [41r]) and "To make A orring pudding" (Pudsey [48v]); I threw a small seventeenth-century dinner party, then wrote about my experience for a local food magazine. As I wrote in that article, while the vague instructions made me doubt that the recipes would turn out, they did. The bread recipe specifies no quantities or baking time, and the oven temperature depends upon the "Judgement of the Baker." So I used my best judgment, and the dough rose beautifully and the bread was at least as good as the sourdough recipe I have been making for years. Likewise, when I had read through the trout recipe in advance, I was not sure what the contributor meant by "let your Liquor / boyl vp to the height before you put in your fish," but in the actual cooking, the broth bubbled up to the top of the pot and I knew it was time to add the trout, which cooked perfectly. And even though I was somewhat hesitant about the seasoning of eggs with sugar, cloves, and nutmeg, the result did appeal to my guests' and my tastes. Similarly, it was not until the actual enactment of the recipe that I realized the orange pudding was a custard (and a very good one). Perhaps most important, however, was that in making each recipe, I had to improvise – I could not find pennyroyal, marjoram, or winter savory in my local produce store in the middle of a Canadian winter, so I left those out or substituted other herbs. Similarly, it seemed wasteful to throw out the egg whites left over from the pudding, so I put those into the fritter. But I know the cooks who wrote these recipes also depended on seasonality, local availability, and variable harvest, and they improvised and were economical, so in some sense it was my *altering* of the recipes that made them true to the spirit of the seventeenth-century housewife's experience. When I shared the recipes in the article, I included my own notes under the original text, noting, for example, that a navel orange works just fine for the pudding if a Seville orange is not available; I thus became an active participant in a kitchen conversation begun at least four hundred years earlier – and which, I have just realized, I continue above in writing that the orange custard was "a very good one." The fact that my mom helped me with some of the cooking – she is the one who expertly flipped the "frittar" (which was, we learned, not a fritter but a frittata) – made it that much more authentic.

The historical and cultural information embedded in these recipes means that it is impossible to directly adapt them for a modern reader. So many layers of translation would be needed that it would render the exercise pointless: one would simply not be left with a seventeenth-century recipe. It is not enough to modernize "turmentill" to "tormentil" to make a "plague water" recipe easily accessible to a modern reader. Almost everything about this recipe, including its placement in the Granville manuscript between a recipe for hartshorn jelly and a recipe for ink, feels strange. As Spiller notes, seventeenth-century recipes "are sometimes hard to read in part because they point to a physical and sensory reality that extends beyond the page" ("Printed" 526) – and understanding the recipe means at least recognizing the difference between this reality and our own.[18] If one wishes to glimpse the seventeenth century through a kitchen window, then one must read receipt books not as modernized cookbooks but as historical, cultural texts, and it is precisely the things a modern reader/cook finds peculiar that are valuable in illuminating the difference in world view. Besides reading these texts in as authentic a form as possible, the active process of actually working through the recipes elucidates the inevitable gaps that still exist between the seventeenth-century experience and our own. Close reproduction of these recipes depends on their cooking on a hearth, and indeed the smell of the hearth, and the sounds of the farmyard and the market. It is not enough to simply acquire pennyroyal or marjoram, but also to know when they are in season, and perhaps where they grow in the wild, and to go to the work of picking them, and to know what virtues they contain (and what "virtues" really means), as well as to know how to adapt the recipe when they are not available. Such an activity makes clear how one could use each recipe (or indeed a single ingredient or technique) as a starting point for an extensive analysis of the recipe's embedded meanings and cultural associations;[19] this is, as Ezell notes above, the kaleidoscope nature of receipt books. Clearly, our understanding can only be imperfect. The best we can do is fill in the gaps as fully as we can, keeping in mind the historical and cultural context out of which the recipes arose as we work our way through the

---

18 If one is looking for a modern cookbook inspired by historic recipes, these already exist; one good one is Francine Segan's *Shakespeare's Kitchen: Renaissance Recipes for the Contemporary Cook*.

19 As noted above, Spiller does just this in her article "Printed Recipe Books in Medical, Political, and Scientific Contexts." This is also a common focus of *The Recipes Project*, a collaborative online resource about historical recipes.

language, and the preparation, of the recipe. Already, I admit, something is lost in the transcription and printing of receipt books; a major part of their meaning is tied to the sense of intimacy a modern reader feels with the people who contributed these recipes in their own handwriting nearly four hundred years ago. However, as not everyone can access the vaults of the Folger Shakespeare Library, or even the scans on *Perdita*, no perfect solution to this problem exists, and at least these transcriptions and select scans provide some access to the artefacts, in the way that looking at a photo of a painting provides some access to that painting.

The sharing of recipes is, of course, a practice that continues today, and in some ways both handwritten recipe notebooks and online recipe-sharing sites carry on the tradition of the receipt book (and hence of the orally transmitted recipe before that). The persistence of recipe sharing and its adaptability to new forms of media reflects the important intertwining in human history of food and language. The recipe connects these two most elemental physical and social needs. It is deeply powerful because it communicates an understanding of the transformation of nature that enables the regeneration from death to life (and here we must forgive Bakhtin's use of gendered language):

> In the act of eating, the body transgresses ... its own limits: it swallows, devours, rends the world apart, is enriched and grows at the world's expense. The encounter of man with the world, which takes place inside the open, biting, rending, chewing mouth, is one of the most ancient, and most important objects of human thought and imagery. Here man tastes the world, introduces it into his body, makes it part of himself. Man's awakening consciousness could not but concentrate on this moment, could not help borrowing from it a number of substantial images determining its interrelation with the world ... (Bakhtin 281)

The sharing of food was so intricately tied to conceptions of utopia in the late medieval and Renaissance periods because folk culture recognized eating as an overcoming of mortality – not just symbolically in the feast, but also physiologically in a "concrete, tangible, bodily" way (Bakhtin 283) because the miracle of regeneration extends deeper than culture; it is, Bakhtin might say, nature's essential truth. It is thus entirely true that "well-worn recipe books occupy a space between the sacred and profane. They contain learning that is critical and life-sustaining. In recipe texts, women accumulated valuable, often arcane knowledge about the mysteries of birth and death" (Theophano 89).[20] The recipe is the means by which we share our most basic human experience. The recipe reflects life: it continues from one generation to the next and yet contains endless variations, it carries memory yet depends upon adaptability, and it is motivated by survival yet is inherently temporary and irreproducible; it is the least fixed of all forms, and perhaps the most resilient.

---

20 One might see a particular example of the importance of recipe books in the resistance, through recipes, by women in the Terezin concentration camp. See *In Memory's Kitchen: A Legacy from the Women of Terezin*, edited by Cara de Silva.

Note on the Text

This edition offers a semi-diplomatic transcription. My first aim has been to preserve the richness of the original texts, including their peculiarities, to allow the texts to speak most fully and honestly of their time and origins. However, emendations have been made where necessary for accessible and unhindered reading of the text. My textual approach generally follows conventions used in manuscript courses at the Folger Shakespeare Library.

Original spelling (such as u/v, i/j, and double f) has been retained in this edition, although thorn has been replaced by "*th*" and long s by "s." Original capitalization and punctuation are also retained; however, borders, underlines, line fillers, and flourishes/decorative marks have been omitted, and a single end-punctuation mark is retained when the manuscript contains multiple or repeating end-punctuation marks (regardless of the form, as there is a continuum of end-punctuation and end-decorative marks). Connected words (such as "Ared cabbage"), split words (such as "a nother"), and repeated words have been retained to my best judgment. In a few instances where the reader might struggle with meaning, omitted letters are supplied in square brackets (as in "w[a]y" or "tops of min[t]es"), as are, rarely, omitted words (such as "for [lack] of it") and clarification of unclear words (such as "an earthen pot well nealed [sealed]").

Superscript letters are silently lowered. Abbreviations are expanded, with supplied letters in italics; there are a few exceptions to this rule: "Mr" and "Mrs" are not expanded, abbreviations using apostrophes (e.g., slic'd) are not expanded, numbers and some units of measurement are not expanded, the abbreviation "viz"/"vizt" (meaning *videlicet*, or "namely," and used to introduce a more precise explanation of what has come before) is not expanded, and brevigraphs such as "&" and "&c" (meaning "and so forth") are not expanded. Tildes are expanded when they represent an abbreviation, with the supplied letters in italics; if they do not represent an abbreviation, they are considered otiose and are omitted. All diacritics are retained in the Spanish, as they affect pronunciation.

Interlinear insertions appear between carets. Words corrected in the manuscript by imposing one character over another are represented by inserting the new character between two carets next to the character it is replacing, and cancelling the replaced character. For example, when "if" is altered to "it" by transposing the "f" into a "t," this alteration is represented as "if∧t∧." Words blotted out or crossed out in the manuscript are struck through. Where an entire section is crossed out, the section is struck through uniformly and a footnote describes the larger marking. Inkblots and intentional scribbling-over and rubbing-out of words have rendered some words indecipherable. I have indicated these areas thus: <....>, with one period representing one letter to the best of my perception. Footnotes are used to explain textual ambiguities.

It was not possible to reflect page-for-page original layout in this edition. However, lineation of the original manuscripts is maintained; in the places where this was not possible due to line length, the carry-over words are right-justified on the next line. Page numbers and foliation following each manuscript's particular system are indicated in the margins, with added numbers in square brackets; these have been placed in the left margins only for consistency. Titles have been bolded for design clarity. Catchwords and their punctuation have been maintained. Marginal annotations and manicules are placed in the outer margins, closest to the line in the manuscript next to which they appear.

Modern English translations of Mary Granville's Spanish recipes are placed at the end of the section transcribing her work; these translations are my own, with the assistance of Ann de León at the University of Alberta.

Changes in hand are indicated in the footnotes.

THREE SEVENTEENTH-CENTURY
RECEIPT BOOKS

MS V.a.430:
Receipt Book
attributed to Mary Granville and
Anne Granville D'Ewes

Textual Introduction

This receipt book is attributed by the Folger Shakespeare Library's catalogue to both Mary Granville and her daughter, Anne Granville D'Ewes,
and is dated c. 1640–1750. It was acquired by the Folger from bookseller
W.A. Meyers in October 1965; no further details on the book's history
are outlined. The manuscript is 21 cm tall by 16.5 cm wide. The vellum
cover has two metal catches, but the clasps are gone. The watermark
is a foolscap with a seven-pointed collar; the *Gravell Watermark Archive*
lists a similar watermark as FCP.012.1 and notes that it was in use in
1625.

The inscription "Mrs Ann Granvills Book / which I hope shee will
make / a better use of then her mother / Mary Granville" then, in
another hand, "Now Anne Dewes / Bradley 8 September. 1740" is written on the inside front cover. The outside back cover has "MW" and
"MC" written on it. Many pages are missing, and some pages have
stains or holes in them, although, as with most receipt books, the manuscript is quite clean. This manuscript begins with remedies rather than
recipes, which is somewhat rare (although not unique) amongst receipt
books. Then, starting at page 7 with "To boile a hanch of Venison," the
manuscript then contains intermingled recipes and remedies, and there
is a gradual shift toward a greater proportion of recipes.

The Folger includes some historical information about Mary Granville
in its catalogue description of the work:

> This book was given to Anne D'Ewes at the time of her marriage to John
> D'Ewes in 1740 by her mother Mary Granville, who was herself the daugh-
> ter of Sir Martin Westcomb. Both Sir Martin and the Sir Martin before
> him, (his father?), were for years the English consuls in Cadiz and this

book contains a group of recipes from these years, many dated at Cadiz, 1665–1687. There are also some household recipes, including several from different countries for making ink. Sources are sometimes given.

The D'Ewes family, the entry further notes, lived in Bradley, Worcestershire; this is also indicated in the inscription on the inside front cover. As Mary would have been a child (or not yet born) during the writing of the Spanish recipes, the manuscript was perhaps begun by her mother or an aunt, and not Mary herself. Thus, the recipe "To make double Incke kalled In ffrench ancre Luisante / this is the way and receat My brother Mr / John wescombe gave mee in January 1671" is likely a reference to Mary Granville's uncle. A John Wescombe was consul of Bayonne from approximately 1662 to 1688, and he was the brother of Martin Westcomb; the phrase "My brother Mr John wescombe" must therefore be the words of Sir Martin Westcomb's wife or sister, the mother or aunt of Mary Granville. Such a history explains why Mary Granville of the manuscript's inscription regrets not having made better use of the receipt book: she did not begin it, but received it by gift or inheritance from her mother or aunt. However, as the Spanish recipes appear in a different hand from those that begin the work (and we might assume that these recipes were indeed written by the mother or aunt), perhaps Mary Granville's mother or aunt *also* received the manuscript by gift or inheritance. If this is true, then Mary Granville is the third-generation owner of the manuscript, and Anne D'Ewes the fourth. Thus, while Mary Granville and Anne D'Ewes are chiefly associated with the manuscript by the library's cataloguing system and consequently by scholars, it is quite clear that the work was begun generations earlier.

Further information on the family is available through the *Oxford Dictionary of National Biography*: Mary Granville and her husband, Bernard, a Royalist colonel, lived in Wiltshire in southwest England; Bernard's brother George was Lord Lansdowne, whose wife's recipe for French bread is included in the manuscript. The *National Archives* has in its holdings "a letter of condolence" from Lord Lansdowne to William Wyndham, and "Lady Katharine Windham's" powder recipe is also included in the manuscript. Besides Anne, Mary and Bernard had another daughter, also named Mary, and a son, also named Bernard. Daughter Mary was active in court circles and was known for her paper collages of flowers. Son Bernard was a supporter of music and personal friend of George Frideric Handel, who willed Bernard a Rembrandt painting, possibly returning a valuable gift that Bernard had previously given him (McLean 598). Correspondence between the sisters Mary and Anne was published by Anne's granddaughter Lady Llanover, herself a Welsh baroness and author of a published cookbook, *The First Principles of Good Cookery* (1867).

Despite the Granville family's social standing, the recipes and remedies in this book mostly call for humble ingredients. Hog's soil, cow dung, and hen dung (often used medically) are the most obvious, but numerous references to penny loaves and widespread native English plants such as ivy, yarrow, and bindweed are other examples. That said, some recipes and remedies in this manuscript do call for exotic and expensive ingredients. Gold, for example, which does not appear in the receipt books attributed to either Constance Hall or Lettice Pudsey, appears in a number of remedies in this manuscript (sometimes in the same remedies as hog's soil). Likewise, some recipes call for large quantities of certain difficult-to-obtain ingredients; "To make Cynamon Water," for example, calls for a pound of borage flowers and a quarter of a pound of rosemary flowers – a quantity of blossoms that would have required hours of work by a servant or else money for purchase. A similar mixture of basic and specialized tools and techniques is reflected in this receipt book: while some recipes suggest sinking spices for mead in a canvas bag with "pebblestones," swinging wet herbs in a cloth to dry them, or using a feather to ice macaroons, others call for stills.

It is not entirely clear who actually made the recipes and remedies in this manuscript. The inscription at the beginning of the book suggests that Mary Granville was not a serious cook, although that does not mean that the woman who began the book, or Anne, or others, were not. Considering the Granville family's social and economic standing, they would have employed cooks and other servants, and remedies such as "The white oyntment for any Itch" (2), which calls for two or three hours' grinding and pounding of the ingredients with a mortar and pestle, suggests that at least some recipes and remedies were perhaps carried out by a servant. The recipes assume skill on the part of the cook or practitioner: "A Medicine for the Greensicknes" calls for the concoction to be stirred "with an easy hand" (8), and "To make Bread A la Roine" depends upon the cook's knowledge and expertise in calling for "good Flower of good wheat, ground in a good mill," and then in noting "the oven must not bee heated too much nor too / little but according to the Judgement of the Baker" (10). And clearly the contributor of Hand A considered herself an expert; as she writes at the end of "To make a water for a Squinancy," "This is the best medicine for a sore Throat that ever I met with" (11). There is likewise a sense of repeated practice and familiarity implied by these recipes; "A Receipt to make Meath," for example, notes that "if the hearbes bee dry it will doe as well as if they were green" (13) – suggesting, of course, that the contributor has tried the recipe both ways. It is in this same recipe that she comments on her own varied results, suggesting that "long running" made her own mead strong, and that if it were made at Michaelmas "it will / not bee ready to drinke till lent but the smaller you make it the / sooner it will bee ready for drinke" (13). In other cases, comments were added by a later contributor; the heading for one recipe "To make Meath" is followed by the words, in another hand, "*the* best Way" (17). A letter "x" before, after, or next to some recipes might indicate that they were tried and deemed not good (see this before "A Recept for hams of Bacon" [208], for example). The Spanish recipes reflect new ingredients and, perhaps in the case of the recipe to get rid of bedbugs, new needs. A number of recipes are repeated, often with variations, such as those for French bread and ointment for the rickets, or identically, such as "To make Lemon Wine" ([191] and [195]). The recipe "To make clouted cream" (206) is repeated (210), but without the speculative comment that it might be good with apple pastry. Throughout the manuscript, the comments and corrections and tweaking of the recipes reveal their intimate engagement with the text – both with the recipes, and with the language itself. The latter is evident through corrections to spelling and to capitalization, as when the contributor (presumably Mrs Gloster) of "To make Raison Wine for Elder Mrs Pain of Glosters Way" (143) cannot decide which case to use and suggests that the practitioner "put a Tile Stone on the Bung or the / bung."

This receipt book shares a number of recipes and remedies with printed texts, although in some cases there are important variations. For example, while "To make the greene Ointment" is similar to the green ointment recipes common in printed texts in its use of an array of herbs, the note that it should be made in the month of May, and its service as somewhat of a cure-all, this version is rare in calling for snails rather than deer or sheep suet or hog's grease. Other recipes offer slight variations to those in the Countess of Kent's *A Choice Manual*. "To make Oyle of Saint Johns worte" is much like the Countess of Kent's "Oyl of Saint John's Wort," for example, although while the recipe in this manuscript specifies that the glass filled with the oil and herbs be buried in warm horse dung, the Countess of Kent's simply states that the glass should be kept in the sun or water. Other recipes and remedies are similar to those in Philiatros's *Natura Exenterata* of 1655 and in W.M.'s *The Queen's Closet Opened* of 1659.

A number of hands are evident in this receipt book (approximately twenty-three); these are listed in the footnotes. Many recipes include attributions. Some are famous or at least known in other works, such as Doctor Chambers, whose medicinal water appears in Hannah Woolley's *The Queen-Like Closet* (1670); Doctor Burges, whose recipe here is almost directly copied from Philiatros's *Natura Exenterata*, although the qualification at the end is the writer's own; Doctor Butler, whose "Receipt against a consumption" is similar to W.M.'s "China broth for a Consumption"; and Doctor Buggs, who is referenced in George Thomson's *Loimotomia, or, The Pest Anatomized* (1666) but whose "sirrup of Violett" does not seem to appear in other printed recipe books. John Westcomb, the source of an ink recipe, is, the contributor states, her brother. And "Lady Katharine Windham," whose recipe for "Powder for Convulsion fitts" appears in the manuscript, is likely Catherine Wyndham (d. 1731), wife of Sir William Wyndham, baronet and politician.

The other attributions are likely neighbours or simply acquaintances of the various contributors: Mr John Rutters (whose name serves as the title of the recipe), Goodwife Lawrence, Mrs Patts, Thomas Blothers, Mrs Margaret Melborn, Mrs Lake, Mrs An Melcombe (who procured Mrs Lake's recipe), Mr Leonard Wilkes, Colonel John Belasyse (who had Mr Wilkes's recipe with him), Captain William Webbers, Mrs Rebecca Ash (who might be the same as Mrs Rebeca Ashan), Juan Baqueriso, Mr William Fens, Doña María Leal, Mr Henry Sheers (who gave his recipe to Marshall Howard), Captain Francisco del Poço (who gave his recipe to the consul, Martín Bisconde, otherwise known as Martin Westcomb), Captain Felpes of Bristol (who gave his recipe to Mr John Emilli), Señor Lucs de Molina, Mrs Tauerner, Mrs Pain of Gloster, Mrs Mary Hills, Mrs Looks, Mrs Carryl, Doctor Lower, Mrs Badge, Mrs Landsdown, Mrs Capel, Mrs Salvage, Mrs Berker, Mr Hugh, Mr Bamber, and Mrs Rogers.

This manuscript has been exhibited at the Folger Shakespeare Library on numerous occasions (1998, 1999, 2005, 2009, 2011).

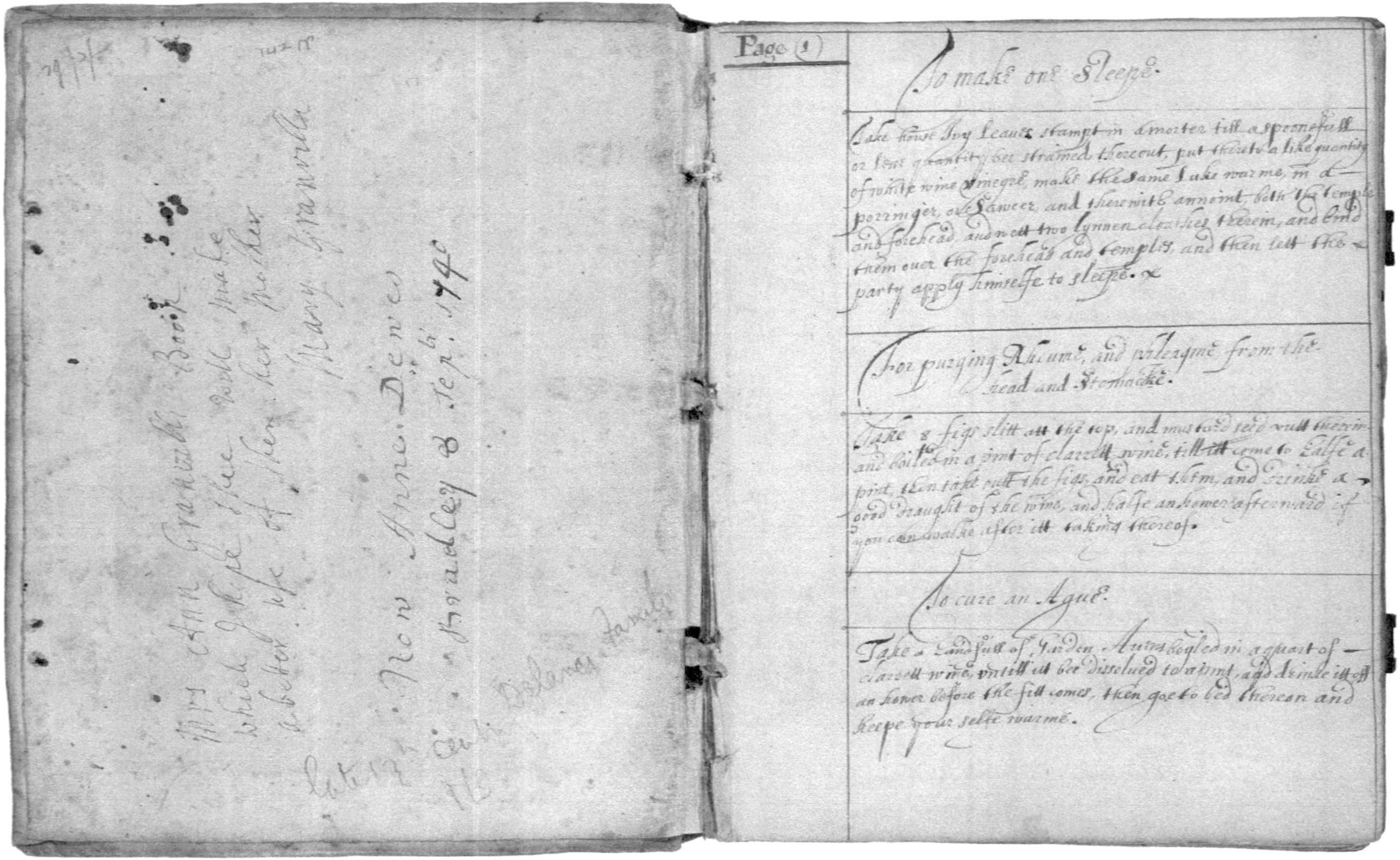

To make one Sleepe.

Take some dry leaues thoroughly dried...

For purging Allume, and Dragagant from the head and Stomacke.

Take a Fig, slitt att the top...

To cure an Ague.

Take...

Fig. 1.1 Folger MS Va.430, inside front cover / p.1. By permission of the Folger Shakespeare Library

Receipt Book

[inside   Mrs Ann Granvills Book
front   which I hope shee will make
cover]   a better use of then her mother
          Mary Granville[1]

          Now Anne Dewes
          Bradley *8 September*. 1740[2]

          late seventeenth century Delaney Family MS.[3]

Page (1)   **To make one sleepe.**[4]

Take house Ivy Leaves stampt in a morter till a Spoonefull
or lesse quantity bee strained thereout, put thereto a like quantity
of white wine vinegre, make the same Luke warme, in a
porringer, or Sawcer, and therewith annoint, both the temple
and forehead, and wett two lynnen cloathes therein, and bind
them over the forehead and temples, and then lett the
party apply himselfe to sleepe.

---

1 This inscription is written in Hand L, most likely that belonging to Mary Granville.
2 This inscription, most likely in Anne Granville Dewes's own hand, might be an
   adult version of Hand O (similarity in certain letter forms, such as minuscule
   w, supports this possibility). Both the above inscription and this one appear at a
   90-degree angle in the inside front cover.
3 This information appears on an angle in the corner of the inside front cover, and
   was likely added by a bookseller or librarian, so a hand has not been assigned to it.
4 From pages 1 through 60, all recipes but one are in the same neat italic hand (Hand
   A), and include carefully drawn horizontal lines separating recipes and vertical
   lines indicating margins. This hand is distinctive in that it includes a small c-like
   mark or small circle over many letters, especially e, but also f and s. Sometimes
   "in" combinations appear as "ni" but I have assumed that this may just be careless
   dotting. Page numbers in this hand are always on the left-hand side; the first page
   has "Page (1)"; then there is simply the number in parentheses. It is not known to
   whom this hand belongs.

For purging Rheume, and phleagme, from the head and Stomacke.

Take 8 figs slitt att the top, and mustard seed putt therein
and boiled in a pint of clarrett wine, till itt come to halfe a
pint, then take outt the figs, and eat them, and drinke a
good draught of the wine, and halfe an hower afterward, if
you can walke after itt, taking thereof.

To cure an Ague.

Take a handfull of Garden Auins Boyled in a quart of
clarrett wine, vntill itt bee dissolved to a pint, and drinke itt off
an hower before the fitt comes, then goe to bed thereon and
keepe your selfe warme.

(2)   ### A medicine for a burne· or Scald.[5]

Take litharge of gold, and oyle of each 4 ounces, of vitrioll
three ounces bare waight, of hogs soile two ounces five drams
and a halfe, take your litharge· and oyle· and boile them
smipering on the fire, untill itt will sticke to a Sawcer,
then take your hogs soyle, and putt to the litharge· and oyle·
and boile them together till it will sticke, then take the
vitrioll and putt to them, and lett itt simper a little while
and then power itt into a Bason of cold Water, and then
make itt up into Rowles, and keepe it for your vse.

A Medicine for a searecloath.

Take a pint of oyle of oliue, and seeth itt till it simpers
then put in halfe a pound of red Lead beaten to powder
and well seirced, stirre them together continually, till
they cast a little blacke, and then dippe the cloathes in itt.

The white oyntment for any Itch.

Take a quarter of a pound of litharge of gold 4· ounces
of oyle of Roses; 5 ounces of the best white wine Vinegre

---

5   The meaning of the dot after "burne" is unknown; however, its appearance in this
    manuscript and throughout the Pudsey manuscript indicates this punctuation mark
    was not uncommon.

putt all these together in a Morter, and grind or pound
them, for the space of· two· or· three howers, till they
bee well mingled, & soe apply it to *th*e place grieued.

(3)   **A Medicine for a sore Breast.**

Take a pint of new milke, boile it very well, then take
a peny Loafe, grate it and put it into the milke, and boile
it thicke to a poultesse, then put into it a little saffron,
and a little barrowes grease, Lay it to yo*ur* Sore, and it will
heale if it have holes without tenting of itt.

**An Excellent Medicine for a Sore breast with the Ague,
it will both breake it, and heale, without any other thing.**

Take a pint of the dregs of ale or new beere, then bruise, a
good handfull of flax seed (alias linseed) boyle this till itt
bee thicke as a poultis, and put into it two spoonefulls of lin
seed oyle, for want of that, take oyle of roses, or Barrowes
Grease, (butt the linseed oyle is best) and apply itt to your Breast
if it bee not too farre past, it takes it away without breaking
att all.

To make the greene Ointment

Take Eight pound of butter in the moneth of may fresh
without salt, a pottle of black snailes, your butter being melted
in a Kettle, then putt in your blacke Snailes and lett them
boile halfe an hower Stirring them all the while, then
take itt off the Fire, and take two handfulls of Rosemary,
of Balme, of Lauender, of Lauender cotten, of Southernewood of
corsemary, of Elder Leaves, of Buglas, of Brookelime, of
Camomile, of sage, of Bay leaves, of hearbegrace, of mint, of
wormewood, of each of These two handfulls, which must
                                                    bee=
(4)   Bee gathered in the heat of the day for they must not bee
washed, but shread, and bruised in a morter then set your butter
againe vpon the fire, and putt in all your hearbes, letting them
boile till it comes to an ointment, when your hearbes bee halfe
boiled, put in a porringer of cow dung, and hen dung newly

made put all these together to boile *with* your spices as followes.
3 quarters of a pound of the best frankincense, two ounces
of nutmegs sleted, two ounces of mace bruised, when it is
boyled to an ointment take itt off the fire, and straine itt,
and soe lett it stand two dayes, then clarifie it upon coales, &
soe put it up for your use, This is an approoued good
oyntment, for any bruise or old ach, as alsoe for the spleene
or the Gout. itts alsoe good for a wrench or spraine=

A Medicine for sore Nipples

Take an ounce of Bee wax, an ounce of Deere suett, and
halfe an ounce of fine Suger, a quarter of a pint of rose
water, boile all these together till it bee salue, and spread
itt upon a cloath, and lay it to the nipple warme, This
will heale any choppe. or skinne broken in the nipples.

Mr John Rutters

Take woodbind Leaves, Sage, Bramble tops, Plantine,
and Red Roses, of each halfe an handfull, boyle them in
3 pints of Barly water to halfe the quantity, to which
when it is strained cleare, ad sirrup of Violette and Syrrup
of mulberries of each an ounce, burnt allum powder, halfe
a dram, spirit of Vitrioll ·3· or 4 drams, rose water an ounce
mix them al together for your vse.

(5) ### Goodwife Lawrence her Salue.

one pound marking pitch.	¼ of a pound of deere Suet
one pound of Rosen.	½ a pound of Barrowes grease.
3 penyworth of turpentine.	¼ a pound of mutton Suett
½ an ounce of mithridate.	1 handfull of hissop
3· or 4· spoonfulls of honey	1 handfull of Sallindine
1 ounce of Bee wax.	1 handfull of camomile
1 ounce of oyle of spike	1 handfull of smallidge.
1 ounce of oyle of Roses	

The deares suet and Barrowes Grease beat in a morter
together, let them stand 3 dayes couered close, then boile
them together with all the other things except the oyle of
Spike and oyle of Roses, which must bee put in, when the
others bee boiled, and strained; for a Bruise take some
of this and melt itt and putt in to it hoxy croxy an ounce=

To make Balsamum

Take halfe a pound of Turpentine, a pint of Sallad oyle,
fower ounces of yellow wax, an ounce of storax, liquid oyle
of hypericon, red Sanders, mirhe of each one ounce, oyle of
camomile, oyle of Roses oyle of firre; oleum balsamiae
oyle of Baies of each fower peny worth, dragon Blood Six
pennyworth, orris powder an ounce, damaske powder an
ounce, oyle of mirhe, & oyle of Juniper of each fower peny=
=worth oyle of cedar, and oyle of dill, of each three peny=
=worth, one dram of Camphire, Lastly of corrall Pearle
and amber finely powdered, with powder of gold a
quarter of an ounce first in an earthen pipkin make
                                                your=

(6)   your wax liquid, and in another your turpentine, then putt
them together, next put in your sallad oyle and lett
them boile a little while then put in your storax liquid,
and then your oyle of hipericon, and lett them boile a
little then take it from the Fire, and put in your
Sanders, and stirre itt till itt bee almost cold then draine
out the water att the Bottome, att a hole which you must
make in the pipkin, then melt it againe, and put in
all the Rest of the forenamed things, and stirre itt till
itt bee cold, and it is Finished.

A Receipt of water for a sore throat or mouth.

Take of knot marjoram, Sage, mother of time, of each
two handfulls, shread them small, & boile them in 3
quarts of water vntill 3 pints bee consumed, then
straine out the hearbes, and put to the liquor a
quarter of a pound of english honey, and lett it boile
a little, then skum itt and straine itt againe and soe
keepe itt for your vse.

To make Oyle of Saint Johns worte.

Take a quart of Sallad oyle of the best, and put it into
a glasse putting therto as much saint Johns worte, as you
can well stop into itt, keeping it very close, with a peice
of parchment, and then sett it in horse Dung couered
over for the space of nine Dayes, casting warme dung
euery day vpon itt Thus doing itt will bee
very good.

(7)   **To make an Oyntment for a Bruise.**

Take a quart of Elder flowers green from the Tree, dryed
by the shadow in the space of 12 howers, then beat them
in a morter of stone, and put thereto a pint of beane flower
finely boulted, and being compounded in a Morter, put
them into a glasse or gallipot, adding thereto a quart of sallad
oyle, with halfe an ounce of fenigreeke or more being finely
beaten and seirced, the meale and elder flowers must bee bea=
=ten till they come to the likenes of paste, before they come to
bee put into the glasse of oyle, or into the fenigreeke, where=
of you may adde an ounce if you please, the grosse substance
of the oyle you may vse in manner of a plaister, this vse of
this oyle is thatt you must annoint your greiued place by the
fire, chafing it in with your hand, then apply thereto a
red Cloath, and soe lett it lye from one dressing to another
keeping the party grieued very warme, especially if itt
bee in Winter.

To boile a hanch of Venison.

Boyle it in water and Salt, and after it is halfe boiled, stuffe
itt with a little beefe suet, and sweet hearbes, and nothing
and nothing in the stuffing saue the Grauey, put to it
a little Clarett wine, with 2, or 3· yolkes of egs, and a little
Sampire cut small, then cut Brewes into the dish, and
Soake them with the fat of the venison and keepe it hott.
if you will boyle it with Colloflowers, boyle them alone, and
after put them into a pipkin, with the Remainer of the
Grauee, and Some sweet Butter and some, three or 4
Anchoues. &c

(8)   **A Medicine for the Greensicknes**

Take 6 ounces of new filings of steele, wash them, cledne [clean]
And heat them red hott in a crucible, then quench
them in fower pints of Rhenish wine, doe thus thrice
then ad to the wine halfe an ounce of nutmegs, three
drams of Cynamon, two scruples of cloues, one dram of
dryed citron pill, fower ounces of Suger, let these
stand together in awarme place 4 dayes together
then power off the wine with an easy hand not

stirring the powder in the Bottome.
Take first 4 spoonfulls of this wine in a morning,
fasting, and exercise for an hower after, but eat
nothing for 3 howers space, after the taking of it,
and after ·4 dayes encrease your dose to six spoon=
=fulls and perseuere in that quantity. And.
Every 8· or 9 dayes take this following purge. (vizt)
Take sena two drams. agarick one dramme, Romane
Wormewood one scruple, Rubarbe two scruples, ginger
halfe a scruple, mace 7 graines, infuse them in
sucory water, warmed 12 howers, then boile it a little
lightly to 4 ounces, then lett it coole and adde to the
liquor strayned six drams of syrupus Augustanus.

(9)   **The Wound Water.**

Take Bolearmeniack 4 ounces, white coperis 4 ounces, cam=
=phire one ounce, then beat the camphire and coperis into fine
powder, and boile them in a little black earthen pot continuall
=ally stirring them till they bee melted, and become thinne
and hard, againe, and soe dissolved to a fine powder, as it will
bee with a soft fire, and long doing them; then beat the
Bolearmeniacke, to powder likewise, and mingle them
together, and keepe the powder in a bladder, and when
you haue occasion to vse it take a pot of Running water
and set it on the fire till it beginnes to seeth, then take
it off, and put thereto, two spoonefulls of powder, and
Stirre it a quarter of an hower, & let it stand untill
it bee cold, and when you will vse itt let it bee of the
Clearest, and put it in an earthen pan, and set it on
the fire, and make it as hott as the party can suffer it,
when you bath the sore bee bathing of it a good while
very well, and if it has a hole in it, syringe it, still very
hott, halfe a dozen tymes one after another, till it come
as cleane out as it went in, then lay thereon a fowerfold,
woollen cloath, scalded well in the water that you are
sure it bee wet through, then bind vp the Sore with
the wet Cloath on it, and bee sure to keepe it very warme
with many double woollen cloathes let this bee done twice
a day att least, This water is alsoe good for sore eyes.

(10)   **To make Bread A la Roine**

Take good Flower of good wheat, ground in a good mill
make leauen with flower, and beere not bitter, and warme,
yet not boiling, the leauen must bee made of the third
part of all the Flower which is to bee vsed, then make
the paste somewhat soft, and in the moistning of itt
put in milke somewhat warme, egs butter, and salt, putt
in butter sparingly, of the Rest you cannot put in too
much, the oven must not bee heated too much nor too
little but according to the Judgement of the Baker.

For the cough.

Take Aquavitae halfe a pint, 6 figs cut in halfe
about 20 raysins of the sun whole with one ounce of
white suger candy then burne[6] it to a syrrup and of
that syrrup take 3 nights together a small propor=
=tion about one spoonfull when you goe to bed and
god keepe you.

To make Doctor Chambers his water

Take a gallon of white wine it must bee Gascoigne
wine, then take ginger, mace, cloues, annis seedes,
Fennell seeds, carraway seeds, and galingall of each of
these a dram, then take sage, spearmint = thyme,
and wild Thime, Rose=mary, Cammomill, Lauander tops
and pellitory of spaine of each of These one handfull,
                                              Then–
(11)   Then Beat the spices small and the hearbes alsoe; and
put them all into the wine, and let it stand 12 howers,
stirring it often then distill it in a Limbecke, and keepe
the first water, for that is the best, the second is good too
butt not soe good as the first, this is a most excellentwater
for weake people.

---

6   It is impossible to determine for certain, but "burne" might be written over "boile,"
    even though boiling seems to make more sense here.

To make a water for a Squinancy.

Take a pint of running water, and make it ready to boile
then take a handfull of dryed red roses and put therein &
lett them stand in that hot water about halfe an hower,
then straine the Roses from the water, and put in 3·
or 4 drops of oyle of Vitrioll and as much syrrup of mul=
berryes as will sweeten it; this is the best medicine for a
sore Throat that ever I met with.

A Soueraigne Balsum.

Take a quarter of a pound of yellow wax cutt it in small
pieces, and put it into an earthen panne; or pot with a pint
of sacke, then melt it on the fire, and when it is all melted,
take halfe a pound of venice Turpentine, and wash it very
well in Rose water, then take apint & a halfe of oyle of oliue and
poure both the oyle and the Turpentine into the pan when
the wax, and the Sacke is well melted, then boile them alto=
gether with a soft fire, untill they bee well incorporated
then take it from the fire, & let it coole, and when it is cold take
away the cake from the sacke, then melt it againe and putt
into it an ounce of the best red Sanders, & soe stirre it conti=
=nually till itt bee cold.

(12)   ## To make an Admirable good Water against Melancholly=

Take a pottle of sacke, and put it into a Jarre glasse.
such an one as you may stop close, put into it 3 handsfull
of Rosemary flowers, 4 handfulls of wallflowers, either
double or single. also of Burrage and Buglas, and mary=
=gold Flowers of each a handfull, of cowslip a handfull
of pinkes 6· handsfull, the redder the better, of damaske
Roses, 3 handsfull, of Balme ·6 handsfull, such of these
Flowers, as have white bottomes they must bee cut off, then
you must ad halfe an ounce of Cynamon, and two ounces
of nutmegs, and one ounce of Annis seedes, you must
bruise your spices, and your seedes, then ad three peny
weight of saffron, put these things to your flowers
and Balme, and let them stand two dayes stirring
them once or twice a day, then put it into a still, and
past up your still close, lett it run into a glasse that

hath two graines of muske tyed in itt, you must not
lett it distill too fast for if you doe it wilbe the
smaller, and you will haue the lesse. in all this water
you must have 6 ounces of white suger candy beaten
itt is very good for them that are heauy hearted, and
haue a heauines in their Spirits; take two or three
spoonesfull att a time and it will comfort you very
much.   Probatum est.

(13)   **A Receipt to make Meath.**

Take to six gallons of water, six quarts of honey, or
as much honey as will make it strong enough to beare an
egge the breadth of three pence aboue water, when the
honey is dissolued in the water put your honey and water
together into a cleane wooden vessell, over night, and temper
it well together, and soe let it stand till the next day that
the honey may bee dissolued well, before you set it on the
fire, then put it on the fire, in a Kettle or broad panne
and boile it well att least an hower, and scum it as long as
any scum will rise, then take halfe a handfull of egremony, &
as much pelitory of the wall, and wash that cleane, and boile
them in itt some halfe an hower more (if the hearbes bee
dry it will doe as well as if they were green) then take halfe
an ounce of nutmegs, and cynamon, & soe much ginger, bruise
the nutmegs and Cynamon but not too small, and slice the
ginger thin, and small, then put the spice into a little canvas
bag, and put little cleane pebblestones in the bag to make itt
sinke, and when the meath is boiled enough put the bag of
spice in the Kettle, and take it up presently off the fire, for the
spice must not boile in it, but scald, then power the meath into
a cleane vessell againe, the same you tempered it in, and soe lett
it stand, and coole, and let the bag of spice lye still in it, and the
next day you may tonne it vp, you must tye a thrid to the bag by
which it must hang in the vessell, and not lie in it, if your vessell
you intend to fill bee six gallons, you must take soe much water, and
allow the honey for wast in boiling for it will wast soe much if not
more, and if the vessell bee not quite full, it matters not much for this
kind of drinke, but if it be full it is the better, this receipt is as it is
usually made. but if you like it not soe strong, you must take five
quarts of water to a quart of honey (but I think it was the long keeping

that made mine soe strong, if you make it att michaelmas it will
not bee ready to drinke till lent but the smaller you make it the
sooner it will bee ready for drinke; you must not tonne vp the
very dreggs into the vessell.

(14)   **To make Poppy Water.**

Take a pottle of Angelica water, and a pottle· of
Annis seed water; take thereof a quart or three
pints, take of poppies about halfe a pecke, when the
Blackes are clipped off the leaves, then put them
into the water and let them lye a day or longer
till they looke whitish, then straine the water
from them, and put therein as many fresh pop=
=pies againe to that water, and let them stand till
they bee whitish, and straine them as before, and
Soe repeat it Seven times in all, and then putt, and
then put the water into a great glasse, with the
other water, and put therein an ounce of cynamon,
an ounce of nutmegs sliced, and halfe an ounce of
cloues steepe these fowreteen dayes in the water,
then straine the water from the spices. and put there=
=in twelve graines of Bezar and a pound of fine
suger candy, then hang in the glass six graines of
muske and Sixe graines of Ambergreece; This
water is very good for a surfett.

                 An excellent water for a consumption

Take Turnips and pare them and slice them very
thinne, and put them into a pipkin that will hold
fower quarts, and Fill itt with your Turnips
then put in fower spoonesfull of rosewater, as
much white wine, and a root or two of Ennula campana –
(15)   Campana, then cover it vp close with paste, att the Top bake
itt in an oven with browne Bread, and when it is baked straine
itt through a linnen cloath, and when it hath stood till itt
be cleare, then drinke six spoonesfull of it in the morning
and at fower of the clocke in the afternoone.

To Take out the holes of the Small Pox.

Take 2 quarts of sherry sacke, and one quart of white wine
vinegre, halfe a pound of bitter Almonds, two handsfull of
Rosemary tops, 30 whites of egs with halfe the shells, distill
all these together, and then put to it one ounce of Suger
candy wash *with* it 3· or 4 times a day. probatum est &c=

+[7]

For a Consumption

Take snails in the shells halfe a pecke, wipe them very cleane
with a cloath, and put them into an earthen pott, with a good
quantity of sage. that the said snails may skowre themselves &
let the pot bee well couered that they get not out, and soe lett
them stand 24 howers therein, with an awle pricke every one
of the snailes, through the shell, then take them and fill the
holes with browne suger candy then put them into a Bag
and hang the bag upon a naile, soe that it touch not the
walls, and set a Bason vnder to receive the water that
will droppe from the same, then put it into a glasse
with a quarter of a dram of confectio Alkermis; take
a little in the morning; afternoone, and at night, if you
would keepe it for your vse, till winter it must bee boiled,
and the Scumme taken off.

(16)

For A Consumption (vizt)

Take a pottle of Goates, or Red cowes milk, with two
handsfulls of colts foot, and halfe an ounce of annis seedes, and
halfe a pecke of shell snailes, fresh purged with salt, then
wash them and put them into astill, with a soft fire, and
when it is distilled sweeten it with the finest loafe suger,

---

7 The + sign might, like the Latin phrase at the end, indicate that the recipe was tried
and "proved." The recipe for mead on page 17 of this manuscript includes the same
sign, and they both might have been added by Hand D, as this hand likely also
contributed the comment on page 17, and because Hand D's recipe on page 104 is
also accompanied by the same sign.

and take 6 spoonefulls att 7· of the clocke in the morning,
six spoonesfull att 11· at noone, six spoonsesfull att 4·
of the clocke in the afternoone, and 6· going to bed, if
the party bee troubled with the spleene, distill with
itt a hand full of Tamariske.

To make Syrrup of Succory with Rubarbe.

Take of french Barly, the rootes of Smallidge, the rootes
of fennell, the rootes of Asparagus, of each two ounces; of
the hearbes, Succory, Lyon-tooth, Endiue, of each two hands
full, the hearbes llettuce, liuerworte, femitary, and hops,
of each one handfull; maiden hair, white maiden hair,
centerach, lycorish, winter Cherries, Dodder, of each Six
drams boile these in 12: pints of water to the consuming
of the third part; in which decoction being strained,
infuse all night 6 ounces of Rubarbe; of spikenard 6· drams
then straine itt and ad to itt 6 li of suger; clarified with
the whites of Two egs, and boile itt gently to the con=
=sistence of a syrrupe, you may giue two or three spoones=
=full of it, and itt will purge gently.

(17)   ### To make spleene Ale.

Take to 4 gallons of Alewort a handfull of harts tongue
a handfull of Egræmony, a handfull of Dockrootes
scraped and sliced, twice as much Tamariske, a good quan=
=tity of liuer=wort. boile all these in the wort, and when
it is ready to tonne vp, put into your Vessel a handfull
of wormewood being a little bruised, and soe att 3· or 4
daies end, drinke it att 7 of the clocke in the morning
and 4 in the afternoone. &c. you must yearst itt as
other Ale, and putt in what other hearbes you please.

A water to cure pimples in the Face.

Two ounces of litharidge of gold in fine powder, boile it
the space of a quarter of an hower, in a pint and halfe
of distilled vinegre, then straine it and put to it 4·
ounces of oyle of Tartar, wash with it every night
when you goe to Bed. and if you find it too sharpe
put oyle of Almonds into it

To make Meath. *the* best Way[8]

+   To one quart of honey take 8· quarts of water, put
them together, hang it over the fire, and when it boiles
scum it cleane, then put thereto an ounce and a halfe
of these spices, (vizt) Ginger, Cynamon, mace, and nutmegs.
this quantity you may put to 8 quarts of honey
then keepe it boiling for an hower and a halfe, and
better; it being boiled put it into a cleane Tub, spice

                          And

(18)   And all, and let it stand till the next day, then tonne
it vpp spice groundes, and all together, the Tub must bee
quite full and you must stoppe it very close, and when
itt hath stood 3 weekes or a moneth you must bottle it vp.

To make A<...> mirabilis[9]

Take ·3 pints of sack, one pint of Aquavitæ and halfe
a pint of the Juice of cælandine, cloues, mace. ginger
nutmegs, cubebees=cardamomum, galingale, meliots
Flowers, of each a dram, well bruised together and put
them into a glasse to infuse 24: howers, then still itt
with a very soft fire, and let the still bee pasted vpp
close, you may add juice of mint if you please; if you
haue a glasse still it is best. and sweeten it with white
suger of candy; The virtues of this Water are very many.

To make Quince Marmelade with Jelly white, or Red[10]

Take a pound, and a halfe of double refined suger, boile one
pounds to a suger againe, beat the other halfe pound, and
set it by, Take quinces and grate them, then straine them
as quick as you can through a Jelly bag, or apeice of cotton

---

8 The words "*the* best Way" have been added in another hand, which appears to be
   Hand D.

9 Part of the title is covered by an ink blot; however, the intended third word is
   most certainly "Aqua," although the descender (which reaches below the ink blot)
   indicates that it is in fact "Agua."

10 The "red" version of this recipe seems to involve a bit of magic: simply covering the
   pot and adding a bit of water to white quince jelly causes the colour change. "The
   manner of distilling a water of honey" below (38) seems to involve a similar trick.
   However, there may be a chemical reaction happening similar to the "purple of

till it be as cleare as white wine, then take parboiled
quinces halfe a pound, cut them in pieces and put them
into that suger that is not boiled then put the boiled suger
to them alsoe, and a pint of that Juice that was strained,
and one spoonefull of water then boile them as fast as you
can till it will Jelly let not the Fruit bee above the
liquor, you must make the Red the Same way; onely
you must put in 3 spoonesfull of water, and cover it
a little &c=

(25)[11]   **To make a plaine cake.**

Take to Six pound of flower, three pound of sweet
Butter rubbed in the Flower, one pound of sugered
Carrawayes, a quarter of a pound of fine suger beaten
mingle it with the carrawayes, one pint of thicke creame,
one pint of Ale yearst, knead your cake and lay it before
the fire to rise halfe an hower, and when you goe to
mold it, put in your carrawayes and suger, and soe lett
it stand 3 quarters of an hower in the ouen.

To make a Fricacee.

Take an onion and cut it in halfe, and fry it in a pan
with a piece of sweet butter, till the butter tast well of
the onion, then take 4 pigeons, and parboile them, then
cut them into pieces, you make take larkes alsoe, and cutt
them in halues, put them into the butter and fry them
a good while, then take a quart of oysters well washed,
letting the liquor stand till it bee cleare, and then put
itt to them againe, and soe put your oysters into the pan
to your pigeons, and when your oysters bee more then halfe
boiled, take the yolkes of seuen egs beaten & mixed with

Cassius" distillate that Pat Collins mentions in a comment on The Recipe Project
blog ("About").

   C. Anne Wilson writes extensively of the interest in colour in medieval European
cooking – an interest that originated in Arabic cooking and clearly carried over
into the early modern period. Red, white, and gold were common colourings (the
former with red currants, sanders, or dragon; white with mixtures of ingredients
including almond milk, cow's milk, rice, breadcrumbs, and chicken; gold with
saffron) (*Appetite* 16–26).

11   Pages 19–24 are missing from the manuscript.

a little wine vinegre, nutmeg, and cynamon according to
your taste, put these into your pan stirring it altogether
till you thinke it thicke enough, and to put into your
dish you may ad apound of Sawsages to it if you please.
I Thinke that leamon wilbe better then Vinegre.

(26)   **To stew a Calues Head**

Take a calues head let it bee halfe boiled, then cut it in
pieces, and season it with nutmeg, and salt; stew it with
a quart of wine put to it two onions cut in quarters
with a good quantity of samper, and a small bundle.
of sweet hearbes, lett this stew altogether till you thinke
they bee almost enough, then take a pint and a halfe
of oysters, put away some of the liquor from them, &
season it with a little wine large mace, salt and an onion,
set them ouer the fire to take the Rawnes from them.
then put them to the other things with some of the
liquor, and apiece of sweet butter, take ared Cabage
boile it in water and salt, with the bones of 4· or 5
anchoues, when it is boiled enough take it vp & cut itt
into quarters, and lay it about the dish. if you
please you may put in the Juice of a leamon.

To make a Pye.

Take a handfull of spinage another of lettuce; al=
=most as much of sorrill as both the other, parsely, and
sweet hearbes a top or two, when you haue washed
them, cut them a little, put them Into your paste
with butter suger, and a little nutmeg. any fruit
that the season of the yeare will afford, some
little pieces of flesh as veale mutton or lambe.
when it is baked put in a little white wine, or
Sacke and Butter. &c=

(37)[12]   Bottle and set them vpon soft embers and let them boile
leisurely the space of two howers, then take them off, and set
your bottle by for a day, and a night, then straine it out fr

---

12   Pages 27–36 are missing from the manuscript; the recipe at the top of page 37 is thus
     partial.

from the spice, and put it into your Bottle againe, then take
a pound of browne suger candy, bruise it and put it in, and
6 graines of muske tied in a linnen rag, and soe put it into
the bottle, and thus you may keepe it all the yeare.

To make Cynamon Water.

Take fower gallons of canary sack, and halfe a bushell of
Damaske roses buds, and a pound of burrage flowers, a
quarter of a pound of rosemary Flowers, two pounds of rei=
=sins of the Sunne stoned, two pound of cynamon, steepe all
these in your sacke, and distill them in a limbecke, in the
put that it runs into put a pound of white suger candy
broken into peices as big as a nutmeg, and apint and a
halfe of Juice of pippins.

To make a pretious drinke good for the wind in
the stomacke, or to bring off any meat or
drinke that lieth vpon the stomacke.

Take two quarts of small aquavitæ, and put into it cowslipp
flowers, sage, rosemary Flowers, and sweet marjoram of each
a pretty handfull, of pellitory of the wall a little, cynamon and
nutmegs of each halfe an ounce, fennell seedes, annis seedes,
corriander seedes, carroway seedes, grumwall seedes, and
Juniper
Berries of each a dram, bruise your spices, and your seedes
seuerally
a handfull of reisins of the sun stoned, and 2· or 3 figs sliced,
put all these
into a wide mouth'd glasse, then set it 20 daies in the sun, and
stirre itt e
euery day with a little sticke, then straine it out and put therein
halfe a pound of
fine suger, and let it stande in the sun till the suger bee melted,
stirring it about sometimes.

(38)   ### To make Sirrup of Vinegre=

Dissolue a quarter of a pound suger in 6 spoonesfull of
Rose water, and a quarter of a pint of wine vinegre, and
Boile itt to a sirrup.

The manner of distilling a water of honey.[13]

Take two pound of the purest white honey being both
cleare, and pleasant in taste, which put into a body of glasse
being soe big as 4 of the 5 parts may remaine empty the
same past strongly aboue settling the head after on itt
and a receiuer aptly to the nose of the still when you
haue thus done then make a gentle fire vnder itt
att the first but after increase the fire to heat more
and more, vntill certaine white smoake appeare in the
head of the glasse body which ma[i]nly coole.
and turne it into water by wetting of linnen clothes in
cold water, and lay on the head and nose towards the
Receuer, for that turneth into water as red as bloud, and
being all come put it into another glasse stoping the mouth
close, which let stand soe long vntill the water become very
cleare, and in coulor like to Rubie, now it being on this wise
as aforesaid distill the same againe in Balmeo maria,
and soe often repeat this vntill you haue distilled itt
Six, or Seven times ouer that the coulor bee changed
and in the end be like to the coulor of gold, which then
is most pleasant of sauor, and soe sweet that nothing
may bee compared like to it in fragrantnes of smell, itt
doth dissolue gold, and prepareth it to drinke, itt is alsoe
very comfortable to all those that are apt to haue swoun=
                                                    ding=
(39)   swounding fitts, and are vsed to faintings in the stomacke,
in giuing to any one two or 3· drams to drinke, likewise if
you wash any wound or stripe with this water it doth in
small time heale the same; this pretious water doth mar=
=velously helpe the cough, the Rheume the desease of the
Spleene, and many other deseases scarce to be beleiued;
This water was administered, to a person sicke of the palsie
for the space of 46· daies, and hee was by the mightie helpe
of god, and this miraculous water, throughly healed of his
desease, alsoe this helpeth the falling sicknes, and preser=
=ueth the body from putrifying, soe that by all these wee

---

13 As with the red quince marmalade recipe on page 18 of this manuscript, this recipe –
    essentially lengthy directions for heating honey in a still – seems to involve some
    magic. The recipe suggests that a white vapour will be given off, and that this will
    cool and condense into a red liquid, and then a gold one.

may learne that this is as it were a divine water from
heauen, and sent from God to serue vnto all ages.

To preserue Walnutts.

Take some walnuts about the latter end of June or the
beginning of July when the shells are like a Jelly or
before they bee tuffe then pare the vpper thin skinne off
like an apple, and make a hole with a Bodkin through
euery one of them, put them in water and shift them twice
a day for 4 daies, then boile them till arush or straw will
goe through them, Then way them, and take as much
suger as they way, and put as much water as will make
itt a sirrup, and when the suger is melted put in your
walnuts, and for halfe a pecke of walnuts you may allow
halfe an ounce of cloues, an ounce of cinamon, and halfe an
ounce of ginger, or els butt a quarter of each, boile alto=
gether till the walnuts be prety tender, then take
out the walnuts and boile the sirrup as for other things.

(40)   ### To boile a capon larded with leamons·

Take the capon being scalded and bruised and put him
into a pipkin, with a fagot of sweet hearbes, and strong
mutton broth, put in a little large mace, one nutmeg quartered
and soe let it boile till hee bee almost tender, then take
him out and lard him thick with leamons, put to your
Broth manchet, and the yolkes of 2 hard egs, garnish
your dish with stewed pares, and Barberies and Season
itt with suger.

To make hipocras for a consumption

Take a pint of malmesey, and as much wormewood water
put them into a fair glasse of a pottle or more, and putt
thereto an ounce of cinamon, two drams of case ginger
which is pure and white within, bruise the cinamon, and
ginger great, and put it into a glasse, and put to this
fine suger, 4 ounces or more, and soe let it stand fast stopped
three dayes, and at the third dayes end give it to the sick
6 spoonefulls in the evening and as many in the
morning and let it bee warme and at euery time
you take of it shake the glasse.

To make Harts horne Jelly.

Take a quarter of a pound of harts horne scraped
boile it gently in a pottle of spring water, till you see
by taking of some vpon the point of a Knife, and laying it on
a dish that it gelly then straine it and sweeten it to your
taste with suger, rosewater, and Juice of leamons.

(41)   ### To make plague Water.

Take red Egrimony; wormewood, sage, salandine, balme
mugwort, dragons wood sorrell, scabius, wood betony,
browne mayweed, Avens. Angelica, turmentill, pimpernel, carduus
benedictus ~~of each a pound~~ Ennula campana rootes, burnett
marigolds, featherfew ^ of all each a pound^ =two ounces of
hartshorne, and two pound
of rosemary; mingle all these together, and chop them very
small, and then steepe them in 5 gallons of the best ~~white~~
~~wine or~~ sack ·3 daies, stirring it once a day, then still itt
in a common still with a soft fire.

Doctor Burges his direction ag*ains*t the plague.

Take 3 pints of malmesey, and boile therein a handful of
sage, a handfull of rew, till it be wasted, then straine
itt, and sett it over the Fire againe, and put thereto a
pennyworth of long pepper, halfe an ounce of ginger and
a quarter of a pound of nutmegs, all beaten together then
lett it boile, a little, and take it off, then put to it 4 peni=
=worth of mithridate, 2 penyworth of London Treagle, and
a quarter of a pint of Angelica water, keepe this as your life
above all wordly Treasure, take it always warme both
euening, and morning, a spoonefull or two if you bee infec=
=ted, and sweet thereupon, if you are free of infection
three quarters of a spoonefull, at morning, and halfe a
spoonefull at night is sufficient, in all the time of the
plague; vnder God trust to this for this neuer did faile
either man woman or child, this is alsoe good for the
measles, smallpox, and other Kinds of Deseases _

(42)   ### To make = Inke = Verie Good

☞   Take a quart of snow or raine water, and a quart of
Beere vinegre, a pound of galls bruised, halfe a

pound of coperis, and 4 ounces of gum bruised; first
mix your water and vinegre together, and putt itt
into an earthen Jug, then put in the galls, stirring
itt 2· or 3 times a day letting it stand 8· or 9 daies, a
and then put in your coperas and Gumme. as you
vse it straine itt. &c=

To make Almond Puddings

Take a pound of the best Almonds, put them in
water over night, and in the morning they will blanch
when you haue blanched them beat them with a
little rose water; take alsoe 12 egs, and boile them
hard, and chop them very small; mingle them with
your Almonds and 6 penny loaues, grated and
sifted, seuen egs beaten, with three pound of suet,
a little Cynamon, mace, and nutmegs, and as
much suger as will sweeten itt very sweet, wett it with
as much creame, as will make it not too thinne
and soe fill them in your gutts, and boile them,
butt Note that a little boiling will serue.

(43)   ### To make the cocke water.

Take of Burrage, Buglas. 2 handsfull of each, tyme penny
=royall, Rose mary flowers, one handfull of each, a pound of
reisins of the Sun stoned one pound of currants, halfe a pound
of dates, 2 quarts of sacke, 2 quarts of new milke, and a
cocke well beaten not washed but dried with a cloth, and put
itt into these things whilest itt is warme, and still them
altogether in an ordinary still, and let the water drop
into a glasse, with suger candy and leafe gold in itt, well
beaten, together with Some magesterium of pearle if
you please, you must take of this water 4 spoonefulls
before dinner an hower or two, and as much att fower
of the clocke in the Afternoone.

A Drinke for the Ricketts

Take two good handsfull of scurvie grasse, 4 handsfull
of water creasis, 2 handsfull of brookelime, one handfull
of Harts tongue, one handfull of lungwort, 2 handsfull of
liuer wort, one handfull of Betony, and one handfull of

egrimony. wash them purely cleane, and swing them well in
a cloth, that there bee noe water in them, and beat
them well in a stone morter, and put thereto a quart of
red cowes milke warme from the cow, then straine them
through a Fine cloth, put it vp into a Bottle, and
let it bee close stopped, and let the child drinke of
itt. It must stand in avery coole place.

(44)   **An Ointment for the Ricketts**

Take a pound of fresh butter well beaten, or
washed out of the Chirne, clarify itt, and take two
handfulls of woodrose or spurrey, shread itt very
small and boile itt with the Butter a good
while leisurely and when you vse itt haue a care
the child take noe cold; annoint the Breast
and belly of the child, spreading the breast
and stroaking downe the Belly; keepe the child
warmer those dayes you annoint him, then att
other times.

                    To make Jelley of Calues Feete

Take two pair of calues Feete, open them and
take out the knott of fatt in the middle of them, then
boile them in two gallons of water vntill it come
to apottle, keeping it cleane scum'd all the while,
Then let it stand till it bee cold, and take off the fatt;
put to this one pint of sack, one pint of white
wine, coriander seedes, nutmegs, ginger, cynamon,
mace, Rosewater, and suger, to your taste; put
in these ingredients when itt is cold, then lett itt
boile on the Fire, and cleanse it through a
Jelly Bagge, till itt bee cleare enough, you
may ad Juice of leamons if you please, and
itt will tast the quicker.

(45)   **To make a thicke creame.**

Bring 2· or 3· Cowes according to the quantity
you will make, as neare the place you set your creame
in as may bee, and milke them with all the speed
that you can, soe that the milke may bee strained as

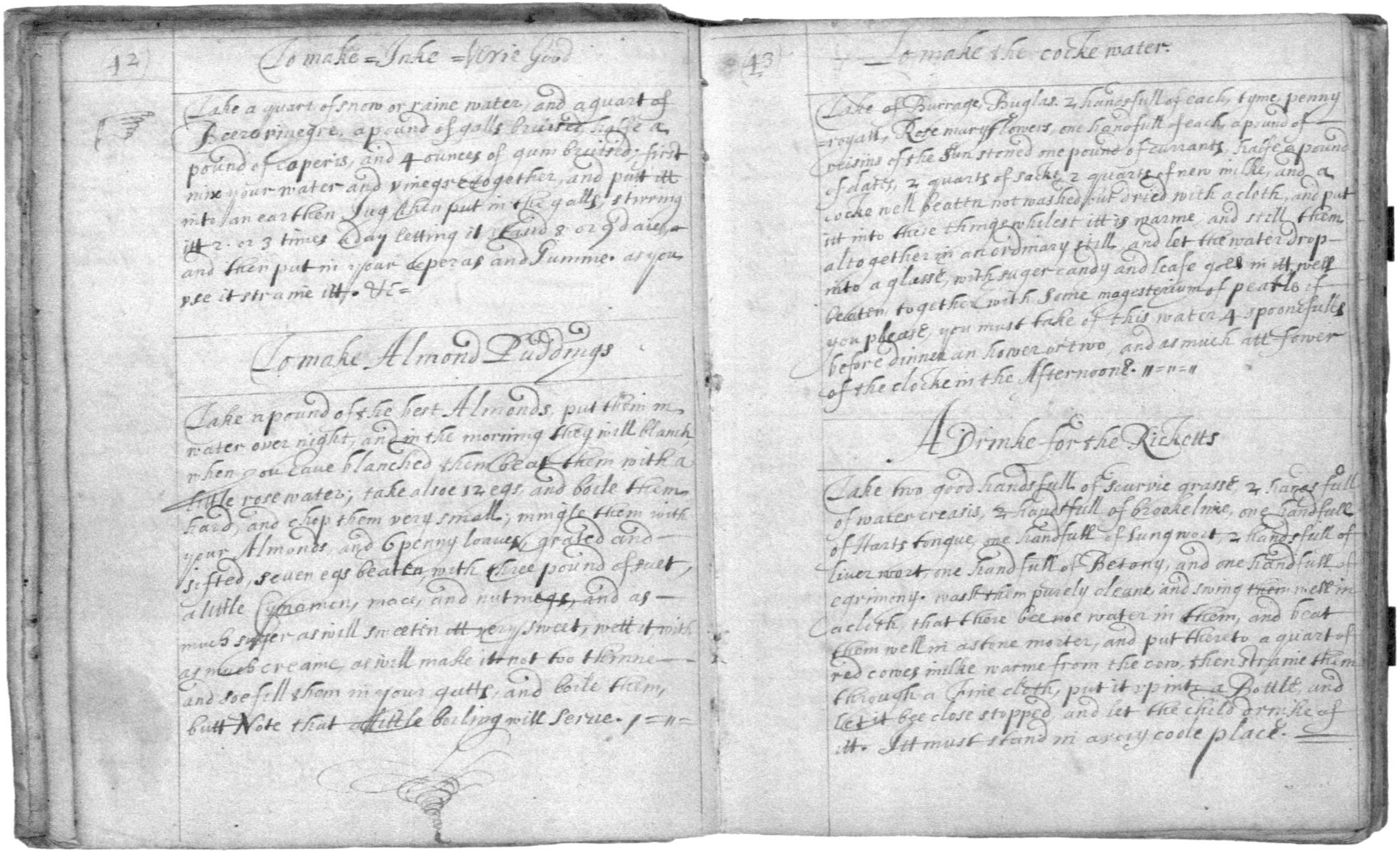

Fig. 1.2   Folger MS V.a.430, pp. 42/43. By permission of the Folger Shakespeare Library.

hott as possible you can into the pans, for the warme=
=nesse of the milke from the cow is the reason of the
thicknes of the creame, soe lett it stand 24 howers
if you thinke itt will keepe noe longer sweete, and
then take itt vp as thick as the creame will afford; &
you will find itt a very thick creame, and cleane
another Taste[14] if you exactly obserue the Rule.

To make a Friccacee of Veale.

Take a Breast of Veale, cutt itt in small pieces
and lay it in water a quarter of an hower to make
itt white after that take a skillet and put in a pint
of clarrett wine, and a pint of water, and a whole
leamon after you have taken away the pill of itt
and put in salt, and when this boiles, put in your
meat skum itt often, then put in a quarter of a pound
of Butter, then take 12 cloues, halfe a nutmeg, and
2 or 3 blades of mace, and a little pepper, and beat all
these together, and put them into the skillet, if this bee too
much spice you may put in according to your liking, alsoe put
in a few sweet hearbes, then take 6· yolkes of egs, the Juice of a
leamon
and one orange, & a little of your broth beat all these in a
porringer
take off from the fire your skillet, & put in these, then take itt
vp and serve itt in.

(46)   ### To make a possett

Take two quarts of very sweet Creame, and
when it boiles take itt off the Fire, and stir itt
least itt curdle, putt into itt *the* yolkes of Six new
laid egs, finely beaten with a little Creame, before
the cocks treads bee taken outt, sett itt two or three
minutes over the Fire againe, stirring itt continu=
=ally, then putt itt into the Sacke (w*h*ich must
bee ready att the Same tyme) thus; Take the
third part of a pint of the best Canary, and putt
into itt 3· nutmegs quartered, 3 quarters of a

---

14   In other words, a completely different taste from other cream recipes.

pound of suger, sett itt on the Fire till itt come
to a sirrup, then putt in your creame as afore=
=said; if you like itt you may lett 2 graines of amber
greece boile in your Sacke.

An excellent approoued plaister for *the* spleene *which* hath cured divers giuen ouer by the Phisitians=

Take halfe a pound and halfe a quarter of Deers
suett, as much wax, and olibanum, Rosen, and
Frankincense of each halfe a pound, masticke,
and camphire of each halfe an ounce, of the best
Turpentine halfe a pound and halfe a quarter,
melt all butt the Turpentine, and the Camphire
and=

(47) And when itt is melted, stirre in the Turpentine and
Camphire, then power all into a Bason, the bason hauing
a quart of white wine in itt, and worke itt into little
Rolls, and soe Keepe itt, lett the Camphire and all bee
throughly Dissolued before you power itt into the wine.
probatum est:

A Receipt to take away the red spotts out of the Face after the small pox are gone.

Take of Femitary water a quarter of a pint, wild tansey
water a quarter of a pint, sulphur vivum, a quarter
of an ounce vnbeaten; 3· or 4 leamons, powder of cam=
=phire a quarter of an ounce, and a pint of the best white
wine, Then wring the Juice of the leamons into a thing
by itt selfe, and boile the pith with the two waters and
the camphire; and when itt is cold, mix itt with the Juice
of the leamons, (when you haue strained) you must straine
the leamons alsoe, then poure itt to the white wine, and
lett itt stand 5· or 6 daies in the Sunne.

Another Receipt

Take ½ a pint of white wine, 2 leamons, 4 graines of
powder of camphire, and a pint of milke; boile the milke
and putt the Juice of the leamons into the white
wine, and when the milke boiles make possett

take of the curd, and then putt in the Camphire and
lett itt boile.

(48)
An Ointment to take the spotts out of the Face after the small Pox=[15]

Take an ounce of deeres suet, cut it small, & put it into
a pipkin with ½ an ounce of camphire; melt them together
and take of sulphur vivum 2 peny worth, beat ~~them~~
it very small, and sift it, and put it in when the other is
almost cold.

A very good ointment for a tetter or any Itching

Take of lithridge of gold, beaten, and Searced into very
fine powder, halfe a pound, and put itt into amorter
and stirre itt well Sometimes with oyle of Roses, and Some
times with wine vinegre, till you haue consumed the
Best part of apound of the oyle, and halfe apound of
the vinegre, by which time itt will bee an ointment
and whitish, you must doe itt with a wooden pestle _

A Receipt for a Consumption

Take Dandelion, wood Sorrell, scabius, watercreses,
bloudwort, yarrow, and parseley, of each of these one hand=
=full; liuerwort parsely rootes, and fennell Rootes, of each
of these, two handsfull; red rose water one quart, red Cocke
Chickens six, hunted to Death, and chopped into little pieces
all parts except the gutts, the hearbes must be chopped, which
when you haue done distill all these in a common still, with 20·
or 30 pieces of gold, and when the water is distilled, put therein a
quarter of an ounce of prepared pearle ¼· of an ounce of pre=
=pared corrall, ½ an an ounce of confectio alkermus, and 2 ounces
of manus Christi, and then giue 3 spoonefulls to him to drinke
att a time that hath need of itt.

(49)
Doctor Butlers Receipt against a consumption

Take China rootes thin sliced 2 ounces, steepe them 12
howers in 8 pints of fair running water, letting itt stand all

---

15 The title of the recipe is in Hand A, but the body is in Hand B (unique to this
recipe). There is no indication of the identity of the Hand B contributor.

the Tyme warme, and close couered in an earthen pipkin
or Iorne pott, then sett itt on a cleare fire to boile with a cocke
Chicken, and a piece of Veale; keepe it cleane scum'd, then putt
to itt raisins of the Sunne, and Currants of each 2 handsfull;
maiden hair and Colts foot, of each an handfull; licorish
scraped and Bruised two stickes, 4 dates, 3 blades of
large mace, and the bottome of a manchett, boile all these
together in the Pipkin, with your broth till itt bee
of a reddish coulor, and bee not in quantitie above a
a quart, then straine the Broath, and bruise the
Chickens bones all in astone morter, and straine the
Juice into the broth, then sweeten itt with suger candy
and Drinke a good draught warme 2 howers before
Dinner and supper dayly, for 12· or 15 daies using still
your ordinary Diett.

To make Mackaroones

Take a pound of Almonds laying them in cold water
two daies shifting the water twice a day then blanch
them out of that water, and pound them in a stone
morter, with halfe a pint of Damaske rose water, till
they bee small, then take a pound of hard suger, and
beat with them, then put them in a dish, adding the
broth of 4 whites of egs, and neere a peny white loafe
grated, and searced through a siue, then make them
Boile=

(50)   Boile a little, and soe drop them on wafers cakes
in fashion of a macaroone, washing them over, with
the froth of egs with a feather, and scrape double
refined suger on euery one of Them, which will Ice
them, then put them into an oven, which must bee as
hott as for manchett, looking to them that they doe
not colour too fast, and when you conceiue they bee
baked, take them out, the finer your suger is itt
makes your mackaroones the better, and the whiter
they will looke.

To make Violett Cakes.

Take Violets, and cutt off the white ends of the
leaues, put them into a pewter dish, and sett them

into the oven after white bread hath been baked
therein, the heat whereof will dry them, which done
beat them to powder and sift them through fine
Taffany, Then take gum dragon, and steepe itt
in rosewater till itt bee like starch, then take 4
ounces of fine suger beaten and Searced, and make
paste with your gum, that which you make must
bee pretty stiffe, putting as much powder of the
violetts thereto, as will coulor itt according to your
owne desire, Then roll itt out like paste very thin
and cutt them into what Flowers you please, laying
them on glasse plates to dry, if you will haue
your cakes red put 2, or 3 drops of Juice of Leamons
to itt, if white nothing but suger and Gum.

(53)[16]   **To make Diett cakes**

Take ten of the palest coulered hen egs, taking the skin
and cock Treads from them, and putt them into a
deepe stone pan, that will hold about a pottle, Then
put a pound of double refined Suger finely beaten vnto
Them, and soe beat them with a stick made flatt att the
end about an inch broad, some 3 howers neuer letting
them stand still, in the Interim heat an oven as hott
as for house hould bread, when the oven is hott take a
pound of fine flower, and stir into the egs, and suger
with a few carraway seedes, and a little Amber
greece, and muske, they must bee baked on tin or
pewter plates, which must bee buttered within the brims
and then drop a spoonefull and halfe of your bater, on
each plate, and soe sett them into the oven, not aboue
3· or 4· att a time, because one must stand att the ovens
mouth, with a slice, and turne them as they see occasion,
when they rise vp in the middle, and looke yellow, they
bee enough, when you haue baked them all take
them off the plates, and lay them on white paper,
setting them into the oven, some three howers after,
(when itt is almost cold to hardin.

---

16   Pages 51 and 52 are missing from the original manuscript.

(54)   **To make Doctor Buggs sirrup of Violett**

Take Violetts picked and cutt, and put them into
a deepe gally pott, then heat water seething hott
euen ready to boile but it must not boile, and poure in
as much of that water into the Violetts, as when the
Violetts are sunck you may presse aspoonfull of water
over them, then couer the pot close with double paper
and sett it in warme embers, but take heed they bee
not too hott for if they bee it will spoile the coulor
of the Juice; let the pot stand in the embers, about
18· or 21 howers then presse them out as hard as you
can, and take to apint of Juice almost 3 poundes
of double refined suger, beaten and Serced, then mix
the Juice and suger well together, you must not lett
the Juice come into any mettall, but put it into the
Same, or other stone pott, which couer close with paper
picked full of holes, soe sett the pott into a skillett
of cold water, setting it one the fire to boile till the
Sirrup hath awhite crust on the top of it which
crust take not off for that will keepe the coulor of
the sirrup, when you haue occasion to spend any
of itt make a little hole in the Crust, and power out
the sirrup Through itt.

(59)[17]   **An Approoued medicine for the Hickockes**

Take such a proporcion of warme milke from the cow
as the party is in case to take, for it may bee administred
to one very weake, giuing itt to them very often if need
soe require.

To make Paracelsus plaister

Take ·6 ounces of sallad oyle, one ounce and halfe of
bee wax, 4 ounces and halfe of lithridge of gold, one ounce
of Amoniacum, and one ounce of Bdelium; Galbanum,
opopanax, and oyle of baies of each of these 2 drams; two
drams of tapis calliminaris; two drams of Aristolochia;
both long and round, two drams of mirrhe, and two drams
of frankincense, and one ounce of Venice Turpentine, the

---

17   Pages 55–8 are missing from the original manuscript.

powders to bee beaten seuerally, first powder the lithridge
of gold, and searce it very fine then boile itt with the
wax and oyle till itt will not stick to your finger
being cold, Then before it be cold putt to your
gummes, but first dissolue them together in white
wine vinegre, and straine them into itt, lastly
ad to itt the powder, the oyle of Baies and the
Turpentine soe make itt vp into Rolls. &c=

(60)   **A Medicine for one that is in a desperate
fitt of the stone, and that cannot vrine.**

Give the party a glister of halfe a pint of possett
ale, wherein pellitory of the wall and parsely haue
been boiled, put to the strain'd liquor as much as
a wallnutt in quantitiy of Castill, spanish, or hard
soape, dissolued in the warme liquor, and foure
spoonefulls of Irish Butter mix all and giue itt
the party luke warme, for a glister, lay the party
on his backe vpon a bed, lift him up by the legs thatt
his body may Rest vpon his shoulders shake him
well divers times, to se if the stone may bee remoued
backward from the neck of the bladder, Then
putt him in a bath, up to the necke, or onely to
the short ribs, keeping itt in a Temperate heat
by the fire side, giue him a draught of possett ale,
and 3· or 4 hiue Bees dryed and beat to powder,
whilest hee is in the Bath, where lett him remaine
an hower, make a poultis of leekes, parsely, and
Black soape beaten together with a little fresh
Butter, apply itt warme to the bottome of the
Belly, next aboue the Share Bone, and
betwixt the cod and Fundament. &c=

88[18]   **To make Sirrop of Jilliflowers,[19]**

Take of flowers the whitts cutt of, one pound of them and
infusse them all night in 2 pints of springe Watter In a

---

18 Pages 61–87 are missing from the manuscript. Page numbers are underlined as of
this point, but I have considered the underlines to be decorative marks and have
not included them. Recto page numbers appear in the top right corner of the page.
Even numbers are now on the recto pages.

19 Beginning with this recipe, numerous hands appear in the manuscript. Some of

balmeum, In the morninge strayne them out and add to the
licquor fower pound of the best Loafe shugger then sett
it ouer a gentle ffyre vntell the shugger bee Disolued
Without boylinge Then strayne it Leist there bee
Anye drosse in the shugger takenge of all the
Skumme ass it Risseth In the same manner you
maye doe it With sack onlye 3 pound of shugger
Will bee Enough and mee thinkes the Sirrup much
better;

To cleanse Teeth Well,

Take A quantitye of Powder of Corralls as much
Powder of the pomye Stone mingle it With a little
honnye and musk and soe keepe it and Applye it
at your need of Rubbing your Teeth _

89 ### To Pickle ffrench Beanes

Cutt of the stalkes of the Beanes and Laye them
In Watter and salt for about a Weekes space then
take them from that Watter and green them in
fayre Water and When they are Verie green
And drained from that Licquor Put them Into
The Vessel you intend to keepe them addinge
White Wine Vineger and Salt to them couer
them with an oylie Paper and Sett them
by for your Vse in the Winter _

An Excellent Receat for A soare Brest to keepe it from breaking ore for anye other swellinge one it ore for any bruise viz, Mrs Patts

Take in Equal quantitiye of honny And Aqua Vitta and
Stirr it Well together over the ffyre vntel it bee a little
thicker then oyle Then Beath your brest Well With it

---

the hands reappear later. The use of Hand C in consecutive recipes from pages 88
through 91 suggests that these recipes were perhaps contributed in one sitting by
a relative or neighbour. This is a loose, messy italic hand; its generally light touch
contrasts with dark inkblots in some graphs.

over the coales and dipp a cloath in it and Laye it
Moringe and Eveninge vntell you fynd Ease

90　　　**To cause sleepe in feauors ore any other Distempers[20]**

Take the yolk of anew layd Egg a large nuttmegg gratted
as much bay salt as halfe the nutmegg beaten the salt must
bee Verie fine mix these Well together and spred it vppon a
fine Lynn cloath take the cold of one it and applye
it to the forhead and the temples and let it soe Lye six
howers and if need doe Require it you maye doe it agayn
but Obserue that commonlye the first time does
the Worke of Causinge Sleepe _

To Cure A Canker in the mouth ore the mouth anye Waye Soare

Take a quantitie of hony and halfe that quantity of Roach Allum but
burne it and beat it to powder then mix it with the hony in a pewter
ore silver dish heat the End of the tongues ore the like Iron redd hott
and then stirr the Allum and honny together with the said Iron
heating it still hott vntill the Ingredients turne black and then vse
it three ore fower times a day with a little Ragge vppon a stick

91　　　**To Marrianate Soles Ore flownders,**

ffrye your fish first as you would doe to Eat it and
haue in a reddines Whit winne Vineger two ore three
Cloues of garlick bruised Ten cornes of Peper craked
Laye your fish in the Sawce and turne it once a day you
Maye Eat it as it is done ore keepe it at pleasure and the
Sauce you must obserue must bee accordinge to the
quanitiye of your ffish _

For Aches thomas Blothers Seare Cloath,

Take a quarter of a Pound of White Lead one ounce and a quarter
of Ceruse Three Large leaves of gold halfe a pynt of sallet
oyle put the oyle in a broad Erthen pann skillet set it one the

---

20　This remedy is a bit complicated because of the contributor's ambivalent use of
"one" and "on," and "off" and "of." Her note to "take the cold of one [linen cloth]
and applye it to the forhead and the temples" thus likely means to "take the cold off
on [the linen cloth]"; that is, to warm it slightly.

ffyre a little While then put in the ceruse and stir it
With a stick tel it bee cleare and black, then make it
vpp in Rolles Spread it one a cloath and Lay it one
Warme Where your payne is and let it lye one vntel
it falls off of it Selfe _

92   **To Make a cake Mrs Margaret Melborns Way. Viz**[21]

Take fower pound of flower three pound of Currans Verie Well pickett
and dryed after washed three ounces of fyne shugger a quarter of an
ounce of these spices mace nuttmeggs and synamon fynlye beaten
mingle all these together take tenn Eggs halfe the Whites taken
away halfe a porrenger of ale Last beat these Well together and
put it to your other things, Then take a pynt and quarter of
thick creame boyled melt halfe a pound of sweet butter in it
and let it stand tell it bee but blood Warme then mingle it
With the other things it Will bee soe thin that you must sett
a hoope one your paper and power it into it It must bee
baked in a quick ouen and Eaten New,

**To Cure a quartan ore doble quartan
ague giuen me for Excellent by a Portuges**

Olibenum mastick and safran mixt with one peny
worth of Venice Terpentine of Each 1 d Worth beaten to
powder Lay it one your navell one hower befor the
fitt comes Playster Wayes / Cures all manner of Agues

93   **To Make Juyce of Liquorish Mrs Lakes Waye Viz**

Take a pound of English Licquorish scrape and kutt into small
peeces sliced and bruised and put it into a deepe gallye pott
and put into it Coultsfoott Watter horehound Watter Isope Watter
Scabius Watter of Each of these a pynt Tye vpp the pott verie
closse and sett it in a skillet of Watter let it boyle in *the* Watter
ffower howers then take vpp the pott and take out *the* Licorish
and Beat it verie small in amarble morter put it in to the

---

21 Hand D (comment on 17 (bottom recipe), 92–102, 104–9, 111–23). As the second
recipe in this hand was given to the contributor "by a Portuges" and then the
Spanish recipes follow in this same hand, perhaps this is Mary Granville's
mother's or aunt's hand, and Hand A was that of an ancestor or perhaps even of a
professional scribe, if the manuscript was initially a gift.

pott agayne to the same Licquor and let it boyle in the skillet
of Watter fower howers more then strayne it out into a
silver basson and sett the basson one a skillet of boyling watter
vncoverd that the thinest part of the Licquor maye
evaporate then add to this apound of white shuger
candie finlye beaten and searced and when it hath
melted well together power it in to severale cheynie
dishes and sett them in the sunne ore a stove and stirr
them euerie daye with a wooden knife soe keepe it in
a stove till it is stiffe anough to roule vpp into
knots ore lozenges you Maye add in the making
vpp of it alittle musk ore ambergrisse if you please
and dipp your finger in powder of Licquorish to keepe
the powder from stikinge to the Stuffe drye them in a
stoue ore in the sunne, This is most Excellent
for consumtive coughs of the Lungs –
This Receat Mrs An   finis /
Melcombe procured mee /

94   **To Make Excellent Orenge Watter Viz_**

Take two quarts of the best sack halfe a pynt of
aqua Vita ore brandye Wine then take the Rynds of halfe
a hundred of orenges pare them as thin as possible that
noe White appeare one them then steepe them all Night
ore 12 howers in the said Licquor then still all with a
soft ffyre and your still must bee Luted vpp which
is pasted that noe ayre come in and this water you
must sweetned with shugger candie ore the best Loafe
Shuger as you please the first quart is the best every
time you still /   finis

95   **Mr. Leonard Wilkes Receat for Good chocolate**
          And the mixture it oft to haue of things

A Milliar <.> 1000 Cacaus tosted & soe taken
the husks off Beinge Computted fower pounds Neat
     Requires 3 Ounces of Synamon
               6 Bynillas
               3 pownd of Shugger
If you please to put Muske to it a dram will serue for
ffortye ore sixty pound to put it in your chocolate you must

beat it in a morter with some white shugger and when
your chocolate is redy to bee taken of the stoue you must
mix it
You must haue a great Care in the Tastinge of your
cacao perpetually stirringe of it while it is one the
ffyre for not to burne which if it happen will giue it a
badd tast
You must tost it in anew Cassuela *that* hath not been
vsed befor for not to giue it a badd tast
Yo*ur* Spyces must bee sifted ass fyne as possible to
preuent any settlinge in yo*ur* chocolate dish at the time
When it is taken,
Coll*onel* Jo*hn* Belasyse
had *the* receat with hime   Cadiz 4th 8<u>ber</u> <u>1665</u>

96   **For the Eys Mrs Rebeca Ashan,**
        Excellent Receat of a Powder for them Viz

On ounce of Prepered Tuttye
On ounce of white shugger cady [candy] beaten & searced
On ounce of *the* powder of Skutell Bone ore shell,

To all thes Powders as Much burnt Allum beaten
fyne ass much as will Lye one A groate
Mingle all these together and blow thes powders
once a day into *the* Eyes with a quil,
You must distil some Rotten Pepins and Wash *the*
Eyes with it vppon a ffether the Watter of it,

        To make Inke *the* spanish Waye Viz

☞   To 3 Alcarrasas of Rayne Watter
        2 quartillos of winne vinegre   ☞
        8 ounces of gaules
        4 ounces of Copres
        2 ounces of gomme Arabicke
Stirr thes things frequently in an Erthen
pott for 7 ore 8 dayes & when you vse it

97   **A Receat for any Bruise an Excellent thinge**

Take 1 pynte of ffayre watter 1 pynt of *the* best
winne vinegre 1 handfull of peny royall greene

is best, use drye yff noe other 6 ounces of Lichorish
slyced and kutt small and soe let it simper in the
aboue said Lichour but not to boyle fast, and let the
quart boyle to 1 pynt litle more ore lesse and
boyle it in anew pipkin and soe boyle it vpp
the licqourish you may chew it in your mouth
as longue as the vertue last, take the Licqour
for a bruise, chauffe ore shortness of breath
and alsoe to bringue one to a stomack take
two ore three supps and fast alwayes one
hower ore two after & soe vse it at your pleasure

98   **To Make orenge Bisquit**

Take orenge Peells and watter them all night next
day boyle them verie tender shifftinge the watter
once in the boylinge then scrape out all the white
pulpe leaueinge onlye the redd rynde verie thinn
and beat them verie fyne in a stone morter, to this
you must put all the meat of the orenge first
boylinge it in a silver Tankard in seething watter
a good whyle the boylinge soe is to take away all
the rawnesse, put away all the Juyce as cleere
as you canne without squeesinge ore wringinge pick
owt all the hard skinns and seeds and put the pure
pulpe soe boyled to the beaten orenge peeles and beat
them boath together, but befor you put the pulpe to
the peeles you must waye the peells and to Euerie
halfe pownd of peells you must waye one pownd
and halfe of doble reffynde shugger verie fynlie
beaten, then beat your pulpe peells & shugger all
together untill it bee well mingled, then let it
stand in the morter till the next day, then
beat it well agayne and spred it upon peeces
of glasse ore plates and when it is a little dry
you maye kutt it into whate shape you please
99   And then sett it in your stoue, yff you dry it hard
you must take all the meat cleane out of the
orenges Peells befor you watter them and the meat

soe taken is it which must bee boyled in the said
Tankard

. finis /

Captain William Webbers Receat for the
Cureinge of most paynes & aches
Cadiz 1669

Take a pynt of white ffrench winne in a
pynt pott 10 leaues ore blades of mace 30
spriggs of sweet murgerim Tyde with a thred
put boath these into the said winne & boyle them
vntell ¼ part bee consumed Then strayne it
through a cleane lyninge cloath into
another vesell and beinge strayned retorne
it into the same pynte Pott & reafill it
with good sallet oyle with ·2 spoonfulls
of white shugger, now thus brew them together
Vntill comes to bee noe warmer then

100   can bee suffered to drinke, and then drinke
The same ffastinge in a morninge in your
bedd then off shirt & couer your selfe verie warme
head and all for an hower lyinge fflatt one
your back, Then one hower more with hott
cloathes from the ffyre continewally frotinge
ore wypinge all the bodye ouer then begin by
little and little to take off the cloathes
from the bedd to coole your selfe by degrees
but still wypinge that noe sweat returne
into the body for the space of an hower
and soe repeat the medecin as you
fynd it needfull for a Totall Cure

finis /

101   ### Mrs Rebekah Ash her most
Excellent Powder for the Eyes

Take one ounce of Prepared Tuttye one
ounce of shugger Candye the whitest, beaten
and serced one ounce of the powder of scutlebone

to all these powders as much burnt Allum
beaten fyne as will lye one a groate, *then*
mingle all these together and blow these
powders once a day into the Eyes with a quill
you must still some Rotten Pepins and wash
the Eyes with some of the watter noat that
the burnt alome   London   x
must bee alsoe searced /

Para haser buena Tinta[22]
Cadiz 6 de noviembre, Juan
☞ ### Baqueriso guarda de nauio
que asido M*aest*re de escreuir y contar

Alna a sumbre de agua llouidiza sin sisar
3 oncas de agallas negras rompidas de vn golpe
3 oncas de caparosa
1 vna onca goma arabiga
Mejido todo en esta olla nueba puesta en la sombra por
doce dias y meneada 2 veses al dia con palo de higuera
hondido decrus al Cabo solo, y cita saldra muy buena
Tinta=

102   ### Mr W*illia*m ffens receat to make rare
          ### Inke given mee in Maalaga Ano <u>1646</u>

☞ Take halfe a pound of Gaules blacke & small &
break them in as few peeces as you canne & steepe
them in three pynts of fountayne watter for 2 dayes
then boyle the said watter with the gaules vntill they
consume to the quantitye of one Pynt *then* take the
quantitye of three quarters of an ounce of copris
and put in it & then put it ouer the ffyre agayne vntill
it boyles vpp a little then take it off and put it a cooling
and there will proceed good Inke you may strayne it
yff you please,
          Nota *that*

---

22 Modern English translations of the Spanish recipes are listed at the end of this
    transcription.

said Inke must bee made in anew Erthen Pott and all
the whyle its one the ffyre, & off vntill it bee cold
it must bee stirred; finis;

103   **To make double Incke kalled In ffrench ancre Luisante²³**
this is the way and receat My brother Mr
John wescombe gave mee *in* January 1671

☞   To three pynts of ffrench wine must put one pound of gaules
which you must putt in an Earthen pott Eather in *th*[e] sunne
ore neere *th*e fyer soe *tha*t it may heat without boylinge duringe
three dayes, stirringe it with a stick of a figue tree three
fower or more times a Day=

It will bee good after *th*e Tow ore three dayes Infussion to aproch
it neere *th*e fyer for fower ore fiue howers time, *tha*t it heat w*i*thout
boylinge and afterwards when its Could to Straine it through
a Linnen Cloath= you must afterwards take one ounce of copres
and put into it, w*i*th halfe an ounce of arabicq*ue* gumme, all well
pounded & stirre it from time to time vntill you see *tha*t all is well
dissolued,= & afterwards must adde to it halfe an ounce of
vitriol ^of^
roman and Let it all remaine duringe three fower ore more
dayes, and finally you must straine said Incke a second
time through a Linnen Cloath, & put it in yo*ur* Botle the w*hi*ch
you must Leaue Exposed to *th*e heat of *th*e sunne duringe
6 ore 7 dayes fore *th*e more you Leaue it *th*e more it will
shyne & obseruinge these things you shall haue perfect

[106]²⁴ +   **Recetta de Doña Maria Leal mi**
Comadre p*ar*a hazer Agua de Ambar

9 libras de rossas limpias
½ aroba de vino de Lucena
2 onzas de clauo de comer

---

23 Hand E appears for this one recipe. The note on the page (in Hand D) makes
evident that this hand belongs to Hand D's brother, Mr John Westcomb. See also
"Receta del Capittan Franc*isc*o del Poço ..." on page 110 of this manuscript and the
corresponding note regarding Consul Martin Bisconde.
24 Pages 104–5 are missing from the manuscript. Page numbers are no longer
indicated on recto pages; I have included them here in square brackets.

2 onzas de canela
2 onzas de nues muscada
4 onzas de benxui
1 onza de ostoraxe
1 Puño de Alxusema
½ libra de Cimienta de Treuol[25]
½ quartillo de aguardiente de Cauessa

Todas las especias y lindas[26] refferidas bien
mixadas y Echar todo en vn lebrillo ama=
sando con fuerca de brassos hasta que se aya
embeuido todo el vino y despues echar en vna
tinaxa ô orza tapar muy bien con vn couertor
dexando todo estar nuebe dias y despues sacar
ô destilar todo por Alquitara con poco fuego, y a
los picos de las Alquitaras atar vnos Algodones con
vna poca de Algalia y a cada asumbre de esta

107[27]   Agua se eche vn quartillo y medio de Agua
rozada vn quartillo de agua de azaxar y
medio quartillo de agua de Treuol Todo
esto echar en vn perol ô Olla nueba
muy bien tapada y dexar hervir vn
poco y a esta cantidad se eche vna
adarme de Ambar dos de Algalia y
media de Almiscle y vn papel de
Poluos de Ambar y despues desbaratar
todo esto en vn Almires Caliente y
echar todo esto, en los flascos quando
el agua esta caliente tapandole muy
bien y poner dichos flascos al sol quanto
mas sol mexar estara dicha Agua de
Ambar /
                    Cadiz Año de 1676=

---

25 I.e., trebol (b is written as v, and then the letterform is u).
26 In the original manuscript, the "das" in *lindas* is written as a superscript.
27 Page numbers are no longer underlined from this point on in the original
    manuscript.

[108]   **Mr Hen*ry* Sheers receat Given My lord**
                  marshall howard for pe*r*fummige of
                  lether an Excellent way <u>año 1670 Jan*uar*y</u>

4 ounces of Ambar ⎤
2 – muske   ⎥
1¼ – Ciuit   ⎥
3 – oyle Jesemi   ⎬   Proportion of *the* Ingredients
3 – Gum Dragon   ⎥
2 Pyntes rosse watter ⎦

The Ambar is first beaten small in a morter by it
selfe and afterwards is put to it oyle of Jesemi w*i*th
which it is agayne beaten and mixed verie well ore
Elce the ambar will wast in the Dryinge, beinge well
mixed w*i*th oyle of Jesemi w*hi*ch requires 3 howers labour
they then put to it Gumm dragon disolued in rosse
watter and strayned through a fyne lyning cloath
beinge thus mixed they put to it the Ciuet stirring
and well mixed together then they put in the
muske which is first well beaten in amorter by
it selfe and Temperd w*i*th rosse watter, still
puttinge in and Tempringe the Composition
therewith vntill it bee of the Consistance
                                    of thicke Cream
109   it is Applyde by asmall spunge and one
quarter of one howers Sunne in Madrid, viz
Sol de Membrilla aboute the month
of Jully p*er*fects the worke
the proportions aboue mencioned
        pe*r*fumes viz
7 Cordouans 4 of *the*m beinge Twice layd one
7 kidd skrins for fans
6 payre of weamons Gloves
                           finis /

[110] **Memoria Como se hace El Picadillo de xigoter de Carnero**[28]

Primera mente sepica la carne, y despues selaua bien y lue=
go, sepone en vna caçuela, a sancochar con agua, y su sall, y
vnos axitos picados=
Tenestando medio sancochada sesaca y seba êchando en
vn Almirez, y seba malando, por si hubiere algun nerbe=
suelo en la carne por mal picado, por este camino sepuede facil–
mente quittar,= Lluego se echa en vna caçuela acoçer, ^con
                                    manteca de puerco^ y sele=
éeba suespeçeria de ^nues muscada,^ azafran, Canela, Clauos,
                                    decomer, y Pimienta
Yantes de sacarla, para lamesa, levanten vnas Yemas de
huebos con suagrio de Limon, y sehecha enla Caçuela
todo y semenea, y de alli selleua este Plato de Pica=
dillo ala Messa=
          Receta del Capittan francisco del Poço
          de Rota quela Remitio a Cadiz al Sr
          Consul Don ^n^[29] Martin Bisconde
          a <u>22</u> de Agosto de <u>1682</u> /
Ojo, con su manteca de puerco ô manteca de flanders /

111 **Receta que me dio vn Relixioso en
Orleans a 23 de mayo Juebes <u>de 1675</u>
por cosa muy cierta para matar y destruyr
chinchas en las camas y Paredes**

Azoge, Hiel de Buey ô Vaca, Vinagre
fuerte, y cal, seca;
Misturar todo en Proporsion y battir y despues
de hecha pasta, ponder della alos abuxeros

---

28 Hand F appears for this one recipe. The "autograph" at the bottom likely identifies
the contributor as Captain Francisco del Poço de Rota. He says he gave the recipe
to Consul Martin Bisconde in Cadiz ("Bisconde" likely being a Spanish variant of
"Westcomb," as Martin Westcomb was, as stated in the textual introduction, Consul
of Cadiz, and "w" is never used in Castilian). Does this mean that Martin Westcomb
temporarily had the manuscript in his possession? The insertions and note at the
bottom of the page are in Hand D, and are in another colour of ink.
29 It seems a correction to the handwriting (not the word itself) was attempted here;
this correction is in Hand F.

delas paredes y en qualquier parte dela cama
que estubieren y matara todas las chinchas
sin criar chincha alguna adonde dicha pasta
aya estado, esta receta es Verdadera <..>[30]

[120][31]   white Cerus two ounces, Liturage one ounce myrrhe
halfe an ounce, Lapis Calaminarus halfe an ounce
Champhir a quarter of an ounce, white Lead halfe
an ounce, Bolus halfe an ounce, frankincence
halfe an ounce, Turpentine a quarter of an ounce
Rosin a quarter of an ounce, Bees wax foure ounces
oyle of Roses foure ounces, all the things that are
hard must be prepared in fine Pouder, take the
Rosin, Oyle, & wax in an Earthen Pipkin, & boyle
them over a soft fire, then put in all your other
things keeping it Stirring, and Let it boyle a quarter
of an houre, then make it up with cold watter, into
roles, when you vse it must be spread thick vpon
Leather, Prickt with the point of a kniue before
you spread it, one plaster will last a fourtnight
wipeing it euery day,
if it be an old wounde wash it euery day when
you dress it with this watter, a pint of running watter
two or three spriggs of rue, three ounces of honny
a Litle allome, Let all these boyle together softly, till
halfe be consumed, it must be hot when you vse
it,
> A most Excellent Plaister for all kind of
> wounds or old zoars, this receat I had from my sister
> Melborn in Essex the 12th of June 1683=

121   **Para Mejorar y Conseruar Vynillas**

Majar 4: ô 6 vynillas para aliñar vn ciento y avn
ducientos, y en vna poca de Agua tibia desleir dichas
Vynillas Junto con vna poca de azeite bueno ô de Al=
mendras Dulces, y batido muy bien esto, entonces
se vntaran ô fletaran las Vynillas con este ingredien^te^

---

30   This might be "&c" or "Receta."
31   Pages 112–19 are missing from the original manuscript.

caliente poniendose vn dedal de Ante sobre el dedo
pulgar y passandolos vno a vno con el Jugo de dicho
Ingrediente ambos lados de la Vynilla con
este Beneficío se purificaran y temaran nuebo
Jugo, lustre y olor; despues de esto hecho
se tendran al Ayre par vna ora ô dos
sueltas porque atandolas luego se pondrían
majosas y de peor calidad de lo que estauan
antes de beneficiarlas

recetta del Sarjento de vn Ojo Gordian sentura
Fernandes Vecino de Xeres / Cadiz 18
de Settiembre de 1685 = que vino en la flotta

[122]
Cap*tai*n felpes of bristoll his receat given Mr John Emilli in Cadiz, *the* month of Jan*ua*ry 1687 for the Voydinge of Grauel & stone Experienced vpon hime selfe   vizt

Take watter cresses beat & strayne them at y*ou*r need
& drink the quantity of halfe a pynte mixt w*ith* some w*hite*[32]
french wynne ore renish
 thes watter cresses are called in Spanish Verros
 of which s*ai*d nation often times Eate as a good
 Sallet as others Eat lettices
s*ai*d Felpes lerned & procured from *the* mours when
hee was a slaue in Barbery Then much tormented
w*ith* s*ai*d Payne Till hee applyde This remedy w*hic*h
vnder God Did cure hime;

123
Remedio para Affixar Muelas y Dientes vizt

Tomar Dos quar*ti*llos de vino
dos ô Tres coxollos de Torbisco macho
dos ô Tres Agallas
cuatro quartos de sangre de Drago
dos o tres coxollos de romero

---

32   The abbreviated form here is w^{t}.

que quesen todo esto hasta que quede en la mitad
reducido y tibio enjuagarse la boca a discretion
hasta que di*c*has muelas ô dientes esten firmes &c³³
Cadiz <u>22</u> de Junio <u>de 1685</u> en el Officio del
Se*ñ*or Lucas de Molina vn Se*ñ*or liz*encia*do me dio esta
memoria ô receta &C

[124]   **To Make a seed cake Mrs Tauerners way³⁴**

To a pound of flower you must take a pound of butter,
you must drye your flower very well, then rub your butter
into it, then take six spoonfulls of the best alle yest and
twelue egges takeing away 6 whites beat all this very well
together with your hand adding as much cream blood warm
as will weet it, when it is well beaten alltogether you must
couer it with a clean cloath and lett it stand by the
fire to risse about half an hower then take a pound of
sugar carroways and strew them in with your hand mixing
them well together then put it into a hoop with paper
vnder it which with the hoop must be buttered that the
cake stick not then tye the paper closse vp to the
hoop that the cake run not out at the edges, it must
stand in the ouen a bout an hower, the ouen must be
pritty quick and you must haue a care of scorching it.

125   **A very good reseipt for Beef steaks**

You must take the tenderest part of the Beef and cutt
it very thin and beat them very well then strew them
with a little peper and salt, then take some butter
and put it in the frying pan with a pritty larg onion
holle, you must stirr the butter till tis melted that it
dos not oyle, then put in your steaks which must be
kept shakeing all the time they are ouer the fire, and
you must keep them turning, your fire must not be rash
and when they be fryed enough haue the yolks of 2
or 3 egges beaten and mixt with some clarritt wine

---

33 I assume this to be a variant of &c, although it appears &ᵃ.
34 Hand G (this recipe and the next one) might belong to Mrs Taverner herself.

and Juce of leamon and a little nuttmege which putt
into the pan to the steaks takeing out the onion
so toss it vp till it be thick and then serue it up

To make a carrett pudding[35]

Take *the* quantity of three large Carrotts &
boil *the*m tender in Beef broth, then beat *the*m
in a stone mortar to a paist, sweeten it w*i*th
half a pound of sugar or more, some salt &
the greatest part of a nutmeg, a little Orang
flower water, then grate a penny loaf & sift
it thro a ~~sive~~ cullender, then put a pint of
cream scalding hott to your bread, & when it
is a little cool, ~~mil~~ mingle six eggs well beat
& soe put all into *the* mortar together ~~to~~ to beat
[126]   *the*n put it into a Dish with puff paist & soe
~~balk~~ Bake it

A Plain Bak'd pudden

Take a two penny loaf grate it or slice it
thin & scald it in a quart of Milk, *the*n before
it is quite cold put to ^it^ three quarters of a
pound of Beef suet finly shred,[36] a whole nut=
=meg, some salt, three quarters of a pound of
sugar, a quarter of a pint of sack, eight eggs
and soe Butter your pan & Bake it _

To make a Rice pudding

Take *the* ~~thr~~ third part of a Pound of rice
flower, & put it into a quart of new milk
sett it over *the* fire, & keep it stirring till it
is as thick as you wou'd mix a pudding, beat six
eggs, & putt *the*m in with spice, & stir *the*m all to=
=gather soe put it into a dish, & half an hour
will Bake it, if you please put marrow, or
half a pound of butter.

---

35 Hand H (this recipe through 127, 202 lower recipe, 203 lower recipe, 204, 206 finishes
    lower recipe begun by Hand O, possibly 208, 233, 239 lower recipe) is a very messy,
    perhaps shaky, italic hand with no indication of the identity of the contributor.
36 The first letter of this word is uncertain, although "shred" makes sense.

127 ~~To ming~~[37]
To pickle Artichoaks

Cut *the* Bottoms clean from *the* leaves & Choak &
lay *the*m to steep in salt & water for an hour att
least, prepare a pickle with *the* best white wine
vinegar, Horse Radish & Jamaica pepper, if
you please a g clove or two of garlick, when
your pickle is boild, wipe *the* bottoms of y*our*
artichoaks dry, & *the*n put *the*m in *the* pickle
& give *the*m a gentle boil, & *the*n pour off
your pickle & lett it stand till it is luke
warme & *the*n pour it agin upon your
Bottoms & soe lett it remain.

140[38]   ## To make Orange flower Cakes[39]

Dip your suger in watter & set it over a quick
fire Let it boyle til it is almost suger again then
put to, it three spoonfulls of water to the quantity
of half a pound of suger Let it boyle til it is clear
then put in your Orange flowers & Let them boyl^e^
up then pour it out on Silver or china & dry theme
ᴏ^i^n a stove til they come out +

To make them another way

Take a pound of Orange flowers the leaves[40] only
melt 4 pou^n^d of double refined suger with a little
water over *the* fire & when *the* suger is clear and
that you find it begins to candy cut the orange
flowers very small & put them imediately into
the suger and keep them allways stirring take
the pan of *the* fire and spread *the*m all on a great dish
and put *the*m to dry in a place where sweetmeats
are commonly kept putting ^a^ chaffing dish of
                                                                coales

---

37 This title is partially rubbed out, rather than struck through.
38 Pages 128–39 are missing from the manuscript.
39 Hand I (140–1, 153 top recipe, 236 lower recipe) is perhaps that of a child; the letter
    forms are rounded and careful.
40 One would think that this must mean the petals, although the recipe "to preserve
    Orange flowers" below (146) does seem to call for leaves.

141   near, *the*m you must make *the* surrup run al over *the*
dish, when they are almost dry breaek them in
peices and turn *the*m, heap *the* smalest peices one upon
another and ^make^ the surrup run between both–

142   **Lemon Cream**[41]

Take a large lemon & pare of *the* yelow skin as thin as
tis posible ~~then~~ then take *the* skin par'd of to *the* white & put it
into allmost 3 quarters of a pint of spring watter & lett it
lye 3 hours *then* take ~~seven~~ ^nine^ whites of eggs & beat them very
                          well
squse *the* juice of four lemons & half a spoonfull of Orange flower
watter, & halfe a pound of duble refiend suger beaten, stire *the*m
together, w*he*n *the* suger is melted straine it through a tifiny sive
into a sliver skilet or stone pipkin sett it over a quick fire &
keep it sitrring all one way till be as thick as cream *then* ~~tha~~
take it of *the* fire, stirri^n^g it tell it is cold, so put it into
glases.

143   **To make Raison Wine for Elder Mrs**
            Pain of Glosters Way[42]

Five pound of Maligo Raisons clean
pick'd & Chop'd small to one gallon of
water, wine measure; boyl the water &
let it stand 'till it is blood Warm, then
pour it to the Raisons keeping it stir'd
every day for fourteen days, then strain
it off, & put in a Pint of Elder Juice
to every Gallon; & Stir it well togather
then let stand eight Days in the Vate,
then pour it off from the Settlement &
Tun it, & when it hath done Working

---

41   Hand J (142, 166b–71, 181 lower recipe, 184) also seems to be a child's hand, again
     because of the multiple corrections and the light lines on the paper.
42   Hand K (143, 145, 153 lower recipe, 155 top recipe, 182, possibly 192 lower recipe,
     201 comment, 214 comment, 234 middle recipe, 241, 305–6) might be that of
     Mrs Gloster herself, to whom the first recipe is attributed. This hand's frequent
     reappearance in the manuscript suggests that Mrs Gloster was a friend of the family
     or at least a regular acquaintance.

put a Tile Stone on the Bung or the
bung: Slightly In 'till it is fine then
Bottle it off: you must prepare
the Juice as follows[43]

[144]   **To pot Beef[44]**

Take a good ~~hand~~ fat buttock of beef weigh=
ing two stone, a pound of common salt; two oz
of salt petra, 1 oz of pepper a large nutmeg, half
an oz of all spice, a quarter of an ounce of
mace. Beat your spices and salt, & mix 'em all
together very well, & rub your beef well with *that*
quantity, let it lye in itt three nights & 3 days
then bake itt all night with bread, Larding your
beef with a pound of fatt Bacon, & *the* marrow
of two Large bones. put your beef in a pott *that*
will hold itt laying *the* bones at *the* top, & put
in a pint & half of pump water, after your
beef is bak'd take it out from *the* pott & drein
it from *the* gravy and put it into *the* potts
you design to keep it in breaking it smal
with a spoon, & as you break it put in enou*gh*
of it's own fat to ~~keep~~ ^make^ it moist then flat it
145   down even, and as close as you can. When
'tis cold Butter it up for your use. be sure to
pott it hott

**To keep the Juice of Elder to
make Wine at any time**

Pick the Berrys off the Stalks, then
put them in a Pot & draw the Juice

---

43 The recipe to prepare the juice, however, does not follow.
44 Hand L (possibly inside cover first inscription, 144, 180, 181 top recipe, 189–92 top
recipe, 193–202 top recipe, 203 top recipe, 214 title, possibly 216, 236 top recipe,
237–9 top recipe, 240) contains a certain amount of variation, but the majuscule
T, ampersand, and ascender on minuscule d suggest that this is one hand. As this
hand collaborates a few times with Hand O, and also includes "Lady Katharine
Windham's Receipt. / Powder for Convulsion fitts" (239), this might be the hand of
Mary Granville. As noted above, Lady Catherine Wyndham and Mary's brother-in-
law were certainly acquaintances.

in an Oven, then Strain off the
Juice but let it run as long as it
will that you do not bruise the Berrys,
then put it into Wide Pans like
Milk Pans, & in a day or Two there
will be on the Top a perfect thick barm,
which you must scum off, then when no
more rises put it into a Bell-Mettle
Kettle, & boyle it & Scum it as long as
any rises, after which the Juice
will be as fine as any Wine, then pour
it out into a Pan & when 'tis quite Cold
Bottle it & Cork it but not too Close

[146]   ### To preserve Orange flowers[45]

Take *the* Largest flowers you can get, and
to a pound of leives take four pounds of
treeble refined Sugar, bruise the leives a
little between a Napkin, and boyle them
in a good deal of water till they are tender,
if the water grow yallow in the boyling
change it for more, which is likewise boyling
hot, then take your sugar and dip it in
fair water, and put it over *the* fire till his
melted, into a syrrop and twill scum
and when tis cold put your flowers, into
it, cover it close and let it stand all night
then boyle all together till the syrrop
is thick and put it into Glasses or pots
you must boyle *the* flowers in silver or
pewter, and very quick, &.c

147   ### To pickle Walnutts Mrs Mary Hills Way[46]

Take an hundred of *the* Largest french Walnuts
at the beginning of July, before they are hard
shell'd, just scald 'em that *the* first skin may

---

45 Hand M (146) is unique in the manuscript. It is careful and perhaps a bit shaky, and
the page has been finely lined to help facilitate neatness.
46 Hand N (this recipe only) might belong to Mrs Mary Hills herself.

rub off them, throw them into brine *that* will
bear an Egg, for 9 or 10 days changing them evry
other day & keep them close from the Air *then*
dry 'em & make your pickle of good Vinegar,
black pepper, Ginger, of each one ounce,
cloves, mace, & Nutmeg of each half an ounce
beat the Spice *with* a Large Spoonful of
Musterd Seed, boiling your Spice in *your* pickle
put *your* pickle on *them* boiling hot 3 or 4
times. If you see occasion, be sure to keep
them close Stop'd. A Spoonful of this
pickle is good in any sawce. 3 or 4
cloves of Garlick do*es* well if you do not
dislike the tast. two quarts of Vinegar
to this quantity.

[150]⁴⁷   **the Queen of hungarys water⁴⁸**

take two Gallons of the best brandy Ten pound of
Rosemary flowers let them steep in a new well glase^ed^
e^a^rthen pot with a cover to it four or five dayes either
in a warme place or in the sun keep it so close stoped
that it loose none of *the* sp^i^rits and then distill it in a
limbeck *the* head being very close passted on a & as you
draw it of in order write *the* first second and third if you
use it outwardly for baithing it must with *the* strongest=

A receit to pic^k^le oysters

open *the* quantity that you designe to pickle into a basin
wash *the* oysters in the liquor very well then strain it
through a fine sive or thin cloath put the oysters into
the liquor again seasoning them with whole white peper
& mace according to your taste put them over a very quick

---

47 Pages 148–9 are missing from the manuscript.
48 Hand O (this recipe, 152, 154, 206 beginning of recipe, 207, 209, 210 top recipe,
    214 body of the recipe, 215, 216 title, 234 top recipe) is also perhaps that of a child;
    the spelling includes multiple corrections, and again the light lines would have
    facilitated neatness for a young writer. The title of the recipe on 214 was written
    by Hand L and a comment is added by Hand K; the recipe on 216 is completed by
    Hand L. This might be the child hand of Anne.

151

fire and just let them boile up then separate the liquor ^from^
the oysters and put to *the* quantity of a quart three spoonffulls
of Good white wine vinegar and give it a boile or two
over *the* fire then when *the* liquor and oysters both are cold
put them together adding half a dozen bay leaves
if you finde the liquor two fresh you may add a little
salt according to your taste and pray observe they
wont keep above two months

[152]

To pickle musarunes

Take your musarunes wash and Clean them well
in fair water & salt with a peice of flanell when dun
put them into a pipkin or silver skilett and boyl
them fast up in watter & salt then take *the*m out &
and put them into Cold watter till cold then take
them out and lay them upon a Clean Cloath till
dry then to prepare your pickle take good vine vinegar
according to your Quantity of musarunes put into it
mace cloves Ginger black pep^p^er and a nutmeg a
little bay salt & when well boyled let it stand ~~tl~~ till
Cold then your nutmeg will slice also put in your
spice into the musarunes and cover them with your
pickle tye them down close put oyl upon them if
you think fit

153

To make Mrs Looks Balsom

Take a pound of *the* leafe barrow Hog[49] Take of
the[50] skin and beat it well with Rose watter then
Take two ounces of stone Pitch two ounces of
bees waxe a pint of *the* best Oyle Incorporate
these over a soft fire till they be all in one body
Straine it through a cloth then put to it 4 ounces
of oyle of St Johns one dram of spermesity give it
a warm over *the* fire to mixt *them* well put it up ~~un~~
in a pott with two grains of ambergreese–

---

49 In other words, the lard of a barrow pig; see "leaf" and "barrow" in the Glossary.
50 In the original manuscript, thorn is followed by a crossed-out e, with the
    superscript e then placed above.

To make Fritters

To a Pint of Small beer two Eggs
some Ginger & Salt & make it
into a thin batter with flower
let it Stand Stirring it often a
good while before you make them,
you may Slice your apples or
Chop them.

[154]   ### To make wiggs

Take 7 pound of flower & 6 or 7 eggs & a
pint & halfe of good ale yeast put into the
flower some ginger finely pounded then rub
in the yeast and eggs lightly then make it up
into a light past with 2 pound of butter melted
in some new milk just so hot as to melt the
butter then let it stand covered warm by *the* fire
for halfe a hour to rise then you must werk
in half a *pound* of pouderd suger mixed with one
ounce of caraways seeds–

155   Take toddy arack and bath watter
an equal quantity Juice of
oronge sweetend with white
suger drinck it hott & tis
amost sovereighn medicin
for the Colick–

To make Shrub Mrs Carryl[51]

Take *the* rinds of 10 Lemons very thinly
pared & also the juice Strain'd, put both
into 3 quarts of Brandy, & let it stand close
cover'd in ^a^ warm place 2 Days, then boile for
half an hour 3 pints of Spring Water; when
so boiled put to it one pound ^& quarter^ of double
refin'd Sugar, boile it another half hour
& Scum it very well, put it hot to *the* Brandy
& Lemons, & let it stand close cover'd about

---

51   Hand P (this recipe, 234 lower recipe) might belong to Mrs Carryl herself.

30 hours, then strain it thro' a jelly Bag &
put it into Bottles, & when it has stood a
fort'night strain it again into pints–

[156]   **To make *the* red Powder**[52]

Cardus	The roots of Elicampain
Draggons	Gentian
pimpernell	Tormentill of
Scabius or Devills	each a handfull
bitt; of each a handfull	

Slice the roots & shred *the* herbes &
steep *the*m in a quart of good strong
white wine 24 houres or more close
cover'd; take a pound of bolearmonak.
the cleanest from filth and made into
fine powder put itt in a pewter dish
& strain as much of *the* wine from *the*
~~herbs~~ herbes as will wett it as thick
as a hasty pudding. sett itt in the
Sunn and strirr itt 3 or 4 times a
                               Day
157   and as it drys put in more till all
is strain'd hard from *the* herbes then
put in an ounce of Methridate an
ounce of harts horn in powder &
a dram of Saffron in powder or
desolved in a Little of *the* Juce and
mix it all well to gether and when
itt is pretty stiff make it into balls
and dry it in *the* Sunne /

[158]   **A Powder to be given to a woman
in Labour.**

Take some grains of parradice and
the like quantity of Saffron and

---

52 Hand Q (156–66) offers a number of recipes in a loose, messy hand with decorative
capital letters. The & sign sometimes looks like X, but I have used & throughout.
There is no indication of the identity of the contributor.

so of date stones and ^of Cum*m*ine^ as much as all
the rest make all into fine powder and
if the Labour stops give of this powder
15 graines & 10 graines of Myrrh in
powder in caudle or alebury; if it do's
not do give the same quantity once
in two houres; but be sure *the* child
come right for 'tis a great forcer &
ought not to be given But when there
is great Occasion, if *the* after paines
trouble her, give her one dose: ~~of this~~
if you would keep this powder by you make
it up in balls with harts horn Jelly &

159   Dry itt and so itt will keep as
Long as you please /

Docter Lowers bitter Infusion

Take filling of Steel two ounces
infused in milk watter one quart
Gentian watter compound 8 ounce's,
wormwood watter compound 6 ounces,
digest itt cold for 16 Days *then* power
it off from *the* Steel, *then* add to the
Liquor Gentian root half a scruple,
the tops of Century one pugill,
Roman wormwood half a pugill
Cardus Bennedictus seed 2 dram's;
then Digest it again six houres *then*
bottle itt. /
    Take 6 spoonfulls night &
                        morning

[160]   ### To make a very good Plumb Cake

Take seven pound of Flower dried att
the fire: put to it a pound of Lofe Sugar
an ounce of mace and a Little Salt, the
yolks of 30 Eggs *the* whites of 14 well
beaten; 3 pints of yeast, & a Little
orange flower watter a little brandy if
you please. & some musk & amber
greece *that* must be steep'd over night then

take a good quart of sweet Creame,
Set it on *the* fire; & put in five pound
of butter to melt, put *the* Eggs & yeast
through a hare sive into *the* flower & on
the other side *the* Cream with the butter
that was melted in itt warm; mix alto=
=gather very well like a stiff pudding &
throw a little flower on itt & set itt
to the fire about a quarter of an
hour

162[53]　hour till you see itt rise then take
12 pound of Corrinths wash'd prick't &
warmed at the fire. work *the*m into
the Cake pritty quick with some Cittron
and Orange peal if you please then
butter yo*u*r hoop and power itt in,
Set itt in a quick oven and bake itt
about an hour.

To make an orange Tourt or Puding

Take a Cevill orange peal: boyle it
very tender then scrape out all *the*
skinns *the*n put it in a marble mortar
with half a pound of Butter & half
a pound of Double refinn'd Sugar;
beat *the*m well togather till itt be Like
a past: *the*n grate in almost two Naples
Bisketts & take *the* yolks of 7· Eggs.
the whites of 5 & a very little Cream
beat them well & put altogeather w*i*th
the juice of an orange and orange
flower watter to bake itt half an

[163]　hour with puff past crust under and
over itt roll'd very thinn.
Let not yo*u*r oven be too hott.

53　A page-numbering error occurs in the manuscript; the number "161" is missing,
and now even numbers appear on verso pages again.

A Receipt for a Cough.

Take 4 quarts of Spring watter, 2 quarts
of bran; a thick marsh mallow ~~Leaf~~ root
2 ounces of green Liquorish; boyle these
to two quarts strain it & sett itt on
the fire again; To every quart of this
Liquor put a pound of double refin'd
Sugar; a pound of malago reasons
& an ounce and half of Cinamon
Let itt boyle very Slowly a quarter of
an hour; then strain itt again & Drink
of this every night after *the* person is
in bed; a Tea dish full made ^prety^ hott and
as much in *the* morning before they
                                        rise

164   ### To Cure a Flux infaliably

A handfull of Oak bark 2 sheets
of the whitest paper about ~~of~~ an
ounce of Double refin'd sugar boyl'd
in a pint of spring watter then
strain it and put a Large wine glass
full of right french Clarret and
give a glass of it 3 or 4 times a
Day.

To Cure Deafness

Essence of Castor dropt 2 or 3 drops
into the ear and *the*n put a Little
wool to be had in Devonshire street
at the Golden head.

[165]   ### To Make spanish Pap

Take Three spoonfulls of fine rice
flower ~~to~~ ^4^ yolks of Eggs 6 spoonfulls
of Sugar Two of Orange flower watt*er*
mix these Together & put them
into a quart of Cream & set them
on *the* fire stirring of itt till itt
comes to ^a^ reasonable thickness then
put them into cups or glasses.

166   **To make Goosberry wine**

Take 12 pound of green goosberry's as
they are ready to turn and beat them
in a mortar; then to every twelve pound
of Goosberry's put a gallon of rain water
let it stand all night then strain it
out and to every gallon of water put
4 pound & half of ten penny Sugar
& let it stand another night and then
let it run through a Flannel bagg and
then put it into your vessel & to every
ten gallons put a quarter of an ounce
of Issinglass cut small into your Vessel
when it is fine Bottle it.

[166b]⁵⁴   **A receipt to cure any Infir^la^mation or**
                Sweling In the Mouth or throat
                   To make the mouth water

Take of   Rose mary   ⎫   each of these 1
              Red Sage   ⎪   handfull or the like
              Plantan Leaves ⎤   ⎪   quantity of each &
              & roots together ⎦ ⎪   lett them be Clean
              Egrimony   ⎪   wash'd inConduitt or
              Alehoofe   ⎪   spring watter – thro' 3
              Scabius   ⎬   waters Then put them
              Sincfield   ⎪   in a new Earthen
              Wood bine Leaves ⎪   Pipkin which you must
              Bramble Leaves   ⎪   keep one porpose for this
              Cullobine Leaves ⎪   use & put as much
              Ground Ivy Leaves ⎪   conduitt or spring
              Horstale   ⎪   watter to them as will
              Issope   ⎭   just cover them, &
                                    boyle them upon a
                                    moderate fire about
                                    5 hours

---

54   There is a pagination issue here, as two consecutive verso pages are numbered 166
     and 167.

Then take the herbs Clean from *the* water
and take of the best Hony 1 pound to
each Gallon & one quart of water wine
measure of *the* best Common Allum to Each
167   Gallon 1 ounce Then put it upon a soft fire
about a quarter of an hour Then strain it
Thro' a Close hair Cive into an earthen pan
or steen and lett it stand twelve hours untill
it settles or becomes fine, Then you may eather
draw it of from the Lee in a steen or into
Botles for you use Keep it alwais well stopt

To use the several things here mentioned
Take this Method_

Take four or five spoonfulls more or less as
The Malady may require it about blood warm
then take a fine bit of alinen rag & drip it in the
water lapp it upon the end of one of your
fingers and put as much of *the* powder as will
lie upon itt then goe tenderly & touch the
place agrieved as near as you posibly can
& shake of *the* powder upon itt & then take a
Serringe full of *the* water & force itt
as strongly as you Can to *the* place agriev'd
[168]   and let the party Hold it in there
mouth, and gargle it upon the place then
spitt it out into a bason this doe three or
four times together then let them wash there
mouth very well with the water after it
then take a ~~linnen~~ Peice of fine flanel
not new and dipp itt in some of *the* oyntment
very warm^+^ [55] as posibly the agrieved person can
suffer itt & bath *the* out side of *the* place
agrieved very well then take your flanel
& wring itt preety dry & pin itt under
the chin & keep the place very warm
then aply the Plaister as derected and
lett the party Eat a porringer of white

---

55   The meaning of the small cross above this word is unknown.

bread & milk sweetned with double refine
sugar & put a good peice of fresh butter
in itt then goe to bed and ley lay the head
prity high & lay upon the side least agriev'd
Take care your bare hand or finger doe not
touch *the* place agrieved either inside or out
side

169   **To make the pouder**

Take   one ounce of the best white sugar
            Candy of ordinary allum halfe an
            ounce Burn'd and as much Bolearmorick
            as will just couler it red & beat
            them together to a fine powder
            then Cift them through a fine
            Cive & soe use it Keep it dry
            in a box or Gally pot Close
            cover'd

Observe,   The water & powder are suffitient
            to cure any sore mouth or gumms
            or any inflamation in the throate
            where no impostumation does apear
            but if your throat mouth or gummes be
            swelld or impostumated it will require
            the use of *the* plaister and oyntment
            following

[170]   **To make the Plaister**

Take   Two ounces of cumminseed bruse
            them very well in a Glass morter
            & put one handfull of *the* finest
            Rye flower you can gett to *the* seed
            then mingle them together with the
            best white wine vinegar untill itt
            be like a paste then spread itt
            between a sheet of halfe pound
            brown paper for each plaister (make *them*
            both of a size proportianable to *the*
            persons head *who* is to use them) Then
            bake them in a fire shovel untill

they are pritty dry & put one of them
to *the* Gnape of *the* neck and the other
to the mold of *the* head & binde them
on with a fillet that they may not
remove.

171   **To make the oyntement**

Take   A quarter of a pint of *the*
best oyle of olives or Sweet
oyle, one fowrth part of a Rolle
of Diacalum Slice itt very thin
& put itt to the oyle then Sett
itt upon a soft fire untill the
Diacalum be melted & put itt
in an Earthen vesel to keep for
use.

[180]⁵⁶   **Mrs Badge's Plaister**

Take ^of^ the best white Rosin you can get one pound
beat yo*u*r Rosin & to a pound you must take 3
ounces of the best yellow bees-wax Slice it into
Just as much sallad oyl as will melt itt. When 'tis
melted put in yo*u*r Rosin and *the*n put in two ounces
of Common Black pitch Symber it together 'till
'tis all disolv'd *the*n make it up in Roles for yo*u*r
use_

To Make french Bread

Make your milk a little warmer than new milk
to 3 pound of flower half a pint of ale yeast, a
very little salt. mix these together not very stiff
when it begins to rise put it into little wooden dishes
& Let it rise in the dishes when *the* oven is ready
(which must be pretty quick) Turn *the*m upon *the* peal *the*
bottom's upwards. & set *the*m not too close in the oven.
When bak'd rasp or grate of *the* out-sides. flow'r the
Dishes well before you put *the* Bread into Them

---

56   Pages 172–9 are missing from the manuscript.

181   **To make Black Currant Wine**

You must boile your Water & Sugar toge–
=ther a good while till you have scum'd it
*tha*t it looks very clear. then pour it boiling
hot upon your Currants and let itt stand
'till you think it of a good Colour *the*n pour
itt off without pressing the berries much. And
tun itt up. If you find itt don't work of it's self
in a week's time or such a mater bung it up
close. When 'tis fine and *the* sweetness pretty
much Lost bottle itt off. to each gallon of
Water. two pound & half of Sugar. and about
<˃ ^2^ quarts of Currants. You must not bruise
them.

                     To make a potato puding

Take 2 pound of potatos & boyle tender then beate them in
a stone mortar with 3 quarters of a pound of butter till they
are well mixt then add a quarter of a pinte of Sack a
little Cinamon & 8 eggs half an hour will bake itt

[182]   **To Make Puding for a Hare
                       or Stuffing For Veel.**[57]

Take to a penny whit Lofe a quarter of
a pound of beefe Suet or if you please
half bacon Shred them very fine a little
Spinage winter Savory & time a little
onion or Shalot Shred fine mix all these
to geather in a dish Season it with
peper & Salt then Slice in *the* bread &
pore in as much boyling milk as will
make it pretty moyst cover it Close &
lett it Stand till it is almost Cold &
then brake in two Eggs & beat it very
well togeather /

---

57 This line has been added in pencil. In his book *The Pencil: A History of Design and
Circumstance*, Henry Petroski notes that graphite was known and used in England
since at least 1586. Rod-shaped pieces were wrapped in paper or string, or pushed
into hollow twigs or reeds (46–7).

183   **To make plum porige**[58]

Take alarge leg of Beef & Cragg
off mutton to 4 gallons of water a litle
salt in the boyling when the meat is
boyl'd to rags strain it off & sett it by
till it is Cold. the take off all the fatt
& sett it over the fire & putt into it
the quantetty of 3 penny white loafs
gratted & lett it boyle halfe an hour
then put in 2 pound of Currants *that* are
plumped in watter & when they have bin
in a quarter of an hour put in 4 pou'd
of reasons w*hen* they are halfe boyled put in
2 *pound* of pruents & a handfull of salt then take
2 *pound* of suger 1 quart of red wine 1 pint of sack
1 ounce of cinamon 1 nutmeg halfe a quarter
of an ounce of mace 12 or 14 cloues
[183b]   & a little Jemeca peper Beat & sift[59]
all this spice & mingle it with y*our*
wine & suger give it but one boyle
before you use it /

To make minced pyes

To a pound of neats tongs take
^one^ 2 *pound* & halfe of beef suett a pound of
Currants & halfe a pound of stoned
reasons Cutt small one quarter of a p*ound*
of pruents cut also; halfe an ounce of
cinamon halfe a nutmeg 4 or 5 blades
of mace 7 or 8 cloues & alitle Jemeca
peper beat & sift all this spice take ~~fore~~
4 ounces of ^candid^ orenge peale 2 of candid
citron 2 of canded lemon peale *the* rine
of a fresh lemon shred very fine 5 or 6
pipins halfe a pint of sack verjuice & a very
litle suger

---

58 Hand R (183a&b; see pagination issues) appears for two recipes, without any
    indication of the identity of the contributor.
59 There is a pagination issue here, as two consecutive verso pages are numbered 183
    and 184.

184   **The Milk Cordial Water**

Take a Gallon of red Cows milk in the month of may
and distill it in a cold still, then take the water of the milk
so distill'd & add to it Sixty Snails bruised shells and all. also
one handfull of bettony & as much scabius, Houndstongue,
                                                    Liverwort
clary & baume & Eringo roots Five Grains of leaf Gold a quarter
of an ounce of Alkarmes the Gelly that is ~~betwixt~~ betwixt *the* foot
& leg of beef, one handfull of Dates one handfull of prunellos
4 ounces of Double refin'd sSugar Then distill it altogether.
Drink Six spoonfulls at a time first & last~

                       The Plague Water

Take of Sage, Salendine, Rosemary, Rue Wormwood
Mugworth Pimpernell Dragons Scabius Egrimony Baume,
Scordium Centory Cardus Bettony Rosasolis of each a good
handfull, Angelica-roots, Benjamin = roots, Turmindall Ledoary
Liquoras, of each half an ounce slice the roots & wash the
Herbs & dry them then chop them & put *the*m all together into
8 pints of white-wine if *your* wine be small put 20 to it & steep
them in it Two Days & Nights close stopt then put it into an
ordinary Still, & so Distill it_

[185]   **To Make Queen Cakes ~**[60]

One pound of Butter, one pound of
flower, one pound of Sugar; you must
beat the ~~Beat~~ Butter and Orange
flower Water half an hour, then put
the yolks of six eggs and beat it
together, then stir yo*u*re sugar and flower
and Butter well together, then add the
white of an Egge thereto, and set it
into the Oven, but not too hot– To this
Quantity a q*uarte*r of an ounce of mace. sift
some double refin'd Sugar over them just
before you put 'em into the Oven ~

---

60 Hand S (185, 186 lower recipe–188) has a particularly decorative majuscule T; there
    is no indication as to the identity of the contributor.

186   **To Make Elder Wine**[61]

Take 20 *pound* of Malago Raisons, quick rub & Chop them;
put to *th*em 5 Gallons of water, let *th*em stand 10 day's, then
strain *th*e Liquor from *th*em and put into it 2 quarts of the
juice of Elders^=^berries *th*at are full ripe, having been infused
in hot water in a jugg or baked in an Oven, when it is
Cold put it into *th*e Liquor, stirring it 'till it is well mixt
then strain it put it <....> in y*our* Barrell & let it stand 6
weekes before you bottle it, put into each Bottle a little
Loaf Sugar /

                     To preserve Mulberries

To a pint of Mullberries, you must have, two pound of
Loaf Sugar w*hi*ch you must dip in water, & make a thin
Syr^r^ope, when you have Scum'd it, put in y*our* Mullberries
which you must only Scald, and set them by in the
Syrrope, 'till next day, & then boile 'em Moderatly
and set them by for y*our* uses ~

[187]   **To Make a Cake**

Take six pound of flower, six pound of
Currants, 2 pound of Butter, 20 Eggs & use
but 8 of *th*e whites of em' one pound of sugar a
pint & half of new yest, Cinamon; Nutmegs & mace
of each a q*uar*ter of an ounce, a quart of Cream
w*hi*ch when ready to boile take off *th*e fire & slice
*th*e butter into itt. & stirr it together, let it
stand 'till it be not scalding hott, *th*en mingle y*our*
flower spices Sugar & Currants (being wash'd
& dry'd) together then put them all of ^a^ heap
Cross *th*e middle of y*our* pan. beat y*our* Eggs well &
mingle them with *th*e yest, & strain them & pour
'em on one side and *th*e Cream on the Other side of
*th*e flower & mingle all well together. Then double
a Sheet of white paper 12 inches deep.
                                     Sow[62]

---

61 Hand T (this recipe only) is a neat hand with a particular decorative ampersand;
    there is no indication as to the identity of the contributor.
62 "Sow" in the directions below means to stitch the paper, and "compass" likely
    means direction, or, in other words, manner or style.

188   it in what Compass you please with white—
—brown paper at bottom & butter *the* paper when
your oven is hot to *the* degree of baking
penny bread put yo*ur* Cake into yo*ur* paper case
pretty thinn for 'twill rise very much, cover it
with paper that it be not Colour'd too much
Let it stand an hour in the oven ~

[189]   **To make Andules**

A Calves Chaldron ꝑ Boil'd, when cold mince
it fine, Take the like quantity of lean pig meat,
mince that also, to four pounds of *the* minced meat
put near a pound of Bacon fat cut to *the* bigness
of Barley Corns, if you put any Leaf fat, let
it be cut to *the* size of smal Dice, mix that with
the minc'd meat, to 5 pounds of *the* meat, put 10
Eggs well beaten, You may put in half a pint
of good milk, Season it with Salt, peper, cloves,
Nutmeg, & a little Coriander Seed, some Marjorum
Thyme, parsley, & onion, or Shallot, Season'd to
the palate, Stuff your meat into Beviors ropes
cut them in lengths at Discretion. Boyle 'em
as you do Hogs puddings, they will keep
good a month at least, Broile or fry them
when they are to be sent to Table ~

190   **To make Shrubb ~**

Pare 12 Lemons very thin and pull off the White
rinds; Slice them but not through; put t̶o̶ them w*i*th
the peals into 4 quarts of Brandy, let them stand
three Days cover'd close, put to them a pound &
half of Double refin'd Sugar, then take out the
Peels and Squeeze the Lemons, *the*n put in half
a pint of milk and let it Stand one night, after
which add two quarts of french white wine; Strain
the whole thro*ugh* a jelly Bagg 'till 'tis fine, then
Bottle it ~

To make Syrrup of Jilly flowers

Take the quantity of Jilly flowers you design to do, when
you have cut them, put as much boiling Spring water as will

wet 'em, let 'em Stand close cover'd 24 hours; to a quart of
tincture put a pint of Sack, *then* Squeeze the tincture from
the flowers, & to a pint put two pound of Single refin'd loaf
Sugar, melt the Sugar eno*ugh* to raise the Scum, let it ~~stand~~
Simber but not boile; when it's cold bottle ^it^ for use.

[191]   **To make Orange Chees-cakes.**

Take half a pound of sweet almonds, blanch'd, &
beaten fine with orange flower watter, half a pound
of Sugar Sifted, 3 quarters of a pound of Melted Butter,
Let it stand 'till 'tis almost cold, Eight Eggs (leave out
4 of the whites) beaten. Boyle the peel of a Large Orange
very tender in quarters, Shifting the Water 2 or 3 times.
Beat it fine in a Stone mortar, mix them very well
together, make yo*ur* past light, and smal, fill them pretty
full, Lemon peel do's almost as well ~

To make Lemon Wine ~

Take 12 quarts of water & 4 pound of Sugar, boile it
and Scum it 'till it be clear then put in the Peels of 7 or 8
Lemons & boyle 'em in it about a quarter of an hour,
take it off, and put it into an Earthen pott & let it stand
'till 'tis cold, then take the white part of the Lemons off &
Slice them into it in very thin Slices. & put in a pint of the
Best Brandy, work it as you do other wine, & tun it up
let it Stand in the Vessel a month then bottle it off.

192   **To make white Elder Wine ~**

Take 20 pound of Malaga Raisins, Pick'd, & Chop't
boile 8 Gallons of Water, let it stand a while, put
it to the Raisins, with 4 ounces of white Elder Blossoms
the juice & rind of 3 Large Lemons, let it stand 9 Days
stirring it every Day, then Strain it thro*ugh* a hair
Seive, & put to it 4 pounds of single refin'd Sugar
Stirr it well together, & Barrel it up, let it Stand
2 months, & bottle it when 'tis fine.

To Scower Pewter

Take half a peck of Wood Ashes & half
a peck of Lime a little slack'd, put

them into Seven gallons of soft Water
& let it boile one hour Stirring it
often; Let it stand 'till Cold, then pour
it off clear & Bottle it for use
You may use it hot or cold.

[193]   **Palsie Water ~**

Take Sage, Rosemary, Betany flowers Lilly of the
Valley flowers Single Piony flowers, Burridge & Buglos
flowers, Spike flowers, Orange flowers, of each quart;
put 'em into a Large Glass and put to them of Aqua-Vitæ
enough to cover 'em, Stop it close, and tie it down fast with
a Bladder wet in water, then put in as many Lavender
flowers (Stript from the Stalk) as will fill a Large Gallon
Glass, & put in more Aqua Vitæ, let all these stand 6
weeks, then distill it carefully in an Alimbeck then
put to this water Citron Peels dry'd, Piony Seeds hull'd,
of each 6 Drachms, *the*n put in Cinamon bruis'd, Cardimums,
Cubells, Nutmegs, Yellow Sanders, each half an Ounce
Lignum Aloes one Drachm, make these into powder put
them into the Water Jujubes new and good Cut Small half
a pound *the*n Stop the Glass & cork it well as before let
it stand 6 weeks *the*n press out the Liquor, *the*n put to it
prepared pearl, Smarages, Musk & Saffron; of each 10
graines, amber greese a scruple, Red Rose Leaves dry'd
red & yellow Sanders, each an ounce, hang all this in a Sarcenet
Bag in *the* water never to be taken out 'till the Water is Spent.
Give 40 Drops to a man; 30 to a woman in Crumbs of Bread &
Sugar Especially against the new, full, & Change of the Moon ~

194   **To make Snaile Water; for a Consumption**

Take the chips of oranges & Lemons, of each 2 ounces
of Ground Ivy 10 handfulls, Hyssop, & Coltsfoot 6
handfulls of each Nutmegs beaten, an ounce & half,
^a peck^ Snailes wash'd in whitte Wine & broken in a quart.
Let them be Sprinkl'd with a quart of Canary, &
let them stand 12 hours, & after add to them of New milk
12 pints, Distill them in a rose still, take 7 Spoonfulls

of *the* distill'd milk, & *the* ^like^[63] quantity of new milk, morning
& at the hour of rest, & every 4 hours, & when you do
not use new milk, Sweeten it with a Spoonfull of the
following Surrup.

To make Surrup of Snailes ~

Take a quart of 3 pints[64] of white Snailes with the
Shells, wipe them very clean, & put them in an Earthen
pott, with a Laying of Fennel at the Bottom, & upon
that, a Laying of Snailes, & so between every Laying
of Snailes, a Laying of Fennell, then cover them
over
[195]   with fennell, this being done in the Evening, Let
them stand all night, and in the morning wipe them
one by one, and prick them, & fill them up, the Shells
with the Snailes with double refin'd Sugar, of^r[65] white
Sugar Candy finely beaten. then put them in a clean
Strainer, Laid an hour before in red rose water, then
hang it upon a Gally pott, *that* the juice of the Snailes with
the Liquor may drop into it, then put up that Syrrup
into a close glass, and take a Spoonfull of it, in the
mor^n^ing,[66] & as much at night when you go to Bed, you
must cover the pott close, when you Lay the Snailes with
the fennel, Laying a weight upon it, Least the Snailes
get out ~

To make Lemon wine

Take 12 quarts of water; & 4 pound of Sugar, boile it &
Scum it 'till it be clear, *then* put in *the* peels of 7 or 8 Lemons
& boyle *the*m in it about a quarter of an hour, take it off &
put it into an Earthen pott, & let it Stand 'till cold. Then take

---

63   This insertion is in different ink from that used for the rest of the recipe, although
the hand appears the same.
64   While "of" does seem written here, "a quart *or* 3 pints" makes more sense.
65   The correction is made in another ink; the hand is unclear.
66   The inserted n is also in a different ink from the rest of the recipe, and the hand is
unclear.

*th*e white part of *th*e Lemons off & Slice 'em into it, in very thinn
Slices, and put in a pint of *th*e best Brandy; work it as other
wine, & tun it, Let it Stand a Month in the Vessell &
Bottle itt ~

196   **To make Cinamon Water**

Take a quarter of a pound of Cinamon, break it Small
into 3 quarts of Water, over night, Stopping the Vessell
close you put it in. on the morrow put it into a Still
*th*e half of it, & as near as you can guess, unless your
Still be Large, if so you may draw it at once then
pour over it 2 quarts of the best Brandy & 2 quarts
of your Lees of white wine, Still it very gently, a very
~~Sme~~ Smal Quantity of fine Sugar put into the Bottles
that receives it is enough, for 'tis apt in it Self to be
Sweet, your water will be Strong eno*ug*h, If you draw
a Gallon from yo*u*r Still, and draw one quart of Smal
by it Self, which is very good for uses; ^where^ the Strong
cannot be used. Five quarts in all ~

[201]⁶⁷   **To make French Bread Lady Lansdowns⁶⁸**

Take a peck of flower, make a hole in the flower & pour in
a pint of milk blood warm, stir it very thin, put then to it half a
pint of milk, & half a pint of yeast, *th*en mix them together thin &
cover it thin with flower, then let it rise a q*u*a*rt*er of an hour, then take
as much milk as will mix it all, then add half a handfull of salt
& a quarter of a pound of Butter melted in*t* the milk both. Mix
itt together not too Stiff, & lap it up in a warm cloth, then make
it up in roles and let it Stand a quarter of an hour, and put
it into the Oven imediately ~

To make an Apple pudding

Take ten apples, scald *th*em & make them into paps, then take *th*e yolks
of 8 Eggs, & two ~~spoonfulls of~~ whites, *th*e crumb of a penny Loaf, one

---

67 Pages 197–200 are missing from the manuscript.
68 The attribution might be in a different hand from the rest of the recipe, perhaps the
    same hand as the note at the end. Its spacing apart from the title suggests that the
    attribution was added at a later time.

nutmeg grated, half a pound of Butter melted, the Eggs must be well beaten & strain'd through a sieve, put in a Spoonfull of orange flower water (or sack), then mix 'em very well together, & sweeten it to your tast, let the dish be well butter'd before you put in your pudding then put it in the oven, being moderately hott, & let it Stand a quarter of an hour ~

add a little grated lemon peel & if
the apples are mellow some of the
Juice[69]

202   **To make Shrewsbury Cakes /**

Four pound of flower: two pound of Sugar, both dry'd & Sifted one pound and half of new butter, the Salt & butter milk clean wash'd out, rub it in the flower & Sugar, 'till it all Looks like grated bread: then with 2 Spoonfulls of rose water (in which was) a nutmeg Sliced. & Steep'd all night) & 6 Spoonfulls of fair Water make it up into a past: flat & role them out into what bigness you please, but not too thick, the oven must not be too hot_

The past for cheescakes ~ or tarts

A pound of flower, a pound of butter, rub the butter into the flower, & beat 3 Eggs and wet it with them.

Nuns Biskett

Take 1 pound of beaten Sugar ½ a pound of beaten and blanched Almonds, 6 Eggs, beat all these togather 'till it's very white, then put in a quarter of a pound dryed flower, the rinds of two lemons grated or shred. bake them in such pans as you doe naple Biskett, sift Sugar over them. you may put candyed orange or Citron Sliced thin into them if you please.

---

69   This note is written in different ink from the rest of the recipe and seems to be in Hand K.

[203]   **To make a pleasant Bitter /**

To 1 quart of brandy take the Peels of 1 doz Oranges
& 1 oz Gentian let it Steep for 3 weeks.
Then put in a little Safron & Cochoneal let that
lye 3 weeks & then filter it off_

For Worms in Man Woman or
Child

Two Drachms of Rhubarb, 2 of Burt^n^t
Hartshorn, ~~one~~ ^one^ of Worm-seed, put them
in a plane Muslin bag, & steep these
in a Quart of Small-Beere twenty four
Hours. give three or four spoonfulls fasting
in *th*e morning, & at four, after noon, fasting
an hour after.
                    Probatum Est:

204   **To make Short Paist Without Butter**

Bake your flower first, then take a quart of
it & the yoalks of three Eggs & a pint of Cream
two ounces of fine sugar & a little salt, soe
make it into paist.

Walnutt water or the Water of Life

Take green walnutts the beginning of June
beat them in a mortar, & distill them in an
ordinary still. keep that water by it self.
Then about midsumer gather more and
distill them as before, which alsoe keep by
it self. Then take a quart of each & mix
them together & distill them in a Glass-still
& keep it for your life.
     The Virtues of this Water are as follows
good for dropsies & palsies drank with wine fasting,
one drop in *th*e eye cures sore Eyes, it help Conception
drinck there of one spoonfull at a time in a glas of wine
once a day. good to wash *th*e face with, Good for all
infermitys of *th*e Body, drives out all corruption of
inward bruises, dranck moderatly with wine, kills

worms in *the* body, drinck much of it you shall live
till *the* world is weary of you. it recovers soure
wine in four days clos'd stopp'd

[205]   **A Drink for *the* Ricketts**[70]

Take 6 or 7 Leaves of Hartstongue, of Liverwort and of Hy=
sop, wild yarrow, wood betony, Coltsfoot, Plantane, Egrimony, violet
leaves, strawbery leaves, maiden hair, alehoof, of each of these
a handfull, Liquorish an ounce, anyseeds a Spoonfull, Currans a
quarter of a po*u*nd, 4 lent figgs sliced, 2 dates stoned, Raisons of
the Sun ston'd a handfull; boyle all these in 3 quarts of running
water, 'till it comes to a quart, strain it off & put in to it
an ounce of brown Sugar Candy & give *the* child 3 or 4
spoonfulls of it every day at 4 in *the* after noon & at
night

Oyntment for *the* Ricketts

Take Camomile, Featherfew, Rosemary, Lavender, Southern Wood,
                                                                Bay=
Leaves, Rue, Hysop, Thyme & Alehoof, Then take a pound of unwashd
butter boyl it skym it clean, *the*n take of each of *the* aforesd herbs a
handfull, chop *the*m very small & boyl *the*m in *the* butter half a quarter
of an hour, *the*n strain it off & anoynt *the* child with it morning
& night for 3 weeks or a month together on *the* breast and
backbone & rub it well in before *the* fire, opening *the* breast
with both hands as you do it.
    The drink is to be took at *the* time
    you use *the* oyntment w*h*ich is to be
    made with may butter & used spring &
    fall.

206   **To make syrop of Violetts**

Take three quarts ^of^ violetts: put a full pint of boiling
water, which must be kept close cover'd twenty

---

70 Hand U (205) appears for the two recipes on this page and is distinguished by its
    minuscule e; there is no indication of the identity of the contributor.

four hours. then strain it off & put your pint of
tincture cold upon 2 ll[71] of double refin'd sugar
finely beten; stir it often in a day: & in a weeks
time the sugar will be disolu'd the violets must
be pick'd the leaves[72] from *the* green: & *the* heel of
the violets must be put to the leaves   end

To make clouted cream

Take a gallone & half of new milk[73] sett it on
a clear fire & lett it boil then put in one quart
of sweet cream & stir it about a little while
over *the* fire, then pour it into two or three pans
and cover it till the next morning then take it
of carefully with a Skimmer & put it into a dish
one upon another, some eat it with sack & sugar
but I think it excellent with aple pasty.

[207]   ### A Reci'p for black Cherry water

Take 12 pounds of black cherryes clean pick'd
from the stalks bruse *the*m in a stone mortar
then put them in a earthen pan & pour upon
*the*m 2 quarts of *the* best Canary & 1 quart of *the*
best french Brandy Distill this in a cold still
with a clear fire keeping a wett cloth on *the*
top of *the* still from this quantity you may
draw d^6^ quarts of very good water

---

71 The abbreviation/symbol appears as either two looped, crossed, minuscule l letter
forms or as a majuscule U with looped, crossed ascenders; if the former, it might
be a variant of li or lb, which signifies pounds, and if the latter, it might signify the
Roman *uncia*/German *unze* or ounce (approximately 28 grams). Considering the
fondness for sweetness in the period, and the fact this is a recipe for syrup, this
recipe likely called for two pounds rather than 56 grams of sugar. "To make Surrup
of violetts" in the Hall manuscript calls for one pint of water to one and a half pints
of sugar and "a good quantity" of violets (27).
72 As is the case in other recipes, the "leaves" here must refer to the petals.
73 Beginning with "milk," the rest of this recipe is written in a new hand (Hand H).

208 **A Recept for hams of Bacon**

x

Take a peck of spanish salt four ounces of
peter salt and fiue pound of the bronest
suger you can gett put all these into as
much water as will beare an egg to the
breadth of six pence the pickle must not be
boild, put in your hams lett them ly three
weekes in the pickle which will, keep a
quarter of a year when you find it begins to
decay then you must boil it and scum it
and this will be fitt againe to put in fresh
hams when you take them out of the pickle
dry them well with a cloth and rub them
ouer with any kind of fatt then hang them
up and make afire with sawe dust or
muck of the stable: to dry them do not let
them hang to long in the chimney: if you
do beef thus it is admirable to eat
fried or broiled as your rasures of
[209] bacon, to make dutch beefe they must be leane
peeces but the other must be fatt, this pickle is
uery good to salt tongues this quantity of
pe^i^ckle will couer 4 hams and 5 or 6 tongues
Beat the salt peter very fine before you put it
in:

To make a very good cake

>[74]

Take a bare peck of flower 6 pounds of currats
half anounce of mace, half anounce of cinamon
a quarter of an ounce ^of^ cloves as much nutmegh
half a pound of ^fine^ sugar & as much rose water as
you please beat your spice, & put that & your
fruit with a lettel salt into your flower, then

---

74   This line is crossed/rubbed out and is illegible.

take cream or new milk as ^much^ you think fitt
dissolue tharein 2 pound of fresh buter

208
210[75]   then put it in a basin with the sugar & as
pint of sack knead it with with a pint of
Ale yest till it rise under your hand let
all things be ready & your ouen hot
before you go to knead the cake,
                        half this quantity
                        makes a larg cake

To Make clouted Cream_[76]

Take a Gallon and a half of new milk,
set it on a clear fire, and let it boy'l,
Then put in one quart of Sweet Cream,
and stir it about a litle while over the
fire, then poure it out into 2 or 3 pan's,
and cover it til the next morning, then
take it of carefully with a skimmer, and put
it into youre dish one upon another, Some
[211]   eat it with wine and Sugar.

The Head Pills. Mrs Capels Receipt,

Take of the roots of round Birthworth,
Gentian, Ditanum, Amber, white wax,
venice turpentine, Myrrh, Chalk of each
2 drams, Methridate three drams, 2 ounces
of Aloes, & as much Syrrup of Marsh Mallos
as will make it into Pills. Take three – 4 –
or 5 – of them goeing to bed, and breakfast
of gruel the next morning.
     These pils, are good for any pains

---

75 Although the correct page number is written below the incorrect page number, the
    incorrect one is not crossed out.
76 Hand V (this recipe through 213) is a messy hand that uses a variety of minuscule
    e forms and sometimes has curled ascenders on the minuscule d. This might be
    the hand of Mrs Capel, to whom the second recipe is attributed, or Mrs Salvage, to
    whom the the third recipe is attributed.

or desorders in the head, Cholick in the
Stomack, any sharp or Cancerous humour
Rheumatick pains, stone, gravel, or
ulcors in the Kidney's, the Gout, worms in
children, and has often cured the green
sickness when steels would not, it is also
good for Melloncholy, & causes sleep, and
212   and may be taken 2 or 3 times a week
as you se occosion. and requires no
confinement:

To Make Red Powder
Mrs Salvages way

Take three pints of white wine,
& put to it of Tormentill roots, Angelica,
Pimpernell, Dragon and Carduus of
each one handfull, shred them small
before you put them into the wine,
let them infuse 12 hours, then take
a pound of the best Bole Almanack
then pour upon it so much of the
wine as will make it as thin as
Batter, and Set it into the Sun to dry,
stirring it every hour; when it is dry
[213]   wet it again till itt hath soaked up all
the wine: at the last wetting put to it
Methridate, Diascordium, powder of
Elecampane, Burnt Harts horn, and
Crabs eyes, of each one ounce, Saffron
and prepair'd pearl of each three drams
let it stand in the Sun till it is stif
enough to make into Balls, and then
make them up, and let them dry in *the*
Sun if the sun be not hot enough you
may dry them in a stove.
  You may ad to it two
  drams of powder of Virginia
  Snake weed root.

214   **To make almond Cheese cakes**

Blanch & beat half a pound of Almonds
as small as posible with as much orang:
flower water as will keep 'em from oyling
then put to 'em half a pound of fine
sugar three quarters of a pound of melted
butter and ^x x 8 eggs mix & beat 'em all well togather x^ bake
'em in a quick Oven in
patty pans In past made with flower a
& butter if you beat *the* whites of *the* Eeggs
all to froth by them selves twill be *the*
better & grind the Almonds as you doe
mustard thay will be finer then thay
can be pounded

Yow must put but half a
pound of Butter, and strain the
butter thro' a sive, & put the
Eggs the last thing when the
Butter begins to grow Cool.[77]

[215]   **To make Almond Milk**

Bake 2 spoonfulls of Barley & a quart
of watter the barly must be boyled In 3 waters
And the 3ed water must be put to the <꞉꞉꞉>
Almonds. To a pound of Almonds 4 quarts
of water The almonds must be Blancht
and beaten very well with Oringe-
flower water, then put the Barly water
to the Almonds mix it well to gather
and strain it, put it into bottles & into
each bottle a Littele Sugar

216   **To make surrup of gilliflowers**[78]

Take one pound of clipt flowers and as
much juice of Lemons as will wett 'em very well

---

77 This last note is added in another hand (perhaps Hand K).
78 As with a few other titles, this one is shifted far right in the original manuscript; the
    contributor did not seem to accurately envision the length of her title in relation to
    the width of the page.

than take three pound of Sugar dipt in water, & boyled
to a Syrrop, you must Press out the Liquor of *the*
flowers hard & pour it into the syrrop upon the
fire stir just once about with your spoon & take
it off speedily, 12 Lemons comonly makes 2 quarts –

To make a Whipt Pudding

Whip the whites of ten Eggs, beat extreamly
and mix some flower & cream or milk with
the eggs a little Salt & either Butter or Marrow
bake it and it hott

To make Calves foot Jelly

Take 2 feet, 2 ounces of Hartshorn, & boyle it in
four quarts of water & boyle it till comes to two quarts, then
pour it out & let it stand till 'tis cold then scum off all the fatt
on the top and take away all the dross of the Bottom then
mix with it one pint of white wine or Rhenish wine, the juice

[233][79]   ## To make the Divine Oyntment

Take 22 ounces of Ox Marrow, well clean'd
from strings or bones, steep it ten days togather
in spring-water, shifting the water twice a day.
then take it out of the spring water, and
steep it in Rose-water four & twenty hours,
then take it out & put it into a fine linning
cloath & hang it up to drain the water from it.
afterwards get Benjamin, Storax, Cyprus and
florence orris-roots of each one ounce
Cinamon half an ounce, Cloves & nutmegs
of each one drachm, all which must be well
beaten & powder'd, then mix in the marrow
with a spoon, afterwards put it into a pott
of two quarts, which must be well clos'd with a
lining cloath, & flower with the whites of Eggs that
the steam may not goe out. put *the* pott into a kettle

---

79 Pages 217–32 are missing from the manuscript.

of water which must boile three hours togather with
a moderate ~~heat~~ fire, reckning from the time it begins
to boil, you must have another kettle of water
boiling to fill the other as it waists, alway keep=
=ing water up to the neck of the pott, after three
hours boiling take it from the fire & strain it thro a
fine lining cloath, & put it into potts.

234   **To drye artichoake bottoms**

Boyle them as usually till the leves take well from the
bottome on some flat thing & put them soe into an oven,
after things ar drawn out of it when it is to be soposed it
is allmost cold that thay may be but just dry
keeping their green Colour

Syrrop of Elder

Put the Berrys into a Jugg & Stop it close.
then put it into a kettle of water & let
it simmer over the fire till all the Juice
is drawn out; & to a pint of Liquor Put
a pound & ¾ of sugar, & boyle it to a Syrrop

x

To scow'r Irons

Take wet Sand, scow'r your Bars with
it, then wipe 'em dry with a linnen
Cloth, afterwards rub 'em with Woollen.

[235]   **Mrs Berkers Receipt:**[80]
                To Make a Seed Cake

Take a pound of Butter, wash it in Rose Water,
then work it with your hand till 'tis as thin as
Cream, then take a pound of flower well Dry'd,
and a pound of double refin'd Sugar finely beaten
Two Ounces of Carraway Seeds, three thimbles
full of pounded mace, mix all the dry things

---

80 Hand W (235) appears for one recipe, and is perhaps that of Mrs Berker herself.

togather and put them by degrees into the
Butter then mix them well togather then beat
9 Eggs, half the Whites, and 3 or four Spoonfulls
of Sack Put these into the other Ingrndients, beat
it all well with your hands, having your Oven
ready put *your* Cake into the hoop and have
a double paper Butter'd to put over it if there
is Occasion_
   One hour will bake it.

236   **Mr Hugh's blist'ring plaister**

Take Burgundy pitch Eight ounces, Venice
Turpentine & Cantharidis finely powder of each
two ounces and a half; Mix these ingredients
Well together over a gentle fire, little or
much of this may be made, by abating or
encreasing the Ingredients proportionably.

               To make a Perfume

Put into four ounces of Spirit of wine (that will burn all
up) two scruples of Ambergrece, & one scruple of musk, tye
them in a rag with a bit of lead to make 'em sink hang it
in the middle of the Spirit of wine & Set the glase in hot
water till *the* Spirit has desolved the musk & Ambergrece,
Stop the glase with a Cork stoped with hard wax or dip *the*
cork in hard wax – a drop of this will perfume a quart
of any Liquor

[237]   **To pott Salmon ~**

Take a whole Salmon, and Splitt it, and wash it very
clean, and scrape out the blood *that* is Settled at the
back bone, then cut it into severall pieces, then
Season it with cloves mace, Jamaica pepper, black
pepper, and Salt to your discretion. Then put it into
a pot close down, and cover'd with butter on *the* top and
a Layer of butter at *the* bottome, when it comes out
of the Oven, bone it, and let it Stand to drain the
Gravy from it, When *the* Salmon is drein'd & cold, then
press it, or, pound it, If you think it not Season'd eno*ugh*
add more in the potting of it, of all Sorts the butter

that is baked with it will go a towards covering it.
~ If you pot it in pieces it requires more Seasoning

238   **A Receipt for the Dropsie**

Take of Sena	6 ounces
Polipodium Roots	6 ounces
Bay berries	4 ounces
Annis=seeds	3 ounces
Ash keys	3 ounces
Sasafras	2 ounces
Bind Weed	2 ounces
Rubarb	4 Drachms<.>

Bind Wheat, (Alias) Wave Wind, one handfull.
Bruise all your Ingredients & put 'em all into a
bag, and let 'em hang in 4 Gallons of Ale 7 Days
It must be drank as Common Beer 'till Well:
The Same Ingredients will Serve twice, & be very good
the Second time If you immediately put the Same quantity
of New Ale, and let it Stand 7 Days as before
directed, and Drink it as before Directed _

[239]   **Lady Katharine Windham's Receipt.**
               Powder for Convulsion fitts ~

Take the Herb call'd Lady's Smock Strip the Blossome
clean from the Stalk & dry the Large Green Stalks
by themselves, & the Blossoms by themselves, then
mix 'em and powder 'em & sift it through a fine Sive,
Give to a young Child as much as will lye on a
6 pence, to a Man, or Woman a Spoonfull, three
Days before a new Moon, & 3 days after, & the
Same before and after the full Moon ~

          Mr. Bamber's Medicine for an Horse has the
                        Grypes

Take one handful of Green Onion tops, & one handfull
of Marsh Mallows, put them into two quarts of
water and boile it to one Quart, then put in
to it two onions chop'd and half a pint of

Turpentine, strain it, and give it to the Horse,
or Mare, warm.

240 ### A Receipt to make Veal Glew.

Take a Leg of Veal, cut of all *the* fat. Make a
very strong broth of the Leg & Strain *the* Same
through a Sieve; that it may be very clear, when
this is done, put the broth into a broad flat
Stew-pan that will hold it all and set it upon a
high Chaffindish of Charcoal, & Stirr it Continually
about, that it may niether burn nor boile the
whole time it is upon *the* fire, which must be about
7 hours; After this set it by for a Day or two, &
then cut it out of the pan, and Scraping off
the Sedement (if any) put the clear Jelly into
a China dish, and place it upon a Stewpan
of hot Water, placing the Stew pan upon a
Chaffing dish of Coals; the Water in the pan
must be kept boiling, 'till by the Steem the
Jelly grow of a Glewy Substance, which :

it[81]

[305][82] ### To get out Iron moulds

half a pint of Juice of Sorrel,
half a p*int* of Lemon juice, of
salt & vinegar a spoonful, boyle
it togather & bottle it for use,
it must be used hot & wash'd out
as soon as done

For a woman as soon as brought
to bed.

Gasgoin Powder & spirmacite one
Scruple Dioscordium 1 scruple &
½, & juice of Alkermes to make
it into a bolous, to be taken at

---

81 The rest of this recipe is missing.
82 Pages 241–304 are missing from the manuscript.

x[83]   night with a drought of Pennyroyal
Doctor Stephens Water, ~~three parts~~

306   **The Red Powder Mrs Rogers**

Take of Cardus, Rue, red sage Lillys of
the valley; Tormentile, pimpernel, Dragons
Bitony, Angelica, Scabious, Speedwell,
of each one handful, Snakeweed one
handful wormwood half a handful Vervain
Agremony of each a quarter of a handful
shred & bruise the herbs, & infuse them
in two quarts of white wine in a jug[84]
Close Stop'd, & set it in the sun nine days,
then strain the wine from the herbs, then
take a pound of bole armoniac finely powderd,
then put as much of the wine after it is
press'd out as the powder will take up, &
set it in the sun to dry & as it drys up; put
in more of the wine stiring it two or 3 times
a day 'till all the wine is dry'd up in the
powder so as to be fit to work like paist,
then put in the same quantity of each sort
of herb as is infused dry'd & powderd,
one ounce of Diascordium, an ounce & ½ of
of Mithridate & ounce & ½ of Venice Treacle

---

83   The meaning of this x is uncertain; it might mean "&" or it might suggest omitting
"Doctor Stephens Water."
84   The j is actually a hybrid j/g.

Translations of Spanish Recipes in the Granville Text

To make good ink
Cadiz 6 of November, Juan
Baqueriso navy guard
who has been a teacher to write this and tell of it

heaping *azumbre* of rainwater
3 ounces of black galls, ground
3 ounces of copperas
1 one ounce gum Arabic

Mix all ingredients in a new pot placed in the shade for
twelve days and stirred 2 times a day with a fig branch,
only to a depth of the top layer and you will get very good
ink

Recipe of Doña Maria Leal a
midwife to make amber water

9 pounds of clean roses
½ *arroba* of Lucena wine
2 ounces of cloves
2 ounces of cinnamon
2 ounces of nutmeg
4 ounces of benjamin
1 ounce of storax
1 pinch of lavender
½ pound of clover seed
½ *cuartillo* of the first spirits drawn from the still

Mix all the above the spices and flowers well,
then put everything in a basin,
kneading well until it has
absorbed all the wine, and then put it in a
tinaja or an *orza*. Cover it very well with a lid,
set it aside nine days and then take it out
or distil in an alembic on a low heat, and at
the tip of the alembic place some cotton with
a bit of civet musk and to each pottle of this
water add a *cuartillo* and a half of rose water
a *cuartillo* of orange flower water, and

half a *cuartillo* of water of clover seed.
Put everything in a metal dish or a new pot;
cover it tightly and let it boil
awhile, and to this quantity add an
adarme of amber, two of civet musk and
a half of musk and a paper of
amber dust and then crush
all these in a warm metal mortar and
put all this in the flasks when
the water is hot. Seal tightly
and place said flasks in the sun; the
more sun there is, the better this said amber water will be
    Cadiz year 1676

Recipe for *Picadillo* of Leg of Lamb

First prick the meat and then wash it well and then
put it into a frying pan, lightly boil it with water, salt and
some minced garlic
Once cooked al dente, remove the meat and pound it in
a metal mortar, and keep pounding it, for if any nerve
appears in the meat as a result of poor chopping, in this way it
is easy
to get rid of it= Then put it into a cooking pot ^with pork grease^
and add
the spices ^nutmeg^ saffron, cinnamon, cloves, and pepper.
Before taking it out to carry it to the table, beat a few egg yolks and
eggs with lime juice, pour everything into the pot
and stir it all and thus carry this plate of
picadillo to the table=
    Recipe of Captain Francisco del Poço
    de Rota who sent it to Cadiz to the
    Consul Martín Bisconde
    22 of August 1682
Note well: use pork grease or butter from Flanders/

Recipe given to me by a monk in
Orleans Thursday 23 of May 1675
for a sure way to kill and destroy
bedbugs in the beds and on the walls

Whip ox or cow bile, strong vinegar
and lime, let dry;
Mix everything in proportion and beat and then
put this paste in the holes
of the walls and in any part of the bed
where the bugs may be and kill all the bugs
without leaving any baby bugs in whatever place said paste
is applied, this recipe is true [&c *or* Recipe]

To Improve and conserve vanilla

Crush 4 or 6 vanilla pods; to season 100 or even
200, and a bit of lukewarm water dissolve said
vanillas together with a bit of good oil or
sweet almond oil, and having beaten this well together, then
the vanilla will be smeared or spread with this ingredient,
warm, putting your first finger over your
thumb and passing them one by one with the juice of said
ingredient both sides of the vanilla with
this improvement it will purify and will have a new
juice, lustre and scent; after this is done,
set it uncovered outdoors for one or two
hours because if they were stuck together then they would become
clumped and of worse quality than they were
before improving them

Recipe from the sergeant of a a one-eyed sergeant
Fernandes citizen de Xeres / Cadiz
18 of September 1685, who arrived in the flotilla

Remedy to make molars and teeth stick
vizt

Take two *cuartillos* of wine
two or three hearts of male spurge flowers
two or three galls

four quarts of dragonsblood
two or three hearts of rosemary

cook all of these together until it has reduced by half;
when it is lukewarm wet the mouth to your liking
until said molars or teeth are firm
  Cadiz 22 of June 1685 in the office of
  Señor Lucas de Molina a gentleman lawyer gave me this
  account or recipe

MS V.a.20:
Receipt Book
attributed to Constance Hall

Textual Introduction

This receipt book is attributed by the Folger Shakespeare Library to Constance Hall and dated 1672. This date appears on the title page, and "Receipt 1672" is also tooled in gold letters onto a title label affixed to the binding; the even spacing of the letters/numbers suggests a typeholder was used, which would mean that neither the current binding, nor perhaps the second binding from which the label originated, is the original, and that this manuscript might have been rebound twice. The book is 19.2 cm tall by 15.1 cm wide. The edges of the pages are dyed red. The unidentified watermark varies. Only half the book contains recipes (the other half is blank), suggesting that it was bound before it was used as a receipt book.

The title page of this work is particularly decorative. Emily Bowles Smith has written about this page and the evident practice of handwriting in the manuscript in her online Folger Library essay, "'Let them Compleately Learn': Manuscript Clues about Early Modern Women's Educational Practices." (Anne Kendall Cater's receipt book, also in the Folger collection, is similarly decorated, with skilled drawings of fish and women's heads on a number of recipe pages.)

Little is known about Constance Hall, although her name appears in Anne Denton's prose miscellany, which is also in the Folger collection. The *Perdita Manuscripts* biography of Denton notes that Constance was the daughter and co-heir of Francis Hall (esquire) of Ledbury. She married Anthony Biddulph in 1680. Sir Bernard Burke's *A Genealogical and Heraldic Dictionary of the Landed Gentry of Great Britain for 1852* adds that Anthony was a high sheriff, and that the couple had three sons: Robert, Francis, and Michael. The note "A London Receipt" alongside "To make a Sack possett" (20) also suggests that the owner of the manuscript at that point lived outside London. The biographical information available on Hall (both what is there and what is *not* there) suggests that she was not of equal social standing to Mary Granville. This receipt book does not, furthermore, include remedies calling for gold, as does the Granville manuscript, and it attributes fewer recipes to people of high social standing (indicators which, however, as explained in the historical introduction above, are not definitive).

This receipt book contains mostly culinary recipes, with occasional remedies interspersed here and there. Perhaps accordingly, the ingredients called for are generally not as exotic as those in the Granville manuscript (although musk and ambergris are listed). The remedies generally contain very detailed instructions for use; while both the Granville and Hall manuscripts include plague water remedies, for example, only the latter suggests that "your first sort being / the strongest you may give to old folks your / midle sort to any and your third to Children / but what ever sort you give mix some of your / Last sort with it," and then the final instruction "you must not lett your / fier be to hot vnder your still and those / drugs that are too harde to Cut beate in A / morter but not small" (14). These specifications might indicate particular familiarity with the recipe – although they could also indicate unfamiliarity and hence the need to copy it in greater detail.

The culinary recipes make wide use of local ingredients, such as broombuds to replace capers, and measurements are sometimes homely: "To preserve Apricockes green" calls for fruit "about *the* bigness of pigeons / egges" (2v). However, this measurement is not as rustic as it might sound, as pigeons were predominantly kept by manor lords (Cooke 18). And other recipes do call for imported ingredients, sometimes in enormous quantities: "How to make A Cake" calls for ten pounds of currants! The cake was probably either meant to feed many people in a large, middle- or upper-class household or to last over a few meals: "the gargantuan size of many dishes, possibly reflect[s] the origin of a recipe in a household (or published cookery book) where meals were designed to produce leftovers" (Pennell 248). This receipt book also includes some "foreign" recipes, such as "To make freanch Bred" (47), which is directly followed by "A ffrigisee" ([47v]), although these were not necessarily novel. While a number of culinary historians have regarded François la Varenne's 1655 *Le Cuisinier François*, which appeared in English just two years after French publication, to have had major influence on English cooking, Joan Thirsk does not see this work as truly revolutionary; she notes that many of la Varenne's techniques were already in use in England, due to *earlier* contact with French, Italian, and Spanish recipes (*Food* 111–12).

A number of recipes are repeated throughout this manuscript, some with subtle differences; others appear to have been directly copied from the same source or one from the other. Recipes for stewed lamprey, apricot cakes, hashed calf's head, sugar puffs, and others appear twice in the manuscript; those for almond pudding appear three times; those for orange pudding and rice pudding appear four times. Such repetition might indicate writing practice.

This manuscript shares a number of recipes with M.H.'s *The Young Cook's Monitor* (1683); "To make a quaking puding" ([22v]) and the three recipes that follow in this manuscript also appear, in the same order, in M.H.'s publication. Likewise, this manuscript's recipes for plague water (14) and whitepot ([9v]) are very similar to those in Sir Kenelm Digby's *The Closet of the Eminently Learned Sir Kenelm Digbie Kt. Opened* (1669). The Hall manuscript's recipes for surfeit water (27) and "lugaillus Balsom" (Lucatellus's balsam) ([42v]) are also similar to those in John Pechey's *The London Dispensatory* (1694). It is difficult to know whether the contributers to the Hall manuscript copied these recipes from these print sources or whether the print sources – including M.H.'s – copied from this or another manuscript.

Other sources appear to be friends or acquaintances. There are far fewer attributions in this receipt book than in the Granville manuscript: only Mrs Beale, Lady Hull, Mr Parkers, Mrs Best, Madam Buttler, and Doctor Morus are listed, and each shares one or two recipes. Doctor Morus was likely local; his name does not seem to appear in other recipe books of the period (unlike that of Doctor Stevens, whose curative water is common in both receipt books and published cookbooks).

The various hands in which this manuscript is written (approximately sixteen; indicated in the footnotes) show significant diversity in letter forms as well as punctuation and spelling. Letter sizes in Hand G are particularly irregular, especially C/c and S/s. Many Hand B recipes end with a series of short lines, while Hand J ends most recipes with a virgule or a slash. The contributors also treat line breaks differently; in some cases, the word is simply broken (without punctuation) and continues on the next line – as with "an" then "chovies" in "Sauce for all sorts of boyled fish" (8). In other cases, the author seems to change her mind in beginning a word at all; she crosses it out and begins again on the next line – as in the recipe "To make lugaillus Balsom" ([42v]), where she writes "tur," crosses it out, apparently rethinking the amount of space until the end of the page, and begins again on the next line: "turpintine." There are a number of repeated words in this manuscript. The variant spelling does not seem to reflect archaic or regional or phonetic spelling forms, but rather mistakes, and in these cases I have not included them in the glossary. Where their meaning is, I think, obvious, I have simply left them alone in the text; examples include "corch" (scorch), "chrush" (crush), "curst" (crust). As explained in the Note on the Text, where a word's meaning might be unclear I have included the correct word in square brackets; examples include "lald [laid]," and "nealed [sealed]."

This book was exhibited at the Folger Shakespeare Library in 2006–7 (the title page) and in 2011 (page 27).

Fig. 2.1 Folger MS V.a.20, fol. 1r. By permission of the Folger Shakespeare Library.

Receipt Book

[fol. 1r]   Constance

                                        Hall

                                        Her Booke

                                        of Receipts Anno

                                        Dominj 1672[1]

[fol. 1v blank]

[fol. 2r]   **To preserve Apricocks Ripe**[2]

Take your Aprecocks & weigh them & to a pound
of them A pound of sugar finely pounded and
sifted, After they are weighed pare them verry
thin then slit them one *the* crest side & fetch out
the stone, then put a laying of sugar in *the* Bottom
of *the* platter w*hi*ch don put in your Apricocks one
by one & cover them w*i*th *the* Remainder of *the* sugar
then cover them and let them stand all night
the next day set them one some coles and let them
boyle softly turneing them as you see Occassion
before they are ready set them by and let them
stand all night one *the* Morrow boyle them vp
and when they are cold put them up in Gallypots
You must preserve them *the* same day they are
                        Gathered

---

1   It is not entirely clear if the hand of this title page matches any of those within the
    receipt book itself. It is likely Hand A.
2   Hand A (2–3) is a neat, mixed hand, combining the backwards minuscule secretary
    e with otherwise italic forms (perhaps differentiating this hand from that of the
    title page). The majuscule P is distinct for its spur to the left of the letter (such as
    "Preserve" in the title and "Plumes" in the ninth line).

[fol. 2v]   **To preserve Apricockes green**

Take green Apricocks about *the* bigness of pigeons
egges pare them verry thin and as you pare them
put them into faire water, before they are pared
take *the* waight of them in sugar, when they are all
pared boyle them in 2 or three waters & while'st
they are boyleing in the Last water take another
skillet, & disolve your sugar in soe much water as
you conceave will make sirrup to boyle up
your plumes[3] when the sirrup is boyled and
scummed take them out of *the* water and put them
in *the* sirrup and keep them boyling A pretty pace
for they will not be apt to breake when They are
somewhat tender slit them one the side & take out
the stone and put them in againe and let them
boyle tell they are green clear and the sirrup
thicke then take them of the fire and let them
stand tell they be almost cold then put them vp
in gallypotts or glasse they must be kept turned or
else one side will be greener then the other

3[4]   **To preserve Quinces Amber Colour**

Take of *the* ffairest quinces you can get and Core them then
coddle them in faire water as tender as you can without
Breaking then take a pounde and a halfe of poulder shuger
to one pinte of water Clarify your suger and let it boyle to a
full sirrup then pare A pound of your quince and put into it
take some of *the* cores *tha*t you scrape out of your Quinces and
picke *the* cernells Cleane from them then take about halfe an
ounce of *the* Cores and sow in litle bagges and put into *the* boyling
of *the* Quince and with *the* backe of your spoone chrush *the*
                                                        baggs as they
boyle up boyle them as fast as *the* quince will suffer you & when
your si^r^pup begineth to turne amber Colour take up a litle
of it in a spoon and see whether it will gelly: if it gelly it is

---

3   While the recipe is for apricots, it does indeed call for plums at this point.
4   Page numbers are included on the recto pages of the original manuscript.

enough then take up your Quinces and put them in a pott & make
your sirrup prety cold and then power it into the quinces but
if you finde your quinces be enough and sirrup doe not gelly take
vp your Quinces and boyle your sirrup vp againe as fast as you
can make it boyle and then coole it and power it to your
quinces take them as soone as they are gathered of *the* tree or
else they will not gelly;

[fol. 3v]   **A Recipt for the seare 'Cloth[5]**

Take Half a pinte of sallet oyle, and a
quarter of a pound of red Lead, put this in
a new pipkin, and sture it, let it boyle tel
it be blak then put in a Lettel rossel Bees
waxe permacitty then boyle it a gaine &
then take it of and dipe in your Clothes –

A Receipt to make a Caraway Cake

Take 3 pound of fine flower, a pinte of
Creame, a pinte of aile yest & mixe your
flower, Creame & yest together and make
it stiff as for a manchett then sett it to
the fire while your oven heats, & when
it is almost hott then worke in a pound
of Caraway Comfitts and put it into
the oven; Butter and then strew in your
Caraways;

4   **How to make A Cake**

Take to a pecke of flower 4 pound of Butter
Crumble it verry fine among the flower, 10
poundes of Currants, 1 pound of stoned Rays

---

5   Hand B ([3v]–[7v], 8 lower recipe–[10v], 12 lower recipe–[13v], [14v], [15v], [16v]–18
top recipe, [18v], [19v], [21v] lower recipe–24, 42–[46v], [48v]–49, 57–[59v] top
recipe, 62–[62v], 63 begins recipe) is a loose italic hand that often uses a majuscule
C. Minuscule t and r are sometimes very similar in form, and minuscule p looks
similar to y. Recipes in this hand often terminate in a series of short lines or plus
signs. This is one of the most common hands in the manuscript, and so is perhaps
that of Constance Hall; however, it does not seem to be the same hand as that of the
title page.

ons, Chopped small 1 ounce of mace and a
half, one ounce of Cloves one ounce of nuttme
ggs aquarter of A pint of good Rose water;
and dessolve in itt 2 or 3 of the best muske
plumbs a little safforn a quarter of a pint
of mallego sack, halfe a pound of Carraway
Comfitts 3 quarters of sugar, and a little
salt, mix all these together; then putt 2
quarts of Cream, and as much good ale
yeast, it will take up most of it: the Currants
must be putt in when the Bread is made it
must not bee kned; one hower and a halfe
will Bake itt;

[fol. 4v]   **To Bake Beef Like venison**

Take Buttake beef cut it in preaty thin
slises, take A way all the skins, then take
bacon cut cut in thin slises, lay A peace
of bacon beteen <e>very peace of beef, then
beat it together with a roleing pin, then
take a prety deyl of peper salt nutmeg
mace and Cloues all beaten, and seson your
meat with it, then take a quart of clarrit
wine and sprinkell it all ouer the meat,
so let it lie all night, next day put it into
a round pot and bake it with the browne
bred put past round the pot about the
edg to keep it close when it come out of
the ouen power of ^out^ the graue from it, &
let it stand a while and setell, then
power of the top of the graue, and put
it to the meat again then couer the
meat with Clarified butter then lay
A wait upon your meat to keep it
Clos –

5   **To make Curd Loaues**

Take A porringer full of cheise curd four
eggs whits and all & as much flower as
will make it pretty stif then take a littell

ginger nutmeg & sum salt make them
up into loaves and set them into an ouen
with a prety quick fier when they begin
to Chang colouer take them out & put
melted butter sack & suger to them and
so set them –

How to make sausages

Take A pound of the lean of a leg of ~~pork~~
po^r^ke cut out all the sinnows then shrid it
prety small and beat it in a stone morter
till it is very fine then mingell a pound
of beef suit shrided prety small then
seson it with peper salt & nutmeg a hand
full of sage shrid, a littill perssly & time,
put in a littill grated whit bread when
you make them up mingel sume yolks of
eggs you must fry them with sweet butter
let let them fry leasurly till they be prety
brown #

[fol. 5v]   ### To make A creem puding

Take to a quart of creem 22 eggs put out 6 of
the whits mix with it 6 spoonfulls of fine
flower, sweeten it to your tast, put in sume
salt a nutmeg, a littill sack half a pound of
Allmonds blanched and beaten very fine
with rosewater, mingell all together then butt
ter and flower a cloth well, & tye it up put
it in boyling water 2 hours will boyl it, when
you make this puding you may beat the
almonds ouer night –

To make an oatmeall puding

Take A porringer of oatmeall beaten to
flower a pint of creem one nutmeg foure
eggs 3 whits beaten a quarter of a pound of
suger a pound of beef suit, minced prety
small mingell all these together and so bake
it, an houer will bake it –

6   **To make an allmond Caudell**

Take 3 pints of ale boyle it with sume Cloues
and mace, slice sume white bread in it
then have redy beaten a pound of blanch
allmond ~~ana~~ an stran them out with a
pint of whitwine and thicken the ale with
it, sweeten it to your tast, besure you skim
the ale well as it boyleth –

To pickell broombuds

Take your buds before they be yellow one the
top, make a brine of viniger & salt, which
you ~~sum~~ must doe only by shaking it to
gether till the salt is mellted then put
your buds in and keep them stirred once
a day till they be sunk with in the pickell
besure to keep them Close couered –

To make A very good cake

Take A quarter of a peck of flower a pint
of creem ten eggs no whits beat the eggs
very well, 3 quarters of a pound of butter
gently mellted, pour a littill ale yeast one
the flower a quarter of a pint of rosewater
with sume musk & ambergreec dissolued
~~itt~~ in it, seson it with a penyworth of mace
and Cloues a littill nutmeg finely beaten /
[fol. 6v]   3 pound of currants well washt pickt and
dryed, a pound of allmonds, blanced & beaten
with sume rosewater to keep them from oyl
ing, half a pound of suger beaten very small
mingell all these together with your hands,
then let it lie before the fier to rise a hour,
Couer it with a Cloth then make it up, & put
it in a hope, or paper round it let not the
ouen be to hot nor to cold sumething more then
an hour will bake it, Against you draw it
have redy sume ros^e^water and suger finely beat
en and well mixt together, & wash the top of
the cake with it and set it into the ouen to dry,

To make whit pudings

Take 6 peny white lofes grat them, take 12
eggs all the white, beaten very well, then put
them to the bread, shrid in a good quantity
of beef suit, sume so rose water nuttmeg and
salt, sweeten it to your tast, a good many
currance, mingell these all together, and fill
the gutts there with,

7

To pickell barberries

gather your barberries when they be dry pick
pick out the fairest of the bunches and put
them in an erthen pot pick the smallest ons
from their stalks and boyl them in water
and salt till the liquor is strong then stran
it and put in sume red wine and when
it is cold power it one the barberries –

To make puff past

Take A quart of flower, the yolks of 4 eggs
2 whits a littill cold water mingell it with
the flower and mold it up then role it a brod,
and take butter and lay all ouer then fould
it up again thoroughly beat it with a roleing
pin, so lay butter as at first and fould it up
again so doe nine times together and make
it up in what fassion you pleas –

To make suger cakes

Take A pound of flower half a pound of
suger beaten and sifted, mingell it with the
flower, then take half a pound of butter &
crumbell it in to the flower and suger then
take the yolks of 2 new lald [laid] eggs 2 spoonfull
[fol. 7v] of sacke 2 spoonfull of creem, beat all those
together and put them in then mold it all up
together into a past and role them out thin
and cut them with a glas & lay them upon
papers or plates very well butter and flow
ered, so set them into the ouen & becarefull

of them for a littill matter bake them, the
ouen must be prety quick but not to corch

To make an allmond creem

Take half a pound of allmonds and blanch
them and beat them in a stone morter now &
then put in a littill rosewater to keep them
from oyling then have a quart of thick creem
put your allmonds into a littill of it and stran
it once or twice till all the verty be out of
them then grate in a quarter of a nutmeg
a littill mace sume rosewater and lofe suger
to your tast then put in the rest of the creem
and boyl it till it come to a pape then power
it forth into a sillver dish or a ston one when
tis cold strow sume cumfits of all collers on it
and serve it –

8   ### To Stew Oysters[6]

Put your oysters in a Stew pan one by
one to avoyd gravill then strane the Liquor
and put it to them, with sume verges
or wineger put a whol oynon sume
whole peper a Lettel wintersauery sume Larg
mace, & as they boyl scum them very
clean, when they are enough put in a
good peece of Butter & shak it till it is
thick then put ^them^ in a Dish & serve them
with slict Lemmon on the top –

Sauce[7] ~~sauce~~ for all sorts of boyled fish

Take sume whitwine put in it sume an
choueys shelot sume stewd oysters

---

6 Hand C (this recipe only) is a rounded italic hand, and the recipe ends in a
   decorative mark that might be a monogram.
7 This word is in one (unidentifiable) hand; the rest of the recipe is in Hand B.

minct small sume mace a sprig of time
and winter sauory boyl all these well to
gether then take out the herbs and beat
it up very thick with butter and power
it ouer the fish –

[fol. 8v]   **to candy angelico**

you must part the leaus from the stalks
and split the stalks that bee of any bigness
but the little ons may goe whole you must
boyl them tender in spring water and
when they are very tender you must dry
them very well in a clean cloth and couer
them up whilst you make a surrop you
must take the wait of them when they are
boyled of duble refined suger and put
to it as much fair water as will iust melt
it and boyl it in a puter bason or silver
and when you begin to find it prety
thick try with a spoone and hould it up
and let it run from the <∴> spoons and when
it hang like a hair as it falls you may
put in your angelico and stur it a bout
till all the suger hang about it you may
put in a few leaus raw in to the candy and
when they be prety dry that you see the
suger hang a bout them you must lay
them out vpon paper tell they are quite
dry if they want stoueing you must stove
them in a stoue or ouen after bread that
is if they grow damp –

9   **To make Cheas Cakes**

Take to as much curd as a gallon of milk
will make a pound and quarter of Butter
3 quarters of a pint of creem being first
Boyled with sume grated Bread and a
littill grated nutmeg, then put it to the curd
put in 5 eggs 2 whites very well Beaten put
in a littill flower sume rosewater & suger

to your tast But before you put in these ingred
ence you must beat the curd in a ston morter
then put in these a Boue [above] mentioned ading sume
currants you must beat the Butter with the
curd Let the creem and Bread be cold before
you put it to the curd, then make your curst
with cold water, and Butter crumled into the
flower 2 yolks of eggs sume creem a littill
rosewater so mould all these up together and
make it into what fasion you pleas –

[fol. 9v]   **To mak[8] To make A whitepot**

Take a quart of creem, take 8 eggs half the
whits Beat them very well and put them
into the creem bruse an nutmeg and sume
mace and in it, slice in sume candyd lemonn
and oring peel and citturn seson it with
rosewater and suger to your tast then
haue a deep dish well Buttered and lay
sume sippits of whit bread cut very
thin at the bottom and sume pretty great
lumps of marrow upon them you must ston
sume reasons and Lay sume of them between
the bread and marrow then power on the
third part of the creem then lay sume more
sippits reasons and marrow as before and
power on a nother part of the creem then lay
on all the rest as before and power on all
the creem so bake it in a uery soft ouen
~~of~~ of a yeallow brone,[9] one marrow bone
will doe, half an houer will bake it –

10   **To make a sak possit**

Take a quart of creem and boyl it with
sume mace in it then take the yolks of 16

---

8 It is not clear why the author began her title again. Although the T is not perfect, the
first attempt is not crossed out.
9 I.e., brown. Sir Kenelm Digby's cookbook includes a similar recipe for white-pot
and says that when the bone marrow turns brown, the white-pot is done. Most
other white-pots (including those in the Countess of Kent's book) do not include
bone marrow.

eggs beat them very well, and when your
creem is prety cool put it to your eggs
and make a smoth custard of it, then take
all the whits of the 16 eggs and beat
them with a wisk up to a high snow
when it is half Beaten put in 3 spoonfulls
of sack and to of Lofe suger and beat it
up to gether, then take half a pint of sak
and put it in an bason and put in suger
enough to sweeten the hole possit put in a
littill nutmeg and set it upon a chaffing
dish of coals & Let it boyl then put in your
custard s^t^uff uery hot stir it round well
together, Let it stand but a very littill
while after, one the fier remember to keep
out sume of the snow to lay on the top of
all then Leaue stiring when that is put
on, haue redy a dish hot to couer it close
and serue it, take it of the fier assoon as
the snow is in –

[fol. 10v]   **Recept for making a broune ~~ffre~~
ffrigasie**

take halfe a dosen Chickens and fleigh
them cut them up in quarters breake
the bones of them very well stew them
in a pan very well with a fagot of <·>
sweete herbs larg mace whole Cloue<·>s
a pint of sake a pint of white wine a
pint of clarret halfe a pint of aquavie
a peice of lemmond and an onion Chop
small pouer your Liquor from them
stew it vp with a couple of anchovies a
handfull of oysters thicke it vp with a
Couple of yelkes of eggs a slice of sweet
butter lay your dish with sippets garnish
your dish with force meats garnish your
dish with all sorts of pickles dish it very
hot soe serve it in –

[fol. 11r]   **Aqua Mirabilis**[10]

Take Gallingall Cubebu, Cardomums, mellilet
Flowers, Ginger, Cloves, Nutmegs and mace, of
each one dram a Pinte of Aqua Vitæ, three pints
of sack, or white wine, one pinte of the Iuice of
Cellendine Let those ingredients of Druggs
and spices being Grossely beaten be infused in
the Liquors and Iuices one night, then distill
them vntill all be run out and let the Extract
fall into a Glasse in which you haue put halfe
a pound of white sugar Candy or hard Sugar
and take two or three spoonfulls when you
are in bed or in the day as Occasions serue

[fol. 11v]   **To make the Duke of Yorks**
                       Cakes[11]

<..
....>[12]

Take one pound of fresh butter and
one pound of powder sugar which
being well mixed with your hands
take seven eggs well beaten and put
them to the Aforesaid mixture this being
don then take one pound of fine fflower
dryed upon A Chafeing dish of Coals and
put into it one halfe of the fflower and
about A quarter of one hour the other
halfe mixing it well together and then
take halfe one pound of Currants and put
into the Aforesaid mixture the Currants
being boyled a little before to fill them

---

10 Hand D (this recipe only) is a neat, straight hand. It uses a long s and dashes as
    fillers at the ends of lines. There is no indication of the identity of the contributor.
11 Hand E (this recipe only) includes a back-slanting, looped ascender on the
    minuscule d and a top-looped majuscule C. There is no indication of the identity of
    the contributor.
12 The first two lines of this recipe are scribbled out and are indecipherable.

12   **To Make a Seare Cloth**[13]

Take fouer peniworth of Sallett Oyle one peniworth
of stone pitch one peniworth of red lead boyle it
to gether over Coales softly till it looke black Then dip
the Cloths in it; Haue a care it doe not Boyle ouer

To make Spiretts of eleder

Gether the berries when they
are full ripe pick them Clean from
the stalkes and leves put them in
to a wooden vessell and mash
them well; to a bushell of berries
put a bottel of fair water and to
four bushells put a quart of alle
yest and a small cake of leaven
Crumbled in to the yest then pour
the yest all over the berries then
Couer them Clos with a couer, and
once in to dayes put them dowen
and stirr them all to gether so
let them stand firmenting: 9 or
[fol. 12v] 10: dayes then distill them in a
ly^m^bick in your distilling you
must keep your pot allwayes
boyling and about three parts
full and, from three gallans of
licker you must take a quart
of good spirit and as much at
the second rvning which you
may put them in to a fresh still
full of the lyquer;

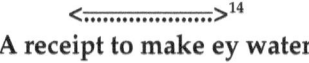

A receipt to make ey water

take a penyworth ^of^ aris root

---

13 Hand F (this recipe only) uses a mixed hand that includes a secretary minuscule e.
     There is no indication of the identity of the contributor.
14 The initial title is scribbled out and is undecipherable.

cut small and a penyworth
of white Copeirs pond small
put it both into a quart
of runing water shake it
well to gether –

13   **To make exlent biskitt**

take a pound of lofe suger well
dreyed befor the fyer pound
and scarced and set a gain to
the fyer and three quartes of a
pound of fine wheat flower
10 eggs leaue out to whits beate
them half an hour then put
in the svger hott and beat the
eggs and suger to gether to
hours when the ouen is redy
which must be as hot as for
manchet s[t]rain the flower and
what caraway seeds you will
butter your tins will and bake
them not to browne the neuer
the eggs are the beter when they
are baked drey them befor the
fyer;

[fol. 13v]   A<.> ~~Resipe for the cloth~~
               A Resaite for the mollin oyntment

Take halfe a pound of may butter
frese out of the Cherrn and one
handfull of mollin leves and
one handfull of rose Campon
leves made Clean and sredid
then boyl them ^all^ well to gether put
In on penywoth of bees wax and
sume rose water then boyl it a
littel more and then straine it
and to penyworth of the oyle of bayes
and ^put it in^ with the bees wax

14   **To Make the Plague Water**[15]

Take of Woodsorrell Rosemary Sage rew Saladine
Avens mint Baum Cardus fetherfew wormwood
Angelecoe Dragons Tormentell Scabious Egremoni
Betoney Scordium Centry pimponell may weede
Sun dew and Motherwort of Each A quarter of
A pound virginian Snake weed one ounce the
Rutes of Elocompane piony and Tourmentell of
Each two ounces Liquorish two Drams
Exodore two ounces Annicedes two ounces
Cut your earbs but not very small slice the
ruts and liquorish beate the seeds then put
them into an earthen pot well nealed [sealed] power
vpon them 4 quarts of sack or two of white
wine and 2 of sack which you please
Lay the the ruts and the seeds and the Liquorish
at the bottome of the pot then cover your
pot Close and let it stande 40 howers then
Still it of in a cold still, your first sort being
the strongest you may give to old folks your
midle sort to any and your third to Children
but what ever sort you give mix some of your
Last sort with it you must not lett your
fier be to hot vnder your still and those
drugs that are too harde to Cut beate in A
morter but not small

[fol. 14v]   **for making of a hash with a Calves head**

take your Calves head and parboyle it
very well cut the one side of it in thin
slices take it and se stew it ouer the fire
with a quart of white wine a pint of

---

15 Hand G (14, 15, 16, 19, 20–[21v] top recipe, 19, [24v]–25 top recipe) includes
    varied letter sizes, especially c/C and s/S, and it is very difficult to determine the
    contributor's intention in capitalization. There is no indication of the identity of the
    contributor.

grauie and a pint of strong broath
a fagget of sweet herbs an onion chopt
small a couple of anchouies an hand
full of oysters stew it very well togeather season it with a littel peper
and sault take the side of the head and
season it well with peper and sault &
sweet herbs chopt small wash them
well with the yelke of an egg broyl it
vpon a gridiron thicken it vp your
hash with a couple of yelks of eggs
put the one side in your dish garnish
your dish with sippets all sorts of pickled
pickled oysters slised, limmond force
meats sossinges dish it vp hot and serve
it in –

15   **To Stew A Carpe**

Take A Carpe Alive, scower him well with Salt
then scale him or not as you thinke fitt
then open him power into his belley A little
vineger and rub him within with salt w*hic*h
will make him bleed freely then take
him with his blood and Liver and put them
into A Shallow Stewpan or Keetle then
take of time Swett marjorum and parsley
a prety quantyty with A Sprig of winter
Savory and rosemary binde them in little
bundles and put them to your carpe with
A blade or two of mase A peece of
Lemon peele and three Anchoves then
power vpon him as much Clarret wine
as will well cover him Cover your stew=
=pan and sett it one A quick fier till
it be sufitiently Stewed then take the
carpe and Lay it with the broth into the
dish and power vpon it A quarter of A
pound of fresh butter well bea melted and
beaten with halfe A dozen sponfulls of
the broth the yoacks of two or three Egss,

and some of the hearbs shreded if you will
soe serve it vp.

[fol. 15v]   **for making of pust past**

take a quarter of flower two pound of
butter fouer eggs breake a litle butter in
the flower woorke it vp put three coate
of butter two of flower for boyling of
the Aple take a littel Cloves and mace
and cinamon and put it in the aple and
put a littel sider in for Coullering the
aple red take a penniwoortth of
scuchineale pound it in a marter
take a littel rose water and put into
it stur it well to gether in the aple to
Couler the aple yellow take a pennywoorth
of safrron dry it well at the fire beate
it in a marter then boyle it in the aple
with the rose water to couler *the* aple purple
take one penny woorth of turnsole boyle
it in the aple to Couler the aple green
take a handfull of serrill or spinnage
use the iuice of it ~~ste~~ stir it in the aple /

16   **To stew A Carpe Another way**

Take A Live Carpe Gut and scale it give it
A cut in the neck Lett it bleed well then take
the blod Clarrett and watter as much as will
Just Cover it their must be as much Clarret
as watter A little viniger A bundle of Sweet
herbs whole mace Cloves whole pepper
nutmeg Salt and onion or Shallot A peece
of lemon peele Stew them in A Stew
pan or deepe dish over A Chafindish
of Chartcole they must Stew very gently
for feare of Brakeing when they are
Enough take Some of the Liquor and
Sett it over the fier with three or foure
Anchoves when they are desolved put in
Some butter beate it all up. very thick
with two or three yoaks of Egss you must

take care the Egs doe not Curdle you
may put in Stewd oysters if you please
and soe serve it vp.

[fol. 16v]   **to make snow**

take three pints of creame and the whits
of eight eggs strain them to gather with
a littel rose water and as much suger as
will sweeten it then take a bundle of reeds
and beat your cream as the snow riseth
take it of with a spoone in a cullender
that the thin may run out when you
haue snow anough to couer a dish take
the cream that remains and boyle it
with hole cloues and sinamond till it
bee thick then strain it and when it is
cold put it into a dish and lay your
snow upon it and seru it vp –

to make sasinges

take two pound of ientle line[16] of a
hodg and one pound of the leane and
beat it to gather in a morter and when
it is a nough season it with peper
and salt and spice then roul it vp
in <...>les[17] and fry them in a pan with
butter

17   **A very good water for a feavor**

Take halfe A pound of mint as much
Balme A quarter of A pound of
popys a quartre of a pound of card
vs halfe A quartre of a pound of
wormwood halfe A pound of
angelica shred the herbs and steepe

---

16 As noted in the Glossary, "line" likely means loin, while "ientle" is "jentle" or
"gentle," meaning tender.
17 There is an ink blot over the first part of this word in the manuscript, but the word
is almost certainly "roles" or "rowles."

them all night in 4 quarts of new
milke to ounces of cin*n*amon A hand
full of maregould flowers and one
handfull of burage flowers distill
it in A Could still 3 quarts of good
water will come out of it –

[fol. 17v]   **to make biskets Mrs Beales way.**

take seuen eggs and devide the yolks
from the ~~wh~~ whits then beat vp the
whits with a burchin rod in a deep
pan till they frothe very much then
put in the yolks and beat them well
to gather then put into them a pound
of the best powder shuger and a
pound of fine flower still beating
with a slice then drop it vpon paper
and sift some lofe suger ouer them
and bake them in a an oven not to hot
when they bee colered on the top take
them of the papers and put them on
a siue into the ouen a gain to dry –

18   **A most excalent glister for**
                   the spleen and wind

Take A pinte of new milke boyle
in it a handfull of Camamile
flowers or Camamile put to it
when it tis strained to spoonfull
of pouder shuger and 5 drops of
spirits of Castor –

to Cause Sleepe in a weake Porson.[18]

take white Popey seeds and sow them in
to litell bags either tifaney or ~~lanel~~ and

---

18   Hand H (this recipe, 25 lower recipe, 51–[52v] top recipe) is a round, decorative
     hand. The curled letters and the spelling suggest that this contributor is a child, as
     does the crossing out of the recipe at the top of 51 before it is begun again below,
     which might reflect an immature frustration.

put them in a litell anyseed water and
at night a ploye them to each tempell
warm it before you A ploy it to the place

[fol. 18v]   **to make Bisket**

take to pounds of sifted suger and to
pounds of fine flower and sixtene eggs
and put them in a crock and as you beat
ẙ your eggs put in a handfull of flower
and a nother of suger till it is all in
strew it in very light then put in four
spoonfulls of sack then beat it vp as
hollow as you can for two houres and
neuer let it stand still then put into
it coliander seeds and caraway seeds
as many as you think fit beat them
a gain a littel then drope it with a
spoone vpon tinn sheets being ~~butr~~
butored before into littel round bisketts
then sift them ouer with suger and
flower and put them in an oven not
to hot when they be bakeed pare the
botom of them and put them in a
seue [sieve] and papers between every row
and when the oven is allmost cold
put them in a gain to harden then
keep them in a dry place –

19   **to Make A Cake**

Take six pounds of fflower five pound of Curants one
pound of Reasens of the sun Cut and stoned one pound
and A halfe of butter one quart of Creame one pintt of
Barme take tenn Eggs and beate them with two or three
sponefulls of Rose watter Keepeing out two of the whites
take half A sponefull of sallt two penyworth of Cloues
and mace one pound of loafe shuger two ounces of
dates one peece of sifforne one leamond of muske
and ambergreace each one graine

How to mix it

Take your flower and put it into A pann or trind and
soe make A hole as big as you thinke will holde your
wetting first put in the salt and spice then put in A quar=
=ter of A pounde of your shuger beaten very small then
put in the barme and Eggs take your Creame and make
it soe hot as to melt the butter and then sturr it
togeather and see that it be not to hott to scald the
Eggs then putting it into the rest take some flower
and strew gently over it soe setting it by the fier and
let it heave [heat?] one hower or more after it hath
stood as long as you please then take it and kneyde
it putting in halfe the muske and ambergb^r^ease then
lett it stay vntill your oven be ready and when
your oven is A gooing to be sweept then take
and <...> mix in it your fruite and suckitts and beshu
=er you doe not lett it stay long after the fruite is
in out of the oven in the meane time while your
Cake is in the oven take the remaineing part of the
shuger and pound and sift it then take it with the two
whites of the Eggs and beate it all the while your
cake is in the oven if it be too thicke then
put in some Rose water and the rest of the muske
and when you thinke it is baked Enough then draw
and put on your Iceing.   and then Eat it as fast as you
Can.

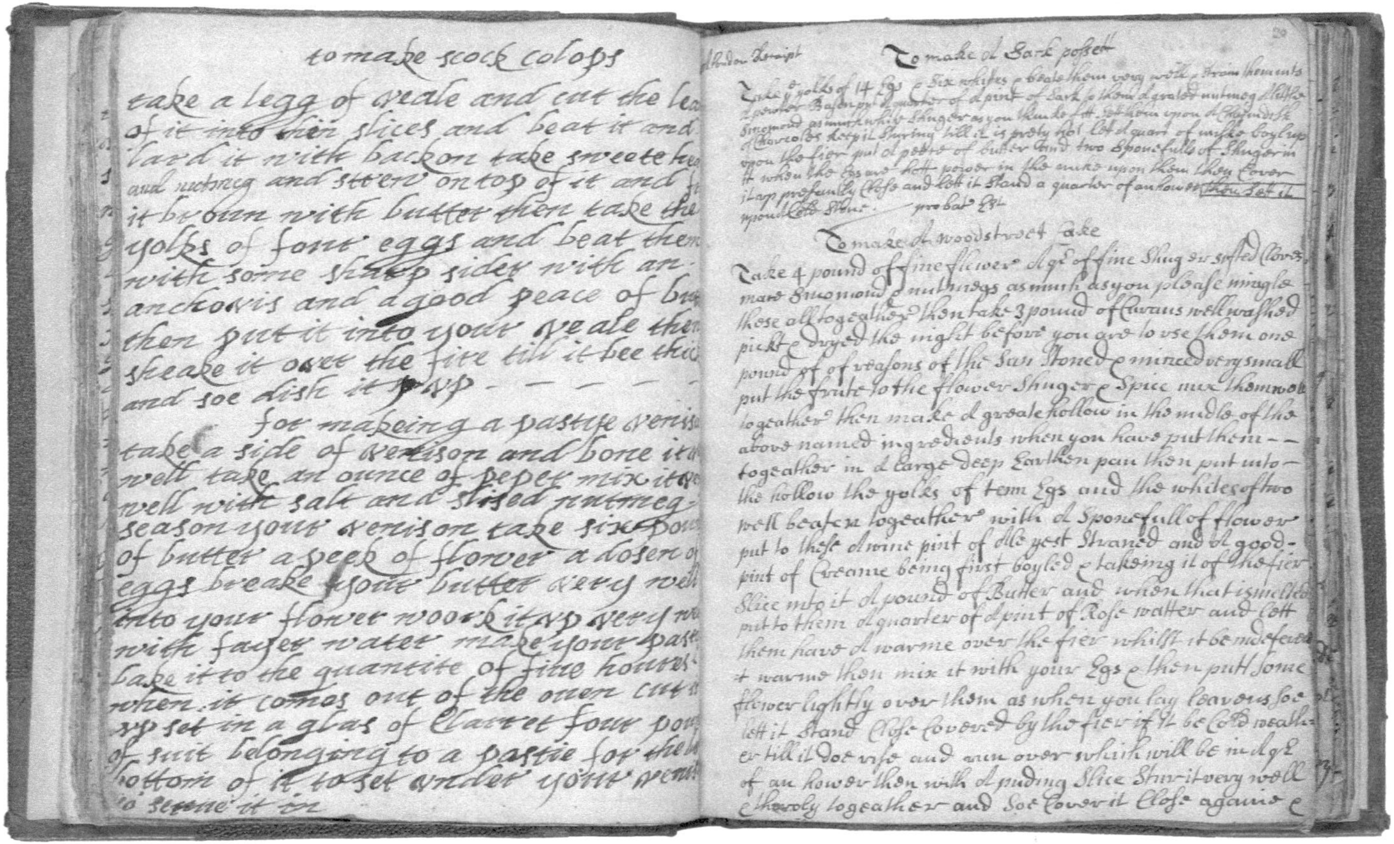

Fig. 2.2 Folger MS V. a.20, fols. 19v/20r. By permission of the Folger Shakespeare Library.

[fol. 19v]   **to make scock colops**

take a legg of veale and cut the lean
of it into thin slices and beat it and
lard it with backon take sweete hearbs
and nutmeg and strew on top of it and fry
it broun with butter then take the
yolks of four eggs and beat them
with some sharp sider with an
anchovis and a good peace of butter
then put it into your veale then
sheake it over the fire till it bee thick
and soe dish it ~~vp~~ vp –

for makeing a pastye venison

take a side of venison and bone it very
well take an ounce of peper mix it very
well with salt and slised nutmeg
season your venison take six pounds
of butter a peek of flower a dosen of
eggs breake your butter very well
into your flower woork it vp very well
with fayer water make your pasty
bake it to the quantite of fiue houres
when it comes out of the ouen cut it
vp set in a glas of Clarret four pounds
of suit belonging to a pastie for the ~~bon~~
bottom of it to set vnder your venison
so serue it in

20   A london Receipt
               To make A Sack possett

Take *the* yolks of 14 Egs & six whittes & beate them very well &
                                              strain them into
A pewter Bason put a quarter of A pint of sack to them A grated
                                                nutmeg A little
sinomond as much white shuger as you thinke fitt sett them
                                              vpon A Chafindish
of charcoles keep it sturing till it is prety hot lett A quart of milke
                                                         boyl up

vpon the fier put A peece of butter and two sponefulls of Shuger in
it when the Egs are hott power in the mi[l]ke upon them then Cover
it vp presently Close and lett it stand a quarter of an hower then sett it
upon A Cold Stoue. probat*um* Est

To make A woodstreet Cake[19]

Take 4 pound of fine flower A q*uarte*r of fine Shuger sifted Cloves
mace sinomond & nutmegs as much as you please mingle
these alltogeather then take 3 pound of Curans well washed
pickt & dryed the night before you are to vse them one
pound of of reasons of the Sun Stoned & minced very small
put the frute to the flower Shuger & Spice mix them well
togeather then make A greate hollow in the midle of the
above named ingredients when you have put them
togeather in A large deep Earthen pan then put into
the hollow the yolks of tenn Egs and the whites of two
well beaten togeather with A Sponefull of flower
put to these A wine pint of Ale yest Straned and A good
pint of Creame being first boyled & takeing it of the fier
Slice into it A pound of Butter and when that is melted
put to them A quarter of A pint of Rose watter and lett
them have A warme over the fier whilst it be indeferen
:t warme then mix it with your Egs & then putt Some
flower lightly over them as when you lay leavens soe
lett it Stand Close Covered by the fier if it be Cold weath=
er till it doe rise and run over which will be in A q*uarter*
of an hower then with A puding Slice Stir it very well
& thoroly togeather and Soe Cover it Close againe
[fol. 20v]   lett it Stand an hower in the intrim prepaire your
papers thus to bake it in the botome papers must be A
sheet of browne & white paper that which goeth round
about the Cake must be duble white of A yarde & half
long & halfe quarter & naile depe when you have sewn
your papers to geather in A round forme to the botome

---

19 This recipe calls for the cake to be baked in a mould made of papers sewn
together. The paper that will form the sides of the mould must be a yard and
a half long; when they are sewn together, they must be "halfe quarter & naile"
deep, a measurement that must mean "half *of a* quarter of *a* nail." A nail in English
measurements of length was two and a quarter inches, so one eighth of this length
would be just over a quarter of an inch.

Soe high as you intende the Cake Shall Come then
with A Spone put your Kake into this Coffin & Soe into
the oven and their lett it Stand 3 *quarters* of an hower
then draw it & Ice it thicke over and Soe sett it in
againe & lett it Stand A *quarter* of and hower then draw
it and when it is Cold pull of the papers.

How to bake the Above named
Cake

Your Oven must be heated as it is for white Small
loves of Bread & before you sett it in you must
sweepe the oven & Sett up the Stone halfe A *quarter*
of an hower or Else it will Crack the Cake.

you must be shewer to butter the inside of your
papers before you putt your Cake in that they
may Come of without Sticking.

21

To make A Lumbard Py
Secend Cource[20]

Take A Couple of two peneyloves grate them very
well take halfe A pound of Currans three kidnes
of veale or for want of them the flesh of pullett
Capon turkey or rabitt Chopt it very Small mix
it well togeathar Season it well with Cloves
mase and A little Salt worke it vp very well
with A pint of Sack the yoaks of fower Eggs A
glass of Roas watter Sweeten it well with
Shuger make it up in Round balls Rais your
Coffin lay it well in the bottom with Sweet butter
Lay them in your Coffin take halfe A pound
of marrow and put in with them take halfe
A pound of Canded leamond oringe peale
Ringoe Roots & dryed dates lay them all in

---

20 The title of this recipe highlights the fact that many dishes contained both savoury
and sweet ingredients. Although this recipe calls for various meats, it also calls for
cloves, mace, rose water, candied citrus peel, dried fruit, and preserved fruit, and a
last step is to "Sweeten it well with / Shuger." Sweet pies, meanwhile, often called
for marrow or suet (such as the Hall manuscript's rice pudding on fol. 23).

Slices & peeces in your quarters whear you
see Conveniant take likewise halfe A pound
of preserved peaches & Aprecocks and doe
the Licke Bake it & take halfe A pint of
Sacke for the makeing your Caudle the
yoaks of two Eggs Sweeten it well with
Shuger A peece of Sweet Butter thicken it
very well over the fier put it into your
pye when it Comes out of the oven &
Soe Serve it in.

[fol. 21v]   **To make Cheescakes**[21]

you must Sett very tender togeather 4 quarts of new
milke & halfe A pint of Creame and when you have
got it Cleane from the whey you must beat it in
A morter with A wooden pesteell till you be shuer
the Curd be all broke then put in Sume thing about
A quarter of A pound of fresh butter and beate
it till you cannot see any of the butter then
take it out of the morter and mix it with the
yoaks of Six Eggs & three whites A nutmeg half
A pound of Currans allmost halfe A pint of Cream
three Sponefulls of Shuger A little Rose watter
this quantyty will make Just Six in the patypans

**Annother way to make
Chese Cakes**

take a pound of iordane almons and blanch
them in cold water and beat them in a
morter putting to them a littel rose water
and fire to them now and then to keep them
from oyling you must beat a dusen of eggs
yolks and whits and mix them <.>with a
quart of creame and let them run throw
a seeue and then put your almonds and
creame and eggs to gather and set it ouer
a charcole fire sturing it that it maynot not
burn to and when it doth begin to heat you
may store [stir] in half a pound of currans and

---

21   For some reason, this whole recipe is shifted right in the original manuscript.

put what suger you think fit when you
find it begin to turn a littel take it of and
let it stand till it be cold –

22   **To make a tansie**

Take a quarte of new cream
and a qurter of a pound of
napell biskets grate them
and put them into the cream
and a grated nutmeg and 2
penyworth of spinnig and a
handfull of tansy pick it and
and wash it very clean and
swing it in a clean corse
cloth put in the straind throw
a hare sefe²² take 14 eggs mtake
away 6 of the whits and bete
them very well and strain them
in to the Juice then put the cream
in and sweten it very well put
in a littell salt put it into a
cleane skillit put in a bout 2
ounces of fresh butter and
melt it and shake it all a bout
the skillet then put in the tansy
and set it ouer the gentell fier
and keep it stiring tell it is as
thick as batter then take a round
tin puding pan and butter it
[fol. 22v] well then put in your tansey and put
it in an ouen that is not to hot and half
an hour will bake it then put it on a
plate or a maserene and squis the Juice
of 2 orings upon it and good store of
double refind suger beten small garnesh
with slices of carue [carved] oring and qurters
if you bake it in a frying pan it most
be with a gentell fire but an ouen is beter

---

22 In other words, strain the mixture through a hair sieve.

To make a quaking puding

Take a peny lofe and grate it take a
pinte of cream and 8 eggs put away
the whites bete them very well grate a
nutmeg and 2 sponfull of rosewater mix
all these together a littell salt and as much
suger as will make it plesent let your
puding cloth byle in water a littell
then squse it out and spreade it ouer
with butter then strew it ouer with
flower and lay it in a bason put in the
puding and tey it vp clos one hour will
boyle it for sa[u]ces a littell sacke and a
quarter of a pound of sweet butter
and a good sponfull of fine suger set it
ouer the fire and melt it thick and scrape
lofe suger <...> vp on the puding
and round the brims of the dish pour
on the sauce so serue it to the table
you may coler it with Juyce of spin
nage or cowslips or uialets or marygolds

23

To make a rice puding

Take a qurter of a pound of rice and boyle
it in a quart of milke tell it be very tender
then put it in to a cullinder and let all *the*
milke draine from it beate it in a marter
grate in a qurter of a pound of napell
bisket a pint of cream and 6 eggs a
grated nutmeg a littell beten cinnamon
2 sponfulls of sack a littell rose water a
littell solt and as much suger as will
seson it to your taste then take a cloath
dipt it in boyling water and butter it
ouer well and strew it ouer with flower
and ~~boyle it~~ tey it vp clos and boyle it
one hour make sauce for it with butter
and suger melted thicke pure it one the
puding scrape on suger and beten cin
namon and serue it to the table if you

bake him then put in halfe pound of
currans and halfe as many resons and 3
qurters of a pound of beff suet sred on hour
will bake it the ouen must not be to hot

[fol. 23v]   **To make an Allmond puding**

Take half a pound of almonds and blanch
them bete them in a morter with 3: or 4 spon
fulls of rosewater grate a qurter of a
pound of napell bisket or the crum of a
peny lofe a littell beten mace a litell salt
and as much suger as will make it plesent
a pint of cream and 8 eggs take away
half the whits bete them very well and
straine them throw a hear sefe mix it
well to gether dip a cloth in boyling ~~war~~
water and squese it out hard then butter
it all ouer and put the puding in it and
tey it up clos and let it boyle quicke on hour
take a qurter of a pound of smoth suger
almonds or blanch almond and stick
them <<>>vpon the puding 4: sponfulls of
sack a good pece of fresh butter and melt
it thick and sweten it and pour it all
ouer the puding before you stick the
almonds scrape sume fine suger on the
brims of the dish so serue it vp –

24   **To make an oringe puding**

Take the pels of 4 good oringes and boyl
them in a good quantity of faire water
on hower then pour it away and put
as much as at first and boyle it as be
fore on hower and so doe for 3 times
then put them in to could water and let
them ley all night ~~tha~~ take them out and
dry them in a cloth and bete it in a stone
morter very fine and halfe a pound of
napell bisket grated and on quart of
cream and: 10: eggs take away halfe *the*

whites bete them very well and strain
them in to the cream grate a small nut
meg and put in a littel salt & halfe a pound
of good suger ster it well to gether then
~~heave~~ haue a thin sheet of pufpast and
flower the bottom of a depe pewter dish
lay on the pufpast then put the puding
halfe a pound of good fresh butter
butter it all ouer the puding in small
peces then couer it with a nother sheet
of pufpast not to thick and cut it with
fine works & on *the* brims of *the* dish on hour
will bake it.

[fol. 24v]   **for a Quinsey or Sore throte**[23]

Take Sallet oyle large mace & red Sage boyle
them togather annoynt the throte & lay a red
cloth on it to keepe it warme

for Convoltion ffitts

Take Rosemary Stamp it & Straine it & give
it on a Sponefull of beare before the fitt or
new mone

Doctor Morus his Purge

Two Ounces of mannah 3 Scruples of Salt
prunella in a quart of Whaye

for the Green Sickness

Take rosa Sollis new gathered beat it into a
conserve with Suger lett the party eate as
much as a nuttmegg fasting fast 2 hours
after it vseing exersise in a weeks time it
Shall Cure them

---

23 The copying of the entire sequence of short remedies from [24v] to 26 in one hand
and to [26v] in another suggests that, as Emily Bowles Smith notes above, someone
indeed used this manuscript to practise her handwriting.

for the Stone

1. Take a pint of Beane watter 8 ounces of
    marsh malloes take 2 spoonfull at a time

for Stomach wormes

2. Take 3 bunches of Lavender cotton boyle it in
    a pint of new milke take night & morning
    fasting

for a Sore Throte

3. Take allum fine Suger planton watter honey
    of roses Surip of mullberys of each a little quan*tity*
    to gargle the throte.

for the falling Sickness

4. Take young ravens when they are ready to fly
    bake them with browne bread till they are
    powder mix it with honey till it is an electuary

25   ### for a Sore Brest

Take Hemlock & oatemeal & lilly roote a handfull Chopp
these togather & make a plaister anoynt the place
with warme milke twice a day

for a Spraine or bruse

Take a handfull of bay leaves 2 handfull of Camom
ell. Rosemary & Sage of each one handfull Chop them
them togather & mingle them to gather with may
butter put them in a Seller nine days Clarefie it
& keep it for your use

a Glister for wormes

boyle a little wormseed & Southenwood & Sentry in
posset drinke Sweeten it with brown Suger drinke
it 3 weeks togather

To pickle Mushrooms

Pick them and wash them in 3 or 4 waters
with a good deal of salt then put then [them] into
a kettle with a good quantity of salt without
any water so let them boyl till they be
tender make the pickle of white wine
vineger nutmeg mace cloves ginger peper
and put them up hot
If you have but a few you must boyl them
with a little water.

[fol. 25v blank]

26   ### For a quinsey or sore Throte[24]

Take sallet oyle large mace red sage boyle
*the*m together and anoint *th*e throte lay a red cloth
on it

For convulton Fitts ~

Take rosemary stampt it stram it give it in
a spoonfull of Beere before *th*e fitt or now

Doctor: Morns his Purge

Two ounces of manna 3 scruples of salt
Prunella in a quarte of Whay

For the Greene Sickness

Take Rosa-solis new gathered beate it into a
consarve w*hic*h [with] suger let *th*e partey eate as much as
a Nutmeg fasting fast 2 houres after it vseing
Excercise in a weekes time it shall cure them

---

24 Hand I (26) copies a sequence of remedies from [24v], presumably in order to
practise handwriting, as the page is carefully lined and there seems to be a
half-attempt at a majuscule T in "For the stone" that is abandoned and then begun
again below (not copied). The contributor does not quite get it all right: see "stram"
rather than "strain." However, the contributor is likely not a child just learning to
write; she uses a mixed hand, the letter forms are confident, and the writing has a
consistent slant. There is no indication of the identity of the contributor.

For the stone

Take a pinte of Beane watter 8 ounces of
March mallowes take 2 spoonfull at a time

For Stomack wormes

Take 3 Bunches of Lavender cotten boyle it
in a pinte of new milke take it Night and an
amor[25]

[fol. 26v]   ### For a Sore Throte[26]

Take allum fine Suger planton water
honey of rosses Surrup of Mulberryes of Each
a Little quantity gargle *the*· Throt /

ffor the falling Sickness

Take young Ravens when they are redy to
ffly bake them with Browne Bread tell they are
Powder· mix it with honey tell it is an Electuary

ffor a Sore Brest

Take hemlock and Ottmell a handfull of a
Lilly roote chop those to Gether and make a
Playster Anoint the plase with warme Milke
Twice a day /

ffor a Spraine or Bruse

Take a handfull of boye Leaves 2 handfull
of Camomell Rosemary Sage of Each one

---

25 It seems the contributor broke off in her copying of the recipe from [24v].
26 Hand J ([26v]–[41v]) also copies a sequence of remedies from [24v] and 25, again
    perhaps with the aim of practising handwriting, before adding new recipes. It is a
    secretary hand and ends most recipes with a virgule or a larger slash. Letter sizes
    are also varied with this hand; again, the ambiguous letters are usually c/C and
    s/S, although v and w are also sometimes scarcely distinguishable. This hand
    includes earlier conventions such as double f. There is no indication of the identity
    of the contributor.

handfull Chop them to Gether mingle *them·* to gether
with may Butter put them in a Seller Nyne days
Clarifie them and keepe them for your· vse /

A Glister for wormes

Boyle a Little wormehood and Sowthernwood &
Sentry in possett drink Sweeten it with Browne
Suger Drink it 3 weekes to gether /

A nother medson for the stone

To a quarter of a pinte of white wine put as
much Black Cherry water 2 ounces of Surrip of
Lemond as much Surrup of Mallows Take 4
Spoonefull in a Morneing and 4 in the
Affter Noone /

27

A drink for a Cough

Take a handfull of ffiggs a handfull of reasons
2 ounces of dates an ounce of greene Liquorish
halfe an ounce of Aniseeds a quarter of an ounce
of Elicum pane boyle it halfe a way Sweeten it
with halfe an ounes of Suger Candy Drink it
Night and Morneing /

To make Surfitt water

Take a Gallon of the best Aquevitæ put it in
a greate Glass bottle then put it into it Resons
of the sun Ston'd white Suger Candy of Each 2
pounds, nutmeg Cominout[27] Cloves beaten of Each
an ounce Liquorish sticke Sliced Anyseed Beaten
of Each 2 ounces Then add to it a quart of Red
popie water and a pinte of Damascke Rose
Water Stopp up the Bottle Closs Shacke it once
a day: you may make a Second sorte of water when

---

27 As noted in the Glossary, "cominout" likely meant "cinnamon," as this ingredient is
called for in similar recipes in M.H.'s *The Young Cook's Monitor*, Hannah Woolley's
The Queen-Like Closet (1670), and others.

you have Drawne of the first by puting in halfe
the Quantity of waters /

To make Surrup of violetts

Take a pinte of Spring water and a pound & halfe
of Double Refin'd Suger and boyle it tell it be
a Surrup then take a good quantity of violetts and
beate them well then put them into the Surrup
when it is over the fire and lett it stand a
Little then Straine it out and put it up for
Your· vse /

[fol. 27v]   ### To make a Cake

Take 5 pound of fflower dry it 5 pound of
Currants cleane pickt washed and Dry'd 3 quarter
of a pound of Suger one quarter of a Ounce of
Sinnimond 3 Nutmegs and a little Salt mix
them all together then take a quarte of Creme
warmed a pound and halfe of Butter melted a
good pinte of Ale Barme 16 Eggs halfe the
whites Beaten them very well soe put your·
currants and Butter and Barme and Eggs into
the flower mix it all to Gether put it before
the fire to rise a bout a quarter of an hower
if will you may put Sack into it and Ice it with
Double refin'd Suger and Rose water and a
Spoonefull of Storch Beten on way all the while
Your· cake backes and then <...> power it on the
   Topp /

To make Schotch Scollops

Take a Legg of vele and cut the ffleshey parte
into Thin Slices as a Shilling and as broad and
as Long as your· fore finger then hack and beat
them with the Back of the Knife then fry them
Browne and not Enough over a quick fire then
take them out & keepe them hot then put in A
pinte of Stroung broath or Clarrett or gravie and
2 Sollots or a Onion spriggs of time 2 of Sweete

margerum 6 of parsley mince them first and put
in Anchoves a halfe nutmeg as much pepper and
Cut a quarter of a pound of the fate of Bacon Cut
as small as peace Soe lett it Stew vp and put in
the collups and lett them Stew all together /
Two minuits and put in 6 yocks of Eggs Beaten
with a Spoonefull of viniger and a quarter of a pound
of Butter so Shake them together tell it is redy
to boyle and Soe Serve it up So you may fry
forse meate vele Sweet breads and Lamb stones
and Bacon Rround them and put in oyesters· and
Such things Larde it then plese /

28

How to make Sawce for ffresh ffish

Take for any of these Samon Trout or pike
perch Smelts or fflownder· or Plaice or Carpe or Towce
Take 2 Anchoves 2 Sallots and mince w*i*th it halfe
a Nutmeg and cut a Little horse Redish the In
=side of a Lemmon and halfe a pinte oyester· & quarter
of a pinte of gravey or Clarrett and lett them boyle
up then put in a pound of Butter and Stur it tell
it is all melted Soe Serve it up /

How to make forst meate

Take halfe a pound of vele the Same of Beefes
Suit mince it Small then take 4 Sprigs of time
4 of peny Royall halfe a handfull of Spinnige &
parcly a Nutmeg grated as much pepper a Spoonfull
of Salt, Soe worke this up all together w*i*th 3 or 4
Yolks of Eggs and halfe a peny white Loafe grated
and make Sume as Long and as Bigg as yo*ur*· finger
and Sum rowne and as Bigg as Small as y<..>^a^ Nutt
and fry them for hash or ffrigeces or Potage /

To make a Oyester or most sorts of ffrech ffish Pyes

Take a quarte or two of oyesters and see there
be noe gravell in them then take a quarter of a
nounce of Cloves and mace and much peppe*r* 2

Anchoves 2 Sallots 3 Sprigs of Sweet Margerum
[fol. 28v] Three of time 6 of parcly mince all these fine
and mix them with as much Salt as will lye on
a Sixpence Soe put them in your· Pye and a pound
of Butter a top and halfe a pint of Srimps and
Bake it an hower. then put in a Cawdle of
a pinte of white wine thickened with five
Yolks of Eggs /

The Lady Hulls Pumatum

Take Some of a Leafe of a hogg new Killed take
of the Skin put it into a Basson of cleane
water Shift it 2 or 3 times a day powering out
the Water and putting fresh when you haue so
Shifted it nyne dayes let it set in aplace where
there is no fire then take the best pipens and pare
them and Slice them as you would for friters cut
out the cores clene them take a clene new Erthen
Jugg and Lay a Layer of your Pippens first in the
Bottom of the Jugg then a Layer of the fat and soe
a Nother Layer of then pipens tell your· Jugg is full
then stop it very Close with a Double paper or Cloth
Soty [So tie] it downe then Set it in a Cettle of water
Lay a brick or Something on the tope that no water
getts In soe lett it boyle 2 or 3 howers then take
a fine Cloth and Straine it while it is hot into
a Basson then the next day turne the Cake and
Scrape all the blacke and throw away the water
then beate it in a Earthen or Silver bason 2 or 3
howers Still powering a way the water that comes
from it soe beate it tell it is as white as
Snow then put in Some Rose water to Cover
it all over the Same day beate it very well[28]
29   Rub the Tongues well with the Spice all over but
noe Salt Sticks them with a few cloves bake
them with Butter 6 howers then fill them with
Butter Keepe them for vse the Tongue must be
Cold before it is Stuffed /

---

28 Pages are evidently missing from the manuscript at this point, as what follows
belongs to a new recipe.

To make Seede Cakes

Take 4 pound of flower Scerckt fine a pound
of Butter & almost a pinte of Ale Barme with
a quarte of creme from the fire 4 Spoonfull
of Rose water when you haue mingled these well
together Lay it before the fire to rise halfe an
hower vntell the oven be made cleane let it
be not hotter the for Mainchett Sett up the
oven Lid after it is Cleane take a pound of
Biskets and halfe apound of carraway comefitts
mingled together then mingle your· paste with
these and make it in a Cake and lett it stand
a hower /

To make a Lemmond Sallett

Take as many Lemmons as yow· please put out
all the meate cleane them very well boyle
the rhrines very Tender dry *th*em· well with a cloth
and put them in a pott with viniger and a good
delle of Suger in a Short time they will be fitt
to Eate it is best to boyle the viniger and
Suger to gether first /

To Stew a Carpp

Power clarrett downe the mouth and cutt it
up take out the Gutts and Save the Blood put to
it Spice and Clarrit Onions Anchoves Sweete
[fol. 29v] Hearbs Sume peeces of Browne Bread a
peece of butter take for the Sawce Clarrett
Onion Spice Anchoves and the bread *that* was
Stew'd with· it masht fine and Straind through
a fine Cloth take as much as will thicken
the Butter and 2 yolks of Eggs /

To make an Orenge Pudden

Take 2 orenges either dry or wett beate *th*em
in a mortor tell they cum to a past and
then put to them halfe apound of butter &
beate them a quarter of an hower then put
in halfe a pound of Suger and beate this to-

gether then Take 18 Eggs the whits of 5
and beate *the*m well together then mix this
well together tell it be like butter then Lay
puft paste in the bottom of yo*u*r Dish put it
in the oven to harden before yow· put in the
Pudden into it, for the pudden must Stand
but halfe an hower in the Oven /

Mr Parkers way for a Hash

Take yo*u*r· caves head and boyle it tell it
begins to be a Little Tend*e*r then take it
it up keepe halfe of it whole Lard it with
Bacon and Lemmon peale Take the meate
cleane of the other parte but Saue the bones
ffry some of yo*u*r meate Stew some brile [broil?] the
whole side haue Lambs Stones Sweete breads
oysters Mushrones ffry some boyle some make
Batter of Eggs and fflowers dry Sage Leaues
And ffry them cut the braines in 4 Square
bits flower it and fry them put the bones
vnder the halfe head and pile all the first
<.>meate make <.> on it some Long some round
Stew some fry some /

To make a cold Possett

Take Sweete creme and boyle it w*i*th· some
Lemmon pele and a Sprige of Rosemary
and when it is boyl'd Lett it Stand tell it
be milke warme then haue reddy yo*u*r· possett
pot w*i*th· white wine a Little water the Juce
of Lemmon and Suger as you like it then
Standing on a high stoole power out the
Crem and be as Long a powering of it out
as you can Stur it and Lett it stand an
houer /

To make a whip Possett

Take a quarter of a pinte of Sack or more Season
it w*i*th Suger put it into it apinte of crem put

it in a bred dish then take a bunch of dry'd
Rosemary the Leaues Stript of whip it tell
you see a greate deale of froath rise then Take
it of with a spoone and Lay it on the Possett
cup tell it be full soe Lett it stand a hower or
2 before you Sarue it in you may make
The same with Clarrit or the Juce of
Rasburyes which· Lookes well /

[fol. 30v]   **To make Strawberry ffoole**

Take a quart of Sweete Creme and boyle it with
12 Eggs Leaue out all the whites 3 graines of Amber
grece lett it boyle thick but not crudle then take
it of the fire and put in halfe apound of Suger and
a quarte of ripe Strawberryes Stur all those to gether
and lett it be cold and soe Serue it up /

**How much ~~flower~~ ^Butter^ yow· must put to a peck of
fflower for all Sorts of Paste /**

1. ffor pye and Tarte paste 3 pounds of Butter
    to a peck of fflower and make the Paste with
    Boyleing water /

2. ffor puft paste Eight pounds of Butter and 8
    Eggs to apeck of fflower and mak the paste
    with Cold water /

3. ffor pasty Paste 4 pound of Butter and 6 Eggs
    to a peck of flower and make the Paste with
    Cold water /

    ffor Custard paste Boyleing water and noe
    Butter /

How To Season Custard Stuff

Sett 2 quarts of Creme over the fire with whole
mace and Slise Nutmegg when it is Scalding
hott Straine out the Spice then beate 14 Eggs leave
out the whites of 7 Beate the Eggs and Straine

out *the* Treads mix the Eggs and Creme together
with Suger and Rose water harden the Coffin
and fill it /

31   **How to make Marrow Pudden**

Slice halfe a pound of Biskett in Thin Squares
Slices then take the marrow of 2 bones cut
Square like dices and some Reasen Stones [stoned] and
Slice dates Sitterne and Orrieng and Canded
Lemmon mix these to gether and butter the
Bottom of the dish and Garnish *the* brimes with
Pufe paste and then fill it with a quarte of Creme
4 Eggs and Rose water and Suger and Nuttmeg /

To Season a Devonshire Pye

Cutt a Loyne of Mutton in Steaks and Seasone
them with peper and Salt and Apples and Onions
and a Little faire water bak the Pye 2 howers
when it is baked put in a Little drawne Butter
and Stire it all together /

To make a Carpe or Ele pye

Cutt in peeces the Ele and Season it with peper·
Salt Nutmegg Slice Lemmon and Barrberryes
and currants put butter in the Pye and bak
it 2 howers Schall [scale] and bone the carp Season
it as above put in Reasings and currants
and bake it 2 howers and make a Lear of
verges Butter and Suger and *the* yolke of an
Egg heate it over *the* fire and fill *the* Pye /

To make a Steak Pye

Cut a Loyne of Mutton in Steaks and Season
it with peper Salt and Nuttmegg sweet hearbs &
an Onion a few cappers put Butter in the Pye
and bake it 2 howers when it is baked fill it with
Anchoves Sawce /

[fol. 31v]   **To Season a Rice Pudden**

Boyle a quarter of a pound of Rice in a quart
of milk with Sinement whole and when it is
Tender· put in 4 Eggs and Sack Rose water
and Suger a Little Saffron and Marrow
and Currants and Cover it with Pufft paste /

To Season a Turkey Pye

Bone the Turkey and Larde it with fatt
Bacon and Season it with peper and Salt
and Cloves and mace and Nuttmeg put butter
in the· Pye and Bake it 4 Howers when it is
Bakt. fill it with Clarrifi'd Butter /

**To Season a Lamb Pye
or a vele Pye**

Cut the meate in Steaks and Season it *with*
peper and Salt and Nuttmegg and Suger put the
meate in the Pye and Large mace Sliced Lemmon
and Barberrys and Reasings and currants and Sweete
meats if yow· please put Butter in the· Pye and
Bake it 2 howers when the Pye is baked make
a Lear of white vine and Butter and Suger &
the Yolk of an Egg heate it over the fire
and fill the Pye /

To season a Chicken Pye

Cut the chickens in peeces and Season them
with Nutmegg Suger and Salt and a Little peper
put the Chickens in the pye then Large mace
Sliced Lemmon peele Dates and Barrberryes /
32   Canded Orrieng and Lemmon peele Dates and
Sitterne put butter in the Pye and Bake it 2
howers when it is baked make a Lear of Sack
Suger and Butter and the· yolk of an Egg heate it
over the fire and fill the Pye /

To season Goose Pye

Bone the Goose and Season it with peper and
Salt and Cloves and mace and ginger put
Butter in the pie and Bake it 4 houers when
then Pye is Baked fill it with Clarrified Butter

To make Sweete Water

Take a handfull of Sweete margerum a handfull
of time a handfull of Savory and a handfull of
hisop put halfe apinte of Damask Rose ~~water~~
Leaves Strip the herbs of the Stucks put them to
Steepe in the Rose water with the peele of halfe
a dozen Civill orrenges halfe a quarter of an
ounce of Sinamon the same quantity of Cloves
Mace Nuttmegg with a peniworth of Arras
Powder· put it all together to Steepe for a Night
then Still it of if you Double Still it, it will
Keepe the Longer /

To pott Venson

Take your· venson and beate it very well if
it be very fatt you must take some beafs Shuett
and beate with it *then*· Season it pretty high with peper·
and Salt and a Little Cloues and mace but not
to much of *the*· Latter, Lay 2 or 3 bay Leaues
[fol. 32v]   In the Bottom of the potts and then Lay
your· beaten venson in them Cover it thinn
with butter and cover the potts with paste
when it is Baked very Tender· then draine
it well from the gravie and put it into dry
pots and Kepe out the liquor and cover it
well with Butter /

To make an Orrieng Cake

Take 3 or 4 Orriengs Lay them in water
2 dayes Shifteing *the* water twice a day boyle them
Close cover'd tell they be Tender· take them
out and beate *the*m to a paste, to apound of

pulp a pound and halfe of Sugger with the
Juce of 2 Lemons Either boyle your· Suger
to Candy height & then: Stur in your Juce
and pulp or Else put them on the fire together
while *the* Suger Melted if you doe them *the*·
Latter way *the* Suger must be Beaten and
Sifted Drop *the*m and dry them in a
Stave /

To make a Gelly

Take vnckles of vele lay it in water one
night to take out the Blood put it in a *pip*ken
with a Gallon of Spring water Sett it on *the*
fire Scum it well let it Stew Safely tell it
Gelly Straine it from the meate & lett it
Stand tell it be cold take of all the fatt and
33 Putt *the* Gelly in ^a^ possnet Set it over *the*· fire to
melt put in 2 ounces of Siniment one ounce
of Nutmeggs brused and ounce of Loafe Suger
halfe a Spoonefull of Rose water 3 Spoonfull
of *the* Juce of Orrienges or Lemons *the* whites
of 8 Eggs beaton to a froth. Sett it on *the* fire
not Sturing it till it Boyles up run it through
a bagg offten till it Looks Clear /

To Hash a Calfes head

Take a Calfes head and boyle him Tender· *then*
Cut it in Small peeces and put to it apinte
of Clarrett with a little of *the* broth it is boyld
in and lett it stew gently then put in a good
peece of butter a Nutmegg 2 or 3 whole Cloves
a bundle of Sweete herbs bound up close take
6 onions apeece of fatt bacon cut small
and lett it Stew with 6 Anchoves Cut *the*· bones
and lett *the*m Stew beate *the*m 3 yolks of Eggs tas [toss]
it to gether in apan *the* Dish is Garnished
with hardychockes bottomes Sweete bread and
Lambs Stones /

To make a ffriggasee of Chickens or Rabbi^ts^

Take Chickens or Rabbets flay them and cut
them in Small peeces breake *the* bones take out
the Biggest of them dip it in yolks of Eggs and
fflower made into batter make Strong broth
of any meate you can gett and of *the·* bones
[fol. 33v]   And wast peeces of Chicken put in a
bunch of Sweete hearbs /

To make Cogs Biskett

Take 3 pound of fine flower well dry'd a
Ounce of Carraway Seeds 6 Spoonefull of Suger
Double Refin'd 6 Spoonefull of Ale 6 Eggs
the whites of Two and wett it with warme
Milk 2 peny worth of Safforn lett it Lye
to Rise /

~~Mrs. Bests way for Cleare Cakes~~[29]

~~Take 3 pints of Goosberrys top and Tayle~~
~~them put them in a Skillett with a little a bove~~
~~a quarter of a pinte of water sett them on the~~
~~fire and when the begin to boyle and discoulor~~
~~put in as much water as before by little~~
~~and Little and when it is thin as a pancake~~
~~batter Lett it boyle a quarter of an hower and~~
~~put it in a Canvas Strainer that is Sow'd at~~
~~one Cornner and /~~

To make Goosberry Biskett

Take 2 quarts of Goosberrys put them in a
Large mugg and Sett *the* mugg in a pott Cover'd
Close and boyle them lett not a drop of
water gett in *then* when very Softe take and

---

29   This recipe is crossed out with a large double x. It is written out in full on the next
     page.

pulp them through a haire sive then take *the*
~~plu~~ pulp & whisk it very well puting in *the·*

34 Weight of *the* pulp of fine Scarched double
Refin'd Suger whisk it 3 or 4 howers then
take Square peeces of white paper and make
Coffins put in y*our·* biskett Stuff, then sett y*our·*
Coffen on Tin plates and Sett them in a stone [stove]
and when it will come Clean out cut them
in w*hat* Shape yow· please and Searve it In /

Mrs Bests way for clear Cakes

Take 3 pints of Goosberrys top and taile *them*
put *the*m in a Skillett w*i*th a Little above a Quarter
of a pinte of water Sett in on the fire and when
they begin to boyle & dis couler put in as much
water as before by Little and Little and when
it is as thin as a pancake batter lett it
boyle a quarter of an hower and put it In
a Canvas Strainer *that* is Sow'd at one Corner
and hangh it up and lett it hangh without
Squeezeing and run out only Scrape it a Little
down w*i*th a Spone then take the weight of y*our·*
Liquor in double Refin'd Suger and beate it fine
and put to it Sett it over a Soft fire and Kepe
it Sturing tell it be desolved lett it not boyle
then put them out in Clear Cake glasses not
to thick and they will crome pule [crumple?][30] of *the* topp
Skin and they are the Clearer in all Cakes, Sett
them in *the* stone to Candy turne *the*m and cutt *the*m
into what place yow· please Keepe *the*m turning tell
they are dry *the* Goosberryes are done when they
are Greene w*i*th a Moderate fire /

[fol. 34v] **Scotch Scollops**

Cut thin Slices of a Legg of vele Chopp it
w*i*th *the* bake of a Knife lard it w*i*th Bacon time

---

30 As noted in the brackets, "crome pule" might be a variant of "crumple"; the
meaning here seems to be that if they do not boil, and are placed in glasses that are
not too thick, the surface of them will not crease and they will remain clear.

Lemmon peele dipp it in batter made of *the*
Yolks of Eggs and flower make balls of vele
Sweete hearbs peper Salt Nuttmegg Lemmon
Peele Anchoves all beate Small roule them
^up^ with yolks of Eggs and grated bread fry this with your·
meate in butter when they are pretty browne
power out the butter & Straine to them Some
Strong broth put in gravie (If yow have it)
Anchoves a bundle of Sweete hearbs nuttmeg
mace Slices of Lemmon a Little Solt Sallott
white vine lett it Stew A good while then put
In a Convenient quantity of Butter and
thicken it up with yolks of Eggs /

To make a Cold Hash

Take a Cold cappon or Chicken pule of *the*
Skin & put it in thin Slices & mix with it then
take 3 or 4 Cabbeg Lettis cut it grose and
mix with it oyle vineger and peper Solay it
Like a Star in the Dich and Garnish the Dish
with Lemmon peele and Blew flowers /

35   ### To make an Allmond Pudden

Boyle a pinte of Creme with Siniam*ent*· or nuttmegg
tell it tast well of the Spice then pare *the* crust
of a peny Lofe and Slice *the* crum in *the* creme
as it boyleth take it of *the* fire and cover it Close
tell it be Chocked [soaked?] Softe *that* yow may beate it to
a pap then put to it halfe a pound of Allmonds
reddy blanched and beaten with Rosewater very
findly 3 or 4 Yolks of Eggs a good quantity of
beefes Suit Shred very smale 3 or 4 Spoonfull
of Sugger as much Sake a Little Salt mingle
all those to gether and put them in a Dish
to bake lett not *the* oven be to hott before yow
put it In *the* oven Stick it thick with Resons
of *the* Son yow ^may^ make *the* Pudden with rice or flower
Schoked like *the* Bread and then it must be no
Bread /

To make Clowded Creme

Take a Gallon of Milke boyle it a pretty while
then put 2 quarts of creme Lett it boyle a pretty
while after that put in a Little Salt then put
in a Milk pan in a Coole place Skime
it next morning /

[fol. 35v]   ### To mak a Hash of vele

Cut *th*e vele in thin Slices season it w*i*th
Savory and time Shord [shred] Small and a little
peper apretty deale of Nutmeg grated then
put it in *th*e Dish or Stewpan w*i*th some butter
in *th*e bottom Cover it Close lett it stand on
the Coles a quarter of an hower then put in
a little oyster Liquor a few minced Capp*er*s·
then Sett it on *th*e Coles againe as Long as
before, Dish it out w*i*th Sippetts and take a
hard Egg & Spred *th*e white w*i*th parsly put i*n*
a little into yo*ur* sauce Garnish yo*ur·* Dish w*i*th
the rest then Sred *th*e yolk very Small and
Strew over the meate and soe Searue it up /

A Nother way to pickle Cowcombers

Take Cowcumbers Rub *the*m cleane lay them
In apott take water and Salt make Strong
Brine to beare an Egg lett it boyle and put
it to *th*e Cowcumbers· as hott as yow· can Soe lett
it Stand 24 howers take white wine vineger
and boyle it with Dallfennele seeds Cloves mace
Nuttmegg whole peper Ginger Draine out
yo*ur·* brine and put in yo*ur·* pickle, as hott as
You can /

36   ### To Preserve Goosburys

Take as much Sugger as yo*ur·* Goosberryes weigh
vnpicked and Stoned to every pound of Suger
take halfe a pinte of water when yo*ur·* Goose
=berrys are Clean peck't and Ston'd Sett yo*ur*
Suger and water over *th*e fire lett it boyle

before it be Skin'd put in your· Gooseberrys
and lett them boyle as fast as yow· can possible
^tell^ they be cleare and *the* Surrup thick enough
w*hi*ch will be in less then a quarter of houer yow·
must not put y*our* Goosberrys in y*our·* Glasses tell
they are plumb Run some of y*our·* surrupp
through a Tiffiny into y*our·* Glasses before the
Surrup is to much Yallow'd when *the* Goosberrys
have stud a Little put them up & run the
rest of *the* Surrup upon them through a
Tiffiny /

To dry Goosberrys

Take the fairest Goosberrys you can gett new
Gather'd cutt of all *the* Blacks pick them full
of holes w*i*th a pin take to Each pound of Goos:
3 q*ua*rters of a pound of Sugger take as much water
as will wett *the* Suger then put In goosberrys
and Suger in a presarueing pan and boyle them
tell they are Tender· lett *the*m Lye in *the* Surrup
2 or 3 dayes you may heate *the* Surrup and lay
*the*m on a Silver dish take to Every pound of
[fol. 36v] Goosberrys halfe a pound of Suger boyle
it to a Candy heigh power it on them as
Soone as they are Lay in *the* Dish lett *the*m
Lye 2 dayes Lay them in Glasses to dry in
Shifteing *the*m in cleane Glasses Every day /

To make a Gelly

Take 3 q*ua*rters of a pound of Red Rasberrys
and a q*ua*rter of a p*ou*nd of white[31] put to a pound
of – 3 quarters of a pound of Suger desolue
your· Suger in the Juce of Rasberrys sett *the*m
on the fire lett them Boyle tell you can
See them begin to Gelly take them of
and put them in Glasses /

---

31   In other words, white (unripe) raspberries.

To Preserve Cheny Orriengs

Take your· orrienges and lay them in water
24 howers changeing *the* water 3 times *then*
boyle them in 2 or 3 waters tell they be
Tender· then take them out and lay them
in a Cloth to draine take to Each of the
orrienges one pound of Suger and a pinte
of water and make a Surrup put *the* orrenges
into it Sett them over a few Embers halfe
a hower but they must not boyle, do soe 2
or 3 dayes boyle them in *that* Surrup tell they be
Cleare take *the*m out and set them on a Sive
to draine Soe yow· must make them /

37

To make Appricoke wine with· water

Take to Every gallon of Appricoks a Gallon o̶f̶
and halfe of water and 4 pound of Suger boyle
the Suger to gether power on the fruit, being
put in a Barrell Stop it up Close tell it hath
done workeing after 2 or 3 moneths drawe it
forth into a Nother vessel and put a pound of
Suger to feed it & when you finde it clear &
ffitt for bottleing draw it of yow· may draw a
strong water of the first thus yow may doe any
Sorte of fruit /

To make Clear Cakes of Plumbs

Put your· plumes into a pott Cover'd Close put
to it a Skilett of boyleing water lett *the* Juse be
all out of *the* Skins take to Every halfe pinte
of Juce a pound of Suger Stur it with a spoone
Sett it on warme Ashes one hower put it In
Glasses Sett them on a Stow [stove] turne them
when yow· thinke ffitt /

To Candy Appricoks

Preserve *the*m first till they Looke clear and
no Longer then take them of and lett them Lye
in *the*· Surrup 2 dayes then take *the*m out of it &

draine them clean from *the* Surrups put them in
a dry Glass take a pound of fine Suger and with a
pint of water boyle it halfe an houer Skime it
verry well whe[n] it is cold put as much of it on your·
Apricoks as will couer *them* put them in aStove to
dry put a Little fire to them / Every day /

[fol. 37v]   **To make poppie water**

Take a gallon of the best Aniseed water a
peck of the best poppes when they cum first an
ounce of the best English Liquorish Slice a q*ua*rter
of an ounce of Ginger Slice a q*ua*rter of an ounce
of dates a q*ua*rter of apound of Reasons of *the* Son Ston'd
6 figgs Slice a handfull of Mother time tops
of min[t]es one ounce of nutmeggs grated Steepe
this 9 dayes and lett *the* water be Strain'd and
Soe boyle it up with apound of lofe Suger tell
it comes to a Gallon /

To make Madam Buttlers Red watter

Take halfe a Busshell of poppies and 4 quarts
of Sack 2 quarts of Brandy 2 quarts of Suger
put it in a bottle Sett it in the Sun Close
Stop't lett it Stand 6 dayes then Straine it
hard out take 6 ounces of Liquorish 4 ounces
of dates Cloves ginger Nutmegg mace Each
an ounce Cardimum Seeds Caraway Seeds
of Each an ounce halfe a pound of ffiggs put
all these to gether and lett it Stand 3 dayes in
the Sun then Straine it out put to this halfe
a peck of Clove gilly flowers take 3 q*ua*rter of Suger
Candy finely beaten & put it in a bottle
Stop't Close /

38   **To Preserve Cherries**

Take a pound of Cherries cut the Stalk halfe
of Cross every Cherrie on the Top only rase
of *the* Skin take 3 q*ua*rters of a pound of other Cherries

pule of *the* Stalks & brack³² them without any
water & boyle them tell they cum to *the* couler
of Clarrett Straine them into a Bason and
take a pound and quarter of fine Suger beaten
Smale divide it into 3 parts put one parte into
the Liquor sett it over the fire untell the Suger
be melted take it of and Skime it lett it
Stand tell it be blood warme put in *the* Cheiries
<⋅> yow intend to presarue and lett them boyle
as fast as yow can then strew in one parte of
the suger let them boyle up againe take them
of the fire and Scum them and Strew the other
parte of the Suger lett them boyle as a foresaid· then·
take them with *the* fire with· a Thin Trencher *that* is
Round, upon a pen Knife point when they
be thick take them of the fire put on their
Skins when they are bett^w^en hott and Cold
Soe keepe them /

To presarue Damsons in Gelly

Take yo*ur*· Damsons and Slit them on *the* Side
take to one pound of Damsons 3 q*uar*ters of apound
of Suger boyle yo*ur* Suger and Scum it put in
yo*ur*· Damsons Sett them on the fire w*hic*h must
[fol. 38v] be Softe when yow· presarue them begin to
turne yo*ur*· Suger lett them boyle them with a
Gentle fire have yo*ur*· Gelly made thus take
some Damsons put them into a Gally pott
Sett them in apan of water take a Sive and
Straine out *the* clearest of it take to one pint
of Juce 3 q*uar*ters of a pound of Suger boyle yo*ur*
Suger Candy hight put in yo*ur*· Surrup and
boyle it tell yow see there is a little Scum put
yo*ur*· Damsons in Glasses and *the* Gelly on them /

To make marmalad of Appricoks

Pare yo*ur*· Appricoks and Stone them and cutt
them in Small peeces put them in a Silver

---

32 In other words, "break" or crush them.

Bason to *the* weight of the Apricoks put as
much refin'd Suger put yo*ur*· Suger into a
nother bason Just wett it with water lett
them boyle Severall tell the Suger be Candy
high tell yo*ur*· Appricoks be pap breake yo*ur*
greate peeces *with* a Spoone when yo*ur*· Sugger
is so high put in yo*ur*· Appricoks lett them
Stand on the fire tell they be well mingled
put them in yo*ur*· Glasses when thay are Cold
put them in a Stove keepe *the*m *with* a temperate
heate tell they are Canded all over if you
put red Currants it looks well yow must stone
them put yo*ur* white fruit into Glasses Sticke yo*ur*
red Currants as yow· please /

39 ### To make Gooseberry wine

Take 12 quarts of water and 36 pound of Goose
berryes bruse *the*m *with* water straine them and put
them in 12 pound of Sugger lett it Stand a
ffortnight

To make and Excellent Surfiet water

Take 2 po*und*· of greene walnuts before they be to
hard 2 po*und*· of figgs 2 handfull of reu Slice yo*ur*·
ffiggs and bruse *the*m *with the* walnuts and rew in
a Stone Morter, then put it in a ordinary
Steele put to it one quarte of Sack lett itt
Stand one houer to Socke [soak] *the* Steele being Close
pasted distill it *with* a soft fire puting in
Some Lofe Sugger as it drops, to Sweeten it
to *the* last [taste] *the* best time to make it is at mid
Summer /

To make Surrup of Gilly flowers

Take yo*ur*· Gilly flowers clip of *the* white take to
and ounce of Gilly flower 4 ounces of water
Scolding hott lett it Infuse all night in Stoue [stone]
or Silver pott cover'd close in *the* morneing Straine
them out take double *the* weight of your gilly flowers

in Double refin'd Suger put it into your· pan
power *the* Liquor to it sett it on *the* fire when
the Sugger is melted and your· Surrup Scalding hott
it must not boyle take it from *the* fire /

[fol. 39v]   **To make Aquemerabilis**

Take cubube cardimum golingule mace nut
megg ginger cinaman of Each 2 Drames
the Juce of Saladine one pinte of Juce of Speare
mints Juce of Baline of Each halfe a pinte
violett flowers Cowslips flower Rosemary
Buglas bells marigolds of Each 3 drames
bruse *the* Spice <.......> *the* flowers and *the*
Seed Steepe <..> in 2 quarts of Sack put in
one pint of Angelico water one pint of
Red rose water Steepe your· Ingredience in
Liquorish one night distill it draw it
of in Glass bottles hide it in Sand Sweeten
it with double Refin'd Suger /

To wash Poynt

Take your· poynt and Sope it on *the* rite Side
lett it Lye in water all Night warme your·
Suds and wash it out of *tha*t make 2 Lathers wash
it well out of *tha*t if it be yellow Lay it on the
Grass a night or 2 first boyle it and put it
to some Cold water if yow See it not white
then Sett it to whitten giue it a Lather run
it with water that has no blew after *tha*t run it
in blew water *tha*t is made with Stone blew Starch
it with Holland Starch it on *the* rowng Side Lay it
in a Cloth a Little dry it ^in^ your· hand pule it as Even
as yow· can Lett it not be to dry nor to wett Iron
it not with to hott an Iron lett *the* cloth be pretty
thicke *tha*t it is Iron on if your point be high rais'd
take *the* Gloss of with a dry cloth rub it pick every
purle in his place /

40   **To Stew a Lampry**

When he is Skin'd season him with a little Salt
and pepper· and Sliced nuttmeg all over & in his
belly some Cloves and Largge mace whole and
Some Sliced Lemon and Sume thin Sliced^s^ of
Butter lett him then be rowled round and A Skure
thrust through to turne him with the Liquor
must be apint ^an halfe^ of white wine or halfe white
wine and halfe sider· put a little Butter in
the Bottom of the pan before yow put on the
Liquor and Some thin Slices of Butter upon
the Top of the Lampries when he is stewing
sett the pan over A stoue Charcole fire and
Ad to the Liquor a bundle of Sweete hearbs
and a Sliced onion turne the Lampry often
in the Liquor and when he is Tender· Enough
bruse 2 Anchoves into thin parts and Infuce
mix on of the best of gravie beate a Little more
butter make your· Sauce and thicken it care
fully with the Yolk of an Egg /

                    To Order· calfes feete

Boyle them and Slice them in the middle & noch it
boyle it with 3 quarts· of milk with halfe an ounce of
Sinomon boyle it to 2 quarts then take it
of and Straine it Sweeten it with halfe and
ounce of white Suger Candy and putt to it 6
Spoonefull of red Rose water Drinke of halfe
a porrienger at night and morning /

[fol. 40v]   **To make Rice pancaks**

Take a quarter of apound of rice boyle it
very tender when you can make it Small
with the back Side of a Spoone put as much
milke to it as will make it pretty thin
then with fine flower make it of the thickest
batter then put in 4 Eggs and a quarter of
a pound of melted Butter beate it well
and lett it Stand 12 howers before yow fry

them w*h*ich· you must do w*i*th· fresh Butter
and not make *the*m very thin Strew Suger &
the Juce of a Lemmon over them /

To make A Pudden

Take halfe a pint of crem put to it a
q*u*a*r*ter of a pound of butter then sett it on *the*
fire tell it be hott *tha*t it well melt *the* butter
put in 3 Eggs well beaten and crumbs of
bread to make it thick as for a pancake
butter *the*n put in a Little Sugger and
Nuttmegg a Little Salt 2 Spoonefull of
rose water butter yo*ur*· Dish well and lay
paste a bout it and Bake it three parts
of an hower /

41   ### To make a crem of Pipings

Take 12 pipings and rost them in a dish in
the oven then take *the* Softe of from *the* Score
and *the* Skin and putt it in a dish w*i*th 2 Spon
fulls of rose water a q*u*a*r*ter of fine Suger then
take a quarte of creme and boyle it w*i*th· 2
Yolks of Eggs lett it not cruddle when it is
on *the* fire put in yo*ur*· pipings as before Stur
it all together and put it in a strainer
Sarue it up Garnish *the* Dish as yow please /

To make a crem of Grapes

Take a pinte of ripe Grapes pick them
from the Stalks put them in a Cloth &
Squeeze *the*m tell you haue all *the* Juce lett it
Stand and Settle then take a quarte of crem
& boyle it w*i*th· 2 graines of Ambergreece 2 Spon
full of Rose water as much fine Suger as
will Sweeten it boyle it a quarter of an hower
take it of *the* fire and put *the* Juce in a dish
yow· Intend to serve it up and when yo*ur*· creme
is allmost Cold power it on yo*ur*· Grapes then
it is reddy for yo*ur*· Services to Eate Cold /

[fol. 41v]　　　　**To Pott Beefe**

Take halfe a Buttock of Beefe take of *the*
Skin and cutt it into pretty thick peeces *the*
way that *the* graine Lye beate it the Same
way very well ^season it· with· pep*per*· and salt very well^ & a
　　　　　　　　　　　　　　Little Cloves and mace
if you please then put it into an Earthen
pott w*ith*· a pound of Shuett Shred and Strawed
betwixt the Slices and put the Skin over it
Cover the pott w*ith*· Some paste and Sett it
in w*ith* a Batch of Bread when it is
Baked pull *the* meate fflak from fflake
and when that is done mix the meate
w*ith the* Liquor Stur it all to gether &
put in too Little potts pressing it downe
with a Spoone Sett it into the oven a
Little againe when it is Cold put a
Little melted butter upon it & keepe
it for yo*ur*· vse /

To make Cherry wine

Break all yo*ur*· Cherries open lett them
Stand 24 howers Straine *the*m out worke
them w*ith* yeast lett it Stand a day and Night
a workeing to every Gallon of Liquor put
In 2 or 3 pound of Sugger then put in
your Barrell and Bottle it /

42　　　　　　**To Colleer a pigge**

Take a good fat pigg of a month
or fiue weeks old and kill him and
dres him fit to rost cut of the head
and slit him down the back and bone
him take a handfull of sage chopt
small and to nutmegs a littel mace
a few cloues bete very fine a handful
of salt mix all well to gether and
season the pigg all ouer with it &
roll it up hord [hard] and tey it a boute with
tape and sow it up in a clean linnen

cloth and boyle it in water with a
littel otmell in it well seasoned with
salt boyl it tell it tis tender then
take it out and hang it up in a cloth
that it was boyled in tell it tis quit
cold then put in some water and
otmell as if you weer going to make
a thin water grewell season it well
with salt and put in a pint of white
vine & halfe a sponfull of wholl peper
boyle it all to gether halfe an hour set [let] it
[fol. 42v]   ley tell it is colld take of the cloth and
put in the g̶ pig let it ley: 8 days in
the sowesing then use it as you pleas
it must be eaten with musterd and
suger or with uineyer [vinegar] –

To make lugaillus Balsom

good for a green wound or any bruse
inward or outward to hell the lungs
being taken inward in canary wine
or poset the quantity of hasell nut
Take a quarter of a pound of yellow
bees wax cut it in to an earthen pan
with a pint of canary melt it and
when it is quite melted take it of the
fire take halfe a pound of uenes ~~tur~~
turpintine and wash it in rose water
take a pint and half of the best sallet
oyle and put the oyle and turpintine
in ^to^ the pipkin when the wax is well melt
<.>ed in the wine then boyle them together
with a gentell fire tell they be well cor
porated take it of then and let it coole
when it is throw could set on the fire a
43   againe and when it is throw melted
put in one ownce of the powder of
red sanderse̶ and stir it tell it is
coold then put it in a galliy pot and
k̶u̶^ee^pe<.> it for use –

To make Almond cream

Take half a pound of Jardon almonds &
blanch them beate them in a morter with
4: sponfull of rosewater or oring flower
water put a quart of cream to the almon^d^
and stis [stir] it well then strain it throw a
hear sieue and set it on a slow fire and
let it Just boyle then sweeten it and
put it out into littel chieng dishes and
when it is cold serue it to th table –

To stew pippins

Take large pipins pare them and cut
them in halfaes and core them lay them
in to a stew pan or presoring [preserving] pan and
put as much water as will couer them
and let them boyle about a quarter of
an hour then power out the water put to
them a pint of whit wine a pound of good
suger 12: cloues a quarter of an ounce of
cinnamon a piece of oring an lemon peel
[fol. 43v]   stew them quick when they are clere
they are enof squise on some Juyce of
lemon and dish them vp with fine carued
sippets and stick smoth suger almonds
and peces of canded oringe and lemen
pele and canded cittorn powr on the
syrrip and then strew on some smoth
carrayways on them and on the breds
of the dish and some suger if you wou<.>^ld^
haue them red put in a slice of preserued
quins and keep them clos couered and
stew them ouer a gentell fire –

To make selebu^b^<..>

Take 2 quarts of cream ~~in~~ and sweeten
it and put it in to a bason and squise
in to lemons <.> in to it and on of the pils
put in a quarter of a pint of sack and

put in one drop of oring flower water
take out the lemon whip it with a clean
whiske and put it in your glases halfe
this will fill seauen –

44 **To dry cherrys**

Take :13: pound of cherrys and :2: pound
of suger and wet it with a qurter of a
pint of water stone your cherrys and
boyle them tell they are clere then set
them by all night then draine them out
and lay them vpon sefes and set them
in an ouen to drye that is hot eneof for
whit <......> bread –

To dry pears or aples

Take them at michaelmas and prick
them full of holes and bake them in a pan
then take them out and pres them flat
and lay them vpon a sefe and if the top
be brown dip them in the sirrop and lay
them one by on in a sefe and set them in
the ouen to drye –

To keep goosberrys all the year

Take the goosberrys when they are at
the full growth but not ripe and put them
in to gllas bottles with a wide mouths fill
the bottles and cork them put them in a ketle
of water to scald in the botles hard corked
downe and when they looke white they are
eneof then set them in your seller when they
are quite cold put some rosin about *the* corkes

[fol. 44v] **How to make lemmon cakes**

Take of the purest hard suger if not
duble refine beate it very small sift
it throught a peace of tiffeny and get
the palest coulered lemons because

you must grate the out side of the rind
be shur you grate if [it] on a fine grater
cut your lemmon swecese it and strain
it throught a peice of tiffeny lawn
in a glass then when your suger is dry
put in as much of your Juce of lem
mon as will weet your suger keep
out a pritty deale of <.> your suger
least you should ouer wet it and keep
out sume of your Juce least should
need it you must put in no more Juce
then will make it a littel thinner then
for paste there must be fire vnder it
all the while but soe littel as will but
heat the dish stire your lemmon and
suger together with a spoone put in
as much grated lemmon as you like
and when tis of that thickness you like
drop it on a plate in littel round cakes
then dry them in the sun or at the fire put
them into a box or papers –

45   **To make Barley creame**

Take halfe a pounde of french barley let
it sibber in two seuerall waters in an
earthen pipke close couered then pour
of your water cleane away and put
to it a quart of new milk boyle it
leasurly and close couerd tell all most
all your milk bee wasted away then
straine it th^r^ought a strainer or thin cloth
and season it as you vse it with a littel
beaten cinamon suger a littel Juice
of lemmon and eate a meale for break
fast or supper it tis both cooling and
nourishing –

**An excellent cordial water for ~~di~~
dizzinese: and swimming in the head**

Take four pound of blak cherries bruise
the stones of them and then put them

with the cherries into a glass bottel and
put into them a good handfull of balm
and a handfull of rosemary tops
cinamon nutmegs vpon them all two quar^ts^
of sack stop it close and let it stand twentey
fore hours then distil it of in balneo distel
so much of it that it be weak like Aqua
merabilis sweeten it with white suger candy
to your tast and drink a littel wine glassful
of it in the morning fasting and at night

[fol. 45v]   going to Bed; this cured a lady of a great
dizzinese and swimming in her and mo
many other haue found the like in fallible
effect of it –

To make Bisketts of apricocks or
any other fruite

first paire your apricocks and slice
them into a pott and stopp it downe close
and boyle it in a skillett of water tell
they bee tender then force them throw a
haier sceiue and to 4 ounces of that pulp
haue 5 or 6 ounces of duble refined suger
beaten and scarced put your suger and
your pulpe into severall dishes and heat
them both scalding hott then put them
togather you must continue beating
them 2 hours the longer you beat them
the more glose they will have this you
may doe with any ffru^i^te the thinner
your pulpe is it will require more suger
but the weight and a third part is a
nought for Apricociks and gooseberry

46   **To make Jelly of harts horn**

take two quarts of fair water and six
ounces of harts horn when your water
is warm put in your harts horn and
let it infuse vpon embers all night
then boyle it till the spoon feels very
clammie then st^r^aine it pu and put to

it half a pound of suger or more a
littel sack a spoonful of cinamon water
the Juice of six lemmons and two graine^s^
of amber grecce and so set it ouer a
slow fire tell it will Jelly then put
it into thin glasses –

to keep backe any ill red humor
that comes in the nose or face

Take a lemmon rinde and all cutt in
peices a little camphire and lay it in
steepe in white wine with a littel cam
phire then wash your face with it
euery day prooued –

[fol. 46v]   ### To make ^a^ calves head pie^y^e

Take a calves head being par boyled
cut of all the meat from the bones and
the tongue in peices season it will with
cloves and mace nutmeg and salt let
it steepe all night in a bout halfe a
pint of sack put in half a pound
of beefe suet chopt small the next
morning when the coffin is made put
some butter in the bottom then put in
the meate with the Li^c^quer and a pound
of raissons stoned and chopt small as
much suger as you think will make
the meate a little sweet put in like
wise the yolkes of 10 <.> or 12 eggs whole
and some marrow a bout the bigness
of wallnvets if you please[33] you may
when the py is baked put in some
canded orreng or erringgo root or
lemmon cut in thine slices if it wante
moustur put a slices of butter and

---

33   The words "if you please" are blotted in the original manuscript, but this might be
    unintentional and the words are still legible.

serve it in it will bee baked in an
hour and halfe –

47   **How to make Exelent Pankakes³⁴**

Take a pint of Creme and 3 Eggs and fife
sponfull of fine flower and beat it Well toga=
ther and Melt a quarter of a pound of butt=
er and put to it little nutmeg and salt put it
very thinn in your pan When the pan is very
hot and fry them With out any thing in the
pan and serue them up –

To make freanch Bred

Take hallfe a peek of fine flover a quarter
of a pint of yest then take the whites of to
Eggs <..>^be^at them to a froth then Strai<.>^n^e the Eggs
and yest in to the flov^e^r and temper it to, gether vi=
th water in to a soft past work it with flover and put
it it^n^<.> to severall wooden dishis and let to stan
d half an our or upward flover dishis before you
put it in and remember to let the yest stand all night
in water –

[fol. 47v]   **A ffrigisee³⁵**

Take of Chickings or Rabbits and divide every
quarter into 2 or 3 parts and season it with
cloves mace nutmegs peper and salt then take
A frying pan & heat it moderately hot with
a piece of buttur then put in your meat and
fry it brown then take it out pour a way the
buttur it was fryed in and take some beef
and make some very good gravy and put

---

34 Hand K (the two recipes on this page) is similar to Hand M, but the ascenders are
    taller and narrower (clear on majuscule M and W, and minuscule l and h). There is
    no indication of the identity of the contributor.
35 Hand L ([47v]–48, [49v] comment, 50–[50v] top recipe) might be a child's hand
    because of the curved letters and the variation of letter forms; this contributor does
    not yet seem to have an established handwriting style.

in a bundle of sweet herbs a little sallot
a leaf of mace a glas of whitwine Let that
stue a little and then put in your Chickins
or Rabbits and let them stue well togather
then take a pice of fresh butter and ster
well togather & 2 anchovoies & *the* Juice of a
lemon & Shak it well togather & Garnish *the* dish w*ith*
lemons & oranges & serve it up as hot as you can

48   **To make calves feet Gelly.**

Take a sett of Calves feet and scald off the haire,
then beat it all to peices: put it into a pan or a kettle
cover it over with spring water: put it over the fire
and boyle it all to a Jelly: then take it off the fire, and
streyne it through a thick woollen bagg: let it stand till
it is cold: then put it into a Skillet, put in a dozen glare
of eggs, but whip your eggs first: put them into the said
Jelly, with about a penny worth of Izing glass into it:
boyle it and scumme it well till it comes clear: then
take it off and streyne it againe: then take the Juice
of half a dozen Lemons a quarter of a pound of double
refined Sugar put it with the Juice of Lemons into the
Jelly with a graine of Amber greece tyed up in a ragg and <.>
put into it then put it over the fire and boyle it againe
as long as you see any scumme: then take it up and streyne it
through a very thick cloth bagg: take the first running and colour
it red with a little Lemon and Cochineale: then take the second
running and colour it with a little bit of saffron: the last
running will bee the clearest for white then pour it into
your Glasses to coole.

[fol. 48v]   **To make A orring pudding**

Take the paring of one large sivell
orring and pound it in a morter
tell it is very fine and then mix
it well with 8 ounces of white suger
and then take the yolks of 8 eggs
and beate them and 8 ounces of
butter and melt it with a little
water as you do for sauce and

then <.>mix your eggs and butter
together and after that put it into
your suger and orring and mix
all together and then put it into
puft past and bake it –

49   **To make A rice pudding**

Take a pound of rice and deuide
it in 3 parts and on of the parts poun^d^
and sift it throught a fine shvrch
then take a quart of milk and boyl it
then lett it stand to be cold but first
mix your flower of rice in a porringe^r^
with a little Cold milk then mix it
with the rest of the milk pouring it in
by little and little and sett it on the
fire to thicken and stur it all the
time and when it tis thick put in
some butter still sturing it you must
put in 3 quarters of a pound of butter
and then take it of the fire and still
keep it sturing tell it is all melled then
put in 3 quarters of a pound of suger
and 6 eggs beatten and when you hav^e^
mixt it well together then put it in a
dish and bake it halfe an hour we^i^ll
bake it –

[fol. 49v]   **To Pickel Wallnuts**[36]

Take the wallnuts when you can thrust
a pin in them and take and prick them
and let them ly 9 days in water and take
very good vinagar and boil it and put
as much solt in it as will beare an egg
and put in some jameca pepper in to it
and put it into your wallnuts and stop
them up very close.

---

36 Hand M ([49v]) is a slightly messy yet rounded italic hand. There is no indication of
the identity of the contributor.

To make a Carret Pudding.

Take too penny manchetts and grate them
and half a dozen of Carrets and grate them
and half a nuttmege and a little quantety
of salt ^and 6 eggs^[37] Take half a pound of sugar and
a point of craime. Take half a pound of
butter and melt it. half a Dozen spunful
of sake so mix it all very well togather and put
it into a dish with some butter alb about
the dish let if it stand about an hour and
a quarter in a pretty quick oven.

50

To Make a Lemmon Pudding

Take a two penny lofe and cut him into
thin slices, take a point and a half of
creaim a boil it and put it boiling hot
into the bread and so stive [stir] it take the
juce of two Lemmons cut the out rine
very smal put it into the juce sweeten
it with sugar the quantity of half a pound
which you must put into the lemmon take
the yoaks of six eggs and whits of four beat
them very well grate in a little nutmeg put
in half a dozen spoon fulls of sack, so mix
it all together buter your dish and put into
it a quarter of a pound of melted buter then
put it into the oven three quarters of an hour will
bake it if the oven be prety hot.

To make an Almon pudding

Take a too penny manchett and cut him into
thin slices and a point an half of creaim
boil it, put it into the bread boiling hot
and stive it,<..>take some almons and blanch
them in hot water ^and beat them in a mortor with a little water^
to keep them from oyling
take half a dozen spoonfuls of sack yoaks of

---

37   This note is in another hand; it appears to be Hand L.

eight eggs and *the* whits of six beat them well
together w*i*th some nutmeg and sugar then mix
it all together and put in it a quarter of a pound
pound of melted buter and less then an hour will
bake it.

[fol. 50v]   **To Make a Tansy**

Take a quarter of creaim half a pound of
sugar half a pound of grated bread 16 or 20
eggs well beaten *the* juce of spinnage and
a little tansy as much as will colour it you
must strain it ~~take a handful of flour~~
and a little nutmeg stir it all together and
put it on *the* fire and when it comes thick
buter *the* pan and put it into *the* oven and
half an hour will backe it.

**To Make Wine vineger
or that which will serve for
the same vses alltogather as well**[38]

To 12 gallons of Cider put 3 pounds of
Malego Rasons & 2 ounces of Roach
allum & lett it stand in a vessel in
the sun with the bung only covered
with a Lynnen or hair cloth so that
the aire may come at it for two
months any time from the ffirst of
May to the Last of July & not
Later & in that time it will be
made good vineger fitt for keeping
of pickles or any other vse

51   **To make Mangoe**[39]

~~Take large Cucumbers cut a piece out of the
length of the Cucumbers scrape out all the seeds~~

---

38 Hand N (this recipe only) is distinguished by its ampersand. There is no indication
of the identity of the contributor.

39 This recipe, except the title, is crossed out with a large x. The full recipe follows; it
seems the contributor was perhaps frustrated by her copying errors.

~~very clean ^then^ scour them with salt and water and~~
~~and make brine that will make brine~~

To make Mangoe

Take large Cucumbers cut a piece out of the
length of the Cucumbers scrape out all the seeds
very clean, then scour them with salt and wa
:ter and make brine that will bear an egg and
pour upon them scalding hot ~~water~~ Stive
them close for 24 hours then take them out
and dry them very well with a cloth and
fill them with sliced garlick mustard seeds
and sliced ginger and tie them up fast with
a thread, you must make the pickle of white
wine vineger whole pepper and what salt you
think fit and pour it on hot and stive it
close and so doe for 2 or 3 days once a day till
they be very green.

a day or 2 after you must put a spoonfull of
mustard and some horse radish into the pickle.

[fol. 51v]   ### To make a frigacy of rabbits.

Take rabbits and cut them in little pieces and
season it with salt and nutmeg and put them
in the pan with water to cover them and put
a quarter of a pound of butter in the water
take some parsly and lemon time and lemon
peel shred them very small when it is almost
fryed away put a good large glass of claret and
2 anchoves take out one of the livers and grate
him to thicken it be sure to keep it stirring
and then put half a pound of butter and so sarve
it up.

To pot Venison

Take your venison and beat it very well if it be
not very fat, you must take some beef suet and
beat it then season it pretty well with pepper

and salt and a little cloves and mace but not too
much of the latter, lay 2 or 3 bay leaves in the
bottom of the pots then lay your beaten Veni
son in then Cover it thin with butter and cover
the pots with paste, when it is baked very tender
then drain it well from the gravie and put it
into dry pots and keep out the cold and cover
it well with butter.

52   **To Stew a Lamprey**

When it is Skinned season it with a little salt
and pepper and sliced nutmeg all over and in its
belly, all along and put also into his belly some
cloves and large mace whole and some sliced le=
:mon and some thin slices of butter let it then
be rowled round and a skure thrust through to
turn him with the liquor must be a pint and a
half of white wine or half white wine and half
Cyder and put a little butter into the bottom of
the pan before you put on the liquor and some
thin slices of butter upon the top of the Lamprey
when it is stewed set the pan over a stove char
cole fire add to the liquor a bundle of sweet herbs
and a sliced onion turn the Lamprey often in
the liquor and when it is tender enough bruise 2
anchoves into thin parts and in Juice mix one of
the best of the Gravie beat a little more butter
make your sawce and thicken it carefully with
the yolk of an egg.

[fol. 52v]   **To pot Beef**

Take lean Beef cut it cross the grain in thin
slices beat it very well with a rowling pin then
season it with salt and pepper and salt peter
some mace and a little nutmeg roul it up in
balls so put it in a pot with some slices of
fat over it, bake it five hours then work it toge
ther with butter take out any strings that
remaine then place it hard in the pots and
cover it with butter.

To drey tongues and Westfalio Bacon[40]

Take salt upon salt as much as will lye upon
a Shillinge for one tongue and as much other
salt as you think will doe sett them on the fire
in a Skillet, and keep tha them stiring with a
spoon: till it is very hot, so hott that you cannot
touch it with your hand, lay it upon the tongue
and then rub it very well in, Lay then in a
pan by themselves and a week after salt them
as you did before: and then let them lye till
they are hard. For one Westfalio ham you must
take an ounce of salt of salt and other salt mixt
with it: Doe it as you did your tongues and let them
lye but a week after the 2d salting. before you hang
up your tongues or hams you must all over with
Calves or Bullocks bloud once or twice and <..>^d^ry
them by the fire: then hang them up: when you
boyle them you must not lay them in water nor
boyle them with hay.

53

To Boyle a Calves head

Take a fat Calves head and boyle it in a little
water and salt very tender, take a great deep
dish put into it claret large mace anchoves
stew it till the anchoves are all consumed then put
the gravy of a rosted leg or Shoulder of mutton
a good quantity of oysters either raw or pic^k^led,
but raw are the best, then take sweetbreads of
veal lamb or hogs, and let them be slitt and
fry'd in a pan but not too brown, Slice also collops
lops of your best bacon, and frey them but not
too brown, then put the calves head into your wil
wine which should have all the while some sliced onions
stewed in it. Let your head stew in it till dinner
be ready; and when you send it up lay a good part
of your oysters at the bottome of the dish, and all the

---

40   Hand O ([52v] lower recipe–[56v], [59v] lower recipe–61) is a small, tight italic
hand. There is no indication of the identity of the contributor.

rest ~~ont~~ on *the* top; lay your collops and sweetbreads all
over and lemmon sliced, or with *the* rind and barberyes
you may garnish *the* dish. remember to sred a pretty
quantity of lemmons and put it into *the* sawce and
a peace of butter and so serve it up.

[fol. 53v]   **To keep Cherys for tarts**

To a pound Cherys allow a q*uarte*r of a pound of
sugar and put them togather in an earthen
pot, and past it up very close, set it in a
bakers oven and keep it close till you use it
you may doe a great many togeather.

For *the* wind Collick.

Take a spoonful of ginger and mix it with a
little ale and drink it.

To stay a looseness.

Take a pint of milk 3 ounces of double
refined suger boyle them togeather a little, then
take it off the fire and put in 3 ounces of
old quince marmalet and when it is melted
drink half of it at a time, the older *the* marmalet
*th*e better.

To Make Aprecock wine.

Take a pound and half of lofe sugar 3 pints
of water, put them togeather over *the* fire, when it
boyles take off *the* scum that rises: then take 3
pounds of Aprecocks par'd&ston'd & and put them
into *the* liquor and let them boyle till *the* <.>Apre=
cocks are tender, then take it off *the* fire, and take
the ⋏Aprecocks out, and let it stand till it is
could then bottle it.

54   **To Make a Carrott Pudding.**

Take your carrotts and boyle them very tender,
then scrape them and beat them in a morter,

take eight eggs and too whites, beat them well, put
in 3 or 4 spoonfulls of sack, half a pound of
butter, half a pint of cream, a little salt and
nutmeg, beat all these togeather in a morter till
it is well mingled sweeten it to your tast with
sugar, then put in some grated bread, so
much as will make it as stiff as batter, then
butter your dish you bake it in, 4 spoonfulls of
Carrotts is enough for this quantity, half a hower
will bake it. you may make it of parsnips or Po=
=tatoes.

To Make Lemmon ~~puddind~~ ^Cakes^

Take your juce of Lemmons & set it in a clear
fire and make it very hot but you must not
let it boyle you must put your suger over the
fire in a broad dish and make it very dry
and when it is very hot and the juce is so
to; cast in your sugar with your hands: keep stirring
your juces till it be as thick with the sugar that
it will drop into cakes and not run on the
plate. you may make orange cakes the same
ẙ way and grate some orrange or lemmon
peel into it.

[fol. 54v]   ### To make Aprecock cakes

Take a pound of Aprecocks and pare them and
take out the stones and slice them into half a pint
of juce of white currins then set it on the fire
till it is all mash'd then put to it a pound and
a quarter of double refin'd sugar that is boyl'd to
candy, then stir it together till it be all melted
then put it into glasses and soe put them into
a stove and when they be ready to turn out, put
put them out of the glasses and keep them turning
morning, and evening, dusting them with a little

sugar throw a tiffany and when they be dry
keep them for your use.

To make quince cake in the fashon of jumballs

Take your Quinces and <.> coddle them then pare
them till you come to *th*e whites & put them into
a silver dish and mash them to pap: then set
them on a slow fire, and keep them stirring
till they be dry but be sure you doe not let
them boyle, <....> take half the weight in sugar
boyl'd to sugar again and beaten fine.

To make Aprecocks cakes in *th*e fashon of jumballs

Take re ripe Aprecocks and pare them and put
them into a silver dish & cover then and set
them over a soft fire and when they are very
soft make them into a pap and so dry them
over coles, & when they are dry'd into past & cold
work them up with sugar finely searched so make them
into little knotts and jumball if you please and dry *the*m
this way you may jumballs of any sort of plum or
quince or pipin plums, you must boyle in a jug in
kettle of water and strain the pulpe throw a strainer –

To Make past of rasberries.

Take y*ou*r rasberries gather'd very dry break them with
a spoon small, allow to every pound of rasberries
3 quarters of a pound of sugar double refin'd finely
beaten let them boyle wi*t*hout sugar till it be very
thick then put in your sugar and boyle it but
once up for if it boyle longer you spoile it
put it into moulds or drop it and so stove
it but let not your stove be too hot.

To make orring biscakes both cordiall and pleasant.

Take orringes and pare them and take the thin peel
and lay them in water a day or two shifting the
water once a day; then boyle the peels very ten=
der, then take the meat of the orranges and

55

infuse them in a silver bason drey'n the thin
juce from them and pick out the strings and the
seeds and mingle them with the peel, and beat it
into a very fine past in a morter, weigh it
and take three times the weight of sugar, it
must be double refin'd, beat them alltogether
in a morter then lay them in a plate some=
=what thicker ordinary past so let them dry
in a stove.

[fol. 55v]   **To cand green<.> Grapes or Goosberries.**

Gather them a little before they be ripe, and take
the fairest *that* is with out specks put them into a
skillet of fair water being ready to seeth cover
them, and let them stand on a few co^a^les till the
skins will peel off; then take them from the fire
and peel them and put them into hot water and
lay a cloath over them and a dish over that and
let them stand in embers till they be green, then
take them out and lay them on a cloath to dry, to
a pound of grapes take a pound and a quarter
of sugar, and as much water as will wett it, and
boyle it till it comes to a candy height then
put your grapes into the syrup and boyle them till
they be enough, and so let them by; let the grapes
lye in the syrup 2 or 3 days every day turning them
and at the last lay them upon plates to dry.

To make Aprecock cakes.

Take a pound o[f] Aprecocks and pare them and take
out the stones and slice them into half a pint of
white curri^a^ns then set them upon the fire till it is
all to mash then put to them a pound and a q*uarter*
of double refin'd sugar that is boyl'd to a candy,
then stirr it together till it be all melted, then put
it into what fashon'd glasses you please and so
put them into a stove, and when they be ready to
turn out, put them out of the glasses, and keep
them turning morning and evening, dusting them
with a little sugar throw a tiffany and when they
be dry keep them for use.

56   **To make paste of Quinces or Pipinns.**

Gather the Quinces when they are ripe and dry
and coddle them very tender with out breaking or
cracking the skinns then pare them and scrape the
pulpe clean from the <.>core and take of double
refind sugar equal to the weight of the pulpe
break your sugar into pretty big lumps, and dip
the peices into a porringer of water one by
one till the lumps have suck'd in the water
and so take more water according as the quantity
of sugar requires, then put your sugar into a
preserveing pann. and boyle it scumming it very
clean till the syrup will stand in a drop, in the <.>
mean time let your pulpe of Quinces be beaten
very fine, then put the Quinces to the syrup and
set it on a soft fire till it be scalding hott, but
not boyle for then it will not dry: then put it out
of the brass pan, and set it by till the morning so
put it could into moulds or upon plates and set
them in a stove to dry, they must be turnd, and will
be dry in 3 or 4 days.

To make clear cakes of Goosberries.

Take fair goosberries and cutt the black top off
them then put as much water to them as will cover the
bottom of the skillet and keep them from burning.
then take to 3 pints of goosberries a pint of warm
water but put it in by little and not altogether
and so let them boyle all to mash: then take them
of the fire and dreyn them through a seive then
take the clear and to every pound of juce take a pound
[fol. 56v]   take a pound of double refin'd loaf suger, wett it with
water and set it on the fire and boyle it till it comes
to sugar again, then pour in your juce but doe not
let it boyle, stirr it till it be quite melted and then
put it into your glasses pretty thick, and set it into
your stove till it hath a candy on the top, then turn
them out and cut them into quarters and dry them
upon glass plates.

To dry Aprecocks

Take your Aprecocks, pare and stone them and put
to them half their weight in double refin'd sugar
and let them stand till the sugar is all melted, and
then set them on the fire, and let them boyle till
they <....> and then set them by in
the syrup 4 days but be sure your Aprecocks
be coverd with the syrup, and lay them to dry in the
sun, or put them into the stove.

To make sugar pufs.

Take a pound of double refined sugar, searce it
through a tiffainey sieve put into it 3 whites of new
laid eggs, 3 spoonfulls of orring flower water and
a spoonful of gum dragon being steep'd in orrange
flower water, you must put in some musk braded
very small in a spoonfull of your stuff. if you see it
goeth too thick you may put in it another white
of egg you must beat it an hour an a half or
2 hours not leteing it stand still at all drop
upon pie ple^a^tes, and set it in an oven after
you have d^r^rawn brown bread this you may ice
a cake with.

To make Calfs foot gelley

Take 4 feet drest clean from the hare
put them in too quarts of water
boil them leisurely tell it well
gelley them take out the feet and
let the gelley stand tell it is cold
then take all the fat clear of it
then to a quart of this stif gelley
put a pint of white wine some
Juice of lemmon to your tast 3
quarters of a pound of suger a
stick of cinnamon and a piece of
lemmen pill fine whits of eggs beat
en very well boile all this together
a little while then put it through

a flannell gelley bagg putting it
still through as long as tel it lookes
clear then put it in potts or glases
as you please –

[fol. 57v]   **To make oring butter**

Take fresh butter out of the chur
ne lay it in oring flower water
to give it a taste then boyle 3 or
4 eggs very hard take out the
yelks make them very fine with
the back of a spoone put four tim
es the quantity of butter to the
eggs a little to your taste doe it
throw a dredg box lid with a
spoone the eggs must be exterore
dirary hard boyled and lett a
lone tell they are could –

To make thick Creame

Take a pinte of creame or more <.>
according to the quantity you wou
ld make boyle it then take a spoon
full of flower of rice and mingle
it with the yelk of an egg and so
boyle it a little then take the pulp
of 2 or 3 roste aples, make them all
to mash and put them in and soe
sweeten it to your tast and ster it
that it may not burn when it is col<.>[41]

58   **To make quince pufs**

Take 6 ounces of suger and 4 ounc^es^
of pulp of quinces beat the white
of an egg to froth and put in 2
spoonfulls of the froth into the

---

41 The meaning here is unclear.

quinces then beat them an hour
and drop it on papers and ~~dri~~
dry them by the fire and they
will keep a year this way you
may make pufs of plums –

To make suger pufs

Take a pound of double refined
suger searce it through a tifenny
sive put into it 3 whites of new
laid eggs 3 spoonfulls of orring
flower water and a spoonfull of
gum dragon being steeped in
orring flower water you must
put in some musk beaten very
small in a spoonfull of your stuf
if you see it groweth to thicke you
[fol. 58v]   may put in spoonfull or 2 of
your orring flower water more
and a nother white of egg you
must beat it an hour and halfe
or 2 hours not leting it stand
still at all drop it vp on pie
plates and set it into an oven
after you haue drawne brown
bread this you may Ice a cake

To make pipin Creame

Take the pulp of pipins sett them
on a soft fire and put to it a good
quanty of suger and let it drye
press them well boyle your Cream
and nutmeg and when cold mingle
them together this way you may
make Goosebery Rassbery straw
bery codlings pear plume cream

59   ### To make snow

Take the whites of 5 or 6 egges a
handfull of fine suger and as

much rose water and put them in
to a quart of Creame of the thickes
you can gett beat them all together
as the snow ariseth take it of with
a spoon you must beat with a ~~sti~~
stick cloven in 4 then must you
take a loaf of bread and cut away
the Crust and sett it upright in a
platter then sett a fair Rosemary
branch in the loaf and cast your
snow vpon it with a spoon –

[fol. 59v]　　　　**To make Goosbery wine**

Take for euery 3 pound of
Goosbery 1 pound of suger a
quart of water brus the goosberys
steep them 24 hours in the water
in which time you must stir it
often then let the clear licker ~~ru~~
run of from the goosbery through
a siue to which ad the suger then
put it in an earthon pot and
keep it clos coured for a fortnight
or 3 weeks then draw it in to
botells let them be well corked at
a monthe end it will be ready
to drinke the same way you doe
carrons and rasbery –

To Make a Marrow pudding.

Take the marrow of 3 bones and cut it into
thin slices, then take half a penny loaf and half
a̶ a pound of biskets, and 2 apples ~~and~~ and cut it
all in thin slices and a quarter of a pound of
currans and half a pa^o^und of reasons 2 ounces of
oraing and lemon and 1 ounce of citron cut it all
in thin slices then put puff past round your dish then
begin to fill your dish <….> of every sort till all your
ingredients be in, then take 3 pints of cream and season
it as you doe your custard stuf and put it into your dish
your pudding will aske an hours bakeing.

60

To Make a rice pudding.

Take half a pound of rice and boyle it in milk till
it be very tender, and while it is hot put 3 quarters
of a pound of butter to it and a little spice, beat 6
eggs, and put to it and a little sack, then put in it
half a pound of sugar and half a pound of currans
and a little orang flower water, put puf past round
the dish and fill it, it will it will ask an hours bakeing.

To Make an oraing pudding

Take 3 oranges and grate the rind of them and cut a
slit and squez the juce of them and sq squeeze in the
juce of half a<.> lemon, then take 18 egg but not
more then 4 whites a little sack and a quarter of
a pound of butter sweeten it to your tast put it in
a morter and beat for half an hour then put
past over and under it, and it will aske an <.>hour ^hours^
bakeing.

To Make Ginger Bread.

Take three pints of fine flower, dry it well
put into it a quarter of a pound of good dry
sugar half an ounce of ginger in powder some
anniseeds mix these well together then rub into
it a quarter of a pound of butter till it is
very fine, then warme a pound of and half
[fol. 60v]   treacle blood warme and mix it together, and
if it be not enough you may put a little warme
milke to make it tender, let it ly by the fire
a quarter of an hour before you put it into
the pans and if you please to put any sweet
=meats into it let it be done but just before
it is put into the oven, it requirs more bake
=ing than cake.

For a Consumption

Take comfrey roots dryed, and marsh
mallow roots dryed of each three ounces
scorcernero roots two ounces canded erig

eringo roots two ounces, cut all *the* roots
in little slices, then mix alltogether very
well and devide them into ten parcels
an ounce in a parcell, put one parcel
into three pints of spring water then
let them boyle a very little while
over a gentle fire after that add a
pint of milk and let it boyle till
it come to a quart, every morning
fasting take half a pint, and as much
at five in *the* after noon, it must be
made blood warm when it is drank
61   and when all the ingredients are gone it
must be renew'd, I have heard this receipt has
done wonderfull cures.

For a violent Cough

Take common honey four ounces, oxcemelle=
quills four drams, flower of brimstone three
drams, powder of Liquorish two drams
with as much syrup of grownd ivey as will
make into an electuary, a grown person ~~may~~
must take as much as a walnut in a morning
fasting, and a child as much as a nutmeg.

Another receipt for a consumption *that* has don great cures.

Take *the* gall of a sucking pig and halfe *the*
lights beat it in a stone morter till it is
well incorporated, take as much as a large
nutmeg in a morning fasting and drink
a larg draught of cock broth after it made
of harts horne and french barley *the* receipt
must be renew'd every three days this was
sent out of Holland for an extraordinary
secret.

[fol. 61v blank]

62   **To preserue Barberies**

Take the Largest Barbereis you can gett and
stone them take doubel their waight in suger
put as much water to the suger as will Just
wet it then Boyl it to a candy hight which you
may know by the bubling then put in your
Barbereis and let them Boyl 2 or 3 walms to
gether & ^then^ take them of for long boyling will
take a way the coller so pot them up & keep
them for your use –

              To make Conserue of damsons ~~or pro~~[42]

Take ripe damsons put them in to scalding
water Let them stand ouer the fier Boyling
till they be broken almost to mas then st^r^ain
out the water through a cullider and let
them stand therin to coole then take a way
all the stons and skins, and set the pulf ouer
the fier again and put therto sume red wine
and boyl them till ~~they be almost boyled pu~~
~~in~~ it tis pretty stif, euer stiring it and whe^n^
they be allmost boyled put in a prety quanti
ty of suger, stir all well together and put it
[fol. 62v]   into a gally pot you may make set tart
of it adding a littill rose water –

63   **To make <⋯⋯> ^Rasbury^ cakes**

first dry the raspase ouer a chaffindish uery
dry, then[43] take double Refined suger, beaten
very fine and putt itt into Askillett

---

42 The suggestion at the end of this recipe that "you may make set tart of it adding a
    littill rose water" is curious, as adding rose water would make the conserve less, not
    more, "set" or firm. A near-identical recipe in *The Accomplish'd Lady's Delight* (1675),
    usually attributed to Hannah Woolley, does not include this final note.

43 Hand P (this recipe only, beginning with "take") completes a recipe begun by Hand
    B; it is distinguished by loose descenders, such as p. There is no indication of the
    identity of the contributor.

and As spoonfull or tow of Rosewater
stir itt till begins to melt, then sett
itt over *the* fier and lett it boyl till it
Candys aboutt *the* spoon, then take it
of and putt in *the* Raspase seed, then
take A plate and Rubb and almond on
itt to make itt slip: then drop y*our*
stuffe in little drops on *the* plate
and lett them stand till they will
slipp then lay them on papers
and keep them for your vse, sett
them in Adry place near *the* fier
in *the* same manner make Cakes
of violetts, or any other flowers butt
they must nott be dryed, butt putt
in to *the* Suger green ~

[fol. 63v blank]

MS V.a.450:
Cookery and Medical Receipt Book
attributed to Lettice Pudsey

Textual Introduction

This receipt book is attributed by the Folger Shakespeare Library to
Lettice Pudsey. It is dated circa 1675 in the Folger catalogue, but circa
1700 on the inside cover of the manuscript. The book is 18.2 cm tall by
14.4 cm wide. The original vellum cover has been removed from the text-
block because of its poor condition. Some pages are missing (between
leaves 7 and 8, where stubs remain), and the manuscript contains some
pages with spots and/or water damage, while the last page is full of
tiny pin-holes. The watermark is a one-handled pot with what appear
to be the letters "RO" or "PO" inside; it is perhaps the latter, as this
watermark looks very similar to the *Gravell Watermark Archive*'s listing
POT.229.1, used by the French papermaker Pierre Ollivier around 1650
(suggesting, therefore, that this manuscript might be older than previously thought). The inside front cover includes a small orange sticker
reading: "SOLD BY THOMAS THORNE, Bookseller, 49, Blackett-st.,
Newcastle-on-Tyne, BOOKS BOUGHT."

The original vellum cover has what appear to be two letters (perhaps
EJ), then below these the name "E. Jackson," on the front. The inside
back cover also bears the name "Eliz Jackson." It is thus interesting that
this manuscript is attributed to Lettice Pudsey rather than Elizabeth
or Eliza Jackson, who, one might suppose, is responsible for Hand
A – unless the other back cover note "not her hand" applies to the entire
manuscript, and Elizabeth/Eliza had her initials added to the original
cover upon acquiring the book *after* Lettice Pudsey. This latter possibility is supported by the fact that the back cover name appears to be in a
hand that does not appear elsewhere in the manuscript. Pudsey's own
name appears on folio [7v], after nearly three dozen recipes. This page
announces,

Lettice Pudsey, her Booke
of recipts, These following
are written with my owne hand

and, indeed, a new hand is introduced at this point.

Little is known of Lettice Pudsey, although she might have been from Derbyshire or Staffordshire, as this manuscript includes recipes attributed to two women from this area, Lady Shirley and Mrs Okeover. Richard Aspin has written a biography of Elizabeth Okeover of Staffordshire, who kept a receipt book (c. 1674–1725, MS 3712 in the Wellcome Library), and she might have been the sister or niece of Thomas Okeover, whose other sister Katherine was Lady Shirley. The nature of Pudsey's relationship with Lady Shirley and Mrs Okeover is not clear. The *Oxford Dictionary of National Biography* notes that Edward Pudsey from Derbyshire (the eldest of nine children of Thomas Pudsey) also kept a commonplace book, which included notes on Shakespeare's plays that he had seen at the theatre in the early seventeenth century, although there is no evidence that he was a relation of Lettice's. The only Elizabeth Jackson listed in the *ODNB* is a London antiquarian born in 1763/4 who did not seem to have any connection with Derbyshire or Staffordshire.

This receipt book also contains a mix of culinary and medical recipes. The clusters of medical recipes suggest that the contributor copied each cluster in one sitting from another work. The recipes and remedies both include various comments indicating repeated practice, and also reflect a particular closeness to the land and the work involved in cultivating and collecting ingredients. "To feed chickings geeses or duckes" ([8v]) is a good example, as nothing similar appears in the Granville or Hall manuscripts, and the various recipes calling for "a young cock" or "an old cock" imply that the cook had a choice of animals at hand. Also, this manuscript's extensive use of the second-person perspective, beyond what was common in other receipt books, seems to assume a familiarity with the ingredients and with cooking, as in "take your chickens" or "ffirst adde to your ordinary bruing"; it also enables an intimate sharing of experience with the reader: "To breake the stone," for example, directs: "Take A Cocke of An Eare owld and open him / and yow shall find in his maw Smale white / stones take them and beake them in A Brasen / Morter very fine put itt in good whit wine & drinke" ([4v]). One contributor is particularly direct, crossing out a recipe for pickles and writing, "This Receipt is good for nothing" (56).

The recipes in this manuscript are particularly rustic. Many recipes call for common native plants such as elderberries and gooseberries, and the recipe "To rost a shoulder of mutton in *the* / blood, to look like venson" ([61v]) reveals an attempt to improve upon the presentation of humble ingredients – mutton, of course, being more readily available than venison. At the same time, however, Lettice Pudsey herself might reveal familiarity with the Latin term for the English bulrush, in calling for a medicinal water to be strained through a "sriprius bagg," if by this term she was referring to a sieve woven of *Scirpus lacustris*. (The possibility also exists that there was a local common term, now fallen out of use, for the bulrush that sounded like its Latin name.) However, it is perhaps more likely that "sriprius" is a variant of "cyprus," a silk used in straining.

This receipt book does share some remedies with published works. The remedy for "An Exceding restoratiue for on *tha*t is brought lowe" (3) is similarly described in James Hart's *Klinike, or The Diet of the Diseased* (1633):

Take an old Cocke, and after a long combat with another Cocke, kill him, pull him, and cleanse him of all his intralls; then fill his belly with barlie prepared as it ought, raisins of the Sunne stoned, violet leaves, maidens haire, a little hysop and peny-riall, with a little salt: boile him till the flesh come from the bone, then bruise him well, and squeeze out all his moisture, and of this broth take a good draught. There are yet many sorts of broth used for severall ends and purposes; some to coole, some to strengthen and cherish nature, &c. Amongst restorative broths, there is one in frequent use, especially in consumptions and great weaknesses. (179)

Pudsey's recipe "To kepe *the* Eys cleare and coule from readnes" ([4v]), meanwhile, is almost identical to Thomas Collins's "most singular good Medicine to keep the Eyes clear, cool, and from redness, and to kill the Itching of them" in his *Choice and Rare Experiments in Physick and Chirurgery* (1658) and to John Partridge's recipe of nearly the same title in *The Widowes Treasure* (1588). This latter work also includes a near-identical recipe to the Pudsey manuscript's "To breake the stone" ([4v]).

A few of the recipes in this recipe book are attributed to specific people. Doctor Stevens's water (14) was a common remedy in receipt books. Lady Shirley and Mrs Okeover, mentioned above, each contributed multiple recipes – although the recipes are written in Lettice Pudsey's hand, rather than their own. Cousen Rugley is clearly a relation; Lady Wendy, Lady Folliot, Mrs Risley, and Mrs Kinnersley might have been friends or acquaintances, and their names do not appear in other receipt books I have seen.

As with the Granville and Hall manuscripts, this receipt book is written in a number of hands (approximately fourteen; indicated in the footnotes). The recipes in Hand A were originally written in red or brown ink, and these were then overwritten with black ink, but the headings were not; traces of the original writing and lines are still evident. On folio 4 recto and verso, a wash has been applied that allows the light ink to be more visible; Heather Wolfe, curator of manuscripts at the Folger Shakespeare Library, indicated that she had not seen such a substance used before (personal communication, May 2012).

While this manuscript is roughly contemporary with the Granville and Hall manuscripts, it incorporates some older conventions, such as particular contractions and use of a long, Roman-numeral "i" ("j"). The spelling also includes a great number of variants. Much of the spelling is phonetic and, as John Considine has noted, it seems that the contributor might have been slightly dyslexic, as suggested by her writing of "smallage" as "slam ledg" and "wrame" rather than "warme" as just two examples (personal communication, May 2012).

The manuscript was exhibited at the Folger Shakespeare Library in 2011.

Cookery and Medical Receipt Book[1]

[fol. 1r]   for A Gam*m*on of Bacon[2]

First parboyle y*ou*r vensen w*i*th Bayleaves and let the
water drayne from it and then put it into a vesell
that yow may put vineger and wine to it and then let
it stand tell it be could and if you will lard it
yow may and when you haue soe done then season
y*ou*r venson w*i*th Cloues Ginger pep*er* and Salt and then
close it in course past and when it baked put in <.>
vineger att the vent hole and then stope it close
and shake the past and turne the Bottom upward
and let it stand soe tell it bee almost could and
then turne it againe.

To Boyle a Capon in whit Broth

first take y*ou*r Capon and boyle him in faier water &
salt then take the best of the broth and as much
white wine and let them boyle togeather and put to
y*ou*r Mace and let y*ou*r Currans and pruans boyle in
faier watter and when the Capon is ready to send
in blanch y*ou*r Almons and stamp them and straine
them in the broth and put y*ou*r pruans and Curans
in the broth and lay them vpon the Capon y*ow*
must not let the broth boyle after the Almons
be in if yow have any oringe pils slise them &
put them on if they be to hard take them and

---

1 The inside front cover contains various comments on the length, date, etc. of the
   manuscript, but these are clearly from booksellers and not the compilers/users, so
   they have not been transcribed.
2 Hand A ([1r]–[4v], possibly [5r]) is a mixed hand that uses Roman numerals
   (including a long i) and tildes to indicate double letters (as in the title of the first
   recipe, where there is a tilde over the m). This hand evidently used red or brown
   ink initially, and then the recipes (but not their titles) were rewritten, in the same
   hand, in black ink. As stated above, on fol. [4r/v] some kind of wash has then been
   applied over the title to allow it to be more visible; this wash is not evident on the
   Perdita Manuscripts scan. It is not known to whom this hand belongs.

lay them in water xxiiii houers and boyle them
in faier water tell they bee tender then slise
them and cast them on the Capon with the Broth

[fol. 1v]   **To make a Pudding in a Breast of Mutton**

Take grated bread and ship suet finly shred marigold
peneriall margerum and a littell time all well shred
temper therwith noe other liquor but 3 whole eggs
mixe with them some Mace Cloues Nutmege and
Suger & peper and put itt into the brest and rost itt

To make A Pudding Pie

Take white bread finly grated and fine wheat flouer
3 eggs whits and all a few Cloues Mace peper and
salt a handfull of Curranc temper these together
with sweet Cramme [cream] noe thicker then maybe
stirred with a spoune then put itt into a coffine
or platter let itt bake an hower then serue itt

To make a Fine Dish of Eggs

take viii yolks of Eggs beate them with a littell
rosewater set them on a chafindish of colls with
a littell butter to keepe them from burninge and
when itt is thicke put to itt the iuce of two
oringes and Season itt with Suger remember to
stir itt with a spone tell itt be thicke enough

To make a Sallet of Spinnage

first Boyle itt and chope itt smale put therto
a peece of Butter and a hanfull of Curranc
and let itt boyle season itt with Suger and
a littell vergis <.>

[fol. 2r]   **To make Pease pottage**

Take peascods beate them and straine them a good many
take some persle time mariorum Savery and Burrage
and other herbes set on your pott and let your water seeth
and then put in the herbs and Strained pease and
straine a good quantitie of Bread into itt and put

in a good many of whole pease and let them seeth
and season them with Cloves Mase peper and Salt
and a good peece of Butter and if yow will Sinamon ginger & suger

To make a Curious Sheep's Puddings

Take bigge oatmeale and <.>^p^ecke itt well and steepe
itt in good Cramme or milke 3 howers then put to itt
a quantitie of Suet minsed also Time and parsle
Margerum and Savery finly minsed also peper &
Salt with as much Ships Blud as will culler it
read and noe moore and soe make your puddings
your Suet in quantitie must be as much as all
the rest of your stufe

Broth for Ani that is Brought low³

take a younge Cocke cutt him in peeces and bruse him tho
take the end of a knuckell of veale brused reasons of
the sunne stoned ore hanfull Damusk pruans stoned xx
french Barly a hanfull a quantitie of Annis seeds
then take 4 suckry roots a yonge fenell roote two
parsle roots 4 Burrag roots all picked and cutt in
peeces a quantity of Safforn violett leaves and
Strawbery leaves a hanfull bind them togeather
and seeth them in half a pint of whit wine
and seasen itt withall

[fol. 2v]   ### A good Broth for potch'd Eggs

Take time and Margerum a littell one onion and a peece
of sweet Butter and a littell Suger half a hanfull of
Curranc shred and pare all these things and put them
into i pint of whit wine boyle itt as itt aught then
put the potched Eggs vpon the broth

To make a mans appetite to his Meet.⁴

Take fennell mints persle Centery Bitony Sorrell
of each alike whitbread powder of Sinamon aquavite

---

3 The meaning of "tho" at the end of the first line in this recipe is uncertain. Perhaps
   it is a short form for "through" or "thoroughly."
4 This might be a remedy for loss of appetite.

vergis seeth all these together in good alle and
drinke itt of warme

A made Dish

Take Carret roots pare them boyle them & chop them
smale and put therto 2 or three yolks of Eggs and
a good quantie of Currant and Dates well minsed
with an handfull of grated bread season itt with
Sinamon xj⁵ Suger and ginger bake itt with an hole
open and when itt is to be sent in put therto a good
quantity of sweet Butter: Melted –

Frittars of Eggs and herbes.

Take persle peneriall and Margerum the quantity
of a handfull finly choped put to them vi egges
a littell grated Bread and three or fouer sponfull
of Melted Butter beate them all togeather and
season itt with Salt and Suger Cloues and Mace
beaten then frye itt as you doe a tansy & soe serue itt

[fol. 3r]
To purge Malincoly without grife.

Take halfe a ~~handfull~~ ^ounce^ of Sene on sponfull of Sinamon &
Suger brused a quantity of Burrage flouers infuse all
this into a pint of whit wine 12 howers then boyle itt
and straine itt and Drinke it warme fastinge.

A potion against poysininge

Take Sentery Rue Read fenell wormwood and Tansy
a like seeth them in stale ale with Meth or Treacle
giue the patient to drinke therof hoott, first procuer
him to vomitt with warme water or the like or
with a feather put Downe to his Troate.

An Exceding restoratiue for on *that* is brought lowe

Take an owld Cocke and pull of his Skine quarter hime
and breake his Bones put him into an Erthen pott

---

5 This letter form is not clear, especially since the quantity is not followed by
   "ounces." However, it does look similar to "xij"in the top recipe on [fol. 4v].

putinge therto the Marrow of any oxe and Rosmary
Time and keepe a hanfull of all thes bound together
then Saforn Sinamun garingall Long pep*er* and
round pep*er* of thes ij ounces a hanfull of pruans
smal reasons half an ounce Dats skined 2 or
3 ounces of great reasons stoned boyle all thes
to gether in iij pints and half of white wine
and then administ*er* itt

[fol. 3v]   **A good Drinke for one *that* is horse**

Take half an ounce of Metredate half an ounce
of Suger Candy half an ounce of pep*er* grosly
beaten make a hole in a great white onien
after the head is cutt of and put in thes said
things then put on the head againe and winde
itt up in a pap*er* and rost itt well soe done stamp
and straine itt through with ij pints of stronge
ale and drinke itt mor*ning*: and euininge hott

To cause one to make water

Take parsle and seeth itt in runninge water tell itt
be half consumed then put to itt 2 or 3 sponfulls
of aquavite and giue the sike of the liquor moor
then luke warme and make a plaster of the
parsle in a lin*n*en bagge and lay itt to the
smale of the Belly as hott as itt can be sufferd
and against the heate be gone of the plaster
prepare a smale wooden dish and in the bottom
therof som Bayleaves and vpon that lay embers
and vpon that wormwood then couer itt and bind
the linen cloth vnder the Dish and let the
sicke hould the dish as hoott to his belly
as hee can suffer itt

[fol. 4r]   **For *the* weaknes of *the* Stomake and Dulenes of *the* Braine**

Take 2 hanfulls of Rosmary i ounce of dried Nutmege ij
ounces of Bittony ij ounces of Cloues cutt very smale
and put therto xv pints of good rennish wine then let
them stand together 2 or 3 dayes drinke a good draft
in the beginninge of thy meate for yo*ur* head at the latt*er* end

For Blered Eyes

Take an Egge Shell that is cleane takinge awaye
the Skine within itt and put therto a littell fine coppris
and sett itt in hott imbers and then itt will melt then
skime itt cleane and wash the eys therwith –

For Hearing

Take 3 Drops of your owne watter and dropt into your eare

For the Redd and Watery Eyes.

Take the white of an Egge and beate itt tell itt bee
cleare then let itt stand a night and settell
likwise take the iuce of wormwood and let itt
Stand and Settell then take the clearist of
them both beinge mixt togeather and drope
itt into your Eye

For an ach and pain of the Side.

Take Camomile and bruse itt then take new wheaten
brann mixe them and put itt into a pewter dish on a
Chafindish of Colls put them in a quilted bagge
and aply itt to the painfull plase

[fol. 4v]   ### To kepe the Eys cleare and coule from readnes

Take ij handfuls of plantine i hanfull of housleek
stamp itt and straine itt and lett it settell then
powre out the cleare iuce from the drose
and put therto half as much Read Rosewater
and a quarter of a sponfull of white Sugercandy
in powder then take Lapis Caluminaus as bigg
as your thumb and slak it xij times in the
same water and put ij or iij Drops thereof into
your Eys Morninge and Eueninge

For the wind Collike

Take Sacke and Aquavite ij ounces put therto
a peece of Suger and let the partie drinke itt of

To breake the stone

Take A Cocke of An Eare owld and open him
and yow shall find in his maw Smale white
stones take them and beake them in A Brasen
Morter very fine put itt in good whit wine & drinke

For one that Consumeth

Take a new laid Egge let itt be reare rosted
and put therto a cake of Manus Christi and
lett itt desolue in itt and eate the same
morninge and Eueninge

[fol. 5r]   **Against *the* Dropsye**

Take the flowers of elder and[6] watercreses
hart strange and Rusmary alike still all those
together w*i*th stale Ale and drinke therof

To Cure sore bruses and any plaine sores

Take a pecke of Ashes made of Ashen wood
and make therof iij quarts of Lye w*i*th ij gallons
of runinge watter, then put to that Lye iij quarts
of Cleare and stronge Tanhouse that was not
vsed w*i*th Leather then ad of Aluime and
Madder made in smale powder halfe a pinte
boylinge itt togeather in a large vesell for
runinge out vntell halfe be wasted a waye
stire itt continually and then let itt stand ix
dayse a settlinge then powre out the thinest
and saue itt in glasses to wash sores w*i*th
warme and to aplye w*i*th duble linen cloths
and drese itt iij or iiij times in the daye this
is good for Rebellious Ulcers –

---

6   While the "d" in this hand often looks like a "g," I have considered it a variant letter
form of "d."

To stope a haske

Take an ege and rost itt with Aquavite and then
eate the ege with sinamond powder and Suger

[fol. 5v blank]

[fol. 6r]   **A resete of alle**[7]

Lignam: vita-2 ounces: cartix <.> 2 ounces: Salsar
2 ounces: hermiodachilis 2 ounces sein 2 ounces
camamill flowers: 2 ounces: Sticcadus 2 ounces: annes
seedes 2 ounces: licoris i ounces: a pound and a halfe
of reasons of the Sunne bruse the same and let
it to boilde with the best worte halfe an hour: with
violet leaues: water cresset, strabry leaues ov each one
handfull: a branch or tow of Rosemary: put all into a
linniny bagge into the drinke when you tounne it
vp into the Barrill and there let it lie in the barill
you may drinke thereof after it bee 3 dayes olde

A resepte for a fellon

Take lauender a handfull: a white lilly roote
the white of a egge a spoonefull of english honny
and a sponfull of wheat flower: beate these in
a morter well to gether: and then a plye to the
sore <..> if it breeke put in a little turpityne

for a parfume

Take of beniamind iij oz and a halfe bruse it a little
and lay it in steepe iij or iiij dayes in damask rose
water then take halfe a pound of rose leaues
beaten as small as any Consarue then put in the
benianind and halfe a quart of an ounce of
muske and as much sevet and beat them all together
and make them vp in little peeces: and with a
seele press them betwixt tow rose leaues

---

7   Hand B ([6r]–[7r]) is a seemingly hastily written mixed hand. It also uses Roman
    numerals. It is similar to Hand A, although its minuscule e, for example, is entirely
    different. There is no indication of the identity of the contributor.

[fol. 6v]   **An: oyntment for the fase that is trubled**
with heath pimples or any rednes that
shall afend [offend] the same

Take 3 ounces of oyle of violetes and put into it
one ounce of flower of brimstone: halfe a ounce
of camfeare: halfe a ounce of Cynamon <...>finely
beaten: and searcde: one ounce of the ~~finest~~
whitest sorte of musterd seede beeing well ground
with whit wine vingere and the ioyce of a good
lemone put all this into a cleane woodne dish to
gether: with a ounce of capone greese and halfe
a nounce of white suger candey worke all these
in a ^the^ wooden dish: with a wooden pestelle tell
it come to bee a parfite fine oyntment and
then with a little spunge a noynte the face or
other plase that is affended ether with heath
pimples or rednes this will cuer it probatome

take halfe a pinte of milke: and halfe a
pinte of sacke and make a possite and
straine it throughe a cleane cloth: and
in the morning wash of the oyntement
with the possite

[fol. 7r]   **for a egge pye**

take six egges and boyle them very harde: and then shread
them as smalle as you can then take 2 spoonfull of sinomand
shearched and a quarter of a pound of <...> currendes
and some beefe showit and some suger and a little
cromes and some nutmeag and soe blend it together
like a Bag puding and put it in a cauffin and
bake it

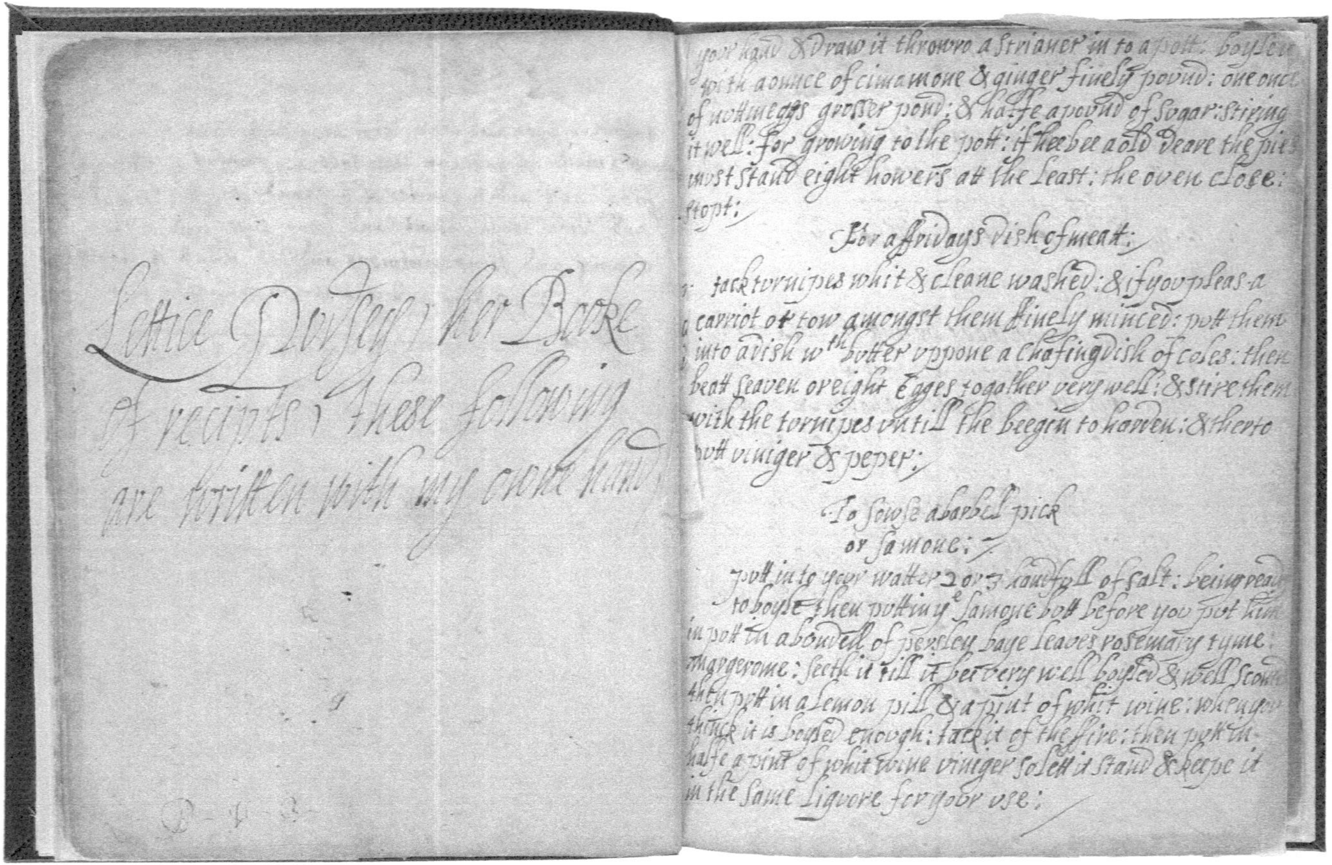

Fig. 3.1 Folger MS V.a.450, fols. 7v/8r. By permission of the Folger Shakespeare Library.

[fol. 7v]   **Lettice Pudsey, her Booke**
of recipts, These following
are written with my owne hand /[8]

[fol. 8r]   your[9] hand & draw it throwro a strianer in to a pott: boyle it
with a onnce of cimamone & ginger finely pound: one once
of nuttmeggs grosser pond: & haffe a pound of sugar: stiring
it well: for growing to the pott: if hee bee a old deare the pies
must stand eight howers att the least: the oven close:
stopt:/[10]

For a ffridays dish of meatt:/

tack turnipes whit and cleane washed: & if you pleas a
carriot or tow amongst them ffinely minced: putt them
into a dish with butter vppone a chafingdish of coles: then
beatt seaven oreight egges togather very well: & stire them
with the turnipes vntill the beegin to harden: & therto
putt viniger & peper:/

To sowse a barbell pick
or samone:/

putt in to your watter 2 or 3 handfull of salt: being ready
to boyle then putt in *the* samone butt before you put him
in putt in a bundell of persley baye leaves rosemary tyme:
margerome: seeth it till it bee very well boyled & well scomed
then putt in a lemon pill & a pint of whit wine; when you
thinck it is boyled enough: tack it of the ffire: then put in
halfe a pint of whit wine viniger so lett it stand & keepe it
in the same liquore for your vse:/

---

8   Hand C ([7v]–[32r], [33r], [34r]–[36r], [37r]–[38r], [39r], [40r], [56v]–[58r] top recipe,
[59r], [60r]–[61r] top recipe, [62r], [64r]–[65r]) is, obviously, Lettice Pudsey's hand.
It is an italic hand characterized by its frequent use of colons and virgules as end
punctuation. It also includes a particularly high number of variant spellings.
Minuscule u and v, and sometimes r, are quite indistinguishable in this hand; letters
reflect the original to my best judgment.
9   This recipe is missing the beginning, as pages preceding this one are missing.
10   As this contributor (Pudsey) quite consistently ends her recipes with this
punctuation, I have retained it.

[fol. 8v]   **To feed chickings geeses or duckes:/**

keepe them in a pen & give them ground malt & milcke[11]
mingled togather: butt noe watter at all: & thay will:
bee so ffatt: that if you tack them not in time thay will
dye with fatt: lett not your malt be groune to small
nor you milck sower: for that will not feede:/

To mack Scurbugrase ale:/

ffirst adde to your ordinary bruing of strick of good
    mault: & of the first runing: tack 5 glanlens [gallons] of
wort: these herbes are for summer: a handfull of water
cresses: a handfull of bruck lime: a handfull of sage red
or greene: a handfull of suckrey: a handfull of femitery
till may putt in a handfull of dock rootes & a handfull
of butter dockrootes: affter may you must putt in noe
dockrootes till michalmas: these must all bee boyled
togather with one handfull of hopes: and a handfull of
scurbuerygrase: a hower & a halfe:/

To mack fretters:/

ffrist tack some stroung ale & som sake: then breake
in 6 eggs the wites & all: & 6 yolks more without
wits: then putt in a lettel salt: & a prety dell of
cloves & mace: then putt in your fflower &:
[fol. 9r]   beat it well & mack it well & thick: then to boyle them:
you must have a flatt pan: or skellett: then putt in your
lard & lett it boyle: but as loung as it popels in the pan:
you must not putt them in: butt affter as fast as you can:
so lett them boyle & stor them: thay will bee enough guickly/

To mack rise pudings:/

tack sweet creame & rise boyle them togather: till thay
bee as thick as for porrich: then put into it 3 or 4 eggs with
the whits and tack out the threads: then season it with sugar

---

11   While most farmers do not feed chickens, ducks, or geese milk today because
birds lack the enzyme to digest lactose, some say that unpasteurized milk is not
problematic because the milk itself contains these enzymes within it.

& nuttmegs: & your marrow finely minct: so fill your pud
dings & lett them boyle well:/

To mack surrupe of lemons:/

tack of the iuce of lemons one pint: of the ffinest
loafe sugar you can gett a pound & a halfe: boyle them
gently opon a soft ffire: & sceming it vntill it come to the
consistance of a surrupe so keepe it for your vse:/

To mack surrupe of violetts

tack of violetts one pound weel pickt putt them into
a earthen pot very cleane: with 3 pints of water: lett
your water bee prety hott: & stop the pot close: sett them
opon a fuw smale <.> coals 24 houres to keepe them in
a moderate heat: but not to seeth: then strane:

[fol. 9v]   of very well: & putt to eveire pint: 2 pound of the
best sugar: then putt it a pipkin: set it in a kettel:
of seething water: when the surrup is ready to boyle
scume it cleane & then lett it sember a quarter of a
hower: so observeing this quantity you may mack
more o^r^lese as you please:/

To mack a nother surrup of violetts of
the best manner to keep couler all yeare:/

tack 2 ounces of violetts very cleane pickt: then
bruse them in a stone morter: then putt them in a
galley pot close covered with iij ounces of running
watter: sett the galley pot in a skellet of watter: *that*
is ready to boyle & there lett it stand for 12 howers:
somtimes stiring it with a selver spone once in 2
howers: covering it close againe: when it is steped
the 12 howers: tack it out & prese it very hard: then
put into it halfe a pound of fine loafe sugar: beaten
to fine pouder: mix them togather in a putter or
selver dish over a chafindish of coales vntill the
sugar bee dissovled: then tack it of & lett it settel;
then scume it: & putt it in a glase bottel close:

[fol. 10r]   covered: be sure you lett it not boyle with the sugar:
if you doe it will lose the clover [colour]:/

To mack conserve of red roses:/

tack red rosebuds: & cutt all the wite from the leves[12]
& part one leafe from a nother: so that there hangs noe
seeds amonge them: then weigh them & putt to everie
pound of roese a pound of searced sugar: then putt *the* roses
in a fare stone morter: & beate them being ever by times
casting in some sugar: beating them very well togather:
till you find the roses very smale: & perfettly fine enough
tack it out & putt it in a glase or som galley pot: when it
is quarter old[13] it is good & not to be used before:/

To mack gouseberrys caks:/

tack of the greenest goosberrys: & pick them; putt them
in a posnit with a lettel watter to shusk them: when they
are scalded soft: then straine them through a cotten st
rainer: keep your stuf wrame one a fuw embers till
you have candid your sugar: to a pint of stuf putt a
pound of sugar: & when your sugar is candid putt in *the*
goosberry stufe: lett it stand a lettel & scume it butt
tack heede it doe not boyle: then put them out
[fol. 10v]   into a glase saucers or putters ones: & sett them in a
wrame plase: & when thay are candid one the top
turne them out with your knife one a pie plate doe
somwhat one them: ether letters or what you please
& lett them stand till thay be dry: then box them:/

To preserve cherries:/

tack of the bigest & farest cheris you can without spots
& stone them putting 2 cheris opon one stalk: to a pound
of cheris a pound of scearced sugar: straw a lettel sugar
one the bottom of your pan: then lay a row of cheris
one by one: cover them over with sugar: then lay another
row of cheris & cover them with sugar: till you have layd
them all: then putt in a spoonefull of fare watter so
sett them one a quick ffier: & boyle them as fast as yo*u*

---

12 As in a few other recipes in this edition, this reference must mean the petals.
13 In other words, a quarter of a year.

can close covered: & as you percive the scum to rise
tack of the dish & scum it very well: & when there
tender tack them vp: & putt one those cheris that
are boyled of: & lay them vp round in sum dish: then
boyle the surrip againe & cume it: then power it opon
the cheris: & when thay are cold putt them: leave
a lettel of the surrip ~~of~~ in the bottom of the dish to cover
them one the top when thay are in the glases:/

[fol. 11r]   **To mack mackeromes:**

tack good allmones a quarter of a pound & blanch them in
cold watter: then to these tack 3 quarters of a pound of fine
searced suger: beat them in a stone morter with a wite of
a egge & rose watter: till it bee a lettel thicker then batter
for fitters: then drop it one waffers & so back them:/

To mack conserve of barberryes:/

tack your Barberrys fall ripe the redest & cleane pickt: as
many as well serve your turne: putt them in a deepe earthen
pot close covered: & sett the pot into a pot with seething
watter: & lett them boyle till thay bee soft enough: so stire
them well togather: & strane them so that non of the seeds
come through: then tack to a pint of that: 2 pound of sugar
then putt the stuf to the sugar & stir it togather: sett it opon
the fier & lett it but boyle to tack of the scum cleane: then
when it is cold putt it in your glases:/

To preserve orringes or lemons:/

tack of the bigest & farest thick rined orringes you can
gett: & finely pare them the out most skinn as thinne
as possibell: then slice them in medell crushing all
the iuce of them forth: then putt in a pan of fare
running watter: as you pare them: letting them stand
[fol. 11v]   for 3 days shifting the water twice a day: then
tack a pan with water & boyle them till you can
thrust a straw through them: but before you must
tack out all the meat cleane out: & when you tack
them vp lay them one a fare cloth & cover them:
then mack your surrip ready: to the weight of them

as much sugar: so boyle them till you thinck thay
are enough: then put them up: leaving surrip to cover
them:/

To mack wite marmalett of quinces:/

tack you quinces unpared & uncored: parboyl them in
fare watter: till you come to some tenderness then pare
them: & tack the purest part of the quince: cleane cut
from the core: beat them in a stone morter till it be
reasonabell smale: & that you percive noe hard lompes in
it: then tack it out of the morter & lay it one a fare sheet
of paper: weight it & tack to evere 3 pound of quince
2 pound of sugar finely beaten: mixt the sugar & the
quinces well togather: put them in a fare posnit or
pan: so boyle it keeping it well with stiring & when
you find it stick to the side of the pan dry: set som
a cooleing in a spoone: that you may gesse when it
is enough: to box it: you may add to it lettel thinne:

[fol. 12r]   sliced preserve orringe when it is boyled enough: then tack it
of the ffire: stiring it till it bee almost coole: then box it:/

To mack a gooseberry foole:/

tack a pint of gooseberrys putt them in a skellet: & put to
them water to cover them: boyle them tender as pap: then
pouer it into a cullinder & rub it through with a spoone: that
the meat may olnly goe through & the skins only stay: putt the
meat againe: into the skellet & put thereto the yelkes of 6 eggs
well beaten with rose watter; & lett it boyle a walme or tow:
sweten it with suger to you licking: if you thinck it be to thicke
mack it thinner with creame: which you must so beate in with
a spoone: that it may not be descerned: while it is hott pouer
it into the dish you will serve it in: lett it stand till it bee
coole before it bee eaten:/

To preserve Apricoks:/

ffirst pare them & stone them: then straw sugar in a dish
& putt them in: then cover them over with sugar: &
lett them stand all night: & thay will bee full of surrip

in the morning: & then boyle them up: add one or tow
more of them to a pound: then a pound of sugar: boyle your
surrip well: & remember to leave som to cover them
affer thay are but [put] vp in glases:/

[fol. 12v]   **To preserve greene walnutts:/**

tack them when you can thrust a nedell thrue them
then lay them in cold watter all night & a day: then
scald them in watter: & pill them: & then scald them
in watter againe till thay bee soft: tack to a pound of
them a pound & a half of sugar: then mack a sirrip &
so putt them in: & boyle them till you thinck thay
are tender: boyle the surrip affer & put them up as
you doe other preserves:/

To mack lipe saulfe:/

tack of the whitest lard & slice it in long thinne
peeces: & lay it in rose watter 2 days: then rost it
opon a wooden spite: & lett it drop in rose watter:
as long as the droping looks whit: & beat it in that
rose watter till it bee very whit: then put away
that watter: & putt to it fresh rose watter: so lett it
stand all night: the next day beat it againe in a
fresh rose watter: so lett it stand 2 days: then tack
it cleane from the watter: & put it in a glase it most
not be to close stopt: nor keept in a hot plase it
will last good half a yeare:/

[fol. 13r]   **For bleared & blodshoten eies:/**

Beat the whit of a egge to oyle: & then beat it againe:
nuw with the Joyce of wormewood: & dipe fine flaxe
in it: & so to bedwards lay it to the eie & it helpeth:/

To draw away a humor:/

tack a toast of rie Bread: steeped in reed wine & when
you goe to bed lay it to your eies & it heelpeth:/

For the humor in the eies a fine plaster

ffirst seeth milke & put it to it leavened whit bread: comin
seeds Beatony: & the claye of the stoping of beare:[14] of each
a lick quantity: boyle them to the thicknes of a poltes &
lay it betwene tow cloths plasterwise: to the temples
of your head: as hot as you can suffer it: so dres it evening
& morning & it will help you in short time:/

An Excelent watter for
the eies:/

tack the destilled watter of eiebright hearbagrase sala
dine browne fennell of each 2 onncs: whit rose watter 8
onnces: of greeke wine 18: onnces: of tutia one onnce:
& a haffe: cloves beaten grose one onnce & a halfe: whit
sugar candy one drame: campher & alose of each halfe
a drame:

[fol. 13v] prepare your tutia in this manner: mack it red hot in
the ffier 6 times: & quench it every time in a pretty
quantity of whit rose watter & the wine mixt togather:
casting it still away & tacking fresh: then pond the
tutia as fine as meale & so putt it into the watters
& wine beeing mixt togather: then prepare the a
loes: in thes sort: but a lettel of the sade watter & with
with the aloes into a morter: & work it well till the
aloes bee dissolved: disolved your campher: then putt
all togather into a doubell glase that is a third part
bigger then to containe the whole: stop it close with
a cork & opone it a parchment: with a past made of
wheat fflower & the whit of a egge worked well to
gather: & layd one: that noe strenth come forth:
this done sett it in the sunne forty days & nights at
the least: shakeing it well 3 or 4 times a day: a smale
drop at a time droped out of a spoone is enough: night
& morning when you use it: the water & wine that

---

14 "The claye of the stoping of beare" is not an obvious ingredient. Probably the
contributor means clay used for sealing beer casks. (Hamlet refers to this practice in
act 5, scene 1, when he describes the dust of Alexander the Great stopping a barrel
hole.) Perhaps this clay would acquire a film of the beer's yeast.

the tutia is quenched in: must bee non of the quanti
tes: mentioned in the compotione: the ingreedience
must not be put from the watters in the glase: & it
will keepe perfettly good many yeares:/

[fol. 14r]   **A sarffiereine: watter devised by D**o**ctor Stewene:**
to my lord arshbisshop of canterburry did wi**th**
it many great cures: keept it a secrett vntill
hee lay opon his death bed: at wh**ich time the:**
Bisshop gott it of him in wrighting as this:/

Tack ginger: gallingallio: cinamon: cordind: cloves: any
seeds: caraway seeds: fenell seeds: of each a quarter of
a onnce: then tack sage: mintce: red rosees: time: pelletory
rosemary: wild time: camamile: lavender: of each a
handfull: beat *th*e spices finely: & bruse *th*e hearbs: smale
putt them all into a gallone of whit or red wine: &
lett them stand so infused: the space of 12 howers oft
times stiring them: then still them all in a limbreke
over a soft ffier: keep the first watter by it selfe it is
the best: the second is good but not so good: this water
preserveth helth: causeth long life: & is good against
many desseases: it is much better if it stand all the
summer in the sunn: it is good against the shaking
of the palsey: it cureth the contractione of senews:
it helpeth the conception: of wemmen that bee:
barron: it killeth wormes in the belley: it cureth *th*e
cold & cough: it helpeth the tooth ach: helpeth
[fol. 14v]   the dropsy: it helpeth the stone: & rines of the
back: it cureth the stinking breath: & macketh
one loock young:/

To aswage any swelling:/

tack whit bread & milk: lett it seeth till it bee:
very thick: then putt to it a spoonfull of bolearmo
lick: & so lay it to the plase pained as warme as the can
suffer it:

for a sore breast:/

tack a quart of new milk: & new oatemeale: aquaviti
sheeps sueuett: lineseeds: pond a good quantity of slam

ledg: boyle all this togather till it bee thick as a has
ty pudding: & lay it to the breast as hot as you can ssofer:

to onointe the stommack:/

tack oile of nuttmeggs & oile of mace: this proved:/

a watter to heale a canker in mouth
or throath:/

tack a pint of ale: & boyle it & scum it: then putt in a
peece of rooch allome: & a quantity of life [live? hive?] hunny as
will season it: & a sprige of rose mary: then boyle them
all togather a good while: scem it very cleane:
[fol. 15r]   this is a Excelent meddiscen: that hath bing trid for the canker:/

To mack a excelent ointment ether
for bruse or sprane:/

tack sage: lavender: lavender cotton: srosemary: baise: wor
mwood: hearbagrase: camamile: of each a good handfull: sred
them: & boyle them in 3 pound of sheeps sewett: deares suewt
capons grece: of each what you please: clovs & mace: nuttmegg
& sinamon: brused very smale of each a like quantity: when
all these are halfe boyled: putt in a pint of brused sneales: &
a good hanfull of hensdung: boyle all these togather: till thay bee
as greene as the hearbs will mack it: then tack it of the ffier:
& strane it into a galley pot: & keepe it for your use: when you:
use it: warme it & aniont the plase pained: rubing it in very
well: before the ffier:: thes is my lady wendys: ointment/

To mack a sceare cloth that is good to lay
opon the plase when it is a ointted:/

tack a pound of Sheeps suwett: one pound of bees waxe: halfe
a pound of rossing: & a lettel frankcomsence: & melt them all
in a skellett: & when thay are all incorperated togather: dipe
in your lining cloth: & when it is cold: role up the seare
cloth: & keep it for your use: this is allso my lady wendys:/

[fol. 15v]   ### pills for the stone: / this is Mrs Risleys:/

tack the wieght of eaght pence: of the best venes
turpetine: & wash it in very good whit wine: till it

look whit: then pouer the wine away: then tack whit
sugar candy: finely beaten: & role up the washed
turpentine in it: made into pills as big as you may
swalloe them with ease: tack all these pills: fasting
in a morning: & fast a hower affter: then you may eate:
your ordinary diatte: it may be thay will work: if not
thay will doe noe harme:/ you may mack affter this
weight & manner: as many as will sarve you to tack
tow or 3 months togather: once a month: for prevention
if you sett those you doe not tack in a oven after a back
of bread is drawne: to harden the out sids a lettel of them
affter thay are roled up in pills in the sugar candy: so
you may keepe them better for your use:/

**The surfett or plague watter: good aganst any
infectionus: deases & to drive anything from
the hart: it is to be made in may or iune:/**

tack sage: saladine: rosemary: wormwood: Balme:
rosasoles: mugwort: pympernell: scabious: egrimonye:
rue = mint =
[fol. 16r]   scordium: cardus: Betonye: Dragon: cowslips fflowers:
marigolds fflowers: of each a larg hanfull: tormentell rootes:
angilico: alycompane: pyonye: zyduiary: lycorich: of each one:
onnce: & a lettel safron: sreed the herbs well & smale: alltogather:
& bruse the roots: steepe them all in a gallon of whit wine: or sake:
sack is better: for 2 days & 2 nights: stiring them once a day: putt
them in a earthen pot: & bee sure to stop it close: you may mack 2
stillfull of thes quantetie if you please: or elce one: destill it in a
ordinary still: tack of the first running one pint: of the second
running one quart: of the last one pint: which is the fittest for
chillderinge: of the first 2 spoonfull will sarve: of the second 4:
of the last for chilldren: 2 or 3 spoonefoll: you may give it at
any time: when you see ocatione: warme it a lettel: & sweeten
with sugar: when you use it: or with surrip of gillefflours: or
violetts: this is my lady Shirleys: recipte:/

**To mack an excelent watter for
the stone & wind collicke:/**

Tack halfe a peck of mother of time: halfe a peck of saxe
fridge: halfe a peck of pelletory of the wale: halfe a peck

of philopendelay: half a peck of grounmile: a quarter of
a peck of bettonye: a quarter of a peck of persley: a quarter
of a peck of reddish leves & roots: a quarter of a peck of
marsmallo berrys: shred all these togather: & putt them

[fol. 16v]   into a very cleane earthen pot: & putt to them 3 quarts
of new milke of a red cow: then destill it: drink a lettle
draught of it in a morning fasting: sweeten with sugar:
/ this is my lady Shirleys recipte:

an aproved pouder: for the stone:/

tack a peck of hawes: when thay have had a frost: pick
them from the stalks: sett them in a oven: & dry them
till thay will pond to pouder: then pond them very
smale: & sifft them: then dry them a gaine: & sifft them
till stons and all be siffted cleane through the siffe:
then tack a good spoonfull once a weeke: in the mor
ning fasting: & drink 2 or 3 spoonfull affter it: of
whit wine: or this watter warmed: & fast 2 howers
affter it: this is my lady Shirleys receipte:/

A receipet for a stich or bruse
in the body: proved:

tack a quart of beere or samle ale: boyle
it: then put in a spoonfull of fennell seed
or anniseed: & 3 or 4 rasers of ginger
sliced: & a bunch of time: when these
are well boyled in tack it of the fier:

[fol. 17r]   and tack a prety deale of stoned hors dung and
straind it into that liquor: that it may tast well
of it & looke greene: & give thereof 3 or 4 spoonfull
wrame at a time: evening & morning:/

[fol. 17v blank]

[fol. 18r]   ### Mrs Okeover's Receipt of Balsom:/

Tack five pints of the best sallett oile: one pint
of the best venise turpentine: halfe a pound of the
best and finest yellow wax: & eight ounces of red:=
sanders everi ounce putt in a paper by it selfe: in

fine powder beeing siffted: first putt the five pints
of oile into a: posnet with a quarter of a pinte of:
Red rose watter: & lett it boyle till the rose watter bee
consumed: then tack it of the ffier: & lett it stand till
it have left bubling: then putt to it your wax and *the*
turpentine: which must bee thus prepared: cutt your
wax in thinn slises: wash your turpentine in a quar
ter of a pint of red rose watter: & beate ^it^ till it looke
very whit: then putt your wax & turpentine: togather
& beeing well mellted: putt them to your oile: & lett
them all boyle togather a quarter of a houer: then
putt in all the sanders: ounce affter ounce very:
softly: stiring it continually least it rvne over:
then lett it boyle a nother quarter of a houre: then
straine it through a new cloath: beeing cleane:
[fol. 18v]   washed: so putt it into a galley pot as you please to
keepe it in: the best way is to tack it of the ffier
when you putt in the sanders: till it bee all stired
well in the oile: least it rvne over: & therefore be
sure your vesell you boyle it in be bigg enough:/

The Vertues of it / Which hath
bing found by experience to have helped
& done much good in all these paines &
Deaseses as ffolowing /

For the running
of the reines as much as a small walnut: 14 days
togather fasting: for any convolsion inward or
outward: for you may both anoint with it &
tack it inwardly: for the paine in the head
anoint the tempells & within the <.> nostrills
for an old sore: or a greene wound beeing aplied
warme: for ani wind in the stomack tacken
inwardly or anoint it: for to gett the fier out
of any burne or scalde: anoint it with it:
[fol. 19r]   I have allso found it most excellent for sore breast
& for swellings: & stopings in the stomack: anoint
the plase & tack it inwardly: beesides it is very good
for biles to anoint them: & to give inwardly the
quantity of a nuttmegg att a time: there is noe feare

of tacking to much: & it is very good for an inward:
bruse: & to drink a draught of sack possett drink affter
it at ani time: when you tack it inwardly: lastly:
it hath helped Divers of the cough of the lunges
& one that had it twenty yeares: by tacking of
it inwardly:/

A singuler good searcloth
for old or greene sores /

Take halfe apond of weather shewett of
the best: & sreed it very smale & render
it but have a care you doe not burne it
in the rendering of it: then strane it
throwe a cloth: then take halfe a pint
of oile of roses: of the best: &
[fol. 19v] & halfe a pound of red lead: & pond it smale
and searce it thorow a hare sive: then
putt it all in a skellet & boyle it: & keepe
it with stirring with a moderate ffier &
lett it boyle till it come to the couler of
a nuttmegg: then take yours clothes &
dipe them in it & hang them up to coole
then cutt your peeces according to your
sores:/ this is my cousen Rugleys receipt:/

for a sore swelling or
a sore breast /

tack halfe a ounce of Balsom a
penny measure of oile ollife one
penny worth of red lead: one
penny worth of Boularniunicke
boyle them togather till they will
stick one a cloth: but tack heede of
over boyleing it: for then it will:
[fol. 20r] bee as hard as a stone: for if it bee a lettel
over boyled: it will teare the cloth all to
peeces: wett the cloth in it when you
think it is boyled enough: & lay it one a
paper to coole: this stufe all the while
it is a boyleing must bee well stired:/

A Receipt to kill a tetterworme /

Tack vinegar & oile of violettes of each a
lick quantitie: & beate them togather
with a knife: & then put in as much bay
salt finely pond: as you can tack upon
yours knifes point: & as much brimstone
finely pond: & beat them alltogather
& Then putt in as much parsley finely
pond: as will mack it thick: then apliy
it all night to the tatter: & in *the* mor
ning wash it of with som bay salt: put
into water: & so lett it goe till night
[fol. 20v]   & then aply it as neede shall reguire:/

To mack oyntment of roses

Tack some hoggs lard lett it bee very
whit & sweet; then wash it in halfe
a dossen severall faire watters: affer
you have done so: beate out *the* water
as cleane as you can: then tack som
red rose budes cutt of the whit ends
& bruse them a lettel in your morter
& then putt your roses & lard all to
gather in a glase or pott stoping *the*
glase close: then sett it in a pot of
seathing water & so lett it stand 3 or
4 howers one the fire: but lett not *the*
water seath after you have putt in *the*
glase of ointment: then strane out *the*
roses & throw them away: you must
shift them with roses in this mannar
6 or 7 times at *the* last time strane it
[fol. 21r]   throw a fine strainer: & beate it till it bee
cold, & lett your roses bee dry gotten:/

To mack *the* laxative whey /

Tack of seney 3 ounces of violett leaves or
flowers sorrel scabious borrage femetory
baulme strawberrys leaves of each one a

handfull: of licorish brused a quarter of
a ounce: of anny seeds & sweet fennell
seeds of each tow drames: putt all to
3 pints of new milk whey: & sett it
one the fire: & so soone as it boyles
tack it & sett it close covered in wrame
ashes twellve howers: then strane it out
hard: & clarifie it with the whit of a
egge: & tack it every morning you must
putt in one handfull of plantan leaves
one ounce of polipodium of the oake
[fol. 21v]   and 2 drames of creame a tartar /

To mack hipocris /

Tack 3 pints of whit wine & putt to it
one pint of well coulered sacke: a pond
of suger a quarter of a onnce of sliced
<.̈.> nuttmeggs: 3 quarters of a ounce of
sinoment broken: halfe a ounce of ginger
sliced: halfe a halfe quarter of graines
halfe a halfe quarter of coriander seeds
& a fuw cloves: bruse all this a lettel:
putt them into the wine in a stone
Juge or pot stop it very close: for
12 howers shaking it offten: then put
to it halfe apint of heten milk & stir
it well togather: & so lett it stand a
hower or more: then pouer it out gently
[fol. 22r]   through a gelly bagg: with a spoute to it
doe it offten till you see it run cleare:/

To mack another plauge water /

Tack of rue: betenny: egremony: scabious:
fetherfuw: selendine: browne may weede:
Bawme: aveirs angellico: cardus: burnett:
sorrell: wormwood: mugwort: pimpernell:
sage: plantane: dragon: marigolds *the* greene
leaves: allicompane roots: scrapt & sliced
of each of these 3 pounds: but of rosemarie
6 pounds: chap them very smale & put

them into 8 gallands of *the* best whit
wine: & cover them very close all a night
& a day: & then destill them in an ordia
ry: still: keep *the* frist running which is
the strongest by it self: & *the* second by
it selfe: beeing weaker / when
[fol. 22v] you give of it warme it & put suger
in it: some 3 or 4 sponefull at a time
is a nough /

How to mack gousberry cakes /

Tack your gousberrys when they bee very
greene & pick them then putt in to
a skellett with a lettel fare water: &
keepe them with shaking till thay
bee soft: then strane them & to
a pound of suger; a pint of this
stufe: you must candy your suger
very hard: then putt in your stufe
& lett it stand one *the* fire till *the*
suger bee melted: & then scum it
bee carefull it stand not on to long
for macking it yellow: then[15]

[fol. 23r]   ### A Receipt to mack bottel watter

Tack 3 gallonds of spring watter & putt to it
3 pound of suger of 6 pence a pound 3
ounces of ginger halfe a ounce of nuttmegs
thin sliced: some mace & a few cloves
beaten: as many as you see or think good
boyle all these in *the* spring watter untill
a quart bee boyled away: then add to it halfe
a ounce of corroander seedes diped in viniger
& dryed before *the* fire againe: & beat them
& when it is allmost cold putt in some
ale barme: to this liquor into a vessell *that* hath
a tap at *the* bottom & when it hath worked

---

15   Pages are missing here.

enough to your mind *tha*t you think it is setteled
enough drawe it forth into your bottels through
a sriprius bagg *tha*t it may run cleare from *th*e
yeast & <....> spicess: when they are corked
[fol. 23v] up so soone as they are filled you must
tye downe *th*e corke or elce they will
flie out all this you may mack ether
summer or winter: & when you pouwer
it out drink it with suger

[fol. 24r] **To mack a fine silleybub /**

Tack a quart of whit wine & tow quarts of
sweet creame & mingdell them <.>togather
with some fine suger: then putt it into
a glase churne & so churne it till you see
it bee thick & frothey: then putt it out into
what silleybub glases or pott as you please

now what quantitie of whit wine you please to
tack at any time ether more or less: to mack
one of: allwaise tack twise as much creame
butt putt noe suger on the top of it: butt
mack it sweet to your licking before /

[fol. 24v blank]

[fol. 25r] **To mack *th*e best sort of beskett /**

Tack halfe a pound of *th*e whit & finest
wheate fflower you can gett; as much fine
scarced suger: mingell them togather: then
tack 4 whole egges & *th*e youlks of 2 more
& putt to them a very lettel salt: & 2 sponfull
of rose watter: putt these to your suger &
fflower: then stir it all togather: & then beat
it in analeyblaster [an alabaster] morter: with a wooden
pestell: a houer or more: till you see it look
whit & very light & puffey: then when it is
allmost beaten enough: putt in ether some
anie seeds or carayways seeds as you like: & when
it is enough: sift some fine suger in *th*e bottomes

of your tinn coffins: so fill them & sett them
in *th*e oven: lett it not bee to hott: for feare
of coulering them: to much: if

[fol. 25v] if you would have them with a crisp thinn
shell one *th*e top: sift with a fine searce
a lettel fine suger one them when thay
goe into *th*e oven: when thay are baked
have a care of breaking it off: & lousen
them out with a knife: /

a ointment

tack some Bueef marrow & whit vergins
wax: a like quantitie as you see good
and a lomp of fine hard suger putt
these alltogather in a skellet with a
sponfull of rose watter so boyle them
till it bee all throwroly melted: cutt
*th*e wax in thinn slices: putt it ^in^ to a pot
it is very fine for sores lipes: or chapes
nanywhere /

[fol. 26r] ### to mack fine suger cakes /

Tack a pound of fine whit wheat fflower
& lett it bee dryed beefore *th*e fier: Then
tack a pound of new sweet butter: & putt
it in lettel bettes to *th*e flower: & halfe a
pound of fine suger scearced & a lettel
pound mace: as you see good to give them
a tast: so mingell these alltogather:
to a past: & then role ^them^ out not very thinne
into lettel cakes opon papers: & have a
care *tha*t your oven is not to hott to burne
them: for thay should look but a lettel
yellow

[fol. 26v blank]

[fol. 27r] ### to mack methegling Mrs Kinnersleys /

tack θ40 & fore quarts of faire water
*th*e 4 quarts are to alow for *th*e boyling

away then putt therein: a handfull of
parsley roots: a handfull of fennell roots
pith them & wash them & tie them
up severall: a handfull of rose mary tied
up: 3 nuttmegs clised: halfe a handfull
of ginger cliced: & 2 pennywroth of
Lickourich cliced: putt these pices in a
thinn bag: then putt all these things
into *the* watter & boyle them till y*o*u
find it is strong enough of them to your
licking: then tack them out: & put to
this liquour: 10 quarts of good honny

[fol. 27v]   then boyle it againe till y*o*u see it
break like unto wort: then tack it
of *th*e fier: & cold some of the wort
then bring it up with Barme, as you
doe Drinke, then putt ^it^ into a ferking
when it hath done working, stop it
close, & let it stand a month or 3 weeks
Draw it out in bottels, putting into
Every bottel a lomp or to of suger
cork them very well, the longer it lys
the better, remember to runn the
wort throwe a sive before you put
it to the Barme /

[fol. 28r]   **to mack Damsons wine /**

take your damsons when thay bee
foll ripe, putt them into a strong
ferking or barell, whole as thay are,
fill your vesell, 3 parts foll of damsons
& then make it up full with boyling
watter, which done, stope the vessell vp
close, & lett it stand 3 weeks, then draw
it out in bottels, potting a lomp of faire
suger, in every bottel, the longer it
lies the better, when you drink it
Drink it with suger /

[fol. 28v]   **How to keep any plumes for**
                 tarts all the yeare /

take your plumes when thay bee
ripe, & boyle as much faire watter
as you see will cover them, when it
tis boyled, putt in your plumes, let
them ly in the watter till the break
the skin, then runn them throwe a
sive, sett the watter by till it bee
cold, & the plumes cold, then putt
them up in a earthen pott, with that
watter, then take some sweet mutton
or beeufe suett, & melte it, & pouer it
opon, the plumes, when the suett is
cold opon them, tie a paper on it /

[fol. 29r]   **The sweete greene ointment /**

Take sage: & rue of each one pond:
bay leaves & worwood of each halfe a
pond; melilot herbe: flowers of camomile
flowers of spike: rosemary: red rose leaves
St John: wort: of each one good handfull:
march mallowes 2 good handfull: choppe
all these herbs as small as can bee: then
weigh them & putt to them: theire weight
of the best Deers suett: then choppe the
suett very small: & stampe it & the hearbes
togather till it looke all greene: then putt
it & five pints of sallett oile: into a pott:
mix them well: & cover it close *wi*th leather
& past: *th*e sides that noe aire gett in: so
lett it stand seaven days: then sett it on
a gentel fier: & lett it boyle stirring it
all wayes:

[fol. 29v blank]

[fol. 30r]   till *th*e hearbs looke somewhat drye: then
             straine it very hard: sett it one *th*e fier

againe: & putt in these oiles: camomile:
roses: white lillies: spike: violetts: turpintine
of each one ounce: mixe all very well togather
& lett it boyle 2 or 3 heates: then putt to
it: gume ladanum: one ounce & halfe:
Beniamin: three Drames: gume storax:
calimas three quartes of a nounce: & all
in fine powder: mix it all very well togather
& strane it againe: then keepe it in potts
close stoped for your use:/
                              this Ointment:
cured *the* dead palsey: & is admirable good for
sore bruses: or any paine preceding of a cold
cause: anoynting *the* plase pained & rubing
it with a hott hand: it is good for aches &
stiches: lameness: shrinking of snewes:
plurisey in *the* sides: & aches in *the* back:

[fol. 30v blank]

[fol. 31r]   **To Make Apricok wine /**

take 3 pound of aprickos – beeing stoned & pared
when they are ripe enough to preserve –
then take 2 pound of suger – & 2 quarts &
a halfe of spring watter & lett them boyle a hower
or more over asoft fier – till thay bee as tender
as when thay are preserved & when thay
are enough poure them into a haire scive
& lett them stand till all *the* lickur bee cleane
runn from them – tast *the* lickour & if you doe
find it to bee to sweet or to thick – you may put
som more watter – as you see fitt & boyle it
a lettel – then when it is throwro cold – putt
it in a vessel – *that* is somwhat to big for it
& cover it – but so *that* it may take som aire
so lett it stand to work & settel – 14 days
then draw it out in to bottels – & stop *them*
close – butt fill them not to full – for fere
they break –

[fol. 31v] then lett it stand 14 days or more before you
drink of it – it will keepe all *the* yeare –
you may either dry *the* apricoks – or make
tarts of them afterwards – & then you
need not pare them –

in this same manner wine of cherries rasberrys
or currons or strawberrys w*hich* is an Excilent
wine & *the* friut is as yousfull as *the* apricoks

for gousberrys wine *the* watter raw not
boyled & *the* berrys not to ripe & bruse *them*

[fol. 32r]   **to mack lemun creame /**

take 4 faire new lemons – chip them very
thinn – cutt *the* chips very smale & putt to
them *the* Juce of *the* lemons – & lett them
stand all night next morning putt to them
6 or 7 whits of eggs & 3 youlks beat them
very well – & put to them *the* lemon Juce –
with pill & all – & a poringer & a halfe of
faire watter – a quarter of a poringer of rose
watter – stir them very well togather – then
straine it throwre a cotton strainer – &
sweeten it with fine suger & musk if you
please – sett it on a chafindish of cools
untill it bee as thick as *the* thickest creame
& it must butt scald not boyle – so putt it
out in to a whit dish – when it is cold
it is ffitt to Eate /

[fol. 32v]   **To make gooseberry Wine.**[16]

Take 24 Quarts of the fruit got dry, pick them
and bruise them, take spring water and boil it
2 hours, when cold, put 13 quarts to the Berrys,
let it stand 12 or 14 hours then draw it off, let it

---

16 Hand D (this recipe, perhaps [56r] the second part of the recipe) is a somewhat
shaky italic hand with a curly majuscule Y. There is no indication of the identity of
the contributor.

run through a scive, and to every quart of liquor
when again measured put 3 quarters of a pound
of powder and loaf sugar mixt. Take out one
pound of the sugar to put into the barrel,
and put one penny worth of barm to it, stop it up
close for half a year, and when you bottle it
put a piece of sugar into each Bottle.

[fol. 33r] **to make surrup of Elderberreys /**

gather your berrys when thay bee
full ripe, pick them, & bruse them
then straine them, & to what quantity
you please to make, take 3 pound of
fine suger, to a quart of that Juce
mixe your suger & Juce, togather in a
tine skellet, & so sett it opon the fier
but not to hot a fier, for you must
bee sure, that it neither boyle nor
simper, but onely to diss<.>old the suger
& to make it throughro hot, softly
stiring it, to bring up the scum, &
skim it very cleane, cold it & bottel it /

[fol. 33v] **How to make *the* Black Searecloth**[17]

Take a pint of sallet oyle, half a pound of red
Lead boyle them togather till <:>they are black,
keeping them with· constant stiring, then put in
a quarter of a pound of rosen, & 2 ounce of
red soft wax, & let *the*m: boyle alltogather about
a quarter of an hourer, then take it of *the* fier
& let it coole a while, & so put it into cold

---

17 Hand E ([33v], [36v], [38v], [39v], [42v], [44r], [47v]–[50r], [53r]–[54v], [56r]
beginning and comment, [58r] lower recipes–[58v], [59v], [61v], possibly part
of [66v]) is a small, relatively vertical italic hand. It often uses a colon under
superscript letters in abbreviated words, and sometimes includes a dot between
words, or within a word, as in "slice·d" ([36v]). The majuscule "T" is also
distinctively wavy in this hand, and the recipes are often marked at the end with
two short wavy lines. There is no indication of the identity of the contributor.

watter, till it is hard enough to role, then make
it into roles, rubing your hands with: butter or <·>
oyle, that it may not stick to them:
this is a very good ~~saulfe~~ salve for a boyle
or any sore /

[fol. 34r]   **to make a faire sort of plume**
suger cakes / Mrs Venables receipt /

Take a pound of fine wheat fflower
dry it very well, a pound of curence
well washt & dryed, a pound of fine
suger scearced, a pound of sweet butter
then take 8 eggs, & beat them well, then
tak an earthen milkpan, & warme it well
putt the butter in to it, & work it, & beat it
with your hand till you make it all thick
& whit, then putt in a lettel of the flower
& still work it with your hand till all
the things bee in, putt in a lettel pound
mace, to your liking, still keeping it
with working, till your oven bee ready
which most bee noe hotter then for
[fol. 34v] manchett, which beeing ready, you must
have some lettel round coffins made
of double broune paper, of what sise
you will have the caks, & pinn them
opon sheets of the same papers which
done butter the coffins about, & so putt
in every coffin a sponfull of the stufe
straw a lettil fine suger opon the
top of every one & flat them doune
with the back of a spone, when thay are
in the coffins, so sett them in the
oven, thay will rise much in the oven
have a great care of burning them
halfe an houer will bake them, while
thay bee hot take them of the papers /

[fol. 35r]   **To make Damsons caks /**

take your Damsons, & coddle them in fare
watter, then pill them, & straine the meat
of them, then sett it on the fier, & lett
it boyle vp, & scum it, then weigh your
suger, & take waite, for waite, candy your
suger to the heigth, & when you see it is
thick Enough, Lay them out in caks /

for an p^E^gge pye/

take six Eggs, & boyle them very hard
& then sread them as smale as you can, then
take some searced cinimon, & 3 quarters
of a pound of currens, & some smale beeufe
suett, & some suger, & a lettil creame &
some nuttmeg, so blend it all to gather Like
a pudding, then putt in some sack, & so put
it in Either, a pye, or fine past in a Dish /

[fol. 35v]   **To mack a neats toung pye /**

Take a neats tounge, & boyle it 3 parts
& then sread it very smale, then take
a good quantitie of marrow, & for want
of marrow take beeufe suett, finely sreed
some reasons of the sunn, some currence, &
cinimon, & cloves & mace, & suger & a lettil
rose watter, season it with a lettil salt, when
your pye, cometh out of the oven putt in
3 or 4, sponfull of sack, so serve it up

To preserve whit quinces:

Take one pound of quinces to a pound of
suger, which suger must bee of the whitest,
& halfe a pint of watter, make your surrup
boyle, & that while, pare your quinces &
core them, then putt them in & lett[18]

---

18 Pages are missing here.

[fol. 36r]   helpe any impostume, in the head, for the
sight, & hearing, or any humer in the body,
or any old sore or new, and allso good to
helpe any ache in the bones /
probatum /

the ordinary blacke salve /

Take apound of oyle of roses, or for [lack]
of it, good sallet oyle, halfe apound of
red lead, put your oyle in an Earthen pot
& sett it opon the fier, & when it is very
hot, put in your red Lead, finely beaten
without any Lumps, & Lett them seeth
togather, but bee fore you take it of,
put in an ounce of wax, finely sreed
& Lett them boyle tongather, stiring them
very well, until such time you think it will
make vp into Roles /

[fol. 36v]   ### To make a orange puding /

Take half a pound of good butter, & melt it as
for sauce, & then put into it, half a pound of
whit suger, or somthing less, as you please, beat these
togather, & then put in 6 eggs, not all *the* whits
when its well beaten, take 2 ounce of candy'd
orange pills, & slice them very thinn, & then have
a dish that youle bake it in, & lay in *the* bottom
of it, a fine thinn past, then put in *the* batter,
& lay *the* slice·d[19] orange, in all over it,
diping it in *the* batter, then have a nother
fine peece of past, & lay over it, so set it
in *the* oven, about 3 quarters of an houer will
bake it /

[fol. 37r]   ### the Black Salve, the Lady Shirley

Take a quart of the best sallett oyle & put it
to a skyllet, that will hold 3 pints, for the oyle

---

19   The meaning of this dot here and in other recipes is unclear.

will boyle high, take care that it boyle not over
put a pound of red Lead finely beaten, into the
oile, & stir it with a stick, a quarter of an houer
togather, then sett it on a charkcole fier, butt
Lett noe flame bee, then putt in an nounc of
good pitch, the oldest you can gett, then putt in
a nounc of pure wax, put the pitch & wax into the
oyle, when tis over the fier, stir it well, allwais
one way & Lett it boyle a pace, when it gotten a
couler, Dipe a cloath into it, if it stick well one
the cloath, & not cleave to your fingers, tis enough
then have a board a Lettle hollow, with Leggs Like a
stoole, oile it very well, then put the salve into it
& have 2 knives well oiled, & stir it vp & downe
till it bee cold Enough, to take into yoor hands,
then take as much as will make a ball, & pull it
Extreamely till the couler of it bee bright, then
[fol. 37v]   mack it vp, there must bee 2 at the macking
it, you must oyle your hands very well, & so
mack it vp into Rolls,   it is good for greene wonds
spraines, Bruises, & any
swellings, beeing sprad opon
Lining cloath,

the oyle of charitie, the Lady Shirleys

Take Red sage, Lavender, rosemary, wormwood
camomile, of each 4, ounces, chop them smale
& putt them into a glas, with a wid tope, then
putt in 3 pints of good sallet oyle, & so sett
it in the sunn, for a month, then straine it
hard out, & then put in as many of the same
herbs, a gaine, with 4 onces, of the smale,
velerion, so sunn it a gaine for a weeke,
then gently boyle it on a soft fier, have a
care it burne not, so straine it & keepe it a
glas, for your vse,   it is good for all sorts
of aches, burns & wonds,
[fol. 38r]   & inwardly taken, a sponfull at a time, for
wemen in childbed, that are brused, & to take
away the great paine, of affter throes /

the Eie watter Mis Lettice Oker^o^vers /

Take of plantaine, & red rose watter of
each a pint, mingle them togather, then
take the stone of Lapis calaminarius, & the
stone, Lapistuticia, putt these stones into *the*
fier, till they bee red hott, then squnch *them*
in these watters, 9 times, then straine it, then
take the stone, of Roman – vitirall – & putt
it into the watter, till it couler it blewish
& noe more, so put the water into a glas bottle
when it is 9 – days old you may vse it, putting
into the Eie – that is greived – 3 drops at the first
then 4 – drops – the next time – 5 – drops dress it
so twice a day, & every time Lett the patience
ly one there back an houer affter – in 3 days
it will cuer, either – pin – web – pearle – or fleame,
in the Eie – prooved /

[fol. 38v]   ### A Backed Tansy /

Take Ten eggs, ^4 whits, half^ a nutmeg three biskets grat:d
as much Juce of spinage, with thick cream, a pint
beat *the* eggs well, mix *the* eggs, biskets cream,
a little Tansy Juce, of theese Juces as much as
will make it Look green, sweeten it to y*our* Tast
*the*n butter y*our* dish very well, set it in *the* oven
no hotter then for custard,

To make a mutton pye,

Season y*our* mutton steaks with savoury spice
fill *the* pye, Lay on butter, & close *the* pye,
when it is backed, Tos up som choped capers
cucumbers, & oysters, in gravy, & anchovy
& drawn buter,

A white Fricasy of Chikens /

Cut *them* in peeces wash *them* well, then put
them into a stew pan, put in as much fair
watter as will cover *them*, season *them* with
nutmegs & salt, 2 anchovies, & stew *them*

till enough, six eggs, a glas of white wine
4 spoonfull of cream, som butter,

[fol. 39r]   **The Blast savle or oiement**

Take a pound of may butter, when it is
new churned, beefore it bee washt, then
take a handfull of houndstongue, a handfull
of parsley, halfe a handfull of mallows, halfe
a handfull of plantaine, halfe a handfull of
mariegold Leaves, sread & bruse the herbs in
a morter, put therto, 2 ounces of Deare suett
boyle all togather on a soft fier, till the <...>
<..> watterie substance bee consumed, then
straine it, throwe a strainer, & keepe it, for
your vse, oynt *the* plase pained with it 2or
3 times a day, for a blast this is prooved /

[fol. 39v]   **A Lemon puding**

Grate *the* piel of 2 Lemons, *the* Juice of one
Lemon, well role:d w*ith* y*our* hand, before it
is cut, *the*n squeeze of *the* Juice, & put to *the*
piell, grate near a penney lofe, make
half a pint of white wine hot, & pour it
upon *the* bread, stir it well togather to
soak, beat *the* yolks of five eggs, half
the whits, mix all well togather,
& suger to y*our* Likeing,

[fol. 40r]   **A Dyett drink, Lady Shirleys /**

take to 6 galons of Alle, 6 hanfulls
of Liverwort, 6 hanfulls of brocklime
& 6 handfulls of clivers, boyle these herbs
in the wort, a Little while, not in all the
wort, butt a Lettle of it, Lett it runn, throw
a sive, & then putt it vp to the rest,
then putt in a bagg, 6 handfulls of
maiden haire, 12 ounces of senea – 10
ounces of polipodyum – 5 ounces of bay
berrys – 2 pound of stoned reasons – 4

ounces, of sweet fenell, seeds – 2 ounces of
any seeds – 4 ounces of duacus – seeds – putt
these in a bagg, with some peeces of stick
tyed to the bagg, so Lett it Ly in the
drink till it bee all gone – drink it
for 10 days, or more or Less, how you
pleas^sssssss^20, a full pint or more, att a time /

[fol. 40v] aslic'd lemon or two, & serve it vp CC:21

[fol. 41r] **A receit how to dress trout**

Take your trout, wash, & dry him with a clean
napkin, then open him, & having taken out his guts, &
all *the* blood, wipe him very clean within, but wash
him not, & give him three scot^c^hes <:.> with a knife
to *the* bone on one side onely. after which take a clean
ketle, & put in as much hard stale beer (but it must
not be dead) vinegar, & a litle white wine, & water,
as will couer *the* fish you intend to boyl; then throw
into *the* liquor a good quantity of salt, *the* rind of a Lemon,
a handfull of slic't Horse Radish root, with a handsom
litle fagot of Rosemary, time, & wintor sauory, then set
your ketle vpon a quick fire of wood, & let your Liquor
boyl vp to *the* height before you put in your fish, & then, if
there be many, put them in one by one, *that* they may not so
cool *the* Liquor, as to make it fall; & whilst your fish is
boyling, beat vp *the* butter for your sawce with a Ladle
full or two of *the* Liquor it is boyling in, & being boyld eno
ugh immediately pour *the* Liquor from *the* fish, & being
laid in a dish, pour your butter vpon it, & strewing it
plentifully ouer with shaved Horse Radish & a litle poun
ded ginger, garnish *the* sides of your dish & *the* fish with22

[fol. 41v blank]

---

20 A puzzling insertion. The repeating s does not overwrite other words. Perhaps the
   contributor was simply practising her writing.
21 These letters might mean &c. They seem to be in Hand F ([40v], [41r], [42r]), a very
   slanting hand with particularly angled descenders. There is no indication of the
   identity of the contributor.
22 The recipe ends on the previous page, fol. [40v], with the sliced lemon.

[fol. 42r]   **A receit how to dress acarp**

Take a carp (alive if possible) scour him, & rubb him
clean with water & salt, but scale him not, then open
him, & put him with his blood & his liver (which you
must save when you open him) into a small pot or ketle;
then take sweet marioram, time & parsley, of each
half a handfull, a sprig of Rosemary & another of
sauory, bind them in two or three small bundles & put
them to your carp, with four or fiue whole onyons, twen
ty pickled oysters, <.>& three Anchouies; then pour
vpon your carp as much claret wine as will <....> ^only^
couer him; & season your claret with salt, cloues &
mace, & *the* rinds of ora^n^ges & Lemons, *that* done, couer
your pot & set it on a quick fire till it be suffic^c^
iently boyled; then take out *the* carp & lay it with
the broth into *the* dish, & pour vpon it aquarter of a
pound of *the* best fresh butter melted & beaten, w*i*th
halfe a dozen spoonefulls of *the* broth, & *the* yolks of
of two or three eggs, & some of *the* herbs shred; garn
ish your dish w*i*th Lemons, & soe serve it vp

[fol. 42v]   **To make a Syrup for a Consumption,**

take three sheeps hearts three pounds of ~~br~~ brown
suger candy & a handfull of rosemary slitt, then
take a lettel of *the* rosmary, & one quarter of *the*
suger candey, & one heart, & put it into a lettel
pan, or any other thing that is fit, & so lay it
till all is in, then power upon it two penny
worth of pimpernell watter, & bake it in an
oven after household bread is drawn, three
or four houres, then strane it, & <.>when it is
cold take of *the* fatt, & it is fitt for use;

                              how to take this syrup,

take one spoonfull every morning fasting
& at foure, in *the* afternoone, & *the* last thing
goeing to bed, & bee shuer to fast 2 houres
after it ~

[fol. 43r]   **to make orange water /**[23]

take 4 oranges & 2 lemons, & pare them
& put *the* parings into a quart of brandy
& lett it stand 9 or 10 days, close coverd
in a gally pott, then take a quart of
spring water, & boyle it, & when it is
cold, putt it to *the* oranges & brandy, &
stire it all togather, then runn it all
throwe a cotton straner, then take a
pound of refined suger, & lett it melt
all in this licquor, without any fier
& when *the* suger is all dissouled then
putt it vp into bottles, close couered,
& drinke it as a cordiall for *the* stomack /

[fol. 43v]   **To make Bisketts**[24]

Take a pound of fine wheat flower sett it to *the* fire
to drye take 10: Eggs leave out 3 whites add 3 spoonfull
of sack & 3 spoonfull of orange flower or rose
water, beat *the*m: together w*ith*: a whisk till *they* froth
very well, then put in a p*oun*d: & quarter of dubble –
refined suggar or fine white powd*er*: sugar: If you use
refind sugg*a*r: it must bee finely beaten & sifted,
keep it constantly stirring, just when *the* oven is hott take
up *the* flower stirr it into *the* Eggs & sugg*a*r: stirring it all one
way till it bee all in, beginn to heat *the* oven when you
begin to beat *the* Eggs & when *the* oven is hott *the* Bisketts are
beaten enough, fold your papers 4 folds & butter *the*m: soe
putt *the*: Bisketts upon *the*m: Just when you putt *the*m: into *the*
oven sift sugg*a*r: & flower upon *the*m: when they are
Baked take *the*m: of *the* Papers Immediately & turn *the*m:
hollow over a Rolling pinn or any other round stick.
                                        W: Oldfeld
                                        His writing

---

23 Hand G ([43r], [45r]–[47v] top recipe, [55v], [61r] lower recipe) is similar to Hand
    C, although the minuscule p, among other letters, is distinct, as is the ampersand.
    There is no indication of the identity of the contributor.
24 Hand H (this recipe only) belongs to W. Oldfeld, as is clearly indicated at the
    bottom of the recipe (in another hand; Hand C?). This hand is quite decorative.

[fol. 44r]   **The receit for Snail watter /**

Take snals ether with or without shells ~~to~~two pounds
leaves of ground Ivy four handfulls, of spotted Lungwort
& coltsfoot each two handfulls, Raisons of the sun stoned
half a pound, figgs four ounces, Liquorice two ounces,
Aniseeds one ounce, nutmeggs a quarter of a <⁖> ounce,
safron, one dram, infuse these in 4 quarts of new
milk, & a pint of sack, all night, the next day
disstill them in a com·on still ~

[fol. 44v blank]

[fol. 45r]   **The Ladys ffolliot salve /**

take halfe a pound of clarified mutton
shewit, a pint of sallett oyle, too ounces
of red Lead sifted fine, a Letle bitt of
beess wax, stir all very well to gather
& boyle it over a gentle fier, & now &
then drop a drope on a plate, to coole
& when tis hard Enough to sprade, pouer
it in a gally pott, & keepe it from the
dust, it is Extream good for any
burne or scald, proved, or a greene
wound or sore –

[fol. 45v]   **This is exseeding good
                      For the Cholick, or faintnes,**[25]

Gu<⁖>^ai^acum chips, an ounce
Elicampane Roots, an ounce
Liquarice slice:d, an ounce
Coriander seeds bruis:d, an ounce
prepair:d senna of Alixandria –
                      an ounce
      infuse all theese in 3 pints of
Anisseed watter, Ten days, then
power the clear into bottles,

---

25   Hand I ([45v]) is perhaps a shaky hand, so might belong to an elderly contributor.

Tak three spoonfulls in a fitt
it may be taken twice a day
if *the* fitt last's
ade ~~half~~ ^a quarter^ of pound of Raisins of the
sun stone:d
<...>[26]

[fol. 46r]   **how to make Lemon ~~Brandd~~ Brandy**

take 8 lemons & pare them very thinn –
then take a quart of brandy & steepe *the*
thinn pillings in *the* Brandy for a week
or 10 days, in an Earthen pott, stiring it
somtimes, then take a pint of faire
watter, & putt there to, halfe apound
of refined suger, & boyle it, up & scum
it, cleane, & when tis cold, mingle *the* brandy
& lemons & this surripe all togather, &
then straine it throwro a cotton bagg
& bottle it, & keepe it for y*our* use –

[fol. 46v]   **for Ebbylon /**

to 4 measurs bruing of malt –
take halfe *tha*t measer of ripe
Elderberrys stript, boyle them in
the wort wi*t*h *the* hops – so cleanse
it, & order it, as other ale – putt
in ginger orang other spice, as
much in quantietie as y*o*u think
fitt /

[fol. 47r]   **to make gingere bread /**

Take a pound of good treacle, a noune [an ounce]
of ginger, finely searced, a noune of
candyd orange pill cutt smale a noune
of lemon candyed pill – cutt smale, & a
nounce of candyed sictren cutt smale

---

26 There are three or four letters written vertically and seemingly backwards here, but
they are indecipherable.

putt *the* ginger, & these sweetmeats, all
into *the* treacle, & mixt it up w*i*th your
hand, w*i*th some fine wheat fflower
till it come to a perfect past, then
role it w*i*th yo*u*r hand in smale roles, or biger
roles – as y*o*u please – *the* roles like *the*
lenth of y*our* finger = or shorter –
lay them on tinn, plats, & dust a
lettil fflower, under them – Bake *them*
in an oven as hott as for manchett
not to scorch them, but to harden them
that they ractle [rattle], togathur²⁷ – when you
[fol. 47v]   take them of *the* plats
doe not keepe them in a moyst place
for they will goe soffter of them
selves=

To make crackneyles /

Take one p*ou*nd of suger & one p*ou*nd of flower, half
a p*ou*nd of butter, 4 eggs, but 2 whits, a spoonfull
or more of careways seeds, ₥mix all these
into a pest, butter pye plats & beat *the*
past on them w*i*th: y*ou*r hand, as thenn as y*o*u
can, when y*o*u put them into *the* ouen, wash
them over w*i*th *the* yoalk of an egg, when *they* are
baked <∴> take them of *the* plats as soon as
ever y*o*u can, & torn [turn?] them hollow –

To make Lemon Jelley /

Take Lemons & rost *the*m: then sques out *the* Juse &
<∴> take *the* full weight of it, in duble refined
suger, set *the*m· on a chafing · dish of coles, there
let it scald till it will Jelly, & looks clear

[fol. 48r]   ### To make orange wine

Take 6 gallons of spring watter, & 12 pound of
the best powder'd suger, & *the* whits of 4 eggs

---

27 In other words, they should be baked enough to rattle together without breaking.

well beaton, put *the*m: in *the* watter & suger, *the*n
boyl *the*m· all three quarters of a houer, & when
it is cold put in 6 spoonfulls of yest, then
take *the* Juce & rine of 25: oranges & let this
work 2 days & 2 nights, then add, if you please
2 quarts of rennesh wine or white wine, so
tun it up in a vessell stoped very close, in
six weeks you may drink it, it is best w*ith*:out
the full quantity of *the* peel ~

To make quincs puding /

take 2 or 3 quinces & parboyle *the*m: till *they* be tender
then pare *the*m: & core *the*m: beat *the*m: in a morter
w*ith*: some suger according to y*ou*r tast, & *the* yolks
of 8 eggs till it is well mixt, then put to it
half a pint of cream, so put it into a dish or
patipans, w*ith*: som past in *the* bottom, & bake it
a quarter of an houer y*ou* may make orange
puding *the* sam way, take *the* rine of 2 orangs, & *the* jus
of one

[fol. 48v]   ### To make allmone cream /

take a quarter of a p*ou*nd: of Jorden allmons, layed in
cold watter till *they* well blanch, then beat *the*m: in
a ston morter, with a lettel rose or orang flower
watter, stran *the*m: w*ith*: a quart of sweet cream,
season it w*ith*: suger, then put it in a clean
skellet, & set it on *the*· fier, stiring it till it
boyl a lettel, then power it into cream dishes &
eat it cold ~

To make allmon bisketts /

take half a p*ou*nd: of blanch'd allmons & beat *the*m:
fine, ading oriang flower watter to *the*m:, *the*n take
half a p*ou*nd: of fine sifted suger, & beat w*ith* *the* allmons
& when *the* suger is well incorperated, beat in
half a p*ou*nd: of fine flower well dryed, by degrees
break in 6 eggs, leave out 3 whits, beat *the*m: in
the morter w*ith*: *the* rest, *the* eggs must be put
in before *the* flower, when *they* are all well mixt
droop *the*m: in lettel biskets, on pewtter plats &

bake *the*m: in an oven when they are brown
at *the* edges, *they* are baked enough, *the* oven must
not be to hott ~

[fol. 49r]   **To reggou a brest of veale**

beat it <.>very well *with: the* flat side of a clever
so put it into watter, & parboyle it till it is
white, flower it very well & fry it in hogs
lard till it is brown, take *the* fat of backon
& cut it into bits, put it into a saspan over
the fier, till it is very brown, then take *the*
backon out, & stire up *the* lickquer *with:* a lettel
flower over *the* fier till it is very brown, but
not burnt, put *you*r brest of veale into this
lickquer; & turn it in till it is very hot, so
put as much very strong gravey to it as well
cover it take a dozen borss [bones?][28] of veal parboyl *the*m:
flower *the*m: & fry *the*m: in butter till *they* be brown
they must be cut in slices before *they* are fryed
so put *the*m: to *the* veal, & boyle *the*m: altogather till *the*
veal is tender, there must be 3 or 4 anchoves
a lettel nutmeg, a bunch of sweet hearbs, a onion
when it · is enough sarve it up in *the* gravey
it is stwe·d in, & squise a letel lemon in, & to
slices of lemon on it

[fol. 49v]   **To make cowslipp wine –**

Take 6: gallons of watter & boyle an hour &
halfe, allow six quarts for wast, then put in
12 pound good suggar, scumm it well, then
take it of, & put it in a vessell to cool, & when
tis a lettel warmer than milk from *the* cowe,
put in 2 pecks of pick'd cowslipps bruis'd,
in a mortar, mix them with *you*r hand, then let
it stand till it be of temper, then put in *you*r
barm, & a bole:dish,[29] stir it as it works, let it

---

28 The two s letter forms in "borss" are questionable. While the transcription is as
    accurate as possible, the word intended here must be "bones." The bones are to be
    parboiled to soften the remaining meat on them, which is then cut and fried.
29 This "barm, & a bole:dish" instruction is not clear; perhaps it means a bowlful of
    barm.

stand two days, & a night, then put *that* liquor
& flowers into a hair sieff, & w*ith* yo*ur* hand squeese,
the flowers well, then tunn it into a sweet
barrell, & see that yo*ur* barrell be full, to work,
when done make it up close & let it stand
3 weeks, then draw it of into a nother vessell,
put in two penneyworth of Isinglass, cut small,
& half a pound of good loaf suggar, stop it close
8 or 10 days, then bottle it, & se that yo*ur* bottles
be very dry, & corks very good _

[fol. 50r]   **how to make meade /**

Take 10 quarts of watter, let it be just at
boyleing, put to it a quart of honney, 1 pound of
lofe suger, let it boyle while any scum well rise
takeing of *the* scum as it rises, then take it of
the fire, & pvt to it 2 Lemons, cut in halfs &
sques'd in, w*ith*: a large rase of ginger slited, &
4 cloves, & a peece of sinement, & a peece of
rosmerey, when it is cold, stran it into an
earthern pot w*ith*; a spigot in, put to it 3 spoon
full, of barme, it well work like Ale for 6 days,
then bottel it, yo*u* may drink it in 3 weeks time
but it well be better if yo*u* keep it 2 months,
it must be a lettel warm when *the* barme is
pvt to it,

[fol. 50v]   **To make mead with Elderberies**[30]

Take very ripe Elderberries, pick them from
the stalkes, put them in an Earthen pot, and
past them close, & bake them in an oven
while the are warm, straine them out, take
a gallen of *the* joyce to twelfe gallons
of water, *tha*t was first boyl'd for an hour
or more, then when *the* water & joyce
is wel mixt & boyld a little, then put in

---

30 Hand J ([50v]–[52v], part of [66v], inside back cover) is a curvy, tight hand in that
words are packed quite close together. Minuscule t is often loosely written and is
only rarely crossed. Recipes in this hand are quite messy, with numerous strike-
throughs and corrections. There is no indication of the identity of the contributor.

one & thirty pounds of honey, boyle them
well for an houer or more *tha*t is till you
think two gallons is wasted, scum it well
all *the* time, as it rises, when it breakes
in *the* ladle i'ts enought, then pour it in
your tubb, & let it stand to coole, when i'ts
cold, put barm to it as warme as you doo
to Ale worke it two days or more if it
happen to be soe cold as not to worke, sett
a pitcher of hott water in *the* tubb, & *the*
heat of *the* water will set it a working
when *the* barme getts a heade, take *the* pitcer
of water out, & beate it as often as you
doe Alle, when it hath worked two or
three dayes, tunn<:> it, & stopp your barrell
close, at five months end botle it, and
it will keep a long time in *the* botle
as hath been prou'd

[fol. 51r]   ~~To make<....>~~
              To Coller a breast of veal to eat hot

Bone it & beat it with *the* flatt side of *the*
clever, *the*n seis'in it with salt & jemecca peper &
a little cloves & mace, *the*n strow it over with some
sweet hearbs cut small & some yolk of egg
*the*n lay a row of baken upon it, cut very thin
& upon *tha*t your hearbs & egg & seisning agen then
~~then~~ roul it up very heard & put it in a cloth ty it
about with a tape & let it boyle 2 hou^e^rs & half
if large veal 3 hours. ffor *the* sauce a little
graue & anchoue & a little white wine & ~~the~~
thicken it with a good deal of butter to be like
fish sauce but not so stroung 3 or 4 youlks
of Eggs is enough.

              ~~To make gooseberys~~
              To make goosberys biskits

scald your goosberys till *they* are soft *the*n rub *the*m
through a siffe take *the* ~~white~~ waight of your

pulp in duble refind sugar, & *the* whits of 2 or 3 eggs
acording as you do for quaintity, beat *the*m together,
for 2 or 3 hours till *they* looke white *the*n drop *them*
upon tinn plates, or pewter in little <:> biskets
sett them to dry in *the* sun, when *the* top is a little
dry turn the~~n~~^m^

[fol. 51v]   **To make scoch collops**

Take a leg of veal, & cutt your· collops very thinn
wright way of *the* veal, & beat *the*m well with a back
of a knife, *the*n seisin *the*m· with· nutmeg & salt & doe
some yeolk of Egg all over them & let *the*m ly<:>
2 hours, *the*n· fry *the*m in butter a little at a time
<.> besure you· do not fry *the*m· too much but till *they* are
a little brown, *the*n· make your sauce of grave
& white wine, 2 anchoves & ~~th~~ thicken it up
with· a little butter, let your sauce be hot
*whe*n· you put your collops into it, so tos *the*m· up toge=
=ther, you may broyl *the* bone of *the* veal to lay
in *the* midle, &, make some forst meate balls
to lay about it, with· some sliced lemon
when you fry *the*m· strow some sweet hearbs on
them, 3 egg will do.

To make a hame of porck.

Take salt peeler & common salt of
each a like, salt *the* gammon 12 or 15
days, turn it every day, hang it ^in^ *the* chimney
where *you* burn wood, for 3 weeks but not
too hot when it is dried enought lay it in
sweet wort for half a day, turn it & when
it is dry, rub it all over with sheeps blood,
& hang it up for use.

[fol. 52r]   **To make a seed cake /**

Take 3 pound of flower, & a pound &
half of butter, with a quarter of a pound of
loafe sugar with· six eggs, & a quarter of a
pint of yeast with a little mace & nutmegs
& creame mix all these together, & set *the*m· <:::>

before *the* fire to rise, Then ~~bu~~put in half a pound
of Carraway comfits, & bake it 3 quarters of an
hour

To season a wett Collar of beif

Take a briskett of beif & bone it & lay it in
water 2 days & 2 nights, & shift it twice in fre<sh>
water, & put in 2 hanfull of salt into *the*
water, & take it out & let *the* water run of it
then season it <:> with half an ounce of cloves
& mace a quarter of Cinnamon, ~~half~~ half a
pound of Bay salt, a quarter of salt peeter, a
little Nutmeg, an ounce of white pepper, then
lay it in a tray, & then putt in half a pint of
Clarett, as much vineger, & let it ly in sesoning
3 days & 3 nights, Then put in halfe a pound of
Anchoves upon it (you must bone them) a handfull of
sweet hearbes; which must <:> be mother of thime,
sweet margerom & winter savory, & soe collar it up
as you doe Brawn & put it into a pot, & put in *the* gravey,
a pint of Clarett, half a pint of white wine vinegar,
[fol. 52v]   bake itt with brown bread, & when it is baked,
turn *the* side downwards, which was ~~down~~ upwards
for an hour, then stretten *the* cloth & lay a weight
upon it, & let it stand 4 houers, & lay it in *the* pickle

A pickle~~y~~ for wet coller of beif

Take as much small bear as will cover it
& as much red sanders as will culler it some
cloves & mace some synnamon[31] an ounce
of salt peter a bunch of sweet hearbs
put all together, & let them boyle one hour,
then strain them & when it is could
put in halfe a pint of white wine
vinegar, soe putt in *the* collar & cover it
close

---

31   The y in this word is actually a hybrid i and y.

To make Elder wine

Take to every gallon of water, 4 pound
of loaf sugar, & about 8 pound of Elder=
berrys when full ripe, let your water boyle
an hour, then put it in an Earthen pot, with an
narrow mouth, to infuse *the* berrys, having before
been wel beaten then take a little ale
yest, beaten with some of *the* same liquor
soe mix it together & let it stand, stirring it once

[fol. 53r]   ## To Regoue a Rabit or any meat /

make a strong broth or gravey of knockels of veal, or any
other bones, let *the*m: boyle till all *the* goodnes is out, put
into it a blade of mace, a few cloves & a Lettel peper,
& a ·crust of bread tosted as hard as you can, & a Lettel
time & saverry, an anchovie or 2, when it is well
boyled stran it through a sive, add to it ether a pint
of white wine, or clarrit, a few pickled oysters, so
haveing stew'd *you*r Rabit, in this Lickquer, boyle it up
& thicken up with· 2 or 3 eggs &· som butter, so serve to
the table, with som mushrooms &· Lemmon pill in *the*
gravey ~

To make Ginger Bread
of allmonds

Take a Lettel gumdragon & steep it in a pint of rose
watter *the* space of one night, *the*n take a pound of *the*
best Jorden allmonds, being blanceed in cold watter,
beat *the*m: in a stone morter, but in beating *you* must
add som of *the* rose watter, w*hi*ch *the* gumdragon was
steep'd in, add to the*m*: som ginger, & som grated bread
& suger, *you*r ginger must be finely sifted, *the*n: knead
*the*m: togather as *you* doe past, & so print in moulds, w*i*th
som search·d suger, & set it before *the* fier to dry

[fol. 53v]   ## To pickel walnuts a hundred[32]

make strong brine to bare an egg
Let them Ly 9 days, stiring them once

---

32   This recipe begins halfway down the page in the original manuscript; the top half is
     blank.

a day, then put them in boyling watter
Let them boyl up, take them out, put
them in a cloth, then take cloves, mace, genger
Black peper, in all one ounce, som musterd
seed, & sherlot, & if you pleas a few Elder
flowers,

[fol. 54r]   **To make Elder Flower wine /**

Take six gallons of watter & twelve pounds
of fine suger, & six pounds of <.>Raisins of
the sun cut small Boil theese togather an
hour, *the*n take of *the* flower of elder, when
they are falling & will shake off, *the* quantity
of half a peck, put *the*m in *the* Liquer when
allmost cold, *the* next day put in six
Larg spoonfull of syrup of Lemons, & four
spoonfull of ale yeast, & three days after
put it in *the* vessell, that it will fill &
stop it close, & let it stand till clear
then Bottle it off, it may stand three or
four months, if not then clear rack it of
into a nother vessell a few day & *the*n
Bottle it, if a pound of suger or Raisins
be added to it, it will be *the* better /

[fol. 54v]   **To make Elder wine /**

Take 20, pound of malago raisons (or raisons of *the* sun)
let *the*m be clean· rubb·d, then shred *the*m: very small
& put *the*m: to five gallons of boyling watter,
the· watter haveing first been boyl·d one hour, Let
*the*m: steep ten days, stiring *the*m: once or twice every
day, then <.....> ^stran^<..> *the* Liquor, through a hair sieve,
& have in readines six pints of very ripe elder-berrys
Juice, stew'd over *the* fier in a pot, put into a caldron
of boyling watter, put it into *the* Liquor cold, & stir
it for some time very well togather, then tun it into
a clean vessel, & Let it stand in a warm place for
two months or ten weeks, then bottle it ~

To make *the* white frigacie of Chickens

[fol. 55r]   or Rabbits.[33]

Take yo*ur*· Chickens, cut *the*m· in pieces to yo*ur*· likeing
and season *the*m· with nutmeg & salt, *the*n· having *the*·
frying Pan w*ith*· Butter in it hot over the fire, Put in
your Chickens & make *the*m· a little crisp, *the*n· take *the*m·
out and Put *the*m· into yo*ur*· stewe pan, some water, &
Anchovie to yo*ur* likeing, & white wine & when
enough, Thicken *the*m ·up with some good cream,
& two yolk's of egg's & Butter some Mushrooms
& sliced Lemmon, upon it.

[fol. 55v]   To pickell Murshroms

gather them in August, & lay
them in water, then shift them in
another water, then take a cleane
cloth & rub them, till you see *they* are
cloane, then boyle *the*m in milk &
water, & a Lettil salt, till you see *they*
are tender – make some Pickell for
*the*m, with water whit wine & wine –
vinger – a Like quantie of Each
boyle it, & putt into it, some cloues
& mace, & whole peper – & salt –
acording to yo*ur* tast, when *the* Lickour
is cold, put *the*m in, & keepe the*m* in
a gallow pott, for yo*ur* vse /

[fol. 56r]   ~~To pickle Cucumbers /~~[34]

~~wipe *the*m with a cloth & put *the*m: into a close~~
~~muge [mug], & make a strong Brine of salt & watter~~
~~Boyl *the* Brine, & put it so on *the* cucumbers,~~
~~then cover *the*m: close, you must put in a lump~~
~~of rock allom,~~[35] ~~into the brine as it boils.~~
~~And this must be thus repeated twice a day utill~~

---

33 Hand K (this recipe only) is a neat hand with long descenders and a single dot
   under superscripts in abbreviated words. There is no indication of the identity of
   the contributor.
34 This whole recipe is crossed out with an X.
35 After "allom," a new hand, seemingly Hand D, takes over the writing of the recipe.

~~you think them green enough. then drain them~~
~~from the brine and rub them dry and make a~~
~~pickle of aleager with what hot spices you please.~~
~~then put a lump of Roch allom in, and some~~
~~dill Boill it and put it on boiling hot to the cucum~~
~~=bers and so keep them close and they will keep~~
~~green fiver or six dyears.~~

~~as for French Beans you cannot miss them if you~~
~~doe but first let them lye a considerable while~~
~~in salt and water.~~
                        This Receipt is good for nothing[36]

[fol. 56v]   **To mack aquamarabiles /**

Tack gubalis – gallingall – cardyment – seeds –
cloves – ginger – nuttmegs – mace – of each a nounce
beaten to powder, Balme – spearmint – both
dryd of each one drame, mellelott flowers
cowslips – rosemary – burich – & mariegold flowers
of each 2 drams – all dryed, then take Juce
of sallindine – one pint – of whit wine 3 pint
a pint of aquavite, angelicoe watter – one
pint, put all these things togather into a
still, in the Evening, & cover them close,
then the next morning stire them againe
& putt *the* still head on, & past it close *that*
noe aire can come in, so still it with a soft
fier, in a common rose, still, keeping wett,
cloths, with cold watter, opon *the* head of *the*
[fol. 57r]   still, draw of your watter by pints, till it
drop lower, then take noe more, put in the
glases you keepe it in, 4 drams of ambergrece
& one of musk, both grun-smale & tied in a
tifiny, & Lett it ly in all *the* time it stills
then take a pint of the first runing, & there
in dissovle a pound of lofe suger, so mixe it
with all the watter, to gather, & keepe it /

---

36 This comment is written in a different hand; as with the first part of the recipe, it
    appears to be Hand E.

To pickell Mushroms

Gather them in Hugoff, &c Lay
them in water, then sh..ft them the
another water then take a clean
cloth & rub them till they be quit
cleane, then boyl them in milld &
water, & a Lettl salt, till 2 feet 2
are tender — make some Pickell for
y[m] with water white wine & some
vinger — a Litle jvanie & of each
boyl it, & put into it, some Loud
mace, whole Pepor & salt —
according to y[r] tast, when y[r] Lickr
is cold, put y[m] in! & Legacy y[m] in
& fellow pint ... for y[r] wife

To pickle Cucumbers

wipe y[e] wth a cloth & put y[m] quite & close
mayt & mak a strong Brine of Salt & water
boyl y[e] Brine, & put it so in y[e] Cucumbers
then Cover y[m] close, y[e] must put in a lump of
if rock allom into the brine or it boil. —
and this must be thus repeated twice a day will
you think them green enough, then drain them
from the brine and rub them dry and make a
pickle of aleger with what hot spices you please.
then put a lump of Rock allom in, and some
dill boil it, and put it on boiling hot to the Cucum-
= bers and so keep them close and they will keep
green five or six years.

as for French beans you ... I ... them & gre...
doe first first for them the a considerable while
in salt and water ...

This Receipt is good for nothing

Fig. 3.2   Folger MS V.a.450, fols. 55v/56r. By permission of the Folger Shakespeare Library.

[fol. 57v]   **A fine ointment for the Skyn /**

Take a keyll, of a young Lamb, putt ^it^ in
some faire watter, & shift it 2 or 3 days
then take it, & putt it in a clean cloth,
& there beat it as you would doe salt; but
very smale, when it is smale enough, putt
it in a fine earthen pott, or silver can, & to
it putt some damask rose watter, a lettle Juce
of lemom, a lettle ambergeese, & musk, tied
in a bitt of laune, then cover your pott, & sett
this in a posnett of hott watter, to infuse, for
some 2 or 3 houers, then take it of, & beat
the ointment very well, with a spone, that it
may look whit, so lett it stand till the next
day, then infuse it as long againe, & then
beat againe, till it look very whit, take
out the musk, & so but [put] it in a glas or
[fol. 58r] pot, if ther bee any watter in the bottom when
it is cold, power it out, & keepe this for your
vse, it is very fine for a pilled skin, or any
            thing that is rough, & for Lipps,

                A wash for *the* fase /

2 ounces of better allmonds, to a quart of
barley watter, & what hungrey watter you please /

                ***The* bitter Draught /**

Take a handfull of cammomile flowers, as
much centuary, & as much roman worm
wood, gention roots ten grains, cardus seeds
a dram, & if you will have it purge, a dram
of sena, boyle a pint of watter & power it
upon *the* ingrediences, let it infuse half
an houer at Least,

[fol. 58v]   **A nother Bitter Draught**
                good for children /

Take century, camomill flowers, topps of celandine
with· *the* roots, & cardus of each one handfull, safron

one scruple, boyle them in two pints of watter, till
one is consumed, then strane it, & give 5 spoonfulls
each morning & evening
give *the* quantity of twenty five, or thrity dropps of
Elixir propietatis, for two or three mornings fbefore
they take *the* Draught,

How to make allmon
pigs pudings /

take half a pound of *the* best allmons; blanched
& puned fine, with som rose watter, then boyl
h[37] A pint of cream, let it be cold a gane, & take
six egs, leave out most of *the* whites, & *the* marrow
out of 2 beefe bones, sred smale, with a quarter p*ou*nd
of beefe suehtt, or somthing more, a penney white
lofe grated, a lettel mace cinament & nutmeg, &
suger to y*ou*r liking; so mix *the*m all togather, &
fill *the*m, boyle *the*m near half an houer /

[fol. 59r]   **to pickle oysters /**

take of the largest oysters, you can get
open them, and save all the Liquor, that's in
them, then take that Liquor, & putt therto
some good whit wine, as much as you see will
bee enough, to putt your oysters in, then putt
to that Liquor, some grose peper, & whole
cloves & mace, what you see good, & as moch
salt, as you think will keepe, them, which
must bee well & high seasoned, so give thes all
togather, one boyle vp, then putt in your oysters
& let them but Just boyle to plumpe them &
noe more, then take them out, & add to y*ou*r
Liquor, a lettle good whit wine veniger, when it
tis cold, & the oysters cold, put them vp to
gather in a earthen pott, close tyed vp, so
                    vse them –

---

37   This h should have been cancelled by the contributor.

[fol. 59v]   ~~To make mead with Elderberries~~[38]

~~Take very ripe Elderberries, pick them~~
~~from the stalkes, put *them* in an earthen~~
~~pott *then* past *them* close & bake them in an~~
~~oven while the are warm, strain them out~~

To make Gooseberry wine /

Take 24 quarts of *the* fruit got dry, pick *them*:
& Bruise *them*: Take spring watter & Boyle it
2 hours, when cold put 13 quarts to *the* Berrys
Let it stand 12 or 14 hours then draw it of
Let it run through a seive, & to every quart
of Liquour when a gane measured, put 3 quarters
of a pound of powder & Lofe suger mixt, save
one po*und*: of *the* suger out, to put into *the* Barrel
& put a Lettle yest to it, stop it up Close, for
half a year, & when y*o*u bottle it put a peece of
suger, to each bottle,

[fol. 60r]   vnguentum[39] album, vnguentum,
nutritum, vnguentum Rosatum,
vnguentum populeum,
any of these ointments mixt together
is excelent good for burnings or
scaldings, or any red inflamation,

confectio, Alkermes a
rare cordiall,/

[fol. 60v]   **to Boyle a carpe /**

take a carpe when hee is alive, gutt him &
scale him but not wash him, stob him to
make him bleede, then take the blood and
as much Claret wine as will b~~l~~oyle him over
head, & putt therin a bundle of herbs as a
lettle <...>rosemary & time & margerum &

---

38   This entire recipe is scribbled out.
39   This list of ointments has no title.

persly, some shaved horsreddish, a pece of
a lemom pill, some hole peper, some whole
cloves & mace, & a nuttmeg cutt in clices,
some eaght or tenn good anchoves, a whole
onion, lett all these boyle togather in the
liquor, a prety while before you putt in the
carpe then when you think it is time to
putt him in, rub him all over with some
pound ginger, then putt him in to the pan
of liquor, & lett him boyle till hee benough put
in a good lump of sweet butter, & season the
[fol. 61r]   broth with salt to your likeing, so take up
your carpe have a care of breaking him
lay him in a dish with as much of the
broth under him as you can, lay opon him
clices of lemom, & garnich the dish with
lemom & scraped horsreddich /

if you have shelott it is much better
to putt in then onion /

**to make a mouth powder, *tha*t is sore or
hath *the* cancor /**

take a Lettle scarlett cloth & burne it to a
powder, & drye a few red sage Leaves
& make it in a powddr, & a Lettle fine
Spanish Bole, shafed smale, & a Lettle
very fine suger, mingle all these togather
& make it in as fine a powder as you can
so keepe it in a Box, for your use /

[fol. 61v]   **To rost a shoulder of mutton in *the*
blood, to look like venson /**

Take a shoulder of mutton new killed, & take
som of *the* blood of *the* sheep, & put to it
a good handfull of salt, & whit breed crumes,
a lettel sreed penney royall, & a nutmeg greated
in, miggle all this like a puding, then let *the*
shoulder liy in it, & cut it up & down, &
~~stuffing~~ stuff it, then skewer up *the* two flaps,

one *the* inside, that it may look, like
a shoulder of venson, then take a peece of *the*
kell of *the* sheep, & lap it in, puting as
much of *the* blood & stuffing all over it as
may be, when it is well rosted, make sauce
of clarrit wine, with: good anchoves dissovled
in it, to yo*ur* likeing, & a lettel sweet butter,
so sarve it up,

[fol. 62r]   **a scearcloth to heale any thing that is**
sore: & very good to heale a young childs
head that is raw or sore:

Tack a lettel deeres suett: a lettel honny: a lettel
sweet bee wax: a lettel rossin: of that the least
for that is drawing: and a lettel francancence:
onley to give it a smell: then tack as much
fresh butter; as the quantity of all the rest
of these things: & so putt them all togather
in a posnit: & boyle them a lettel while: then
skem it: & when it is a lettel cold dipe in
your peces of flacken cloth: of what big
niss you will: & when it is cold lap them
up in papers: & keepe it for your use:

of what quantity you will mack at
a time: you most only add more or
lesse of the things: you may if you
will when it is cold keepe it in lomps
lick saulfe: & so spread opon cloaths /

[fols. 62v and 63r blank]

[fol. 63v]   **To make bisket ella**[40]

take some gume dragon dissolue it in a little rose water
the ioyce of A lemon and A little muske then straine it
through a fine linion cloth then take as much refined sugar
as you will use beeinge beaten and finely searsed take

---

40 Hand L (this recipe and the next one only) is a neat hand with a distinct indefinite
article a, which is written as a small majuscule A. There is no indication of the
identity of the contributor.

the white of ann ege and beate it to froth then take your
gume and as much of the froth of your ege as will make
your sugear in to paste make it not to stiffe then straw
in some annesseeds beeinge huld and made cleane and so
make them op in small loates [loaves?] or knotts put under the
bothome of euery one a wafern cut the loates about the
side as you doo a manchett and pricke them in the topps
soe lay then, on A sheete of paper and bake them litt not
your oten [oven] bee to hott they will doo as well without
wafernes if you straw A little suger opon the peapers you
lay them on

to make almonde cakes

take too ounces of the best almonds you can gett and lay
them in cold water all night in the moringe blanch them
in to A bason of cold water then drye them on A cloth, then
beate them uery fine in a stone morter putting to them A
little rosen water to which you must haue one pound of
refined suger finely searsed redy by you and the white
of ann ege beaten to froth and as you beate your almonds you
must put in some of the suger and a little of the frothe of the
ege intill you haue mingled your almonds and suger into a
stiffe paste then role your cakes thin upon a trencher
and print them then bak them in ann ofen not to hott
[fol. 64r]   and when they are risen drawe them keepe some of the
sugar out to mould them in or else they will stick to
your print

to mack a very good dish of meate:

tack som cold rosted veale: & sreed it very smale:
with som suett: then putt in som currines & reasons
& a lettel sugar: & nuttmege: & a lettel rose watter
so mixt it altogather: & putt it in a dish betwene
tow: peces of puffe past: so sett it in the oven:

to macke a quacking puding:

tack som with greated bread: & a lettel wheat fflowr
with som sweete creame: & 7 or 8 wites of eggs:
butt one youlk: & som sugar & nuttmege: blend it
altogather: & putt it in a cloth: boyle it halfe

a hower: when you tack it vp putt it in a dish
with som rose watter sugar & butter: & if you wish
stick som blancht allmons opone it:

to a pound of quince for marmalet take
a pint of watter /

[fol. 64v]   **to mack a venison pasty:**

tack a peck of wheat fflower: & 14 – eggs: wits
and all: & a quart of creame: & – 4 – pound of
butter: work it up with your hands lightly opon
a tabell: & when it is past role it out: have the
meat boned: & be sure you tack out all the grissels
& sunnues: & season it well with peper salt &
nuttmegg: when your past is ready: lay som suit
in the bottom under your meat: then mack it up
laying the pece of skine that you tack of the meat
one the top of the meat againe to keep it moist with
a lettel grose peper: then garnich your pasty with
past: as you please so sett it in the oven – 4 – howe^rs^
will bake it:

[fol. 65r]   **how to mack Shrewsberry cakes**

tack a quarter of a peck of fine wheat fflower,
lay it one a bord: putt to it one pound of powder
sugar: one ounce of beaten ciniment: a qarter
of a nounce of cloves & mace beaten: mixt
them with the fflower: then break in 3 new
lay egges: & 3 pound of new butter: work it
very well togather: then weigh 4 ounces of
this past to every cake: drive them out
very thinn: & prick them: then back them
one papers: affter manchett or with it if *the*
oven be not to hott:

as I mack it / I tack 3 quarters of a pond of
fflower: a quarter of a pond of fine suger
one egge: a lettel cloves & mace &
& ciniment: & a quarter & a halfe q*uarter*
of a pond of butter: washed in rose water

[fol. 65v]   **To drawe a tooth**[40]

Take a mulberye root beeing gotton in the beginning
of June: and layd in wine vineger: iust nine days
and then dried in the sunn: and pound it to powder
and put it into a fine lawne ragge: and put it
to one tooth that aches: and noe more but that
tooth: and it will draw it: <⋯⋯⋯⋯>

[fol. 66r]   **for the tooth ache**

ff the tooth bee trubled with a blud: let them furst blud
with a nedle: take a sponefull of wheat flower: more
or lesse: and a peniworth of Cloues: and a prity doase
of peper: and kneaded: with stroung water: and
bake it in the embers: and diepe in stroung water
a small quantity: and put it to the tooth: and if the
tooth bee halloe furst prik it: and then a plye it
                    and this may doe you good

                    1709[41]

[fol. 66v]   **For a sore mouth**

Take *the* iner barke of elme & boyle in water /

A pottel is two quarts /

[inside back cover]   not her
                                        hand[42]

            To make meade[43]   Eliz
                                                    Jackson[44]

---

40 Hand L ([65v]–[66r]) is a sharp mixed hand that uses the backward minuscule e and
    has a distinctive, backward-sloping, looped minuscule d. There is no indication of
    the identity of the contributor.
41 Written in another (unidentifiable) hand.
42 This is seemingly Hand J.
43 The recipe for mead does not follow.
44 "Eliz Jackson" is written in a new hand (Hand N).

Glossary of Culinary, Medical, and Household Terms

As food and medicine were intertwined in the seventeenth century, this glossary includes both culinary and medical terms: ingredients, techniques, weights and measures, implements, and ailments. It also includes occasional household terms that might not be familiar to a modern reader. Origins, uses, and supposed properties of ingredients are included as deemed fit. All English weights and measures are listed under the entry for "weights and measures." All entries are included in lower case regardless of their appearance in the original manuscripts, except words that are proper names. This glossary primarily draws from John Gerard's *Herball* and the *Oxford English Dictionary*.

adarme – a medieval unit of weight, equivalent to approximately 1.8 grams (Spanish) (Granville 107)

agaric (agarick) – fungus growing primarily on larch trees; used as a purge (Granville 8)

agrimony (agremony, egræmony, egremony, egrimoni, egrimony, egrimonye) – a plant of the rosacea family, native to England and elsewhere in Europe. Ingested as a medicine to alleviate liver problems and other ailments, and applied outwardly to wounds (Granville 13, 18, 42, 43, [166b], 184, 205; Hall 14, Pudsey [15v], [22r])

ague – a fever (passim)

a la reine (a la roine) – literally, "in the style of the queen"; often applied to a style of bread, and *potage à la reine* is a soup with bread cubes as one ingredient (Granville 10)

alcarraza (**alcarrasa**) – a porous earthen jug whose shape ensured that limited evaporation kept the contents cool; this Spanish term is now quite obsolete (Granville 96)

ale (alle) – a drink made of fermented barley, although sometimes more generally referring to other fermented herbal drinks as well; originally, the distinction between ale and beer was that beer contained hops (passim)

aleager – sour ale; malt vinegar (Pudsey [~~56r~~])

aleberry (alebury) – ale brewed with spices, sugar, and bits of bread (Granville 158)

ale-hoof – *see* ground ivy

alembic (alimbeck, limbeck, limbecke, lymbick) – an apparatus used in distilling; commonly made of glass or copper, it consisted of a rounded vessel with a long beak (passim)

alewort – fermenting malt (Granville 17)

alkermes (alkarmes, alkermis, alkermus) – a red secretion from an insect found in the kermes oak around the Mediterranean region; often used in dyes. *See also* confectio alkermes (Granville 15, 48, 184, [305])

allicompane, etc. – *see* elecampane

almond (allmon, allmond, almon, almonde, Jardon almond, Jordan almon, iordane almon, Jorden allmond) – native to the eastern Mediterranean region; used whole or ground into meals, or pastes such as marzipan, or milk. "Jordan" does not refer to the country, but is a bastardization of the Spanish *jardín*, meaning "garden" (passim)

aloe (alose) – succulent plant first cultivated in the West Indies, but native to Africa, India, China, and South America; used to treat eczema and burns (Granville 193, 211; Pudsey [13r], [13v])

alum (allum, allome, aluim, roach allum, rock allom, rooch allome) – an astringent mineral salt made from a double sulphate of aluminum and potassium; used in baking, pickling (with boiling vinegar), tanning, paper-making, and medicine (Granville 4, 90, 96, 101, [120], [166b], 170; Hall [24v], [26v], [50v]; Pudsey [5r], [14v], [56r])

amber – fossilized resin; considered an aphrodisiac in Arabic medicine and used as an additive in European recipes such as hot chocolate (Granville [104], 211)

ambergris (amber greece, amber greese, ambergrase, ambergreece, ambergreese) – intestinal secretions of the sperm whale, harvested from the sea or beaches; "gris" refers to its grey colour. Used primarily in perfumery, it was also used to scent culinary creations (Granville 153, [160], [193], 236; Hall 6, 19, [30v], 41, 46; Pudsey [6v], [57r], [57v])

ammoniac (amoniacum) – a naturally occurring salt originally collected from camel dung (Granville 59)

andouilles (andules) – sausages or chitterlings (French) (Granville 189)

angelica (angelecoe, angelicoe, angellico, angilico) – indigenous English herb used as a digestive and in fruit recipes to reduce acidity; it was also often candied (Granville 14, 41, 184, 212, 306; Hall [8v], 14, 17, [39v], Pudsey [16r], [56v])

aniseed (annelseed, annes seed, annesseed, annicdede, anny seed, any seed, anyseed) – feathery herb native to Egypt and the Middle East and spread across Europe by the Romans. Used as a flavouring, and medicinally as a digestive, to combat colds, and to increase mothers' milk production (Granville [205]; Hall 18, 27, [37v], 60; Pudsey [6r], [21r], [40r], [44r], [63v])

apricot (aprecock, apricko, apricock, apricok) – fruit native to the Middle East and introduced to Europe by the Romans. Popular in Renaissance receipt books (passim)

aqua mirabilis (agua mirabilis, aqua merabilis, aquemerabilis) – Latin generic term for composite waters of various ingredients (Granville 18; Hall [10v], [39v], 45; Pudsey [56v])

aqua vitae (aquavitae, aqua vitta, aquavite, aquevitae) – Latin generic term for distillates, especially those that are alcoholic (passim)

arabicq gumme – see gum arabic

Aristolochia (birthworth) – a large family of vines and perennial plants. Due to the similarity of the flower to the birth canal, it was also called birthwort and was used since ancient times in childbirth to expel the placenta; however, the plant is now known to be carcinogenic and to cause kidney failure (Granville 59, 211)

arroba (aroba) – a medieval unit of weight, equivalent to approximately 11.5 kilograms (Spanish) (Granville 104)

artichoke (hardychocke) – thistle-like plant native to the southern Mediterranean, introduced to England in the sixteenth century. Not related to the Jerusalem artichoke (Granville 127, 234; Hall 33)

ash key – winged seeds of the ash tree; pickled and used in place of capers in salads, and also used medicinally as a diuretic (Granville 238)

avens (aveirs, aven, auins) – also known as herb bennet, a root used to impart a flavour of cloves (often to ale) (Granville 1, 42; Hall 14; Pudsey [22r])

azumbre (a sumbre) – a measurement of liquids, equivalent to approximately two litres (Spanish) (Granville 101)

bain-marie (balmeo maria, balmeum, balneo) – a cooking vessel in which the upper part is heated by boiling water in the lower part (French) (Granville 38, 88; Hall 45)

balin (baline) – obsolete word for an unknown plant with supposed medical virtues; while various herbals and other works reference this plant, its identity remains a mystery; it might be a misspelling of balm (Hall 39v)

balm (baume, baum, balme) – likely lemon balm, used medicinally since the time of ancient Greece, although it might also refer to balsam. The leaves of both were boiled to combat colds. Lemon balm was also used to dispel melancholy as well as, in a poultice, to relieve insect bites (Granville 3, 12, 41, 184; Hall 14, 17, 45; Pudsey [15v], [56v])

balsam (balsum, balsamum) – general term for oily resin from plants or trees (passim)

barbel (barbell) – a carp-like freshwater fish (Pudsey [8r])

barberry (barbereis) – a sharp-flavoured, pointed berry; more than four hundred species exist and some are native to England. Used in jams, jellies, and sauces, as well as decoratively in meat dishes (Granville 40; Hall 7, 53, [31v], 62; Pudsey [11r])

barm (barme) – ale yeast, which forms as a froth on top of fermenting malt liquors; used to leaven bread (Granville 145; Hall 19, [27v], 29; Pudsey [23r], [27v], [32v], [49v], [50v])

barrow (barrowe) – a castrated male pig; see also "leaf fat" (Granville 3, 5, 153)

bay (baise, boye, house bay) – the leaf of the laurel tree; used as a flavouring and a digestive (passim)

bay salt – salt made by natural evaporation (i.e., in a saltwater bay), often sourced from southern Europe; used frequently in salting of meats (Granville 90; Pudsey [20r], [52r])

bdellium (bdelium) – gum resin similar to myrrh; used primarily for its scent (Granville 59)

bean flower (beane flower) – flour made of beans, likely fava beans or broad beans (Granville 8)

bean water (beane water) – this term is listed in the *Oxford English Dictionary* as simply an attribute of the bean seed; perhaps it meant a broth made of beans, or a strained bean mash (Hall [24v], 26)

beefer (bevior) – an animal that supplies beef (Granville 189)

beer – essentially hopped ale, which keeps longer than unhopped ale. According to Richard W. Unger, beer was introduced into England from Holland in the thirteenth century or earlier. Beer was often purchased – unlike ale, which was made at home – and beer-brewing long remained the work (and business) of men, primarily, Unger notes, Dutch expats in London. See also "small beer" (Granville 3, 10, 42, 153, 238; Hall [26]; Pudsey [16v], [41r])

bell-mettle kettle – *see* kettle

benjamin (beniamind, benianind, benjamind, benjanind) – benzoin gum, an aromatic resin derived from a Sumatran tree and used in perfumes and medicinally as a tonic (Granville [106], 184, [233]; Pudsey [6r], [30r])

betony (betany, betenny, betonye, bettony, bitony, bittony) – a woodland plant widely believed in Renaissance England to hold cleansing and other medicinal properties; used as somewhat of a panacea (passim)

bevior – *see* beefer

bezoar (bezar) – a stone-like concretion found in the digestive systems of certain ruminants; believed to have medicinal properties (Granville 14)

bindweed (bind weed) – a trailing vine of the family *Convulvulus*, of which several varieties exist, and John Gerard states that many varieties are native to most parts of England; used as a laxative (Granville 238)

bind wheat (wave wind) – as the *Oxford English Dictionary* notes, this name was applied dialectically to trailing vines such as honeysuckle, smilax, and tamus; a contributor to the Granville text treats bindweed and bind wheat as distinct (Granville 238)

birthworth – *see* Aristolochia

biscuit (bisket, biskett) – any small biscuit or cake made with sugar; *see also* cog's biscuit, nun's biscuit, Naples biscuit, biscuit ella, etc. (passim)

biscuit ella – Pudsey's recipe title seems unique in Renaissance cookbooks; however, the recipe is similar to those for Italian biscuits, as both call for musk and aniseeds and are "cut like manchet." (Pudsey's recipe differs only in that it calls for gum dragon rather than ambergris.) Plus, "-it ella" certainly sounds similar to "Italian," and much of Pudsey's spelling is phonetic (Pudsey [63v])

bitony, etc. – *see* betony

black pitch – *see* pitch

black soap (black soape) – soft soap made from alkali and fish oil or blubber (Granville 60)

blast – an obsolete term for a swelling (Pudsey [39r])

bloodwort (bloudwort) – the perennial bloody dock, also called bloody sorrel, which has red-veined leaves and is eaten like spinach (Granville 48)

bole armeniac (bole almanack, bolearmeniack, bolearmo lick, bolearmonak, bole armoniac, bolearmorick, bolus, boularniunicke, Spanish bole) – an astringent clay originally

brought from Armenia; used to stop the bleeding of a wound
(Granville 9, 120, [156], 169, 212, 306; Pudsey [14v], [19v], [61r], [64r])

borage (burridge, burrage, burich) – herb native to the Middle East
and Mediterranean countries; leaves and flowers were eaten to
dispel melancholy (Granville 12, 37, 43, 194; Pudsey [2r], [3r], [56v])

boye – *see* bay

bramble – the blackberry bush; the leaves were consumed as a cure
for diarrhea or were boiled with water, honey, alum, and white wine
as a cure for sores in the mouth (Granville 4, [166b])

bray (brade) – to beat small or crush in a mortar (Hall [56v])

brerd (bred) – obsolete term for the topmost surface or edge of a dish
(Hall [43v])

brewes – birds of some kind; while the *Oxford English Dictionary*
suggests snipes, W.R.P. Bourne suggests night herons. There is also
a possibility that the reference in the Granville recipe is a variant of
brewis, bread soaked in broth or pottage (or beef or vegetable broth
thickened with bread) (Granville 7)

brimstone (brimsone) – sulphur; used to treat various skin ailments
(Hall 61; Pudsey [6v], [20r])

brook lime (brookelime, brocklime, bruck lime, speedwell) – a
succulent herb with blue flowers also known as veronica; eaten
as a salad plant and used medicinally as an astringent and to cure
coughs (Granville 3, 43, 306; Pudsey [8v], [40r])

broom buds (broombuds) – buds of the broom plant, pickled and
used in place of capers; believed to be a diuretic (Hall 6)

bugloss (buglas, buglos, gubalis?) – a plant similar to borage,
although John Gerard says that bugloss leaves are longer (798).
Also eaten to dispel melancholy, as well as used to cure wounds
(Granville 3, 12, 44, [193]; Hall [39v]; Pudsey [56v])

Burgundy pitch – resin of the spruce fir, chiefly obtained in the forests
around Neufchâtel, previously part of Burgundy; used medicinally
in plasters (Granville 236)

burnet (burnett) – herbaceous plant; several varieties exist. Eaten in
salad and used medicinally to dispel melancholy and to staunch
bleeding (Granville 41; Pudsey [22r])

burrage, burich, burridge – *see* borage

butter – as with milk, provenance was sometimes specified. The Irish
butter called for in the Granville text was considered to be of high
quality, and might have been made with slightly soured, rather than
sweet, cream for depth of flavour. In 1861, Mrs Beeton mentions Irish
butter, saying that in London it is always sold salted, but it is generally

good (760). It is not clear why the Spanish recipe for "Picadillo of leg of lamb" in the Granville text calls for "pork fat or butter from Flanders," although Holland did produce and export high-quality butter and cheese in the seventeenth century (Prak 94); in *The Merry Wives of Windsor*, Ford notes that he would "rather trust a Fleming with my butter … than my wife with herself" (2.2.286–9) (passim)

bynilla – *see* vanilla

cabbage (cabbeg) – while lettuce was sometimes referred to as "cabbage lettuce," "cabbage" referred to the vegetable we know today; John Gerard says, "This is the great ordinarie Cabbage knowne euery where, and … commonly eaten all ouer this kingdome" (312) – although it only appears once in these three manuscripts (Hall [34v])

cake – general term used to refer to baked items made with flour, sugar, and various other ingredients; in Scotland and the north of England it also referred to a thin oat bread. *See also* clear cake, diet cake, queen's cake, cheesecake, Shrewsbury cake, sugar, Duke of York's cake, Woodstreet cake (passim)

calamint (calimas?) – a genus of aromatic herbs, often used to cure everything from a nosebleed to leprosy (Gerard 688). Calimas is likely a variant, as Pudsey's ointment is similar to green ointments found elsewhere that call for calamint (Pudsey [30r])

calimas – perhaps a variant of lapis calaminarus, but more likely calamint; see both terms

camphor (camphire, camfeare, champhir) – a waxy turpenoid from an evergreen native to Asia, as well as a few related plants. Used medicinally to reduce itching (Granville 5, 9, 46, 47, 48, [120]; Hall 46; Pudsey [6v])

canary – *see* sack

cantharidis – the Spanish fly. Powder made from these insects was used in the treatment of boils and sores, and it was also believed to cure incontinence when ingested (Granville 236)

capon – castrated rooster (passim)

cardamom (cardamomum, cardimum, cardyment) – John Gerard notes that this spice (which he describes as a kind of pepper) came from the East Indies and was used to dispel humours from the stomach and head (1542) (Granville 18, 193; Hall [37v], [39v]; Pudsey [56v])

carduus benedictus (cardus, cartix) – also known as holy thistle; eaten as a salad vegetable and used medicinally in several ways, including as a common ingredient in plague water, and to increase flow of mothers' milk (Granville 41, [156], 159, 184, 212, 306; Hall 14, 17; Pudsey [6r], [16r], [22r], [58r], [61v])

carrot (carret, carriot) – John Gerard describes both yellow and blackish-red carrots, but not orange, and says that they are sweet but not particularly nutritious (1028) (Granville 125; Hall [49v], 54; Pudsey [2v], [8r])

cartix – *see* carduus benedictus

case ginger – *see* ginger

Castile soap (Castill soap, Spanish soap) – olive oil soap originating in the Castile region of Spain (Granville 60)

caudle (cadle, caudell, cawdle) – a thick drink; often ale or wine sweetened and then thickened with egg (Granville [158]; Hall 6, 21, [28v])

cazuela **(cassuela)** – an earthenware pot (Spanish) (Granville 95)

celandine (cellendine, calandine, saladine, salandine, sallandine, selandine, selendine, sallindine) – John Gerard divides this plant into "great" and "lesser" varieties; the former is good for eyesight (1070) and the latter purges the head of "filthy humours" (816) (passim)

centaury (centery, centry, century, sentry) – a woody herb growing plentifully in England, used as somewhat of a cure-all, especially in healing "green wounds" (Granville 159; Hall 14, 25, [26v]; Pudsey [2v], [58v])

cerus, ceruse – *see* lead

ceterach (centerach) – a genus of ferns; used medicinally as a diuretic (Granville 16)

cettle – *see* kettle

Cevill orange, etc. – *see* orange

chafe (chauffe) – a rubbed spot on the skin (Granville 97)

chafing dish (chaffing dish, chafingdish, chafindish) – a portable grate holding coals that served as a small stove (Granville 140, 240; Hall 10; Pudsey [1v], [4r], [8r], [9v], [32r], [47v])

chaldron – the *Oxford English Dictionary* lists the term as an obsolete form of "cauldron" as well as a dry measure of thirty-two bushels. As the latter is certainly not appropriate here, the reference in this recipe might thus mean "a cauldron full of veal," or else it might refer to a specific body part (the entrails, perhaps?), using a now obsolete term (Granville [189])

chalk – limestone, or other geological substances of the same texture (Granville [211])

chamomile (camamill, camaile, camamile, cammomile, camomell, camomill) – herb native to England and other places; used as a calmative (passim)

chap (chape, choppe) – crack in the skin (Granville 4; Pudsey [25v])
cheny orrieng – *see* orange
cheesecake (cheas cake, chees-cake) – unlike modern versions, these "cakes" were a kind of custard made with butter, eggs, and sugar but no cheese (Granville [191], 214; Hall 9, [21v])
cherry (cheiry, chery) – John Gerard lists several species of cherry and notes their use in tarts; he urges sour varieties over small, sweet, wild cherries, which he says "not only breed worms in the belly, but troublesome agues, and often pestilent fevers: and therefore in well governed commonwealths it is carefully provided, that they should not be sold in the markets in the plague time" (1506) (passim)
chicory (succory, suckrey, suckry, sucory) – edible plant with blue flowers; medicinally, it was used to cure fevers and insomnia (Granville 8, 16; Pudsey [2r], [8v])
chieng – *see* china
china (cheynie, chieng) – porcelain dishware (Granville 93, 140, 240; Hall 43)
China root (China roote) – the root of the China plant, closely related to the American plant known as sarsaparilla (and listed as *tsinaw* from Virginia in John Gerard's *Herball* [1619]). Used to cure stomach problems, ulcers, tuberculosis, gout, leprosy, syphilis, and other ailments (Granville 49)
cinnamon (cinaman, cinament, cinamon, cinimon, cynamon, sinamon, sinamond, sinement, siniament, siniment, sinnimond, sinomand, sinoment, sinomon, sinomond, synnamon) – bark from a tree native to Sri Lanka and perhaps China; used as flavouring in both sweet and savoury dishes, and medicinally as an astringent, antiseptic, and stimulant (passim)
cinquefoil (sincfield) – the five-leafed plant *Potentilla* from the Rosaceae family; John Gerard says that it is useful against the bloody flux, poisoning, the falling sickness, "ruptures and burstings of the rim, and guts falling into the cods," and other ailments (991) (Granville [166b])
citron (cittorn, citturn, sictren, sitterne) – thick-peeled, lemon-like fruit grown in southern Europe. The juice was often used as a flavouring, and the peel candied; medicinally, used to stimulate appetite, ease colds, and sweeten the breath (passim)
civet (sevet) – musk produced by the cat-like civet, native to tropical Africa and Asia; imported in powder form to England and used in perfume or to impart an exotic touch to food (Granville [104], 107, [108]; Pudsey [6r])

claret (clarett, clarrett) – the most common wine exported from the Bordeaux area; typically light red in colour (Granville 7; Hall [51v]; 53, Pudsey [42], [52], [60v])

clary – herb native to southern Europe, often made into fritters or to flavour wine. Used medicinally to cure eye problems (Granville 184)

clear cake – a transparent, soft or hard jelly-like confection made of fruit (e.g., raspberry or quince) or flower (e.g., violet) juice and sugar (Hall [33v], 34, 37, 56)

cliver – goosegrass or cleavers, a widespread English native plant that is creeping and has hairy leaves. John Gerard says that it is used to treat spider bites, and that women make it into a pottage with mutton and oatmeal to "keep them from fatnesse" (1123) (Pudsey [40r])

clove gilly flower – *see* gillyflower

clyster (glister) – liquid enema, or a purge to be drunk (Hall 25)

cochineal (cochineale, scuchineale) – insect native to Mexico and South America; its dried and pulverized body is the source of the red dye carmine (Hall [15v], 48)

cocks tread – *see* tread

coffin (cauffin, coffen, coffine) – pastry case for pies and tarts; often reused and only sometimes eaten (Hall [20v], 21, [30v], 34, [46v]; Pudsey [1v], [7r], [25r], [34v])

cog's biscuit (cogs biskett) – "cog" meant, among other things, a small drinking vessel or a dram (usually of liquor); these biscuits might be named after the six spoonfulls of ale called for by the recipe (Hall [33v])

collar (colleer) – any fish or joint of meat that was boned, rolled, and trussed to keep a circular shape, then often pickled or brined before boiling (passim)

collop (schotch scollop, scoch collop, scotch scollop) – thin slice of meat, such as bacon. "Scotch" may derive from "to cut" (Hall [27v], [34v], 53; Pudsey [51v])

colts foot (coltsfoot) – broad-leafed plant used against coughs, although now believed to be toxic; also used to produce green-yellow dye (Granville 16, 49, 194, [205]; Pudsey [44r])

columbine (cullobine) – a higher-altitude plant with bonnet-shaped flowers. John Gerard says that "milk of the leaves" was a popular medicine against a sore throat in his day, although he notes that the only columbine remedy described by the ancients was to mix a dram of columbine seeds with half a scruple of saffron in wine as medicine against jaundice and other liver problems; he also notes that a Flemish doctor gave a powder of the seeds to hasten labour (1095) (Granville 167) comfit (comefitt, comfitt, cumfit) – sugar-coated grain, seed, or aromatic substance. The most common flavours were caraway, aniseed, and coriander (Hall [3v], 4, [7v], 29; Pudsey [52r])

comfrey – plant with blue-mauve bell-shaped flowers; used for healing wounds and reducing swelling around fractured bones (Hall [60v])

cominout – unknown; the contributor of Hall 27 likely meant to write cinnamon, as this is called for in other recipes for surfeit water. See cinnamon

confectio alkermes (confectio alkermis, confectio alkermus) – a compound cordial; see also alkermes (Granville 15, 48; Pudsey [60r])

consumption – tuberculosis (passim)

copperas (coperas, coperis, copres, copris, coppris, Roman vitirall, vitriol, vitrioll, white copeirs, white coperis) – copper, iron, or zinc sulphate, used primarily for tanning, dyeing, and making ink (Granville 2, 4, 9, 11, 42, 102, 103; Hall [12v]; Pudsey [4r], [38r])

coral pearl: see pearl

cordind – unknown; perhaps a variant of either coriander or diascordium (Pudsey [14r])

corduan – The term "cordovan" originally referred to dried leather hide originally from Córdoba; the term sometimes came to mean leather shoes (consider cordonnier, meaning "cobbler," in French). The reference in Granville 109 might thus refer to seven pairs of leather shoes, although one would think that they would require more perfume than six pairs of gloves (Granville 109)

coriander (corroander, cordind?) – feathery plant brought to Europe by the Romans. Used as a digestive, often as a sugar-coated comfit (Granville 44, [189]; Pudsey [14r], [21v], [23r], [45v])

corrinths – see currants

costmary (corsemary) – mint-flavoured plant native to Asia and commonly planted in medieval herb gardens. Called Sweet Mary in Renaissance England for its frequent use as a bookmark in Bibles. Used medicinally as a diuretic and a laxative, as well as to treat various skin ailments, including bruises and blisters (Granville 3)

cowslip (cowslipp) – early-blooming plant, closely related to the primrose. Infusion of the leaves was used as a cough remedy, to relieve headaches, and, according to John Gerard, to cure "all the diseases of the sinewes" (783) (Granville 12, 37; Hall [39v]; Pudsey [16r], [49v], [56v])

crab's eye (crabs eye) – bean-like seed from the precatory vine, native to Indonesia and common in tropical and subtropical parts of the world and often used in jewellery-making. The bean is toxic, although an infusion of the leaves was used to cure colds (Granville [213])

cracknel (crackneyle) – a thin, crisp biscuit that takes on a curved or hollow shape when baked (Pudsey [47v])

crag (cragg) – neck of mutton or veal. Sometimes also called "scrag," although this refers specifically to the lean (and inferior) part of the neck (Granville 183)

cromes – *see* crumbs

crumbs (cromes) – small bits of bread, often used for thickening a sauce or adding texture to a dish (Granville 193, [201]; Hall [40v]; Pudsey [7r])

cuartillo **(quartillo)** – a unit of liquid measurement equivalent to approximately 500 millilitres (Spanish) (Granville [104], 107, 123)

cubeb (cubebu, cubell, cubube, gubalis?) – a type of pepper native to Indonesia. Popular in the 1600s, used both as a flavouring similar to allspice and as a curative for respiratory problems; Pudsey's recipe calling for gubalis is similar to those calling for cubeb (Granville 193; Hall 11, [39v]; Pudsey [56v])

cucumber (cowcomber, cowcumber) – John Gerard describes several shapes of cucumbers. He notes that they are good for the complexion both when applied outwardly and when consumed in a stew with mutton; over-consumption of the vegetable, however, "filleth the weines with naughty cold humours" (911) (Hall [35v], 5̶1̶; Pudsey [38v], [56r])

cume – *see* scum

cumin (comin, cummine, cumminseed) – feathery herb native to Egypt; one of the oldest cultivated herbs. Used to flavour pickles and curries, and medicinally as a digestive and to relieve stitches in the side (Granville [158], 170; Pudsey [13r])

currant (carron, corrinth, curan, currain, curranc, curran, currat, curence, currende, curine, currin, curron) – while red and white currants grow throughout England, "currants" in most of these recipes refers to the black currant, usually imported from Greece (one exception is Pudsey [31v]). Besides being a popular culinary ingredient, they were seen to have medical virtues; John Gerard even notes that the sap from the branches could be used to remove warts and superfluous hairs (876) (passim)

cyprus (sriprius?) – a gauze-like fabric, sometimes used for straining and to reduce inflammation and heal burns (Granville [233]; Pudsey [23r]?)

d – abbreviation of "denarius," commonly used to mean "penny"/"pence"

dallfennell – *see* fennel

Damask powder (damaske powder) – likely a powder prepared from Damask roses (Granville 5); *see also* rose water

Damask rose water – *see* rose water

damiask pruan – *see* prune

damson – a bluish-black varietal of plum; particularly good for making jams and jellies. The name indicates its origins around Damascus (Hall 38, 62; Pudsey [28r], [35r])

dandelion (lyon-tooth) – a jagged-leafed plant with yellow flowers; its description is one of Gerard's most poetic: "upon euery stalke standeth a floure greater than that of Succorie, but double, and thicke set together, of colour yellow, and sweet in smell, which is turned into a round downie blowball, that is carried away with the winde" (290). The leaves were incorporated as herbs into medicine or were (and still are) eaten in the manner of spinach; the plant has long been known for its diuretic properties (Granville 16, 48)

daucus (duacus) – wild carrot known to grow in the Alps and Jura mountains; used medicinally as a diuretic and to alleviate stomach problems (Pudsey [40r])

devils (devills bitt) – the meadow flower scabious, also known as devil's-bit, which was used to improve eyesight and to cure scorpion bites; in instances other than the red powder remedy in the Granville text, it may also refer to ditain (*see* ditain) (Granville [156])

diachylon (diacalum) – originally an ointment made of various vegetable juices, then a plaster composed of boiled litharge (lead oxide), olive oil, and water; used to aid in digestion and reduce swelling (Granville 171)

diascordium (cordind?) – medicine made from the herb scordium, used as a diuretic and a sudorific, and to alleviate stomach problems (Granville [213], 306; Pudsey [14r])

diet cake (diett cake) – the *Oxford English Dictionary* defines diet-bread as special bread prepared for invalids, so diet cake is likely made especially to strengthen an ill person (Granville 53)

ditain (ditanum) – the alkaloid substance derived from the bark, known as dita-bark, of the evergreen *Alstonia* tree, also known as devil's tree, native to southeastern Asia; used as an astringent. Also sometimes referred to as devils (Granville [211])

dock root (butter dockroote, dock roote, dockroote) – refers to various types of cress or lettuce, including sorrel (Granville 17; Pudsey [8v])

Doctor Stevens's Water – Gervase Markham says in *The English Huswife* that this remedy keeps one youthful and that Doctor Stevens took it for years, as did the Archbishop of Canterbury (who apparently drank it in his old age through a silver straw). Markham describes the water as a cure-all; among other things, it comforts the spirit and vital parts, increases fertility, and cures toothaches and bladder troubles (Markham 58–9) (Granville 305; Pudsey [14r])

dodder – a parasitic plant growing on herbs such as thyme and which, as John Gerard writes, is like threads "very much snarled or wrapped together" (577). Medicinally, used to purge melancholy and other "corrupt and superfluous humours" (Granville 16)

double refined sugar, etc. – *see* sugar

dragon (draggons, dragons, dragons wood) – there is some discrepancy regarding this term. Sir Kenelm Digby uses "dragon" to refer to the aromatic herb tarragon, and John Gerard says it is the French term for tarragon (249). However, Gerard also uses the term to refer to the dragon tree growing in Portugal and the Canary Islands, and perhaps native to Africa or South America, that is the source of dragon fruit (1524). The "blood" of the tree is its red sap, extracted by boring into the trunk and used medicinally for its astringent properties (*see* gum dragon). Finally, Gerard also uses the term to refer to blood worte, which he describes both as a type of sorrel and as a bastard rhubarb (390) (Granville 3, 41, [156], 184, 212, 306; Hall 14; Pudsey [16r], [22r])

dropsy (dropsye) – edema or swelling of some part of the body (Pudsey [5r], [14v])

dross (drose, drosse) – dregs, for example of oil or wine (Granville 88, 216; Pudsey [4v])

Duke of York cake – the meaning of this term and provenance of this recipe are unknown (Hall [11v])

dung (of cow, of hen, of hog, of horse, etc.) – dung/soil of various animals was common in ointments and in medicines in both Galenic and Paracelsian remedies; the benefit of each particular dung is unknown (Granville 4, 6; Pudsey [15r], [17r])

dutch beef (dutch beefe) – as this term's use in the Granville text sounds like a particular preparation, it might refer to cooking the meat in the way quills were "dutched" by passing them rapidly through a fire to harden them; if so, this use of the term likely predates the earliest reference in the *Oxford English Dictionary* (Granville [209])

ebulum (ebbylon) – elderberry wine (Pudsey [46v])

egremony – *see* agrimony

elder (eleder) – a common English tree with white berries. The berries were eaten or pressed into wine, while the bark, leaves, and seeds were all consumed to aid digestion and cure stomach ulcers (Granville 3, 7, 145, 186, 192, 234; Hall 12; Pudsey [5r], [33r], [46v], [50v], [52v], [53v], [54r], [54v], [~~59v~~])

elecampane (allicompane, alycompane, elocompane, elicampane, elicampain, elicum pane, ennula campana) – a yellow-flowered herb native to England and many parts of Europe; John Gerard says that the roots were particularly good for curing chest and lung ailments, while an ointment cured "itch, scabs, manginesse and such like" (794) (Granville 14, 41, [156]; Hall 14, 27; Pudsey [16r], [22r], [45v])

electuary – a medicinal paste made palatable by the addition of a sweetener such as honey or sugar (passim)

emula campana, ennula campana – *see* elecampane

eryngo (eringo, erringgo, ringoe) – the root of the sea holly, a common grassland and coastal plant with a thistle-like flower; often candied or pickled, these were considered an aphrodisiac (Granville 184; Hall 21, [46v], [60v])

exodore – unknown. Presumably a rare word distorted beyond recognition in the process of copying; one possibility is that it is a variant of zedoary. *See* zedoary (Hall 14)

eyebright (eiebright) – *Euphrasia*, a small flowering plant that grows across England and was reputed to cure conjunctivitis and weak eyesight (Pudsey [13r])

falling sickness (falling sicknes) – epilepsy (Granville 39; Hall [24v], [26v])

felon (fellon) – a small abscess (Pudsey [6r])

femitary, femitery – *see* fumitory

fennel (dallfennele, fenell, fennell, brown fennell) – John Gerard describes both wild and garden fennel, the former being so common that "it were but lost labour to describe the same" (1031). He suggests that garden fennel becomes wild/common fennel the second year, so must continuously be replanted from seed. Medicinally, fennel seeds, leaves, and roots were primarily consumed to aid digestion and to alleviate kidney problems. "Dallfennele" likely derives from fennel's similar appearance to dill (Granville 10, 16, 37, 48, 194/5; Hall [35v]; Pudsey [2v], [13r], [16v], [21r], [27r])

fenugreek (fenigreeke) – a plant "sowne in fields across the seas" as well as in England, according to John Gerard (1196). The seeds and leaves were consumed as a purge, while the seeds were also commonly ground into powder and used to heal skin problems (Granville 7)

feverfew (featherfew, fetherfew) – a herb with a daisy-like flower; used medicinally to alleviate headache and fever (Granville 41, [205]; Hall 14)

fig (figg, Lent figg) – John Gerard notes that while fig trees are plentiful in Spain and Italy, they must be planted against a south-facing wall in England; he suggests diverse medical uses for figs: the fruit cures skin diseases and lung and throat problems, the leaves treat tuberculosis, and various concoctions and plasters cure hemorrhoids, gout, toothache, and biting by a mad dog (1510–11). A Lent fig (Granville 205) is perhaps a dried fig, since in the northern hemisphere figs ripen in autumn, and since all of the other fruits described here are dried (passim)

filipendula (philopendelay) – a flowering herbaceous plant of the Rosaceae family; used as a flavouring in beer and jams, and medicinally as a diuretic and to ease bladder pains (Pudsey [16r])

firkin (ferking) – a small cask a quarter the size of a barrel (Pudsey [27v], [28r])

flounder (flownder) – a flat fish once common in English seas (Granville 91; Hall 28)

flour (flower) – a wide variety of flours were used in seventeenth-century England, including not only those from grains but also those from pulses, such as beans (passim)

frankincense (francancence) – aromatic gum resin from a species of pine; used primarily for its scent, but it was also believed to heal wounds and improve eyesight. John Gerard also describes a "herb frankincense," the plant *Libanotis*, which was used as a curative for diverse ailments such as swellings and gout (1011) (Granville 4, 46, 59, [120]; Pudsey [62r])

French bread – bread enriched with butter, milk, and eggs (Granville [180], 196)

fricasée **(fricasy, friccacee, frigacie, friggasee)** – mixture of meat and other ingredients chopped and fried, then boiled or stewed in a broth (Granville 45; Hall [10v], 28, 33, [47v], [51v]; Pudsey [38v], [55r])

fumitory (femitery, femitary) – small flowering plant that commonly grows wild in England; a tea of its leaves (often boiled with whey) was drunk to heal skin disease and to cure conjunctivitis (Granville 16, 47)

galangal (galingale, galingall, gallingal, gallingall, gallingallio, golingule) – root of a Javanese plant with a flavour reminiscent of ginger; C. Anne Wilson notes that it became popular in late medieval England with the influence of Norman cookery (*Food and Drink* 280) (Granville 10, 18; Hall [11r], [39v]; Pudsey [14r], [56v])

galbanum – aromatic gum resin from a large, fennel-like plant; used in perfumes and remedies. John Gerard claims that it cures poisoning, regardless of whether the poison "hath been taken inwardly or shot into the body with venomous darts, quarrels, or arrowes" (1058) (Granville 59)

gall (gaule) – fungus growing on a species of oak tree common in southern Europe; high in tannins, galls were often used in tanning and making ink (Granville 42, 96, 101 (*agallas*), 102, 103, 123 (*agallas*); Hall 61 reference is to the gall bladder of a pig)

galley pot (galleypot, gallipot, galliy pot, gallow pot) – small, glazed, earthenware pot used by apothecaries for mixing medicines (passim)

Gascogne powder (Gasgoin powder) – a common curative powder in seventeenth-century receipt books; a recipe for this powder appears in the Countess of Kent's *A Choice Manual*. The relationship to Gascony is not clear, as the ingredients are mostly exotic (Granville [305])

Gascogne wine (Gascoigne wine) – wine from the Bordeaux area of southwestern France; one of the most widely imported French wines into England in medieval through early modern times (Granville 10)

gentian (gention) – small Alpine plant, some species with bright blue flowers; its leaves and flowers were drunk in a tea as a cure for colds and coughs (Granville [156], 159, [203], [211]; Pudsey [58r])

gillyflower (clove gilly flower, gilliflower, gillefflour, jilliflower, jilly flower, pinke) – the carnation, used for its clove-like scent and flavour (Granville 12, 88, 190, 216; Hall [37v], 39; Pudsey [16r])

ginger (genger) – root native to southeast Asia; used in many seventeenth-century recipes (John Gerard notes that it is "right good with meate in sauces" [62]) and used medicinally as a digestive. Case ginger (in "hipocras for a consumption" on Granville 40) is unknown, although it is perhaps whole, unpeeled ginger (passim)

glair (glare) – white of an egg (Hall 48)

glister – *see* clyster

gold – a common medicinal ingredient for those who could afford it, for its supposed healing properties. Sir Thomas Browne, however, wrote in *Pseudodoxia Epidemica* around 1646, "That gold inwardly taken, either in substance, infusion, decoction, or extinction, is a cordial of great efficacy, in sundry medical uses, although a practice much used, is also much questioned, and by no man determined beyond dispute" (85). Litharge of gold is gold mixed with red lead (Granville 2, 5, 17, 43, 48, 59, 91, 184)

grain of paradise (parradice) – peppercorns of *Aframomum melegueta*, a plant native to Ethiopia and also known as Guinea pepper or Malagueta pepper; related to the ginger plant, although John Gerard describes the grains as related to cardamom and says that they warm a weak, cold, and feeble stomach (1542) (Granville [158])

green sickness (greensicknes) – chlorosis, a form of anemia; symptoms include a green pallor to the skin (Granville 8, [211]; Hall [24v])

groat (groate) – an obsolete English coin worth four pennies (Granville 96, 101)

gromwell (grumwall, grun-smale, grounmile) – herb of the borage family; used both as a purple dye and to dissolve bladder stones (Granville 37; Pudsey [16r], [57r])

ground ivy (ale-hoof, alehoofe, ivy, grownd ivey) – creeping herb with purple flowers; used as a diuretic and a digestive – *or*, rarely, periwinkle. Granville lists both "alehoofe" and "ground ivy" in one recipe, suggesting her understanding of ground ivy as periwinkle (Granville 1, [166b], 194, [205]; Hall 61; Pudsey [44r])

guaiacum – a flowering sub-tropical or tropical tree native to North and South America; in the sixteenth and seventeenth centuries it was believed to be a cure for syphilis (Pudsey [45v])

gubalis – *see* buglas *and* cubeb

gum (gumme) – plant resin, such as frankincense or galbanum, etc. (passim)

gum arabic (arabicq gumme, gomme arabicke) – aromatic resin of the acacia tree; used primarily as a stabilizer in dye and ink (Granville 96, 101 (*goma arabiga*), 103)

gum dragon (dragons blood gumdragon, gume dragon) – aromatic resin of the tragacanth legume plant, also known as burnet goat's thorn, native to Persia; John Gerard says that this plant is to be "licked in with honey against the cough" (1330) (Granville 5, 50, 52, [108], 123 (*sangre de drago*); Hall [56v], 58; Pudsey [53r], [63v])

gum ladanum – aromatic resin of a flowering shrub native to Spain and Portugal; used primarily as a fixative in perfumes (Pudsey [30r])

gum storax, etc. – *see* storax

gut (gutt) – intestinal case of animals, used for making sausage and black pudding (Granville 42; Hall [6v]; other references are to the general entrails, or the verb to remove the entrails

hair sieve, etc.– *see* sieve

hardychocke – *see* artichoke

harstrang (hart strange) – also known as hog's fennel, used to treat stomach aches and diverse other ailments (Pudsey [5r])

hartshorn (hartshorne, harts horn) – ammonium carbonate, a salt both naturally occurring and created through distillation of animal hooves and horns; also called spirits of hartshorn. Traditionally used in dyeing, prewashing of wool, and as a source of nitrogen in the fermentation process (Granville 40, 41, 157, [158], [203], [213], 216; Hall 46, 61)

hartstongue (harts tongue) – a fern native to England; used medicinally to cure stomach ailments and snake bites (Granville 17, 43, [205])

hash – a stew of meat, spices, and other ingredients (passim)

haske – *see* husk

hawe – hawthorn berry, and more generally a hedge berry (hawe being a Middle English word for hedge) (Pudsey [16v])

hay – ham was (and still is) sometimes braised in water and hay to tenderize it; the hay imparts a herbal flavour to the ham (Hall 53)

hazelnut (hasell nut) – while this is a common English tree, only one recipe calls for hazelnuts in these three receipt books; John Gerard says that hazelnuts are hard to digest and cause headaches (1440) (Hall [42v])

heave – to cause to expand or rise (e.g., dough) (Hall 19)

heel – in the Granville text's reference to violets, this possibly means the sepals: the green, leaf-like structures at the base of the petals, which cover the petals in the bud stage (Granville 206)

hemlock – a poisonous plant native to England; John Gerard says that even laying the leaves on the body is dangerous (1063), so it is surprising to see remedies in Hall's book calling for its leaves to be used in a plaster (Hall 25, [26v])

herb of grace, herbgrass, etc. – *see* rue

hermodactyl (hermiodachilis) – a bulbous root originally from the East Indies; used medicinally as a treatment for gout and arthritis (Pudsey [6r])

hickockes (hiccups) – as is commonly known, an involuntary contraction of the diaphragm; the spelling here might relate to the fact that Hickock is a relatively common English surname (Granville 59) hipericon – *see* St John's wort

hippocras (hipocras, hipocris) – spiced wine (Granville 40; Pudsey [21v])

hive bee – common honey-bee (Granville 60; this reference substantially antedates the *Oxford English Dictionary*'s first reference)

honey (honny, hony) – the principal sweetener used in English cooking prior to widespread access to sugar; honey type is rarely, if ever, specified in seventeenth-century English recipes (passim)

hoop (hope) – a wood or tin ring used in baking cakes (Granville 92, [124], 162, [235]; Hall [6v])

hops (hopes) – plant used in the making of beer (their inclusion is what traditionally distinguished beer from ale); also used, as John Gerard notes, to "make bread light" (Granville 16; Pudsey [8v], [46v])

horehound – herb with downy leaves native to England; used to treat coughs (Granville 93)

horseradish (horse radish, horse redish, horsreddich, horsreddish) – wide-leafed plant native to England, used to flavour dishes; also used medicinally to cure diverse ailments, particularly in poultices for stomach or hip pains (Granville 127; Hall 28, 51; Pudsey [41r], [60v], [61r])

horsetail (horstale) – a plant growing around bogs in England; used medicinally in ointments to heal wounds, and drunk in medicines to cure diverse ailments including stomach problems and ulcers (Granville 167)

hounds tongue (houndstongue) – a herb related to borage and native to England; known for its foul scent. Used to treat wounds, ulcers, and hemorrhoids (Granville 184; Pudsey [39r])

house bay leaves – *see* bay

house ivy – likely a term used simply for climbing ivy, rather than "ground ivy" or ale-hoof (Granville 1)

hoxy croxy – oxycroceum. The *Oxford English Dictionary* defines oxycroceum as "A medicinal plaster made from saffron, vinegar, and various other ingredients" with attestations ?1425–1873 and variant forms including "oxirocroceo" (fifteenth century) and "oxycrocij" (sixteenth century). See also *Notes & Queries* article by Kristine Kowalchuk and John Considine listed in the Works Cited (Granville 5)

Hungary water (Hungrey watter) – a distillation of wine and rosemary essence, named after one of the Hungarian queens. A common seventeenth-century recipe, particularly in French cookbooks and herbals (Granville [150]; Pudsey [58r])

husk (haske) – a dry cough (Pudsey 5)

hypericum, etc. – *see* St John's wort

hyssop (hisop, hissop, hysop, isope, issope) – an aromatic herb native to England, used medicinally to cure lung diseases, and also as a purge: John Gerard says that it purges "mightely, and that in great abundance, waterish, grosse, and slimy humors" (582) (Granville 5, 93, [166b], 194, [205]; Hall 32)

ink (incke, inke) – only the Granville manuscript includes recipes for ink. They all utilize specific water (snow, rain, or fountain), galls, and copperas, and sometimes vinegar (beer or wine) and gum (Granville 42, 96, 102, 103)

impostumation – a running or festering sore (Granville 169)

iorne – *see* iron

Irish butter – *see* butter

iron (iorne) – iron pots were historically common cooking vessels, as they could be used over an open fire (passim)

isope, etc. – *see* hyssop

isinglass (issinglass, izing glass) – gelatin derived from the air bladders of freshwater fish such as sturgeon; used primarily for making jelly and glue (Granville 166; Hall 48; Pudsey [49v])

ivy – *see* ground ivy, house ivy

Jamaica pepper (Jameca pepper, Jemeca pepper, Jemecca peper) – allspice; a pepper native to southern Mexico and central America with a flavour similar to cloves (Granville 127, [183b], [237]; Hall [49v]; Pudsey [51r])

jasmine (jesemi) – climbing plant with fragrant, star-shaped white flowers used often in perfumery (Granville [108])

jilly flower – *see* gillyflower

Jordan almond, etc. – *see* almond

jujube – fruit of the *Ziziphus* tree, native to many parts of Asia; also referred to as Chinese date (Granville 193)

jumball – a sweet cake, often in the form of an interlaced ring or knot; C. Anne Wilson notes that the name derives from "a gemmel or twin finger-ring" and that "[t]heir texture varied, the paste for them sometimes resembling biscuit bread and at other times short cakes" (*Food and Drink* 269) (Hall [54v], 55)

kell (keyll) – fatty membrane around the intestine (Pudsey [57v], [61v])

kettle (bell-mettle kettle, cettle) – an open metal pot, used for boiling food. Bell-metal is an alloy of copper and tin, and is generally the substance from which bells were made (passim)

knot marjoram – *see* marjoram

knuckle (vnckle) – a large cut of meat from the animal's hindquarters
(Hall [32v])

lady's smock – spring-blooming herbaceous plant with white flowers;
inclusion of this plant in a remedy is rare, and John Gerard says that
this plant's virtues were unknown (261) (Granville 239)

lambs stones – *see* stones

lane – *see* lawn

**lapis calaminaris (calaminarus, calimas?, lapis calaminanus, lapis
calaminarius, lapis caluminaus, tapis calliminaris)** – calamine, a
zinc ore used against rashes, itchiness, and similar skin problems
(Granville 59, [120]; Pudsey [4v], [30r], [38r])

lapistuticia – *see* tutty

lard – besides meaning rendered fat, this term was also used as
a verb to mean to insert little bits of fat or bacon into a piece of
meat by pricking it with a larding pin. One recipe in the Granville
manuscript adapts the term to "lard" a capon with lemon (Granville
40, [144]; Hall [19v], 28, [29v], [34v]; Pudsey [1r])

large mace – *see* mace

lavender – an aromatic herb used medicinally for its calming
properties. John Gerard writes that the flowers, mixed with
cinnamon, nutmeg, cloves, and water, "doth helpe the panting
and passion of the heart, prevaileth against giddinesse, turning, or
swimming of the braine" (584) (Granville 3, [104] (*alxusema*), [193],
[205]; Hall [24v], 26; Pudsey [6r], [14r], [15r], [37v])

lavender cotton – obsolete term for ground cypress, a low, aromatic
shrub native to the Mediterranean region (Granville 3; Hall [24v])

lawn (lane, lawne) – a fine linen cloth (Hall 18, [44v]; Pudsey [65v])

lead (cerus, ceruse, white lead) – chemical compound used primarily
in ointments to treat skin diseases and whiten the skin (Granville 91,
[120], 236 – used here as a weight, not an ingredient)

leaf – sometimes perhaps used to refer to the petal of a flower
(Granville 140, 206; Pudsey [10r])

leaf (leafe) – the fat around the kidneys and in the layers between the
flesh and the skin; regarded as the best lard (Granville 153, 189; Hall
[28v])

lear – a thickened sauce (Hall 31, [31v], 32)

leaven – yeast starter, added to dough to cause fermentation; to "lay
leaven" is to mix the leaven into the dough (Granville 10; Hall 12, 20)

ledoary – *see* zedoary

**lemon (leam, leamon, lemen, lemmen, lemmond, lemom, lemond,
lemun)** – lemons were imported to England primarily from Italy

and Spain in the seventeenth century and fulfilled many culinary uses; medicinally, John Gerard says that lemons helped "stinking breath," cured manginess, and improved the skin (1465) (passim)

Lent fig – *see* fig

lettuce (lettic, lettice, lletuce) – in receipt-book recipes, lettuce is both used in salads and cooked as a vegetable (Granville 16, 26, [122])

li – abbreviation of "libra," often used to mean "pound(s)" (passim)

licorice (licoris, licorish, licourich, liquorish, lycorich, lycorish) – root of the plant Glycyrrhiza, grown in England; used as a flavouring for gingerbread and other things; medicinally, used primarily to treat coughs (Granville 16, 49, 93, [163], [205]; Hall 14, 27, [37v], [39v], 61; Pudsey [6r], [16r], [21r], [27r])

lights – lungs (Hall 61)

lignum (lignam) – lignum aloes or aloeswood, a tree native to southeast Asia that develops an aromatic bark when infected with a type of mould; the aromatic bark is burnt as incense and used in perfumes (Granville [193]; Pudsey [6r])

lily of the valley (lilly of the valley) – a woodland plant with fragrant, white, bell-shaped flowers in springtime; used medicinally against palsy, gout, and various other ailments. John Gerard says that a glass of the flowers placed into an anthill for a month will result in a liquor particularly good for treating gout (411) (Granville 193, 306)

limbeck, etc. – *see* alembic

lime – calcium oxide, created by submitting limestone to a red-hot heat; used in mortars (Granville 111 (*cal*), 192)

line – in the Hall text's recipe "to make sasinges," this likely means loin (Hall [16v])

litharge (litharidge, lithridge, liturage, red lead) – lead monoxide, a natural mineral form of lead; used as a pigment (Granville 2, 17, 48, 59, [120]; Hall [3v], 12; Pudsey [19v], [36r], [37r], [45r])

litharge of gold – *see* gold

liverwort (liver-worte, liverworte) – term referring to diverse plants beneficial to the liver, including agrimony and a type of lichen (Granville 16, 17, 43, 48, 184, [205]; Pudsey [40r])

loaf sugar, loafe shugger, loafe suger – *see* sugar

long pepper (long pep) – pepper native to Indonesia, related to cubeb; commonly used in curries and pickles (Granville 41; Pudsey [3r])

Lucatellus's balsam (lugaillus balsam) – a turpentine-based remedy for bloody urine and for "spitting of blood" (Hall [42v])

Lucena – a town near Córdoba, Spain

lumber-pie (lumbard py) – a savoury pie made with meat or fish and eggs, hence Hall's note that it is for a second course (Hall 21)

lungwort (lungworte) – also known as cowslip of Jerusalem, a plant with hairy leaves, native to England; used to treat lung ailments (Granville 43; Pudsey [44r])

Lyon tooth – *see* dandelion

macaroon (macaroone, mackaroone) – a small sweet cake whose principal ingredients include sugar, egg whites, and ground almonds (Granville 49/50)

mace (large mace, mase) – an aromatic spice derived from the fleshy part surrounding the seed of the nutmeg tree; widely used in seventeenth-century cooking. Large mace is not listed in the *Oxford English Dictionary*, but it is specifically called for in recipes by Sir Kenelm Digby, Joseph Cooper, Thomas Dawson, and Granville and Hall manuscript contributors (passim; large mace: Granville 26, 40; Hall 8)

madder – a plant with a large root, native to Asia but growing in England; the root was widely used to make red dye. Medicinally, an infusion of the boiled root was taken as a cure for ulcers, wounds, and bruises (Pudsey [5r])

made dish – a dish composed of many ingredients; sometimes the dish is simply called "a made dish," in other cases a principal ingredient is given, such as "a made dish of rabbits," "a made dish of apples," "a made dish of artichokes," and so forth (Pudsey [2v])

magesterium of pearle – *see* pearl

maiden hair (maiden haire, white maiden hair) – a fern with a fine dark stem and leaves similar to those of rue; the "white" form is a lighter colour. Used medicinally to cure kidney stones as well as coughs, tuberculosis, and other lung diseases (Granville 16, 49, [205]; Pudsey [40r])

Malaga raisin, etc. – *see* raisin

Malaga sack, etc. – *see* sack

malmesy – a strong sweet wine from Greece, the Canaries, Madeira, and other Mediterranean regions (Granville 40, 41)

manchet (manchett, penny manchet) – fine white bread made from the best, whitest flour available. It was usually sold in small loaves; "penny" would indicate the price of one loaf (passim)

mangoe – a kind of pickle resembling those made of green mangos (often made with cucumbers) (Hall 51)

manna (mannah) – gum of a flowering ash tree native to southern Europe and southwest Asia; used medicinally as a laxative (Hall [24v])

manus Christi – a restorative confection or cordial drink, usually flavoured with rose water, violet water, or cinnamon (Granville 48; Pudsey [4v])

marigold (maregould, mariegold, marygold) – flower used both for its yellow colouring (for example, in the making of butter), as well as in salads; medicinally used to cure toothaches and eye inflammations (Granville 12, 41; Hall 17, 23, [39v]; Pudsey [1v], [16r], [22r], [39r], [56v])

marjoram (knot margoram, margerim, margerom, margerome, margerum, marjoram, murgerim) – an aromatic herb native to southern Europe. Knot marjoram is also known as sweet marjoram. Commonly used as a flavouring, and medicinally as a diuretic and to ease toothaches (passim)

marking pitch – *see* pitch

marshmallow (march mallowe, marsh mallo, marshmalloe, marsmallo, marsh mallow) – a flowering plant native to Africa; medicinally, the root was used to cure sore throats and to cure throat and stomach ulcers (Granville [163], [211], [239]; Hall [24v], 26, [60v]; Pudsey [16r], [29r])

maserene – *see* mazarine

mastic (masticke) – aromatic resin of a shrub native to the Mediterranean region; used medicinally to treat diverse ailments including indigestion and colds. John Gerard also refers to a herb called "masticke," which resembles marjoram and is used medicinally to cure cramps and convulsions (671) (Granville, 46, 92)

may weed (mayweed, may weede) – small, daisy-like plant native to England; often referred to as stinking chamomile (Granville 42; Hall 14; Pudsey [22r])

mazarine (maserene) – a deep plate pierced like a strainer and sometimes placed inside a serving dish (Hall 22v)

mead (meade, meath) – alcoholic drink made of fermented honey and water (Granville 13, 17; Pudsey 50, [50v], [59v], inside back cover)

meliot (melilot, mellelott, mellilet) – plant of the clover family, common in England. Used medicinally as a diuretic and in the making of plasters to reduce swelling (Granville 18; Hall 11; Pudsey [29r], [56v])

mell – to mix or blend (Hall [48v])

meth, methridate, etc. – *see* mithridate

Michaelmas – 29 September; generally, the beginning of autumn and the academic year (Granville 13; Hall 44)

mint (mine, mintce, minte) – a fragrant herb of which many varieties grow wild in England; John Gerard notes that it is "marvelous wholesome for the stomach" (681) (Granville 3, 10, 18; Hall 14, 17, [37v], [39v]; Pudsey [2v], [56v], [14r], [15v])

mirhe – *see* myrrh

mithridate (meth, methridate, metredate) – compound medicine of various ingredients, regarded as a cure-all, including curing poisoning (Granville 5, 41, 157, 211, 213, 306; Pudsey [3r], [3v])

mollin – *see* mullein

mother of time, etc. – *see* thyme

motherwort – diverse plants used to cure uterine disorders or aid in childbirth (Hall 14)

mugwort (mugworth) – *Artemisa vulgaris*, or common wormwood, a weedy plant with wide native distribution, including in Europe. Used to protect travellers from weariness and danger, and medicinally in a plaster to treat pain (Granville 41, 184; Pudsey [15v], [22r])

mulberry (mulberye) – the fruit of the black mulberry is consumed as food, while the white mulberry bush was often used to feed silkworms (Granville 11; Hall [26v]; Pudsey [65v])

mullein (mollin) – sage-like plants with grey woolly leaves, of the genus *Verbascum*; used medicinally as a remedy for sore throat, cough, and asthma (Hall [13v])

murgerim – *see* marjoram

mushroom (musarune, mushrone) – despite suspicions of their inedibility (John Gerard suggests that they are poisonous and cause choking [1584]), culinary recipes for mushrooms are not rare in seventeenth-century cookbooks (Granville 25, 152; Hall [29v]; Pudsey [53r], [55r])

musk (muske) – substance secreted by glands of animals such as the civet cat or the musk deer; used in both confectionary and perfumery, sometimes tied up in a little bag before use (Granville 12, 14, 37, 53, 88, 93, 95, [104] (*algalia*); [108], [160], [193], 236; Hall 4, 6, 19, [56v], 58; Pudsey [6r], [32r], [57r], [57v], [63v])

mustard (musterd) – John Gerard describes a "sauce" made of mustard and vinegar, which is the spreadable mustard we know today. Gerard notes that, besides its culinary uses, mustard was used medicinally to aid in digestion and stimulate the appetite, as well as in a number of plasters; he says that mustard plaster applied to a shaved head helps prevent the falling sickness (245) (Granville 1, 147, 214; Hall [42v], 51; Pudsey [6v], [53v])

myrrh (mirhe, mirrhe) – aromatic resin of a small thorny plant native to parts of Africa and the Middle East; John Gerard notes its use in medicines and plasters to treat various ailments, as well as in perfumery and in the preservation of dead bodies (916) (Granville 5, 59, [120], [158], [211])

Naples biscuit (Napell bisket, Naples biskett) – lady-finger cookies, or sometimes macaroons made with ground pine nuts rather than almonds (Granville 162; Hall 22, 23, 24)

neal – to bake or glaze (Hall 14)

neat – archaic term for ox or cow (Granville [183b]; Pudsey [35v])

nun's biscuit (nuns biskett) – macaroons; light cookies made with ground almonds (Granville 202)

nutritum – an ointment created of an emulsion of oil, vinegar, and a litharge (Pudsey [60r])

oak bark – John Gerard does not have much to say of the virtues of oak bark, except that it is dry and binding (1341) (Granville 164)

oiling (oyling) – many recipes call for rose or orange flower water to be added to almonds when they're pounded, "to keep the almonds from oiling." Adding water or flower water to almond oil works to create an emulsion so that one ends up with almond meal rather than almond butter/paste (and of course the flower water also flavours the meal). This emulsion has the advantage over almond butter that it stays fresh longer rather than going rancid. If a significant amount of water is added, one creates almond milk – which could be used during fish days in place of cow or goat milk (Granville 214; Hall [7v], [21v], 50)

oleum balsamiae – oleum is fuming sulphuric acid; while balsam is also defined above (an oily resin from plants), the precise meaning of oleum balsamiae is unknown (Granville 5)

olibanum – *see* frankincense

olive oil (oil ollife, oyle of olive) – besides its culinary use, olive oil was used, according to John Gerard, for its digestive properties, as well as outwardly to cure joint pain and swelling (1394) (passim)

onion – both white and green onions are called for in seventeenth-century household manuscripts but are not usually specified; besides onions' obvious culinary uses, John Gerard suggests that applying onion juice to a bald head in the sun will bring back hair "very speedily" (171) (passim)

opopanax – resinous gum from the woundwort plant, native to Syria; John Gerard suggests that woundwort cured snake bites and the biting by a mad dog, while mashed leaves of the plant acted as a salve to cure wounds and bone punctures (1004) (Granville 59)

orange (cheny orrieng, Cevill orange, Civill orrenge, oraing, orang, oring, oringe, oronge, orreng, orrieng, orring, orringo, Seville

orange, sivell orring) – as noted by these terms, oranges in England originated in Spain and China (via Portugal). They were served whole or used as a flavouring; John Gerard also notes that a cordial of a dozen oranges boiled with water and mercury sublimate was useful in curing itchiness and mange (1465) (passim)

orris powder (aris root, arras powder, florence orris-root) – powder made from the root of the blue iris; used to scent confections, syrups, and perfumes (Granville 5, [233]; Hall [12v], 32)

orza – tall, glazed, earthenware vessel (Spanish) (Granville 104)

oxymel of squills (oxcemelle quills) – oxymel is a medicinal syrup made with vinegar and honey; squills are the bulbs or roots of the sea onion (Hall 61)

palsy (palsie) – any weakness in the body, sometimes accompanied by tremors (passim)

pap (pape, Spanish pap) – anything of a soft or semi-liquid consistency, often made from bread moistened with water or milk (Granville 165, 196; Hall [7v], 35, [38v], [54v]; Pudsey [12r])

paper – used extensively in baking, sometimes tied onto hoops with string; as paper was relatively scarce in the seventeenth century, pages from manuscripts were sometimes used

Paracelsus plaster (Paracelsus plaister) – it seems that this name was given to plasters containing galbanum and frankincense; Paracelsus believed that mineral substances worked as agents to help the body produce its own healing medicine (Granville 59)

parboil – in the seventeenth century, this term meant both to boil thoroughly and to partly boil, although the former was the original (and, it seems, more common) meaning (Granville 18, 25)

pare – *see* pear

parradice – *see* grain of paradise

parsley (parcly, persle, persly, perssly) – herb used to season dishes, and medicinally as a digestive and diuretic (passim)

pattypan (patipan, patty-pan) – a small baking tin or dish (Granville 214; Hall [21v]; Pudsey [48r])

pear (pare) – a common fruit in seventeenth-century England; the fruit was sometimes made into perry (pear cider), which John Gerard states is good for digestion (1459) (passim)

pearl (corral pearl, magisterium of pearl, pearl of corral, powder of corralls) – obviously, the hard secretion of the oyster; John Gerard describes corrals next to sponges and mosses in his work (1575). "Magisterium" is an alchemical term denoting a pure substance (Granville 5, 43, 48, 88 193, [213])

peel (peal) – a long-handled wooden paddle used in baking bread to transfer the loaf to and from the oven (Granville [180])

peel (peell, pill) – the rind of citrus; used frequently in seventeenth-century cooking, just as it is used today (passim)

pellitory of the wall (pelletory of the wale, pelitory of the wall, pellitory of spaine) – a small plant generally growing on damp rock walls; brewed into a tea as a diuretic and to cure diverse ailments, including coughs and kidney stones (Granville 10, 13, 37, 60; Pudsey [14r], [16r])

penny loaf (peny loafe, peny lofe) – a loaf of bread that cost a penny. Penny loaves and biscuits were often grated into sauces, pastes, and puddings to thicken them (passim)

pennyroyal (peneriall, pennyroyall) – a mint-like plant common in England; John Gerard says that it was used to cure various ailments and to aid in expulsion of the afterbirth, while a garland of pennyroyal worn around the head cured giddiness (672) (Granville 43, [305]; Pudsey [1v], [2v])

pennyworth – as much of an item as could be bought or sold for a penny (passim)

peony (pyonye) – a large fragrant flower. The seed was used in culinary recipes, while the whole plant was believed to contain various medical properties; Gerard notes that the roots were hung around infants' necks to ward off maladies (984) (Pudsey [16r])

permacitty – *see* spermaceti

persly, etc. – *see* parsley

philopendelay – *see* filipendula

picadillo – a dish of minced meat and vegetables (Spanish) (Granville 110)

pike (pick) – a freshwater fish common in England; this fish appears in many seventeenth-century recipes (Hall 28; Pudsey [8r])

pill – *see* peel

pimpernel (pimpernell, pimponell, pympernell) – a chickweed common in England; used to cure diverse ailments, from toothache to tuberculosis (Granville 41, [156]; Hall 14; Pudsey [15v], [22r], [42v])

pink – *see* gillyflower

pipkin (pipke) – a small, round, usually unglazed earthenware pot (passim)

pippin (pepin, pipin, piping, pipinn) – a sweet apple; several varieties exist (passim)

pitch (black pitch, marking pitch, stone pitch) – dark, sticky substance that is a residue of the distillation of wood tar or turpentine, used principally for sealing ship hulls; stone pitch is

the solid form. Also used medicinally to reduce swelling. *See also*
Burgundy pitch (Granville 5, 153, [180]; Hall 12; Pudsey [37r])

plague – the bubonic plague, most likely caused by a bacterium
carried in the gut of a flea. The plague decimated Europe's
population in the fourteenth century and recurred until at least the
late seventeenth century. Curatives for it were common in receipt
books (Granville 41, 184; Hall 14; Pudsey [16r])

plaice – a common European flat fish (Hall 28)

plantain (plantan, plantane, plantine, planton) – any of several
varieties of banana; John Gerard says it is called the Adam's Apple
in seventeenth-century England (1515) (Granville 4, 166b, [205]; Hall
[24v], [26v]; Pudsey [4v], [21r], [22r], [38r], [39r])

polypodium (polipodium, polipodyum) – fern common to England;
its roots were used medicinally in purges (Granville 238; Pudsey
[21r], [40r])

pomatum (pumatum) – an ointment (Hall [28v])

poppy (popey, poppe, poppie, popy) – the seeds were used in
culinary recipes, and medicinally both the seeds and leaves were
used to induce sleep (Granville 14; Hall 17, 18, 27, [37v])

porringer – a small wood, metal, or earthenware bowl, used for eating
out of (passim)

posnet (possnet) – a small metal vessel with a handle and three feet,
used for boiling (Hall 33; Pudsey [18r], [57v])

possett (possit, possite) – a hot drink of milk curdled with wine or
lemon juice (Granville 46, 47, 60; Hall 20, 25, 26, 30; Pudsey [6v], [19r])

pot – "One of the new techniques of the sixteenth century, potting
worked on the principle of smothering the food to be preserved
totally in melted fat, usually butter, lard, or mutton fat, in order to
exclude the air, in a pot or cask, which was then sealed tightly. This
apparently worked sufficiently frequently to merit wide application
even for use on shipboard in hot climates, as described by Boyle in
1663. Sir Hugh Plat described the process as practiced about 1600 or
earlier" (Stead 86) (Granville [144], [237]; Hall 32, [41v], [51v], [52v])

pottle – a container holding approximately one gallon (passim)

poultice (poultesse, poultis) – a paste applied to the body, usually by
means of a bandage or dressing, to encourage healing and relieve
swelling (passim)

powder of corralls – *see* pearl

powder of the pomye stone – *see* pumice

prune (damiusk pruan, pruent, prunello, pruan) – John Gerard
notes that prunes are more wholesome and nourishing than fresh

plums, and that they are often used for "loosening" the belly (1498)
(Granville 183, [183b],184; Hall [24v], 26; Pudsey [1r], [2r], [3r])

puffed pastry (puffe past, puff paist, puff past, pufft paste, pufpast, pust past) – puffed pastry usually consists of numerous layers spread with butter. John Considine comments on the Hall [15v] recipe for apples baked in puffed pastry: "Recipes for apples cooked in pastry do not seem very common in printed books, I suppose because considered too banal; but the colouring raises this one above banality, perhaps" (personal communication) (Hall 7, [15v], 24, [29v], [30v], 31, [31v], [48v], [59v], 60; Pudsey [64r], [126r], [163r])

pugillum (pugill) – a small handful; *see* weights and measures (Granville 159)

pumatum – *see* pomatum

pumice (pomye stone) – volcanic rock, used as a mild abrasive in toothpastes and detergents and on the skin (Granville 88)

pust past – *see* puffed pastry

pyonye – *see* peony

quartan ague – a fever that returns every fourth day (with inclusive counting); one example is malaria (Granville 92)

quarter – in measurements of length, a quarter is nine inches

queen's cake – a small pound cake made with rose water or orange water, often with currants (Granville 185)

ragout (reggou, regoue) – a stew of meat, vegetables, and spices (Pudsey [49r], [53r])

raisin (Malaga raisin, Malago raison, Malago reason, Malego rason, Maligo raison, raisin of the sun, raison, raison of the sun, raisson, reasen, reason of the son, reisin of the sunne, reson, rayson) – this dried fruit was used widely in culinary recipes in the seventeenth century, and medicinally for its purging quality (passim)

rasher (rase, raser) – thinly shaved slice (Pudsey [16v], [50v])

raspberry (rasbery, rasberry, rasburye, raspase, rassbery) – this berry was used in culinary recipes and medicinally for a weak stomach and for curing sores in the mouth (passim)

rear (reare) – slightly undercooked (similar to rare); originally, it referred only to eggs (Pudsey [4v])

red cloth (red cloath, scarlett cloth) – red cloth and red thread have been used in sympathetic magic as cures and as protection from harm since at least the Middle Ages; the practice continues in some places to present times. The cloth or thread is tied around or placed next to a wound or vulnerable part of the body (Granville 7; Hall [24v], [26]; Pudsey [61r])

red cow (red cowe) – most likely the Suffolk dun breed of dairy cow, which is now extinct, although it contributed to the modern red poll breed (Dohner par. 2) (Granville 16, 43, 184; Pudsey [16v])

red lead – *see* litharge

red sage – a plant native to China and Japan used in Renaissance England in diverse remedies for aches and inflammations. John Gerard advises that applying a linen cloth filled with red sage leaves, ashes sprinkled with vinegar, and hot coals to "a grieuous stitch" will alleviate it, and the same concoction, presumably placed against the chest, works for pleurisy (766) (Granville [166b], 306; Hall [24v], [26]; Pudsey [37v], [61r])

resin (rosen, rosin, rossel, rossing, rossin) – aromatic substance secreted by various types of tree (passim); rossel in particular is the residue from the distillation of turpentine (Hall [3v])

rew, etc. – *see* rue

Rhenish wine (Renish wine, Rennesh wine) – wine from the Rhine region of Germany (Granville 8, [122], 216; Pudsey [4r], [48r])

rhubarb (rubarb, rubarbe) – wide-leafed plant native to China, used in culinary recipes; medicinally, John Gerard suggests that it is a bit of a cure-all and purges "naughty and corrupt humours" (396) (Granville 8, 16, [203], 238)

ringoe – *see* eryngo

rock allom, etc. – *see* allum

rolls (rowles) – balls or lozenges that can be kept for later use; many recipes call for a mixture to be "made up into rolls" (passim)

Roman vitriol (Roman vitirall) – *see* copperas

Romane wormewood – *see* wormwood

rosa solis (rosasoles, rosa-solis, rosasolis, rosa sollis, sun dew) – herb sundew; often made into a liquor. Also used medicinally to cure blisters and other diverse ailments; John Gerard says that it also works as an aphrodisiac for female cattle (1557) (Granville 184; Hall 14, [24v], 26; Pudsey [15v])

rose campion (rose campon) – a flower of the carnation family, native to England; John Gerard claims that this plant cures scorpion bites (468) (Hall [13v])

rosemary (rosemarie, rose mary, rose=mary, rosmerey, rusmary) – aromatic herb used widely in culinary recipes and medicinally for diverse cures, including to make the breath sweet and to improve the memory (passim)

rose-still (rose still) – a still used specifically for creating rose water (Granville 194; Pudsey [56v] "rose, still")

rose water (Damask rose water, Damascke rose water) – distillation made from a varietal of rose apparently brought from Damascus (passim; many references, especially in Hall)

rossel – *see* resin

rue (hearbegrace, hearbagrase, herb of grace, herbgrass reu, rew) – dwarfish shrub, native to Europe; used widely in medical remedies to cure diverse ailments, including earache (passim)

running of the reines – gonorrhea (Pudsey [18v])

sack (Canary sack, Mallego sack, sacke, sak, sake) – white wine formerly imported from Spain (including the Canary Islands and Malaga) (passim)

saffron (safforn, saforn, safron, sifforne) – stigma of the crocus flower, which was grown in England in Saffron-Walden and other places; John Gerard says that, when consumed in moderation, this spice makes one lively, quick, and merry (152). Saffron's popularity was largely due to the golden hue it lent food; in *The Appetite and the Eye*, C. Anne Wilson notes the value medieval European cooks placed on food's colour was an influence of Arabic cooking (18). The colour gold in particular was highly esteemed, owing to the belief that it offered longevity – as reflected in Gerard's note (Granville [203]; Hall 4, 19, [33v]; Pudsey [2r], [3r], [16r], [44r], [58v])

St John's wort (hypericon, hipericon, hypericum) – a plant of the *Hypericum* family, used medicinally to counter depression, heal wounds, and cure hip aches (Granville 5, 6)

sallandine, etc. – *see* celandine

salsar – unknown; perhaps this is a variant of salsify, although this edible root (while native to England) does not often occur in seventeenth-century recipes (Pudsey [6r])

salt – according to C. Anne Wilson, salt was harvested from seawater in England since 600 BC (*Food and Drink* 19); bay salt was imported to England from Spain, France, and Portugal since medieval times (*Waste Not* 20)

saltpetre (peter salt, salt peeler, salt peeter, salt peter, salt petra) – potassium nitrate, formerly derived from the interaction of decomposing animal feces and a nitrogen-rich source like lime; used in meat preservation and medicinally to cure sore throats and arthritis (Granville [144], 208, [209]; Hall [52v]; Pudsey [51v], [52r], [52v])

salt upon salt – the *Oxford English Dictionary* quotes W. Brownrigg's 1748 *The Art of Making Common Salt*, noting that this means "bay salt dissolved in sea water, or any other salt water, and with it boiled into white salt" (Hall [52v])

samphire (samper, sampire) – aromatic plant with fleshy leaves that grows on rocks near the sea; used in pickles (Granville 7, 26)

sanders (red sanders, yellow sanders) – red sandalwood, a tree native to India; its bark was used in dying cloth, in cosmetics, and medicinally as an astringent (Granville 5–6, 11, [193]; Hall 43; Pudsey [18r], [18v], [52v])

sarcenet – a very fine, soft silk, used for searcing – its occasional spelling as searce-net indicates the etymology of the term (Granville 193)

sassafras (sasafras, saxe fridge) – bark of a tree of the laurel family, native to Florida; the root was consumed in a tea to cure agues and fevers, and to help women conceive (Granville 238; Pudsey [16r])

savory (saverry, savery) – low-growing herb commonly used to flavour food (passim)

scabious – plant with lavender-coloured flowers, also known as pincushion poppy; used medicinally to cure coughs and to heal skin sores (Granville 306; Hall 14; Pudsey [15v], [21r], [22r])

scarlet cloth (scarlett cloth) – *see* red cloth

scem – *see* scum

scerckt – *see* searce

schvrch – *see* searce

***Scirpus lacustris* (sriprius?)** – an English freshwater sedge from the Cyperaceae family, also commonly called the English bulrush; the updated scientific name is *Schoenoplectus lacustris*. Used in weaving of chair seats and baskets and occasionally thatching; the baskets, or bags, could serve as sieves (Pudsey [23r]?); see also cyprus

scock colops – *see* collop

scordium – water germander. As John Gerard writes, this plant "draweth out of the chest thick flegme and rotten matter" (661); it was also used to cure poisonous snake bites (Granville 184; Hall 14; Pudsey [16r])

scorzonera (scorcernero) – black salsify, a parsnip-like root vegetable; used medicinally to cure consumption, and sometimes as a cure for bites by venomous snakes (Hall [60v])

scotch collups, etc. – *see* collop

scour (skowre) – to rub clean (Granville 15)

scuchineale – *see* cochineal

scum (cume, scem, scume) – to skim off impurities floating in or on a liquid (passim)

scurvy-grass (scurbuerygrase, scurbugrase, scurvie grass) – *Cochlearia officinalis*, a plant often eaten by sailors to avoid scurvy, as the plant possesses high levels of vitamin C (Granville 43; Pudsey [8v])

scuttle-bone (scutlebone, skutell bone) – the cartilaginous pen of a cuttlefish, which is an invertebrate similar to a small squid (Granville 96, 101)

sear-cloth (searcloth, searecloath) – a bandage coated in salve, used as a winding sheet or a medicinal plaster (Granville 2; Pudsey [19r], [33v])

searce (scarce, scearce, scerck, shvrch, search, seirce, serce) – to sift or strain, or the cloth used for doing the same (passim)

senna (sein, sena, sene, senea, senet, seney, senna of Alixandria) – a tropical shrub; its leaves were used in pickling, and medicinally the plant was used as a purge (Granville 8, 238; Pudsey [3r], [6r], [21r], [40r], [45v], [58r])

sentry – *see* centaury

Seville orange – *see* orange

shallot (sallot, sallott, shelot, shelott, sherlot, sollot) – a bulb whose flavour seems to have been valued over that of onions, as evident in Pudsey [61r]: "if you have shelott it is much better to putt in then onion" (Granville [189]; Hall 8, 16, [27v], 28, [34v], [47v]; Pudsey [53v], [61r])

share-bone (share bone) – pubis bone (Granville 60)

shewit – *see* suet

shord – *see* shread

shred (shord, shread, sread, sred, sreed) – to slice (passim)

Shrewsbury cake (shrewsberry cake) – a biscuit-type cake made with rose water and nutmeg or cloves (Granville 202; Pudsey [65r])

shrub (shrubb) – a drink made with either orange or lemon juice, sugar, and rum (Granville 155, 190)

shusk – presumably a variant of husk, or shuck; that is, to remove the dry or hard outer covering, or the skin, of certain fruits and nuts (Pudsey [10r])

sibber – *see* simmer

sictren – *see* citron

sieve (cive, sceiue, scive, seeue, sefe, seive, seue, sieff, sieue, siffe, siue, sive) – seventeenth-century recipes and remedies widely call for ingredients to be strained or sifted (*see also* searce). Often cloth such as tiffany or sarcenet was used, as was finely woven hair (likely horsehair); one recipe in the Pudsey manuscript might also call for an English bulrush sieve (see *Scirpus lacustris*) (Granville 49, 160, 167, 192; Hall [17v], [18v], [21v], 22, [33v], [45v], [59v]; Pudsey [19v], [23r], [31r], [49v], [51r], [54v])

silleybub – *see* syllabub

simmer (sibber, simber, simper, smiper, symber) – to sustain heating just below the boiling point (passim)

sinamond, etc. – *see* cinnamon

sincfield – *see* cinquefoil

sippet (sippett, sippit) – a thin slice of toasted bread, used to garnish a dish and for dipping/sopping (Hall [9v], [10v], [14v], [35v], [43v])

sitterne – *see* citron

skowre – *see* scour

skrin – screen; i.e., the flat part of the fan, often made of kid goatskin (Granville 109)

skutell bone – *see* scuttle-bone

slaked (slack'd) – combined with water (Granville 192)

slit (sleted) – it seems that nutmeg was sometimes added whole to a recipe rather than grated in; in such cases, it was slit (or sliced, as called for in some recipes) to release greater flavour, just as other spices such as mace were bruised (passim)

small beer (small-beere) – weak beer, often served to children (Granville 153, [203])

smallage (slam ledg, smallidge) – plant similar to wild celery or parsley; used medicinally to cleanse the body or to cure persistent colds (Granville 5, 16; Pudsey [14v])

smaragd (smarage) – now-rare term for a precious green stone; an emerald (Granville [193])

smiper – *see* simmer

snail (snal, sneale) – this gastropod appears surprisingly often in seventeenth-century household manuscripts, considering that a taste for it did not endure in England (Granville 3, 15, 16, 184, 194; Pudsey [15r], [44r])

snakeweed (Virginia snake weed, Virginian snake weed) – name given to an American hemlock plant whose roots supposedly cured rattlesnake and other poisonous snake bites (Granville 213; Hall 14)

snow – meringue; egg whites beaten to stiff peaks (Hall 10, [16v], 59)

soil, soyle, etc. – *see* dung

sol de membrilla – An expression (Spanish): *membrillo* is a quince. "Quince sun" is the time of year in which *membrillo* ripens in southern Spain, where the Granvilles lived (it does not ripen until early fall in northern Spain)

sollot – *see* shallot

sorrel (serrill, sorrell) – a small, edible, perennial plant; also sometimes referred to as dock (Granville 305; Hall [15v]; Pudsey [2v], [21r], [22r])

southernwood (southenwood, southernewood, southern wood) – *Artemisia*, a hardy southern European shrub, used medicinally as a diuretic, to cure one of worms, and to reduce swelling when mixed in a plaster with barrow's grease (Granville 3, [205]; Hall 25)

Spanish bole – *see* bole armoniac

Spanish soap – *see* Castile soap

speedwell – *see* brook lime

spermaceti (permacitty, spermesity, spirmacite) – waxy substance derived from the head of sperm whales; used in candle-making and medicinally in ointments (Granville 153, [305]; Hall [3v])

spikenard (spike) – plant native to China, India, and Nepal, whose rhizomes contain an aromatic substance used in perfumery and as a sedative (Granville 5, 16, [193]; Pudsey [29r], [29v])

spinach (spinage, spinnag, spinnage, spin nage, spinnige) – John Gerard was clearly not much of a fan of this leafy plant: he says that it yields little nourishment, is windy, and "easily causeth a desire to vomit" (330) (passim)

spurrey – a sprawling herb native to England; sometimes added to wine, as John Gerard says, "to make men merry" (1126) (Granville 44)

squench (squnch) – to quell or stifle; in the Pudsey contributor's recipe, she clearly means to cool the stones (Pudsey [38r])

squinacy (squinancy) – tonsillitis (Granville 11)

sread, sred, sreed – *see* shread

sriprius – *see* cyprus and *Scirpus lacustris*

starch (Holland starch, stone blew starch, storch) – flour-derived substance used for stiffening cotton and linen cloth. "Stone blue" was indigo mixed with starch, added to counter the yellowing of white cloth. "Holland" refers to special linen made in the Netherlands (Hall [27v], [39v])

stave – while this can mean a thin, narrow shape (such as the planks of wood that are hooped to form a cask or barrel), the reference in the Hall text might instead mean to dry the cakes on top of a stove (Hall [32v])

stean (steen) – a clay pot with two handles (Granville 167)

stechados (sticcadus) – obsolete term for French lavender (Pudsey [6r])

steel (steele) – iron alloy sometimes used in the form of filings to help cure chlorosis (*see* green sickness, above) (Granville 8, 159, [211]); *see also* still

sticcadus – *see* stechados

still (steel, steele) – apparatus for distillation, consisting of a closed vessel (*see* alembic) in which the substance to be distilled is heated and tubes that collect the condensation of the vapour produced (passim)

stitch (stich) – a puncture wound or cramp (Pudsey [16v], [30r])

stive – to boil slowly or stew (Hall 50, 51)

stone pitch – *see* pitch

stones (e.g., lambs stones) – testicles (Hall 28, [29v], 33)

storax (gum storax, gume storax) – aromatic gum resin of the *Liquidambar orientalis* or Turkish sweetgum tree, native to the Mediterranean region; used in perfumery and incense and medicinally to cure colds (Granville 5/6, 106 (*ostoraxe*), [233]; Pudsey [30r])

storch – *see* starch

stove – as a verb, this meant to subject a food to a hot-air bath; the Hall contributor includes this optional step in her recipe to candy angelica (Hall [8v])

strain (s[t]rain, straine, streyne) – while the *Oxford English Dictionary* relates this term in its culinary use to filtering solids from liquids, the term was occasionally used in Renaissance recipes to refer to dry ingredients, as in to sift (passim)

straw – a test for softness (of walnuts or fruit) was whether a straw could pass through (Granville 39; Pudsey [11v])

strawberry (strabry, strabury) – John Gerard says that this berry quenches thirst, takes away redness in the face, and makes the heart merry, while the leaves strengthen the gums and "fasten" the teeth in the mouth (998) (Hall [30v]; Pudsey [2r], [6r] [21r], [31v])

streyne – *see* strain

strick – fast-running (e.g., water) (Pudsey [8v])

succory, sucory, suckrey, suckry – *see* chicory

sucket (suckitt) – food preserved in sugar, either in candied (dry) or syrup (wet) form (Hall 19)

suet (shewit, suehtt, suett, suette, suit) – solid fat from around the kidneys and loins of sheep, oxen, and other animals; used as a fat in cooking (passim; especially common in Pudsey)

sugar (shuggar, shugger, suger, sugger) – John Gerard says that sugar from the sugarcane plant cleanses the stomach and makes the throat clear (38). The more refined the sugar, the whiter and more expensive it was. As of 1650, great amounts of sugar were imported

into England from the colonies and increasingly replaced honey.
One reason for sugar's popularity might have been its preserving
qualities (Hunter 136) (passim)
   loaf sugar (loafe shugger, loafe suger) – sugar sold in hard, conical
loaves and cut then pounded in a mortar for use
   powder sugar (poulder sugar) – sugar sold in a loose form rather
than a loaf
   refined sugar – a common sugar, refined only in its country of origin and often a pale-yellow colour
   double-refined sugar – sugar refined both in its country of origin
and then again in England; this type of sugar was very white
   triple-refined sugar – sugar refined three times and sometimes
called "royal sugar"; this sugar was even whiter than double-
refined sugar (not called for in any of the recipes in the Granville,
Hall, or Pudsey manuscripts)
   sugar candy – refined sugar clarified and crystallized by slow
evaporation
sulphur – *see* brimstone
sulphur vivum – naturally occurring sulphur (Granville 47, 48)
sun dew – *see* rosa solis
sunflower (turnsole) – seeds of this large flower were not commonly
used in the seventeenth century; the term "turnsole" comes from
the French *tournesol*, which literally means to turn toward the sun
(Hall [15v])
surfeit water (surfett water, surfiet water) – any medicinal water
given as a cure for excessive indulgence (passim)
sweetmeat – sweet food, such as cakes, candied fruits, sugared nuts,
etc. (passim)
syllabub (silleybub) – a drink or dish made of milk or cream curdled
by wine and often sweetened and flavoured (Pudsey [24r])
syrupus augustanus – a syrup of rhubarb, as indicated by Nicholas
Culpeper's 1649 *A Physicall Directory*; the recipe also calls for
various flowers and spices, but no indication of purpose is given
(Granville 8)
tamarisk (tamariske) – an evergreen shrub native to China and
the Mediterranean region; its bark and leaves were used as an
astringent (Granville 16, 17)
tanhouse – this term usually refers to the building in which tanning
(for example of leather) occurred. The reference in the Pudsey
manuscript indicates the tannin solution itself, which in England in
this period was usually ground bark in water (Pudsey [5r])

tankard – a tall mug, often made of silver or pewter (Granville 98–9)
tansy (tansey, tansie) – a tall herb with yellow, button-like flowers and bitter-tasting leaves; used medicinally as a diuretic and to cure gout, worms, and the "shrinking of the sinews" (Gerard 651) (Granville 47; Hall 22–[22v]); also a pudding or an omelet flavoured with tansy leaves and sprinkled with sugar (Hall 22, [50v]; Pudsey [2v], [3r], [38v])
tapis calliminaris – *see* lapis calaminaris
tartar (creame a tartar, oyle of tartar) – saturated solution of potassium carbonate, usually derived from grape juice residue that forms a crust on the inside walls of wine casks (Granville 17; Pudsey [21v])
temper – to bring something to the proper state or condition (Granville 13, [108]; Hall 47; Pudsey [1v])
tent – to search, cleanse, and/or keep a wound open with a soft, medicated bandage (Granville 3)
tetter (tetterworme) – skin eruption such as herpes, ringworm, or eczema (Granville 48; Pudsey [20r])
thyme (mother of time, mother time, thime, time) – aromatic edible herb native to England; John Gerard describes it as a cure for various ailments, including poisonous snake bites, the vomiting of blood, the "wambling and gripings of the bellie," and "Lethargie, frensie, and madnesse" (572) (passim)
tiffany (taffany, tifaney, tiffainey, tiffany, tiffany, tiffiny, tifiny) – while this cloth is commonly known as a thin silk, the term was also formerly used to refer to gauze or muslin lawn (a type of linen). It is likely this latter cloth that was used for straining, although another reference in these manuscripts to the use of sarcenet for searcing means that tiffany silk might also have been used (Granville 52, 142; Hall 18, 36, [44v], [54v], [55v], [56v], 58; Pudsey [57r])
tinaja **(tinaxa)** – large earthenware jug, sometimes glazed, with a middle that is wider than its base or mouth; it usually sits on the ground and is used primarily for holding water or oil (Spanish) (Granville 104)
toddy arrack (toddy arack) – liquor made from the fermented sap of the coconut palm (Granville 155)
ton, tonne – *see* tun
tormentil (tormentell, tormentile, tormentill, tourmentell, turmindall, turmentill) – low, herbaceous, edible plant of the rose family; often used in dyeing and tanning. John Gerard also notes that it preserves the body in time of pestilence and cures it of choler and melancholy (993) (Granville 41, [156], 212, 184, 306; Hall 14; Pudsey [16r])

towce – unknown. Evidently a type of fish (Hall 28)

tragon – *see* tarragon

treacle (treagle) – a compound salve with a honey base, usually applied as an antidote to poisonous bites. London, Venice, or other names of origin were often included in the remedy's name; it was also sometimes called *theriac* (a term used generally to signify a healing concoction) and was used interchangeably with "mithridate" (Granville 41, 306)

tread (cocks tread) – speck on the yolk of a fertilized egg; usually removed by straining (Granville 46, 53; Hall [30v])

trencher – a slice of bread (usually dry) used as a plate in the medieval and Renaissance periods (Hall 38; Pudsey [63v])

trendle (trind) – round vessel used in baking (Hall 19)

tun (ton, tonne) – to put into casks or barrels; this is the last step in many drink recipes (passim)

turmentill – *see* tormentil

turnsole – *see* sunflower

turpentine (turpityne, uenes turpintine, Venice turpentine, Venice Terpentine, venise turpentine) – semifluid resin of various coniferous trees (Granville 5–6, 11, 46–7, 59, 92, [120], [211], 236, 239; Pudsey [6r], [15v], [18r], [30r])

tutty (lapistuticia, tutia, tuttye) – a crude zinc oxide, used as an astringent in ointments, as well as a polishing agent (Granville 96, 101; Pudsey [13r], [13v], [38r])

unguentum (allum vnguentum, vnguentum, vnguentum populeum, vngentum Rosatum) – "unguentum" means a salve or ointment, usually perfumed; qualifying words describe a key ingredient in the salve (Pudsey [60r])

urine (watter) – human and animal urine were sometimes used medicinally, as well as for cleaning everything from laundry to one's teeth. Bartholomœus Anglicus wrote in the thirteenth century that urine's drying property makes it useful for cleaning wounds, and that, given in drink, it helps splenetics (Pudsey [4r])

valerian (velerion) – a genus of plants used medicinally as stimulants. John Gerard says that the root was the base for wine and for a diuretic drink and the pounded leaves and flowers were applied to venomous bites – and that even holding the plant prevented hurt by any venomous beast (679) (Pudsey [37v])

vanilla (*bynilla*, *vynilla*) – aromatic pod and seeds from the vanilla plant, native to Mexico and other parts of Central America, as well as Madagascar; this was evidently more common in Spanish than English recipes (Granville 95, 121)

veal glue (veal glew) – brownish gelatin obtained by boiling calves' hooves (Granville 240)

verbena (vervain) – edible aromatic herb used medicinally to ease headaches and inflammations (Granville 306)

verjuice (verges, vergis, verjus) – sour juice from unripe apples or grapes (passim)

vinegar – a common imported ingredient in sixteenth- and seventeenth-century English recipes and remedies; most often, it was made from white wine (passim)

violet (vialet, violete, violett) – small, early-blooming flowers; many species are native to England. The flowers were often sugared; John Gerard says that the flowers were also used medicinally to ease inflammations and fevers and to purge choler. He notes that simply looking upon flowers such as violets causes one to become virtuous: "floures through their beautie, variety of colour, and exquisite forme, do bring to a liberall and gentle manly minde, the remembrance of honestie, comelinesse, and all kindes of vertues" (850) (Granville 54, [205], 206; Hall 23, 27, [39v], 63; Pudsey [2r], [6r], [6v], [9r], [9v], [16r], [20r], [21r], [30r])

Virginia snake weed, etc. – *see* snakeweed

virtue (vertu, verty) – in the context of plants, the *Oxford English Dictionary* notes that this word means "efficacy arising from physical qualities; esp. power to affect the human body in a beneficial manner; strengthening, sustaining, or healing properties" (passim)

vitriol – *see* copperas

vnckle – *see* knuckle

wallflower – small yellow violet, used medicinally to cure cankers and ulcers (Granville 12)

walm (walme) – a boiling of water, or a spell of boiling (length of this time is unknown) (Hall 62; Pudsey [12r])

walnut (wallnuet, wallnut) – white walnuts were young ones that were peeled and then pickled in vinegar or preserved in sugar; black walnuts were the fully mature ones, often eaten fresh. John Gerard says that walnuts are good for curing the biting by a mad dog, and the oil was used to smooth the skin (1441) (Granville 39, 60, 147, 204; Hall 39, [49v], 61; Pudsey [12v], [18v], [53v])

water cress (water creasis, watercrese, water cresset) – leafy edible plant; used medicinally to cure or prevent scurvy and as a source of iron for young women (Granville 43, 48, [122])

wave wind – *see* bind wheat

weights and measures – separate weights and measures existed for dry items, wet items, and ale; a useful guide is Stuart Peachey's *Measures and Dates 1580–1660*. Besides the official weights and measures listed below, many unofficial forms were also used; a recipe in the Granville manuscript calls for three thimbles of mace in a seed cake recipe, while recipes in the Hall manuscript call for apricots about the size of pigeons' eggs and a "convenient" amount of butter, and a syrup to cure a violent cough suggests that a grown person can take "as much as a walnut," while a child should take "as much as a nutmeg." A few recipes in the Granville manuscript call for brine that is salty enough "that it will bear [up] an egg," while a "Receipt to make meath" calls for the following: "Take to six gallons of water, six quarts of honey, or as much honey as will make it strong enough to beare an egge the breadth of three pence above water" (passim)

Dry measures in order of increase:
scruple – approximately 20 barley grains
drachma – three scruples
peck (pecke) – a quarter of a bushel; equivalent to two gallons
bushel (bushell) – four pecks
coumb – four bushels
quarter – two coumbs
pugillum (pugill) – small handful
pennyweight – a unit of weight equal to 24 grains (and formerly 22.5 grains, which was the weight of a silver penny)

Liquid measures in order of increase:
pint – basic measure of liquid; 568 millilitres
quart – two pints
pottel (pottell) – two quarts (wet)
gallon – two pottels

Westphalia ham (Westfalio ham) – an esteemed, dry-cured, beechwood- and juniper-smoked ham made from acorn-fed pigs in the German region of Westphalia. Jennifer Stead says that this ham was originally made from bear or bear cub (76) (Hall [52v])

white lead – *See* lead

white-pot (whitepot) – trifle-like pudding, usually made with bread, butter, cream, and flavouring (Hall [9v])

wigg – a small, usually sweetened, bun (Granville [154])

winter cherry – the small, round fruit of a plant of the nightshade family that is ripe in winter; also known as the cape gooseberry

or ground cherry; used medicinally as a diuretic and to dissolve
bladder stones (Granville 16)

wood betony – *see* betony

woodbine (wood bind, wood bine) – name given to various climbing
plants, including honeysuckle; used medicinally as a cure for
diverse ailments, including a sore throat (Granville 4, [166b])

wood rose (woodrose) – a wild rose; used medicinally to cure the
biting by a mad dog (Granville 44)

wood-sorrel (wood sorrell, woodsorrell) – common name of *Oxalis
acetosella*, a small woodland plant with white flowers (Granville 41,
48; Hall 14)

Woodstreet cake – Woodstreet is an area of London that was once
known for its manufacture of excellent cakes, including wedding
cakes. Sir Thomas Browne notes that he ate them for dinner, and
Samuel Pepys writes in his diary that His Highness loved them
(Wheatley and Cunningham 529) (Hall 20)

wormseed (worm-seed) – name given to diverse plants, including
Artemisia species and certain types of fennel, believed to cure one of
worms (Granville 203; Hall 25)

wormwood (Romane wormewood, wormewood, worwood) –
Artemisia absinthia, used to make a bitter tonic as well as absinthe
(Granville 3, 8, 17, 40, 41, 159, 184, 306; Hall 14, 17; Pudsey [3r], [3v],
[4r], [13r], [15v], [22r], [29r], [37v])

wort – unfermented beer; an infusion of malt or grain. Or a general
term applied to any plant, herb, or vegetable used for food or
medicine (passim)

wound water – any medicinal drink given to cure wounds (Granville 9)

yarrow – a tall plant with small flowers with a strong, bitter scent;
native to England. Used medicinally to cure wounds and ease
toothaches and migraines (Granville 48, [205])

yeast (yast, yearst) – in seventeenth-century England, yeast was
usually derived from the froth skimmed off a fermented vat of ale;
this was then used for baking bread (passim). A contributor in the
Granville manuscript also uses "yearst" as a verb, to add yeast to a
mixture (Granville 17, 25)

zedoary (ledoary, zyduiary, exodore?) – a variety of turmeric, native
to India; the roots are used medicinally to cure stomach aches and
worms, as well as to sweeten the breath (Granville 184; Hall 14?;
Pudsey [16r])

Works Cited

Albala, Ken. "Cooking as Research Methodology." *Renaissance Food from Rabelais to Shakespeare: Culinary Readings and Culinary Histories*. Ed. Joan Fitzpatrick. Farnham: Ashgate, 2010. 73–88. Print.

Anderson, Jennifer, and Elizabeth Sauer, eds. *Books and Readers in Early Modern England: Material Studies*. Philadelphia: U of Pennsylvania P, 2002. Print.

Anglicus, Bartholomeus. *On the Properties of Things*. Vol. 1. Trans. John Trevisa. Oxford: Clarendon Press, 1975. Print.

Anselment, Raymond A., ed. *The Remembrances of Elizabeth Freke, 1671–1714*. Cambridge: Cambridge UP, 2002. Print.

Appelbaum, Robert. *Aguecheek's Beef, Belch's Hiccup, and Other Gastronomic Interjections: Literature, Culture, and Food among the Early Moderns*. Chicago: U of Chicago P, 2006. Print.

Aspin, Richard. "Who Was Elizabeth Okeover?" Online. *Medical History* 44 (2000): 531–40. http://www.ncbi.nlm.nih.gov/pmc/articles/PMC1044326/pdf/medhist00013-0097.pdf. Web. 10 Oct. 2015.

Bakhtin, Mikhail. *Rabelais and His World*. Trans. Helene Iswolsky. Cambridge, MA: MIT P, 1968. Print.

Baumfylde, Mary. *Medical and Cookery Recipes*. C. 1626. MS V.a.456 Folger Shakespeare Lib., Washington, DC.

Beale, Peter. *In Praise of Scribes: Manuscripts and Their Makers in Seventeenth-Century England*. Oxford: Clarendon P, 1998. Print.

Beeton, Isabella. *Mrs Beeton's Book of Household Management*. London: Wordsworth Reference, 2006. Print.

Bland, Mark. *A Guide to Early Printed Books and Manuscripts*. Chichester: Wiley-Blackwell, 2010. Print.

Blencowe, Ann Wallis, ed. *The Receipt Book of Mrs. Ann Blencowe, A.D. 1694*. London: Guy Chapman, 1925. Print.

Borlik, Todd A. "The Chameleon's Dish: Shakespeare and the Omnivore's Dilemma." Online. *Early English Studies* 2 (2009): 8. http://0-literature. proquest.com.fama.us.es/searchFulltext.do?id=R04763905&divLevel=0&ar ea=abell&forward=critref_ft. Web. 16 Feb. 2016.

Bourne, W.R.P. "Fred Stubbs, Egrets, Brewes and Climatic Change." *British Birds* 96 (July 2003): 332–9. https://www.britishbirds.co.uk/wp-content/uploads/ article_files/V96/V96_N07/V96_N07_P332_339_A003.pdf. Web. 29 June 2016.

Bowden, Caroline. "Women in Educational Spaces." *Cambridge Companion to Early Modern Women's Writing*. Ed. Laura Lunger Knoppers. Cambridge: Cambridge UP, 2009. 85–96. Print.

Bower, Anne. "Cooking Up Stories: Narrative Elements in Community Cookbooks." *Recipes for Reading: Community Cookbooks, Stories, Histories*. Ed. Anne Bower. Amherst: U of Massachusetts P, 1997. 38–43. Print.

Bowles Smith, Emily. "'Let them Compleately Learn': Manuscript Clues about Early Modern Women's Educational Practices." Online. Washington DC: Folger Shakespeare Lib. https://web.archive.org/web/20070908163253/ http:/www.folger.edu/html/folger_institute/mm/EssayES.html. Web. 1 Aug. 2012.

Brandon Schnorrenberg, Barbara. "Delany, Mary (1700–1788)." In *Oxford Dictionary of National Biography*. Ed. H.C.G. Matthew and Brian Harrison. Oxford: Oxford UP, 2004. Online ed. Ed. Lawrence Goldman. Oct. 2008. http://www.oxforddnb.com/view/article/7442. Web. 9 Oct. 2015.

Brears, Peter. "The Ideal Kitchen in 1864." *The Country House Kitchen 1650–1900*. Ed. Pamela Sambrook and Peter Brears. Stroud: Sutton, 1997. 11–29. Print.

Bremness, Lesley. *The Complete Book of Herbs*. London: Dorling Kindersley, 1988. Print.

Brown, Katherine. *Receipt Book*. C. 1650–62. MS V.a.397 Folger Shakespeare Lib., Washington, DC.

Browne, Sir Thomas. *Pseudodoxia Epidemica*. 1646. Online. http://quod.lib. umich.edu/e/eebo/A29861.0001.001?rgn=main;view=fulltext. Web. 1 March 2017.

Burke, Sir Bernard. *A Genealogical and Heraldic Dictionary of the Landed Gentry of Great Britain for 1852*. London: Colburn, 1852. Print.

Burke, Victoria. "Manuscript Miscellanies." *Cambridge Companion to Early Modern Women's Writing*. Ed. Laura Lunger Knoppers. 54–67. Cambridge: Cambridge UP, 2009. Print.

– "Women's Verse Miscellany Manuscripts in the Perdita Project: Examples and Generalizations." *New Ways of Looking at Old Texts IV: Papers from the Renaissance English Text Society, 2002–2006*. Ed. Michael Denbo. Tempe: Arizona Center for Medieval and Renaissance Studies in conjunction with Renaissance English Text Society, 2008. Print.

Burman, Barbara. "Pocketing the Difference: Gender and Pockets in Nineteenth-Century Britain." *Gender and History* 14.3 (2002): 447–69. *Wiley Online Library*. Web. 1 Aug. 2012.

Cadman Seelig, Sharon. "Missing, Marginal, Mutilated: Reading the Remnants of Women's Manuscripts." *New Ways of Looking at Old Texts IV: Papers of the English Renaissance Text Society, 2002–2006*. Ed. Michael Denbo. Tempe: Arizona Center for Medieval and Renaissance Studies in conjunction with Renaissance English Text Society, 2008. 217–28. Print.

Camporesi, Piero. *Bread of Dreams: Food and Fantasy in Early Modern Europe*. Trans. David Gentilcore. Cambridge: Polity P, 1989. Print.

Castleton, Lady Grace. *Cookery and Medical Receipt Book*. Seventeenth century. MS Add 940. Folger Shakespeare Lib., Washington, DC.

Cervantes, Miguel de. *Don Quixote*. 1605, 1615. Trans. Tobias Smollett. New York: Modern Library, 2001. Print.

Collins, Pat. Online comment on "About." 2 Feb. 2015. *The Recipes Project*. https://recipes.hypotheses.org/about. Web. 6 Dec. 2016.

Collins, Thomas. *Choice and Rare Experiments in Physick and Chirurgery*. 1658. Online. https://quod.lib.umich.edu/e/eebo/A34011.0001.001/1:7?rgn=div 1;view=fulltext. Web. 8 Dec. 2016.

Considine, John. "Grey, Elizabeth, Countess of Kent (1582–1651)." In *Oxford Dictionary of National Biography*. Ed. H.C.G. Matthew and Brian Harrison. Oxford: Oxford UP, 2004. Online ed. Ed. Lawrence Goldman. Oct. 2006. http://www.oxforddnb.com/view/article/11530. Web. 9 Oct. 2015.

Cooke, A.O. *A Book of Dovecotes*. London: T.N. Foulis, 1920. Print.

Cowan, Brian. "New Worlds, New Tastes: Food Fashions after the Renaissance." *Food: The History of Taste*. Ed. Paul Freedman. Berkeley: U of California P, 2007. 197–232. Print.

Cressy, David. *Literacy and the Social Order*. Cambridge: Cambridge UP, 1980. Print.

Culpeper, Nicholas. *A Physicall Directory*. London, 1649. Print.

Dawson, Thomas. *The Good Huswife's Jewell*. 1587 edition. Online. http://quod.lib.umich.edu/e/eebo/A19957.0001.001?view=toc. Web. 21 Nov. 2016

de Silva, Cara, ed. *In Memory's Kitchen: A Legacy from the Women of Terezin*. Lanham: Rowman and Littlefield, 2006. Print.

Diccionario de la lengua española. 2nd ed. Online. Real Academia Española. http://buscon.rae.es/draeI/. Web. 1 Aug. 2012.

Digby, Sir Kenelm. *The Closet of Sir Kenelm Digby, Opened*. 1669. Ed. Peter Davidson and Jane Stevenson. Totnes: Prospect Books, 2010. Print.

DiMeo, Michelle. "Authorship and Medical Networks: Reading Attributions in Early Modern Manuscript Recipe Books." *Reading and Writing Recipe Books, 1550–1800*. Ed. Michelle DiMeo and Sara Pennell. Manchester: Manchester UP, 2013. 25–46. Print.

DiMeo, Michelle, and Rebecca Laroche. "On Elizabeth Isham's 'Oil of Swallows': Animal Slaughter and Early Modern Women's Medical Recipes." *Ecofeminist Approaches to Early Modernity*. Ed. Jennifer Munroe and Rebecca Laroche. New York: Palgrave Macmillan, 2011. 87–104. Print.

Dohner, Janet Vorwald. "Red Poll Cattle: Heritage Livestock Breeds." *Mother Earth News*. Online. http://www.motherearthnews.com/homesteading-and-livestock/raising-cattle/red-poll-heritage-livestock-zeylaf. Web. 1 March 2017.

Dolan, Frances E. "Tracking the Petty Traitor across Genres." *Ballads and Broadsides in Britain, 1500–1800*. Ed. Patricia Fumerton and Anita Guerrini. Farnham: Ashgate, 2010. 149–88. Print.

Dowd, Michelle M. *Women's Work in Early Modern English Literature and Culture*. New York: Palgrave Macmillan, 2009. Print.

Eggert, Paul. "Textual Product or Textual Process: Procedures and Assumptions of Critical Editing." *Devils and Angels*. Ed. Phil Cohen. Charlottesville: UP of Virginia, 1991. 57–77. Print.

Ellis, William. *The Country Housewife's Family Companion*. 1750. Ed. Malcolm Thick. Totnes: Prospect Books, 2000. Print.

Estienne, Charles (Charles Stevens and John Liebault). *Maison Rustique, or The Countrie Farme*. Trans. Richard Surflet. London: By Edm. Bollifant, for Bonham Norton, 1600. Online. http://gateway.proquest.com/openurl?ctx_ver=Z39.88-2003&res_id=xri:eebo&rft_id=xri:eebo:image:1865. Web. 31 Aug. 2015.

Estok, Simon C. *Ecocriticism and Shakespeare: Reading Ecophobia*. New York: Palgrave Macmillan, 2011. Print.

Evelyn, John. *The Rusticall and Œconomical Works of John Evelyn: The Manuscript Book of John Evelyn*. Ed. Christopher Driver. Totnes: Prospect Books, 1997. Print.

Ezell, Margaret J.M. "Cooking the Books, or, The Three Faces of Hannah Woolley." *Reading and Writing Recipe Books, 1550–1800*. Ed. Michelle DiMeo and Sara Pennell. Manchester: Manchester UP, 2013. 159–78. Print.

– "Domestic Papers: Manuscript Culture and Early Modern Women's Life Writing." *Genre and Women's Life Writing in Early Modern England*. Ed. Michelle M. Dowd and Julie A. Eckerle. Aldershot: Ashgate, 2007. 33–48. Print.

– *Social Authorship and the Advent of Print*. Baltimore and London: Johns Hopkins UP, 1999. Print.

– *Writing Women's Literary History*. Baltimore and London: Johns Hopkins UP, 1993. Print.

Field, Catherine. "'Many Hands Hands': Writing the Self in Early Modern Women's Recipe Books." *Genre and Women's Life Writing in Early Modern England*. Ed. Michelle M. Dowd and Julie A. Eckerle. Aldershot: Ashgate, 2007. 49–64. Print.

Fletcher, John. "The Significance of Samuel Pepys' Predilection for Venison Pasty." *Wild Food: Proceedings of the Oxford Symposium on Food and Cookery, 2004*. Ed. Richard Hosking. Totnes: Prospect Books, 2006. 122–30. Print.

Foucault, Michel. "What Is an Author?" Trans. Donald F. Bouchard and Sherry Simon. *Language, Counter-Memory, Practice.* Ed. Donald F. Bouchard. Ithaca, NY: Cornell UP, 1977. 124–7. Print.

Franklin, Colleen. "'An Habitation of Devils, a Domicill for Unclean Spirits and a Den of Goblings': The Marvelous North in Early Modern English Literature." *The Mysterious and the Foreign in Early Modern England.* Ed. Helen Ostovich et al. Newark: U of Delaware P, 2008. 27–39. Print.

Freke, Elizabeth. *Receipt book.* C. 1700. Add. MS 45718. British Library.

Fumerton, Patricia, and Anita Guerrini, eds. *Ballads and Broadsides in Britain, 1500–1800.* Farnham: Ashgate, 2010. Print.

Gerard, John. *The Herball, or Generall Historie of Plantes.* 1597. Online. 1633 edition. http://quod.lib.umich.edu/e/eebo/A01622.0001.001?rgn=main; view=fulltext. Web. 1 March 2017.

Glover, Stephen. *The History, Gazeteer, and Directory of the County of Derby ... Part II.* Derby: Henry Mozley and Son, 1829. Print.

Goldstein, David B. *Eating and Ethics in Shakespeare's England.* Cambridge: Cambridge UP, 2013. Print.

– "Woolley's Mouse: Early Modern Recipe Books and the Uses of Nature." *Ecofeminist Approaches to Early Modernity.* Ed. Jennifer Munroe and Rebecca Laroche. New York: Palgrave Macmillan, 2011. 105–27. Print.

Granville, Mary, and Anne Granville D'Ewes. *Recipe Book.* C. 1640–1750. MS V.a.430. Folger Shakespeare Lib., Washington, DC.

Green, Monica H. *Making Women's Medicine Masculine: The Rise of Male Authority in Pre-Modern Gynaecology.* Oxford: Oxford UP, 2008. Print.

Grieve, Mrs M. *Botanical.com: A Modern Herbal.* Online. http://www.botanical.com/botanical/mgmh/a/almon026.html. Web. 1 Aug. 2012.

Hakluyt, Richard. *The Principal Navigations Voyages Traffiques & Discoveries.* Vol. 3. London: J.M. Dent and Sons, 1927. Print.

Hall, Constance. *Receipt Book.* 1672. MS V.a.20. Folger Shakespeare Lib., Washington DC.

Harrison, Freya, et al. "A 1,000-Year-Old Antimicrobial Remedy with Antistaphylococcal Activity." *mBio.* Online. doi:10.1128/mBio.01129-15. Web. 26 Feb. 2017.

Hart, James. *Klinike, or The Diet of the Diseased.* 1633. Online. http://quod.lib.umich.edu/cgi/t/text/text-idx?c=eebo;idno=A02758.0001.001. Web. 1 March 2017.

Hobby, Elaine. *Virtue of Necessity: English Women's Writing 1649–88.* London: Virago P, 1988. Print.

Hookes, Mary. *Cookery Book.* 1675–1725. MS Add. 931. Folger Shakespeare Lib., Washington, DC.

Hunter, Lynette. "Nineteenth and Twentieth-Century Trends in Food Preserving: Frugality, Nutrition or Luxury." *Waste Not, Want Not.* Ed. C. Anne Wilson. Edinburgh: Edinburgh UP, 1989. 134–58. Print.

Justice, George L., and Nathan Tinker, eds. *Women's Writing and the Circulation of Ideas: Manuscript Publication in England, 1550–1800*. Cambridge: Cambridge UP, 2002. Print.

Kathman, David. "Pudsey, Edward (bap. 1573, d. 1612/13)." In *Oxford Dictionary of National Biography*. Ed. H.C.G. Matthew and Brian Harrison. Oxford: Oxford UP, 2004. Online ed. Ed. Lawrence Goldman. Jan. 2008. http://www.oxforddnb.com/view/article/71298. Web. 9 Oct. 2015.

Kelemen, Erick. *Textual Editing and Criticism: An Introduction*. New York: Norton, 2007. Print.

Kent, Elizabeth Grey, Countess of. *A Choice Manual*. 1653. Online. http://quod.lib.umich.edu/e/eebo/A47264.0001.001?view=toc. Web. 21 Nov. 2016

Kowalchuk, Kristine, and John Considine. "Hoxy Croxy and Oxycroceum: A Folk Survival from Medieval Latin." *Notes and Queries*. Online. doi:10.1093/notesj/gjs280. Web. 21 Nov. 2016.

Labert Ortiz, Elisabeth. *The Encyclopedia of Herbs, Spices and Flavorings*. London: Carroll and Brown, 1992. Print.

Laroche, Rebecca. *Medical Authority and Englishwomen's Herbal Texts, 1550–1650*. Burlington: Ashgate, 2009. Print.

Laurence, Anne. *Women in England 1500–1760: A Social History*. London: Butler and Tanner, 1994. Print.

Lehmann, Gilly. "Reading Recipe Books and Culinary History: Opening a New Field." *Reading and Writing Recipe Books, 1550–1800*. Ed. Michelle DiMeo and Sara Pennell. Manchester: Manchester UP, 2013. 93–113. Print.

Leonardi, Susan. "Recipes for Reading: Pasta Salad, Lobster a la Riseholme, Key Lime Pie." *PMLA* 104.3 (May 1989): 340–7. Print.

Leong, Elaine. "Editorial Introduction." *Receipt Books c.1575–1800, from the Folger Shakespeare Library*. Online. http://www.ampltd.co.uk/digital_guides/receipt_books_from_the_folger_shakespeare_library/editorial-introduction.aspx. Web. 7 Aug. 2014.

Leong, Elaine, and Sara Pennell. "Recipe Collections and the Currency of Medical Knowledge in the Early Modern 'Medical Marketplace.'" *Medicine and the Market in England and Its Colonies, c. 1450–1850*. Ed. Mark S.R. Jenner and Patrick Wallis. Houndmills: Palgrave Macmillan, 2007. 133–52. Print.

Leong, Elaine, and Alisha Rankin, eds. *Secrets and Knowledge in Medicine and Science, 1500–1800*. Farnham: Ashgate, 2011. Print.

Llanover, Lady. *First Principles of Good Cookery*. Lausanne: Richard Bentley, 1867. Print.

Longe, Sarah. *Mrs. Sarah Longe, Her Receipt Book*. C. 1610. MS V.a.425. Folger Shakespeare Lib., Washington, DC.

Love, Harold. *Scribal Publication in Seventeenth-Century England*. Wotton-under-Edge: Clarendon P, 1993. Print.

Lunger Knoppers, Laura, ed. *Cambridge Companion to Early Modern Women's Writing*. Cambridge: Cambridge UP, 2009. Print.

MacLean, Gerald. "Literature, Culture, and Society in Restoration England." *Culture and Society in the Stuart Restoration: Literature, Drama, History*. Ed. Gerald MacLean. Cambridge: Cambridge UP, 1995. 3–28. Print.

Markham, Gervase. *Hunger's Preuention*. 1621. Online. 1633 edition. http://quod.lib.umich.edu/e/eebo/A06936.0001.001?view=toc. Web. 23 Nov. 2016.

– *The English Huswife*. 1615. Online. 1631 edition. https://quod.lib.umich.edu/e/eebo/A06924.0001.001?view=toc. Web. 1 March 2017.

May, Robert. *The Accomplish't Cook*. 1660. Ed. Alan Davidson, Marcus Bell, and Tom Jaine. Totnes: Prospect Books, 2011. Print.

McKenzie, D.F. *The Panizzi Lectures, 1985: Bibliography and the Sociology of Texts*. London: British Library, 1986. Print.

McLean, Hugh. "Bernard Granville, Handel and the Rembrandts." *Musical Times* 126.1712 (1985): 593–601. Print.

Mendelson, Sara H. "Women and Work." *A Companion to Early Modern Women's Writing*. Ed. Anita Pacheco. Oxford: Blackwell, 2002. 58–76. Print.

Mennell, Stephen. *All Manners of Food: Eating and Taste in England and France from the Middle Ages to the Present*. 2nd ed. Urbana: U of Illinois P, 1996. Print.

Millman, Jill S. "Introduction to the Perdita Project Catalogue 1997–2007." Online. http://www.perditamanuscripts.amdigital.co.uk. Web. 1 Aug. 2012.

Mitchell, Rosemary. "Ogborne, Elizabeth (1763/4–1853)." In *Oxford Dictionary of National Biography*. Ed. H.C.G. Matthew and Brian Harrison. Oxford: Oxford UP, 2004. Online ed. Ed. Lawrence Goldman. Sept. 2014. http://www.oxforddnb.com/view/article/20577. Web. 9 Oct. 2015.

Moffett, Thomas. *Health's Improvement*. 1655 edition. Online. http://quod.lib.umich.edu/e/eebo2/A14059.0001.001?view=toc. Web. 23 Nov. 2016.

The National Archives. Online. http://discovery.nationalarchives.gov.uk/details/rd/08ad1940-a4a5-4b74-8cd0-a4e37262861a. Web. 9 Dec. 2016.

Ostovich, Helen, and Elizabeth Sauer, eds. *Reading Early Modern Women: An Anthology of Texts in Manuscript and Print, 1550–1700*. New York and London: Routledge, 2004. Print.

Oxford Dictionary of Superstitions. Ed. Iona Opie and Moira Tatem. Oxford: Oxford UP, 2005. Print.

The Oxford English Dictionary. 3rd ed. Ed. John Simpson. Online. Oxford: Clarendon P. http://dictionary.oed.com/. Web. 1 Aug. 2012.

Pacheco, Anita, ed. *A Companion to Early Modern Women's Writing*. Oxford: Blackwell, 2002. Print.

Packe, Susanna. *Receipt Book*. 1674. MS V.a.215. Folger Shakespeare Lib., Washington, DC.

Parkinson, John. *Paradisi in Sole Paradisus Terrestris*. 1629. Online. http://quod.lib.umich.edu/e/eebo2/A09010.0001.001?view=toc. Web. 23 Nov. 2016.

–　*Theatrum Botanicum.* 1640. Online. http://quod.lib.umich.edu/e/eebo2/
A09011.0001.001?view=toc. Web. 23 Nov. 2016.

Partridge, John. *Treasurie of Commodious Conceites.* 1573. Online. http://quod.
lib.umich.edu/cgi/t/text/text-idx?c=eebo;idno=A68556.0001.001. Web. 21
Nov. 2016.

–　*The Widowes Treasure.* 1588. Online. https://quod.lib.umich.edu/e/eebo/
A09123.0001.001?view=toc. Web. 8 Dec. 2016.

Patrick, Penelope. *Receipt Book.* 1671. MS V.a.396. Folger Shakespeare Lib.,
Washington, DC.

Peacham, H. *The Valley of Varietie: or, Discourse Fitting for the Times Containing
Very Learned and Rare Passages out of Antiquity, Philosophy, and History.*
London: Printed by M. P[arsons], 1638. Online. http://quod.lib.umich.
edu/e/eebo/A09208.0001.001. Web. 6 Oct. 2015.

Pearsall, Derek. "The Value/s of Manuscript Study: A Personal Retrospect."
*Journal of the Early Book Society for the Study of Manuscripts and Printing
History* 3 (2000): 167–81. Print.

Pechey, John. *The Compleat Herbal of Physical Plants.* London: Printed for
Henry Bonwicke, 1694. Online. http://gateway.proquest.com/openurl?ctx_
ver=Z39.88-2003&res_id=xri:eebo&rft_id=xri:eebo:image:59977:3. Web. 31
Aug. 2015.

Pennell, Sara. "Women, Manuscript Recipes and Knowledge in Early Modern
England." *Early Modern Women's Manuscript Writing.* Ed. Victoria Burke and
Jonathan Gibson. Burlington: Ashgate, 2004. 237–58. Print.

Perdita Manuscripts: Women Writers, 1500–1700. Online. http://www.
perditamanuscripts.amdigital.co.uk. Web. 1 Aug. 2012.

Petroski, Henry. *The Pencil: A History of Design and Circumstance.* New York:
Alfred A. Knopf, 2010. Print.

Philiatros. *Natura Exenterata.* 1655. Online. http://quod.lib.umich.edu/e/
eebo/A89817.0001.001/1:9.189?rgn=div2;view=toc. Web. 1 Dec. 2016.

Philostratus. *The First Two Books of Philostratus.* Trans. Charles Blount. London:
Printed for Nathaniel Thompson, 1680. Online. http://quod.lib.umich.
edu/e/eebo/A54811.0001.001. Web. 6 Oct. 2015.

Plat, Hugh. *Delightes for Ladies.* 1644 edition. Online. https://www.loc.gov/
item/73217891/. Web. 21 Nov. 2016.

–　*Sundrie New and Artificiall Remedies Against Famine. Written … Uppon the
Occasion of this Present Dearth.* 1596. Online. http://quod.lib.umich.edu/e/
eebo2/A09733.0001.001?view=toc. Web. 23 Nov. 2016.

Prak, Maarten. *The Dutch Republic in the Seventeenth Century.* Trans. Diane
Webb. Cambridge: Cambridge UP, 2005. Print.

Pudsey, Lettice. *Cookery and Medical Recipe Book.* C. 1675. MS V.a.450. Folger
Shakespeare Lib., Washington, DC.

Rabelais, François. *Gargantua and Pantagruel.* 1532, 1534. Trans. Sir Thomas Urquhart and Peter Anthony Motteux. London: John Westhouse, 1945. Print.

Randolph, Grace. *Cookery Book.* 1697. MS V.a.301. Folger Shakespeare Lib., Washington, DC.

Recipes Project, The. Online. http://recipes.hypotheses.org. Web. 26 Feb. 2017.

Revel, Jean-François. *Culture and Cuisine: A Journey through the History of Food.* New York: Doubleday, 1982. Print.

Robertson, Una J. *The Illustrated History of the Housewife, 1650–1950.* New York: St Martin's P, 1997. Print.

Ruthven, Patrick. *The Ladies Cabinet Enlarged and Opened.* 1654. Online. http://quod.lib.umich.edu/e/eebo2/A76199.0001.001?view=toc. Web. 21 Nov. 2016

Sambrook, Pamela, and Peter Brears, eds. *The Country House Kitchen 1650–1900.* Stroud: Sutton, 1997. Print.

– "Introduction." *The Country House Kitchen 1650–1900.* Ed. Pamela Sambrook and Peter Brears. Stroud: Sutton, 1997. 1–9. Print.

Saunders, J.W. "The Stigma of Print." *Essays in Criticism* 1.2 (April 1951): 139–64. Print.

Schoenfeldt, Michael C. *Bodies and Selves in Early Modern England: Physiology and Inwardness in Spenser, Shakespeare, Herbert, and Milton.* Cambridge: Cambridge UP, 1999. Print.

Schoonover, David E., ed. *Ladie Borlase's Receiptes Book.* Iowa City: U of Iowa P, 1998. Print.

Segan, Francine. *Shakespeare's Kitchen: Renaissance Recipes for the Contemporary Cook.* New York: Random House, 2003.

Severson, Kim. "Written Recipes Undergo a Makeover." *New York Times.* Online edition. http://www.nytimes.com/2015/10/14/dining/written-recipes-undergo-a-makeover.html?ribbon-ad-idx=2&rref=dining&module=Ribbon&version=context&region=Header&action=click&contentCollection=Food&pgtype=article&_r=0. Web. 13 Oct. 2015.

Shakespeare, William. *The Arden Shakespeare: Complete Works.* Ed. Richard Proudfoot, Ann Thompson, and David Scott Kastan. London: Thomas Learning, 2001. Print.

Sharpe, James. "The Debate on Witchcraft." *A Companion to English Literature and Culture.* Ed. Michael Hattaway. Oxford: Blackwell, 2000. 653–61. Print.

Sherman, William H. "What Did Renaissance Readers Write in Their Books?" *Books and Readers in Early Modern England: Material Studies.* Ed. Jennifer Anderson and Elizabeth Sauer. Philadelphia: U of Pennsylvania P, 2002. 116–34. Print.

Sim, Alison. *Food and Feast in Tudor England.* Stroud: Allan Sutton Publishing, 1997. Print.

Sloan, A.W. *English Medicine in the Seventeenth Century.* Bishop Auckland: Durham Academic P, 1996.

Smith, Lisa. "Imagining Women's Fertility before Technology." *Journal of Medical Humanities* 31.1 (2010): 69–79. Print.

Smyth, Adam. *Autobiography in Early Modern England*. Cambridge: Cambridge UP, 2010. Print.

Snook, Edith. "Reading Women." *Cambridge Companion to Early Modern Women's Writing*. Ed. Laura Lunger Knoppers. Cambridge: Cambridge UP, 2009. 40–53. Print.

Spiller, Elizabeth. "Printed Recipe Books in Medical, Political, and Scientific Contexts." *The Oxford Handbook of Literature and the English Revolution*. Ed. Laura Lunger Knoppers. Oxford: Oxford UP, 2012. 516–33. Print.

– "Recipes for Knowledge: Maker's Knowledge and Traditions, Paracelsian Recipes, and the Invention of the Cookbook, 1600–1660." *Renaissance Food from Rabelais to Shakespeare*. Ed. Joan Fitzpatrick. Farnham: Ashgate, 2009. 55–72. Print.

Spurling, Hilary, ed. *Elinor Fettiplace's Receipt Book*. London: Faber and Faber, 2011. Print.

Staveley, Jane. *Receipt Book*. 1693–4. MS V.a.401. Folger Shakespeare Lib., Washington, DC.

Stead, Jennifer. "Necessities and Luxuries: Food Preservation from the Elizabethan to the Georgian Era." *Waste Not, Want Not*. Ed. C. Anne Wilson. Edinburgh: Edinburgh UP, 1989. 66–103. Print.

Stuart, Tristram. *The Bloodless Revolution: A Cultural History of Vegetarianism from 1600 to Modern Times*. New York: Norton, 2007. Print.

Surflet, Richard. *See* Estienne, Charles.

Tasso, Torquato. *The Householders Philosophie*. Trans. T.K. London, 1588. Print.

Tebeaux, Elizabeth. "Women and Technical Writing, 1475–1700: Technology, Literacy, and Development of a Genre." *Women, Science and Medicine 1500–1700: Mothers and Sisters of the Royal Society*. Ed. Lynette Hunter and Sarah Hutton. Stroud: Sutton Publishing, 1997. 29–62. Print.

Theophano, Janet. *Eat My Words: Reading Women's Lives through the Cookbooks They Wrote*. New York: Palgrave, 2002. Print.

Thick, Malcolm. "Root Crops and the Feeding of London's Poor in the Late 16th and Early 17th Centuries." *English Rural Society, 1500–1800: Essays in Honour of Joan Thirsk*. Ed. John Chartres and David Hey. Cambridge: Cambridge UP, 1990. 279–96. Print.

– "Using Language to Investigate Ellen Chantrill's Recipe Book." *Food and Language: Proceedings of the Oxford Symposium on Cookery 2009*. Ed. Richard Hosking. Totnes: Prospect Books, 2010. 350–9. Print.

Thirsk, Joan. "Agricultural Innovations and Their Diffusion." *The Agrarian History of England and Wales. (1640–1750: Agrarian Change) Vol. 1*. Ed. Joan Thirsk. Cambridge: Cambridge UP, 1984. 533–89. Print.

– "Agricultural Policy: Public Debate, Legislation." *The Agrarian History of England and Wales. (1640–1750: Agrarian Change) Vol. 2.* Ed. Joan Thirsk. Cambridge: Cambridge UP, 1984. 298–405. Print.

– *Food in Early Modern England: Phases, Fads, Fashions 1500–1760.* London and New York: Hambledon Continuum, 2007. Print.

– "Making a Fresh Start: Sixteenth-Century Agriculture and the Classical Inspiration." *Culture and Cultivation in Early Modern England: Writing and the Land.* Ed. Michael Leslie and Timothy Raylor. Leicester: Leicester UP, 1992. 15–34. Print.

Thomas L. Gravell Watermark Archive. Online. http://www.gravell.org. Web. 22 Aug. 2014.

Tryon, Thomas. *The Way to Save Wealth.* London, 1695. Print.

Turner, William. *A New Herball.* 1568. Online. http://quod.lib.umich.edu/e/eebo2/A14059.0001.001?view=toc. Web. 23 Nov. 2016.

Tusser, Thomas. *Fiue Hundreth Points of Good Husbandry.* 1573. Online. http://quod.lib.umich.edu/cgi/t/text/text-idx?c=eebo;idno=A14064.0001.001. Web. 21 Nov. 2016

Unger, Richard W. *Beer in the Middle Ages and the Renaissance.* Philadelphia: U of Pennsylvania P, 2007. Print.

Ure, Andrew. *A Dictionary of Chemistry.* London: Thomas Tegg, 1828. Print.

Wall, Wendy. "Distillation: Transformations in and out of the Kitchen." *Renaissance Food from Rabelais to Shakespeare.* Ed. Joan Fitzpatrick. Farnham: Ashgate, 2009. 89–104. Print.

– "Literacy and the Domestic Arts." *Huntington Library Quarterly* 73.3 (September 2010): 383–412. Print.

– "Reading the Home: The Case of *The English Housewife.*" *Renaissance Paratexts.* Ed. Helen Smith and Louise Wilson. Cambridge: Cambridge UP, 2011. 165–84. Print.

– *Staging Domesticity: Household Work and English Identity in Early Modern Drama.* Cambridge: Cambridge UP, 2002. Print.

– "Women in the Household." *Cambridge Companion to Early Modern Women's Writing.* Ed. Laura Lunger Knoppers. Cambridge: Cambridge UP, 2009. 97–109. Print.

Wheatley, Henry Benjamin, and Peter Cunningham. *London, Past and Present: Its History, Associations and Traditions.* Vol. 3. London: John Murray, 1891. Print.

Wilson, C. Anne. *The Appetite and the Eye.* Edinburgh: Papers from the Second Leeds Symposium, 1991.

– *Food and Drink in Britain from the Stone Age to Recent Times.* London: Constable, 1973. Print.

– *Waste Not, Want Not: Food Preservation from Early Times to the Present Day.* Edinburgh: Edinburgh UP, 1992. Print.

Withey, Alun. "Crossing the Boundaries: Domestic Recipe Collections in Early Modern Wales." *Reading and Writing Recipe Books, 1550–1800.* Ed. Michelle DiMeo and Sara Pennell. Manchester: Manchester UP, 2013. 179–96. Print.

W.M. *The Queens Closet Opened.* 1659. Online. http://quod.lib.umich.edu/e/eebo/A52209.0001.001?view=toc. Web. 1 Dec. 2016.

Wolfe, Heather. "Manuscripts in Early Modern England." *A Concise Companion to English Renaissance Literature.* Ed. Donna B. Hamilton. Malden, MA: Blackwell, 2006. 114–35. Print.

– "Rethinking the Price, Quality, and Social Significance of Writing Paper in Early Modern England." Online brochure item. *The Open University: Book History Research Group.* http://www.open.ac.uk/arts/research/book-history/research-seminar-series/paper-pen-and-ink. Web. 21 Aug. 2014.

"A Woman's Work Is Never Done." Online. *University of California Santa Barbara English Broadside Ballad Archive.* http://ebba.english.ucsb.edu/ballad/30355/xml. Web. 25 July 2014.

Woolf, Virginia. *A Room of One's Own.* New York: Harcourt Brace Jovanovich, 1981. Print.

Woolley, Hannah [unauthorized]. *The Accomplish'd Lady's Delight.* 1675. Online. http://quod.lib.umich.edu/e/eebo/A66834.0001.001?view=toc. Web. 2 Dec. 2016.

– [unauthorized] *The Compleat Servant-Maid.* 1677. London, 1683. Print.

– *The Ladies Directory.* 1661. London, 1662. Print.

– *The Queen-Like Closet.* London, 1670. Print.

– *A Supplement to the Queen-Like Closet.* London, 1674. Print.

Index

Note: References to culinary and medical ingredients, techniques, weights and measures, implements, and ailments are included (with page/folio numbers) in the Glossary.

Studies in Book and Print Culture

General Editor: Leslie Howsam

Eli MacLaren, *Dominion and Agency: Copyright and the Structuring of the Canadian Book Trade, 1867–1918*

Ruth Panofsky, *The Literary Legacy of the Macmillan Company of Canada: Making Books and Mapping Culture*

Archie L. Dick, *The Hidden History of South Africa's Book and Reading Cultures*

Darcy Cullen, ed., *Editors, Scholars, and the Social Text*

James J. Connolly, Patrick Collier, Frank Felsenstein, Kenneth R. Hall, and Robert Hall, eds, *Print Culture Histories beyond the Metropolis*

Kristine Kowalchuk, *Preserving on Paper: Seventeenth-Century Englishwomen's Receipt Books*